Creating Lively Passover Seders

Second Edition

A Sourcebook of Engaging Tales, Texts & Activities

DAVID ARNOW, PHD

Coeditor, *My People's Passover Haggadah:*
Traditional Texts, Modern Commentaries

JEWISH LIGHTS Publishing
Woodstock, Vermont

Creating Lively Passover Seders, 2nd Ed.:
A Sourcebook of Engaging Tales, Texts & Activities

2011 Quality Paperback Edition, First Printing
© 2011 by David Arnow

Library of Congress Cataloging-in-Publication Data
Arnow, David.
   Creating lively Passover seders : a sourcebook of engaging tales, texts & activities / David Arnow.—2nd ed.
      p. cm.
   Includes bibliographical references and index.
   ISBN 978-1-58023-444-3 (quality pbk. original) 1. Seder. 2. Haggadah. 3. Passover—Customs and practices. I. Title.
   BM695.P35A76 2011
   296.4'5371—dc22

                                                                                            2010051488

About the Cover Art:

Plates 54–55 "It Is Our Duty" from the Moriah Haggadah™

Avner Moriah was born in Jerusalem in 1953. He received his BFA from the Bezalel Academy of Art and Architecture in Jerusalem and his MFA from Yale University's Graduate School of Art and Architecture. His paintings have been acquired by the Metropolitan Museum of Art and the Jewish Museum in New York, the Israel Museum in Jerusalem, the Holocaust Museum in Washington, the Skirball Museum in LA, and private collections throughout the world. The artist can be reached in Israel at Rehov Elqahi 57/8, Jerusalem 93807.

Pictured here are six panels from "It Is Our Duty" from the Limited Edition of the Moriah Haggadah™, arranged in pairs from right to left: the Israelites enslaved and the Hand of God bringing them from slavery to freedom; the people being lifted from sorrow to joy and from mourning to festivity.

10 9 8 7 6 5 4 3 2 1

Cover Design: Bridgett Taylor
Manufactured in the United States of America

Published by Jewish Lights Publishing
A Division of Longhill Partners, Inc.
Sunset Farm Offices, Route 4, P.O. Box 237
Woodstock, VT 05091
Tel: (802) 457-4000   Fax: (802) 457-4004
www.jewishlights.com

CONTENTS

—

ACKNOWLEDGMENTS TO THE SECOND EDITION

—

A number of people deserve thanks for helping with various aspects of the second edition. Rabbi Jeffrey Hoffman, with whom I have been studying for the last few years, has been a great sounding board for ideas, a wonderful guide through some of the challenging texts that appear in the book, and a patient teacher. Avraham Holtz, Joel M. Hoffman, Nathan Shapira, and Rabbi Burton L. Visotzky provided good answers to a few arcane questions. I've learned a great deal from the rabbis who have served at Temple Israel Center—Rabbis Gordon Tucker, Neil Zuckerman, Dina Shargel, Tamar Elad-Appelbaum, and Michael Goldman—and Rabbi Lester Bronstein of Bet Am Shalom. Many of their insights have found a home among these pages. Rabbi Tucker also reviewed one of the new chapters in this book.

Special thanks also to Madeleine Arnow, my wife, my sons Adam and Rabbi Noah Arnow, and my daughter-in-law Tamar Arnow for carefully reviewing and commenting on new material. Once again Madeleine has been a great source of encouragement and unfailing good judgment.

Jewish Lights Books . . . What a great publisher and what a great staff! Many thanks to Stuart M. Matlins, publisher of Jewish Lights. Stuart took a chance on the first edition and had the wisdom to propose the second. Emily Wichland, vice president of Editorial and Production, has always been a wonderful collaborator. Erin Ryan edited the second edition and her sharp eye and good judgment left their mark on every page of this book.

PREFACE TO THE SECOND EDITION

—

The Passover journey continues!

Since the publication of the first edition of this book in 2004, my love of the Haggadah has only grown. I've published a number of articles on the subject and had the great fortune of coediting the two volumes of *My People's Passover Haggadah: Traditional Texts, Modern Commentaries* (Jewish Lights) with Rabbi Lawrence A. Hoffman, one of this era's greatest scholars of Jewish liturgy. Working with Rabbi Hoffman and the other contributors to *My People's Passover Haggadah* has deepened my understanding of the holiday and the Haggadah enormously.

Each spring has brought wonderful opportunities to teach about Passover, which in turn have prompted new research. For example, in one course, the notion that the Passover Seder developed as a substitute for the ancient Passover sacrifice stimulated students' curiosity about the sacrifice itself. Those questions ultimately led to a new chapter about Passover as it was celebrated in Temple times and about the role that the concept of sacrifice—broadly understood—ought to play in our lives today.

It also became obvious that the first edition said very little about one of the real highlights of the Seder, the songs. I can vividly remember singing those songs as a child with my grandparents Doris and Jack Weiler at their Seders. With one chapter devoted to *Dayyenu* and another to *Echad Mi Yodea* (Who Knows One?) and *Chad Gadya* (One Kid), the second edition cures that omission. The Seder plate, such a focus of the evening, now also has the chapter it deserves. Many think of this plate as a precisely defined collection of symbolic foods, each of which occupies its designated place, the epitome of the evening's commitment to order. A look at the traditions surrounding the contents of the plate tells a very different story, one of great diversity. This sets the stage for using the Seder plate as a springboard for enlivening the Seder.

And finally, I've become fascinated by the erroneous myth of Moses' complete absence from the Haggadah, an issue only touched upon in the first edition. Some myths are helpful because they actually reveal truth. Other myths prevent us from seeing what stares us in the face. The myth that the Haggadah makes absolutely no reference to Moses is a good example of the latter. "Finding" Moses opens the door to reassessing the common wisdom that the Haggadah denies a human role in the redemption from Egypt and leaves all the responsibility to God.

Readers of the second edition should also know that the book's website, www.livelyseders.com, has been greatly expanded over the last few years. I plan to continue updating the site in the coming years so be sure check it from time to time. But I'm confident that this edition of *Creating Lively Passover Seders* contains enough material for many, many wonderful Seders.

Remember, one chapter of this book a year is all you need to create a lively Seder! If the book helps you do that, "it would suffice"—*dayyenu*!

ACKNOWLEDGMENTS TO THE FIRST EDITION

—

This book would never have been written were it not for the New Israel Fund's interest in publishing a series of eight Haggadah supplements I wrote, which represent a significant portion of the present volume.

The following individuals were kind enough to review chapters of the book: Rabbis Lester Bronstein, Lawrence Kushner, Hillel Levine, Michael Paley, Nahum Shargel, Gordon Tucker, and Abraham Unger, and Professors Judith Hauptman, John Healey, and Lee Levine. Rabbis Gilbert Rosenthal and Burton Visotzky merit extra thanks for reviewing extensive material and for quickly responding to queries. Thanks to Hershel Shanks for his helpful comments. This book has also benefited from many of Riva Silverman's insights on a broad range of topics. Each of these individuals' wisdom has vastly improved the book.

Several conversations with David Goshen also proved extremely enlightening. Robert Friedland; Elliott Malki; Egon Mayer; Joshua Sherman; and Tatiana Light, my Hebrew teacher for many years; served as ready sounding boards for testing out ideas. Madeleine, Adam, and Noah Arnow; Tammy Reiss; and Ariella Sidelsky provided unstinting editorial assistance. For their comments on the entire manuscript, special appreciation goes to Kathleen Peratis and to the director of Hazon, Nigel Savage. Co-led by Basmat Hazan Arnoff, Hazon's Beit Midrash on the Exodus from Egypt introduced me to wonderfully creative approaches to the story.

Weekly study sessions with Elie Kaunfer, a gifted rabbinical student at the Jewish Theological Seminary of America, provided invaluable assistance for translations and deepening my understanding of numerous texts.

Thanks also to Ruth Abram; Michael Balick; E. Robert Goodkind; Betsy Lewittes; John D. MacArthur; Joseph B. Moskaluk; Dina Shargel Projansky; Elliott Rabin; Peter Reimold; Sharon Zoffness; Rabbis Shlomo Riskin and Neil Zuckerman; and Professors Robert Brody, Daniel J. Lasker, and Israel J. Yuval for their help with particular questions or bringing important material to my attention.

My teachers in the Wexner Heritage Leadership Program helped me learn what it means to make a Jewish text come to life. I owe them and all those associated with that program an enormous debt of gratitude.

The librarians of the Dorot Jewish Division of the New York Public Library—Anne-Marie Belinfante, Faith Jones, Roberta Saltzman, and Eleanor Yadin—are simply among the most dedicated, helpful professionals I've ever encountered. And the Jewish Division's collection is one of the best in the world. Thanks also to Laura Schraeger for her tireless assistance. In addition to their time and varied expertise, these individuals have contributed something equally important: unflagging encouragement.

The staff of Jewish Lights has been a pleasure to work with. Thanks to Stuart Matlins, publisher, for his confidence in the concept for this project. Emily Wichland, managing editor, unflappable and pleasant throughout, has provided endless guidance. Alys Yablon's wise editing contributed enormously to the book. Amanda Dupuis, project editor, did a superb job turning the manuscript into a book.

My sons Noah and Adam have blessed me with unlimited opportunities to fulfill the injunction that "You shall tell your children . . ." about the Exodus from Egypt. I thank them for their patience and wise counsel.

Madeleine J. Arnow, my wife, has endured living through something of a nonstop Passover for more than a solid year. For that, along with helping in countless ways, she deserves all my gratitude.

PREFACE TO THE FIRST EDITION

—

Memories of Passover Seders in my grandparents' Manhattan apartment are among the most treasured of my childhood—the smells, tastes, and songs; the faces of friends seen only at Seders year after year; and the dramatic storybook illustrations of the vintage 1952 Haggadah we used, a copy of which sits open to the left of my computer screen as I write this now. The cover is unforgettable: a young wide-eyed boy with a kindly, white-bearded man—who may as well be Moses—gazing together toward the heavens over an open book. But for a child raised in the suburbs, spending two consecutive nights in a building with an elevator also made those nights different from all others.

In March of 1988 I traveled to Israel with Jonathan Jacoby, then executive director of the New Israel Fund, to investigate the implications of the first *intifada*. Following that disturbing visit, I composed a short reading for our family Seder. Each subsequent year I wrote something else. My family liked these and in 1994 the New Israel Fund, with which I had long been involved, published the first of what would become a series of eight Haggadah supplements that comprise about one-third of this book.

I'm neither a rabbi nor formally trained in any area of Jewish studies, so I approach this undertaking with a combination of excitement, trepidation, and *chutzpah*. My formal training was in clinical psychology, but I've pursued Jewish learning in various formats over the years and have picked up things along the way. Passover has been on my mind for a long time. The holiday fascinates me. I've come to love the Haggadah for itself and because it provides such a perfect doorway into virtually every aspect of Jewish thought and experience. If this book transmits some of that love and fascination to you and your Seder participants, it will have succeeded.

INTRODUCTION
—

THE GOAL OF THE SEDER AND OF THIS BOOK

For almost two thousand years, Jews have gathered with family and friends to celebrate the festival of Passover with a Seder-like meal featuring matzah, wine, and questions about the story of the Exodus from Egypt. Today we conduct Passover Seders in almost every country on earth and in scores of different languages. Among the common ingredients at all these Seders is a book recounting the Exodus saga. That book, the Passover Haggadah (which means "the telling"), might be "traditional," "modern," Ashkenazic, Sephardic, Yemenite, Conservative, Orthodox, Reconstructionist, Reform, Post-Denominational, Hasidic, Kabbalistic, New Age, Feminist, Gay, Environmental, Vegetarian, Civil Libertarian, and so on.

But behind the symbols, rituals, and countless Haggadot lies one aim: to help us draw inspiration from the ancient tale of our ancestors' liberation from Egypt as we wage our own struggles against physical and spiritual oppression.

The Haggadah itself expresses this goal in a single sentence.

In every generation, each individual should feel as though he or she had gone out of Egypt.

This book will help you create that feeling at your Seder.

How? As we will see, eighteen hundred years ago, the architects of the earliest Seders developed an approach designed to preserve a healthy measure of spontaneity. They struck a brilliant balance between elements of the Seder that would be fixed and those left open for creativity and change. The Haggadah reflects that spirit when it says, "All who elaborate on telling of the Exodus deserve praise."

Over the centuries, the Seder continued to evolve, but in an ironic direction. The passion for creative elaboration persisted; the Haggadah grew and grew. Eighteen hundred years ago, the Mishnah, one of our earliest law codes or teaching manuals, sketched out a 435-word plan for the Seder. Over the centuries, the Hebrew text of the traditional Ashkenazic Haggadah grew to more than 5,500 words, and that's without a single word of commentary.

Today's "traditional" Haggadah preserves elaborations and additions that evolved over more than a thousand years.

You can read that "everyone who elaborates on the story of the Exodus deserves praise."

You can read about Rabbis who did just that as they discussed the Exodus all through the night.

You can read a complete midrashic exposition on My father was a wandering Aramean mostly composed in the late third century.

You can read how Rabbi Akiva managed to cleverly recalculate the number of plagues from 10 to 50 in Egypt and 250 at the Red Sea.

You can read about how others freely and creatively played with the Exodus story and made it come alive for them. For them, but not necessarily for us!

For most of us, simply reading the Haggadah no longer helps us feel as if we had been redeemed from Egypt. Instead, the experience of reading more than few pages of the Haggadah often makes us feel as if we are oppressed, saddled with an ancient, confusing text that never quite tells the story we expect to hear. Further complicating the matter, the Haggadah lauds a God who saved the Israelites but whose strong hand and outstretched arm seems so very distant from the world as many of us experience it.

Don't get me wrong. I love the Haggadah. But I probably wouldn't if I opened it just for Seders once or twice a year.

The positive feedback I've received from people who have used the texts, tales, and activities in the first edition of *Creating Lively Passover Seders* has convinced me that the Haggadah *can* serve as the basis for great Seders that can give you a taste of leaving Egypt.

At its core, the Passover Seder embodies a dialogue that began millennia ago and continues to this very day. The dialogue reflects the encounter between the Jewish People and our founding story, sacred texts, evolving ritual practice, changing political circumstances, and a shifting cultural milieu. You can get a hint of that dialogue if you consider three things: the Seder developed as a response to the destruction of the Second Temple in 70 C.E.; it found much of its form in the Greek symposium; and it evolved over an extended period when Jews were exiled from the Land of Israel, sometimes living under circumstances in which oppression was very real.

For the Haggadah, reliving the Exodus is not about remembering an event long ago, but about participating in a conversation that aims to shore up our hope and strength for the struggle to make tomorrow brighter than today.

With some background, virtually every passage in the Haggadah provides a springboard for activities and discussions that can help you bring that conversation to life.

HOW TO USE THIS BOOK

—

Unless you have a special interest in the Haggadah or the Exodus story, this is probably not a book you'll want to read from beginning to end. I would suggest looking through it three or four weeks before Passover. Just after Purim would be a good time. Choose one or maybe two chapters to read leisurely. That will help you get in the Passover spirit and give you some ideas you may want to take up during your Seder.

As you'll see, all but one chapter (the first) begins with a passage from the Haggadah, and all the chapters (except the last) are arranged in the order in which those passages appear in the Haggadah. Generally you'll find material you can bring into the Seder when you reach the passage in the Haggadah with which a particular chapter begins. But keep in mind that most chapters also contain material that would be better used at other points during the evening. For example, chapter 18, "Reliving the Exodus: The Story of the Last Night in Egypt," includes a package of activities to do before the Seder begins. Similarly, chapter 14, "Women of the Exodus: Redeemed by Their Righteousness," includes the ritual of Miriam's Cup, elements of which occur toward the beginning and end of the Seder.

Over the years, my family has used some of the material in this book to help set the mood for our Seders. We invite people to arrive about an hour and a half before we plan to sit down at the table. We gather in the living room for about an hour before the Seder begins for an activity or conversation like those suggested in this book.

Alternatively, you might consider beginning your Seder on the early side (depending on your observance of Jewish law), making Kiddush, washing hands, and then dipping parsley (*karpas,* Greek for "hors d'oeuvre"). Then you might serve more substantial dips. These will take the edge off your participants' appetites and create a good atmosphere for discussion.

We've also sometimes divided into small groups, moving into opposite ends of the living room and an adjacent library for small group discussions. Later, during the Seder, each group gets a chance to share *briefly* the highlights of its conversation with the entire group. (If you plan to do this, ask someone in advance to be the group's "reporter.") You'll be surprised how engaging these conversations can become.

If you plan to lead a discussion based on a particular passage from the Haggadah or another selection from this book, it is important to make a copy for each of your participants. That really helps keep things focused.

Another reason for dividing into small groups is that you can devote one group to activities that are particularly suitable for children. For example, "The Last Night in Egypt" includes a version of the Passover story for reading aloud to children (it's fine for adults, too). On the other hand, you'd be surprised how well even five- and six-year-olds can participate in most of the other activities along with adults, especially in small groups.

We then begin the Seder itself, which for our family does include a fair amount of reading from the Haggadah, interspersed with brief questions and occasional discussions.

How long you want your Seder to run and how much you read from the Haggadah will determine how much time you have to bring additional activities into the Seder.

I've found that once people are seated at the table it's easier to read things and to take a few comments that may evolve into short conversations, rather than to plan on numerous extended discussions. Those conversations are best held before the Seder.

Your Seder will also work better if you involve others in leading parts of it. If you do this and want them to work with the material in this book, be sure to make them a copy and send it to them in advance! When copying material from this book for your Seder, please be careful to cite Creating Lively Passover Seders. For public uses, please be respectful of copyrights and the requirement for permission (see page ii). To find a list of the permissions required for reprinting previously published materials included in this volume refer to page 415.

A FEW WORDS FOR SEDER LEADERS

—

As anyone who has led a Seder knows, the Passover gathering generates a range of expectations, joys, and sometimes a few disappointments. Year after year, you hear the grumbling whispers: "When do we eat?" "How long is this going to last?" "It's getting late!" Some come to the Seder hungry for spiritual sustenance, and others are simply famished for a dinner that seems as if it will never arrive. Some find great meaning in the holiday. For others it seems paradigmatic of that rather sad nine-word version of Jewish history. "They tried to kill us. We won. Let's eat." Some would never miss a Seder. Others come because they would be embarrassed not to. For some, it's all about being with family. For others, that's just the beginning.

Many arrive at the Seder vaguely expecting to hear the great tale of the Jewish People's struggle for freedom. Year after year they leave with a gnawing sense of disappointment. The Haggadah comes close to telling the story, but it does so in a way that creates confusion, if not frustration.

Instead of a heroic battle for liberation, the Haggadah recounts an all-powerful God's triumph over an evil, but comparatively impotent, Pharaoh. There's barely even a word about Moses!

Although the activities in this book can help overcome some of these challenges, it's also important to understand the underlying dynamics that contribute to them. Even if a problem cannot be entirely solved, often just having a better grasp of what causes the difficulty changes the way you experience it.

To one degree or another, the difficulties of creating an "ideal Seder," in which all participants actually *feel as though they have gone out of Egypt,* recapitulate the original Exodus.

We know that many of those slaves who *physically* left Egypt remained there *psychologically.* Taking the slaves out of Egypt turned out to be easier than taking Egypt out of the slaves. No sooner did the slaves leave than they yearned to return. The leader of the Seder gets to taste Moses' frustration. His unruly followers were a lot better at lamenting the good old days in Egypt than at celebrating their newfound freedom. The grumbling at the Seder comes straight from the story of the Exodus! Three days after crossing the Red Sea, the Israelites start complaining about the quality of the water. A while later, they whine about being starved for the "fleshpots" of Egypt.

What makes it so hard to stay focused on celebrating the fact that we are free? In part because we take freedom for granted. But maybe on a deeper level we really *don't* feel free. So we find it hard to wholeheartedly celebrate a condition that still eludes us.

The Hebrew word for Egypt, *Mitzrayim,* can also be read *maytzarim,* "narrow straits." To the extent that all of us feel stuck in our own narrow, familiar places—our own private Egypts—we all resist the Seder. We want to leave, but we're afraid. Of course, this is exactly why the festival is so important.

The Haggadah tells it like it is: "Now we are slaves." We all need to confront the enslaved parts of ourselves with hope that "next year we will be free."

An element of tension at the Seder seems to pit those who want to make this night "different from all other nights" against those who want it to remain an ordinary night—an evening that ends "on time" and includes all the regular topics of conversation. This is only part of the picture. The rest is that each of us feels both poles of ambivalence—wanting to make the night different from all others, wanting to become free, and at the same time not wanting to leave our own Egypts. This helps explain why making a "successful" Seder is not such a simple matter.

There's another angle we need to consider. *Seder* literally means "order." In fact, many begin the Seder by chanting a rhymed mnemonic list of the Seder's fifteen traditional elements. Here the tension lies between the urge for freedom in the sense of total absence of limits versus freedom that comes from acting within the bounds of an externally imposed structure. The chaos that sometimes invades the Seder represents the newly freed slave's yearning for unbridled liberty. Anyone who saw the news footage of the looting in Iraqi cities immediately following the fall of Saddam Hussein's regime in the spring of 2003 witnessed an example of the chaos of sudden freedom without order.

It is as if the Seder represents Torah and we are not really sure that we want to accept it. We'd rather enjoy anarchy than constraints upon our personal freedom. If Sinai is the ultimate destination of the Exodus, each of us along the way is tempted by our own golden calves, by our own false gods.

Another challenge involves the dissonance between the comfort of celebrating liberation and the distance, if not alienation, from God the Liberator as depicted in the Haggadah. The truth is that the God of Jewish liturgy (at least of most liturgy) poses a serious obstacle for many Jews today. Without tools to reframe the concept of God, that dissonance often leads to disappointment and frustration with prayer and ritual. For many, the God of the Haggadah has become the elephant, as it were, at the Seder—present in virtually every passage, but ignored by everyone. Neglecting this "disconnect" can seriously undermine the Seder's potential. Chapter 12 takes up some of these difficult issues.

Finally, remember the Haggadah's four children. Each has a seat at the table. That makes the Seder's diversity something of a microcosm of the Jewish world. Working to create a space in which all can feel comfortable during the Seder gives us a taste of what life in today's pluralistic Jewish world is sometimes like and of the unfinished work that lies ahead for the Jewish People when it comes to living with our differences.

As a Seder leader, the more you're aware of these issues, the better you can handle them with grace and sensitivity.

Finally, Seder leaders should realize that having two Seders—with the possibility of two kinds of Seders with different participants—can be a real opportunity! Our second Seder is smaller than the first and often more experimental.

A NOTE ON RABBINIC LITERATURE, THE HAGGADAH, AND TRANSLATIONS

This book includes a good number of passages from rabbinic literature. Dating of rabbinic literature, often an issue of scholarly debate, generally follows the

Introduction to the Talmud and Midrash, by H. L. Strack and Gunter Stemberger, translated and edited by Markus Bockmuehl (Minneapolis: Fortress Press, 1996).

This vast body of literature has much to teach us, but not necessarily about the "facts" of Jewish history or the actual biographies of the sages who appear in its texts. The material was virtually always compiled by redactors over long periods of time, often hundreds of years after the events described. The deeds and even particular teachings of rabbinic figures all reflect the complex motivations of redactors who sometimes sought to elevate a particular idea by putting it in the mouth of a beloved or highly respected sage. These are the texts our tradition has handed down. Like the Bible, they represent a treasure of wisdom about how to live our lives; they are not meant to be history books. The question is not whether events occurred literally as these texts describe them, but what deeper lessons our tradition wants us to learn from a particular story.

All this applies to the Haggadah with the added complication that it has evolved over a longer period of time and exists in more versions than possibly any other Jewish text. The Haggadah, of course, includes many verses from the Bible. But the core of the Haggadah's treatment of them as well as its nonbiblical material derive first from the Mishnah and secondarily from the Jerusalem and Babylonian Talmuds. The Talmuds are essentially wide-ranging commentaries on the Mishnah, the Jerusalem Talmud compiled by around 400 C.E. and the Babylonian Talmud between 550 and 650 C.E. The Haggadah also utilizes various midrashic sources. (For a definition of midrash see "What is Midrash?" on page 360.)

Our oldest Haggadot are manuscripts written in Israel that were found in the Cairo Geniza. They date from between the tenth and eleventh centuries and differ recognizably from contemporary Haggadot. They include three, rather than four, questions, for example, and lack the midrashic elaboration of Deuteronomy 26:5–8. Fourteenth century "copies" of Haggadot attributed to ninth century Geonim—leaders of the great centers of learning in what is now central Iraq—are relatively similar to those of today with the exception that they lack the rituals associated with Elijah and the familiar Seder songs, which were added in the Middle Ages. Beyond this, it is difficult to be more precise about the sources and dates of some of the Haggadah's nonbiblical passages. Take for example: "In every generation, each individual should feel as though he or she had gone out of

Egypt." This passage appears in today's "standard" Mishnah but not in earlier manuscripts from the twelfth and thirteenth centuries. Some of the "standard" Mishnah's language about the night of Passover may actually reflect the influence of the textual traditions found in early Haggadot. References to the Mishnah's treatment of the night of Passover (Pesachim, chapter 10) are based on the text of the Kaufmann manuscript, thought to be relatively free of these influences. It was published in facsimile by George Lewis Beers in 1929 (Haag, M. Nijhoff). A translation of this appears in Appendix I.

I've used the Ashkenazic text of the Haggadah, variations of which are likely used by a majority of American Jews. My "standard" Hebrew version of this text is found in the *The Passover Haggadah* (Schocken Books, 1984), edited by Nahum N. Glatzer with commentaries based on the studies of E. D. Goldschmidt, one of the great Haggadah scholars of the last century. This text, or very similar versions of it, is widely used. It appears, for instance, in the Maxwell House Haggadah, the Silverman Haggadah (Media Judaica, 1979), and the many Haggadot published by Artscroll/Mesorah Publications. Translations of this basic text are based on various Haggadot.

In most cases, I've used the Second (1999) Jewish Publication Society translation of the Bible. However, I have departed from the Jewish Publication Society in choosing to retain the Hebrew, Adonai, rather than using the translation "Lord." When the Talmud, for example, quotes a biblical passage, I've generally retained the translation contained in that passage, because in such cases, the translation of a Talmudic passage and the rendering of biblical verse are often closely related. Unless otherwise noted, quotations from the Mishnah, Talmud, Midrash Rabbah, and Zohar are from the Soncino translation, Davka CD-ROM version. In an attempt to preserve the flavor of these works spanning thousands of years of Jewish history, their original language has been maintained whenever possible, including instances of "masculine God language."

1

A Dish for the Ages: The Seder Plate

. . . צְלִי־אֵשׁ וּמַצּוֹת עַל־מְרֹרִים יֹאכְלֻהוּ:

. . . They shall eat it roasted over fire, with unleavened bread and with bitter herbs.
—EXODUS 12:8

Adorned with pictures or labels specifying its proper content and arrangement, the Seder plate seems to epitomize what the night of Passover is all about—order. The Seder plate seems to embody the essence of ritual, the precise duplication of a series of acts passed down from one generation to the next. A brief look beneath the surface reveals a completely different picture. While the Seder plate contains items that are to be dipped or made into sandwiches and eaten in a certain sequence, the nature and use of those items has varied enormously. For instance, the first reference to horseradish on the Seder plate—in the twelfth century—mentions it as an ingredient in charoset, not as a bitter herb.[1] Maimonides (1135–1204) called for dipping a green vegetable in *charoset*![2]

This chapter will enable you to use the Seder plate as a vehicle for introducing a bit of novelty to the evening—within the bounds of Jewish law—and will help you create an engaging experience. Thinking about the Seder plate this way will not only help your guests appreciate the diversity of Jewish custom, but will model the kind of creativity and freedom that are appropriate for celebrating our liberation from slavery. We'll also provide some background about the elements on the Seder plate with questions for discussion throughout.

CONFUSED?

Despite the fact that Seder plates make every effort to indicate what goes where, many people find these plates to be a source of confusion. Why, for example, do some plates have a place for lettuce and others don't? If what belongs on the Seder plate and how to arrange it confuses you, rest assured you are in fine company. Some of the greatest Jewish thinkers of past centuries have disagreed over these very issues. Why have the contents and organization of the Seder plate occupied so much attention? The short answer goes like this. Seder means "order," and the Seder plate has become a microcosm of concerns about properly carrying out the evening's many rituals. Just as we have a fifteen-word mnemonic to remind us of the correct order of the Seder's fifteen steps, many Haggadot also include a diagram to help people arrange the plate. In fact, some Haggadot provide two or even three different diagrams. But these only beget more questions. For example, many such diagrams specify the location of two or three pieces of matzah, but many plates leave no space for matzah. Where does it belong?

A longer explanation about the complications surrounding the Seder plate involves five factors.

1. The contents of the plate evolved from a fairly straightforward biblical passage about the paschal sacrifice: "They shall eat it roasted over fire, with unleavened bread [*matzot*] and with bitter herbs [*m'rorim*]" (Exodus 12:8). All three traditional approaches to the Seder plate include three core ingredients that evoke the ancient festival—unleavened bread, bitter herbs, and a roasted shank bone (some prefer a chicken neck), representing the absent paschal offering.

2. Our earliest descriptions of the post–Temple celebration of Passover show the influence of customs associated with the Greek symposium. Along with stylized conversation and reclining, the symposium featured multiple dipped appetizers served on a removable tray. All arrangements of the

Seder plate include a bitter herb that we dip in *charoset*, while two arrangements also include *karpas*, a green vegetable, for dipping.

3. Because the Seder became a substitute for the paschal offering, some of the laws that governed the sacrifice were later applied to the Seder—as well as the plate containing the evening's principal symbols. Different interpretations of those laws contribute to different arrangements of the plate.

4. As Jewish texts describing the Seder evolved, ambiguities gave rise to the development of contrasting customs. How many matzot does the Seder require? Two or three? Can we use the same bitter herb for two purposes—first dipping it in *charoset* and later using it as part of the Hillel sandwich? Or does each of these rituals require unique ingredients? Different answers to these questions influenced the contents and arrangement of the Seder plate.

5. Local customs and changing language also added to diversity among Seder plates. For example, one of our earliest descriptions of the Seder lists five acceptable kinds of bitter herbs, the most common choice being *chazeret*, or lettuce, as that word was understood eighteen hundred years ago. In modern Hebrew, *chazeret* means "horseradish"!

EXPERIMENT WITH YOUR PLATE

Although you may have very established traditions of what you put on your Seder plate, these practices have varied enormously in different times and places. Below you will find a wide variety of suggestions for experimenting with your Seder plate as a means of creating a more engaging experience for your guests.

The Seder celebrates freedom, so be creative!

SOCIAL ACTION

In more recent times, the Seder plate has become a vehicle for focusing our attention on issues in the world that demand our attention. During the Soviet Jewry movement of the 1970s and 1980s, many Jews added a fourth matzah, the "Matzah of Hope," to the plate and accompanied it with a reading on oppression and liberation.[3] In the early 1980s, Susannah Heschel began adding an orange to the Seder plate. A rabbi's wife had once told her that "there's as much room for a lesbian in Judaism as there is for a crust of bread on the Seder plate." Rather than violate the laws of Passover and add a crust of bread to her Seder plate, she added an orange. Anita Diamant described the orange as "a symbol of the struggle of people who have been marginalized within the Jewish community; that includes gay and lesbian Jews, and indeed all Jewish women. . . . The orange is a symbol of the juicy vitality of Judaism, which reseeds and reforms and reconstructs itself from generation to generation."[4]

- Choose something to add to the Seder plate this year that relates to a subject of special concern. Explain the matter, lead a short discussion about it, and brainstorm with the group about what concrete actions guests might be willing to undertake to make progress on the issue, such as writing letters to members of Congress, contributing to an organization working on the issue, or writing a letter to a newspaper. Alternatively you might wish to arrange with one of your guests to choose an item to add to the Seder plate and to lead the ensuing discussion. Note: This kind of conversation could well be conducted in your living room before the Seder actually begins.

AROUSING THE CURIOSITY OF CHILDREN

Long ago, the Seder plate became a vehicle for engaging children at the Seder. The Talmud says that we should remove the table—now the Seder plate—before recounting the story of the Exodus, so that children will ask, "Why?"[5] That's why many Haggadot instruct us to remove the Seder plate from the table when reciting the Four Questions. Zedekiah ben Abraham (thirteenth century, Italy) said that the plate contains "toasted grains, types of sweets and fruits to entice the children and to drive away their sleepiness and so that they will notice [the unusual foods] and will ask" questions.[6] (There were precautions, of course—such toasted grains could not violate the prohibition against *chametz*, for example.)

- Add something to the Seder plate that you think will arouse curiosity and stimulate discussion.

KARPAS: A GREEN VEGETABLE?

- Ideally one should use a green vegetable, but in Russia, for example, where greens were not always available, potatoes were traditional, and elsewhere turnips or onions sufficed.[7] This year, try something different, preferably green, for *karpas*!

- One of the most familiar rituals of the Seder comes when we dip *karpas* into saltwater. The symbolism goes something like this. As we anticipate renewal, we remember the salty tears of our ancestors who likewise were redeemed from Egypt in the spring. But saltwater is only one option. Other traditions argue for vinegar or wine.[8] Maimonides, among others, advocated dipping *karpas* into *charoset*![9] Ask your guests to interpret the symbolism that each of these might suggest. If you always use saltwater, consider choosing wine or vinegar this year.

A BITTER HERB?

- The Mishnah mentions a number of options for bitter herbs, including romaine lettuce or chicory (*chazeret*), endive (*ulshin*), and something called *tamkha*, which has been identified as chervil or horehound.[10] If you regularly use horseradish, consider adding one or more of these "bitter" alternatives to your Seder plate this year. If you do, you might want to offer the explanation below.

Although today Ashkenazi Jews commonly use horseradish for bitter herbs (*maror*), this practice dates back only to the Middle Ages. For centuries rabbinic authorities discouraged using the root and permitted just the leaves. Opposition to horseradish root did not disappear until the eighteenth century. Horseradish only began to appear on the Seder plate when Jews began to reside in the northern reaches of Europe, where greens such as lettuce were unavailable or too expensive in the early spring.[11]

CHAROSET Á LA BRICK?

- In 1862, during the Civil War, a Jewish Union soldier described a battlefield Seder: "The necessaries for the *choroutzes* we could not obtain, so we got a brick which, rather hard to digest, reminded us, by looking at it, for what purpose it was intended." Consider serving your *charoset* this year on a brick![12]

A TASTE OF HISTORY

Here we'll explore a bit of history and commentary about the contents of the Seder plate. If you are interested in questions for discussion and activities, you might want to focus on the sections covering bitter herbs and *charoset*.

KARPAS

The designation of *karpas* as celery or parsley, as opposed to any other green vegetable, came about in the Middle Ages.[13] The Talmud speaks only of *y'rakot*, "vegetables." Amram Gaon (d. c. 875) mentions *karpas* among many other options, and Saadiah Gaon (Babylonia, 882–942) says that one recites the blessing over "the type [of vegetable] one wishes, so long as it is not bitter."[14] According to one scholar, the ultimate preference for *karpas* only came about through the influence of the students of Rashi (1040–1105), the great eleventh-century French commentator. Yosef Tabory believes that this group disseminated a mnemonic enumeration of the Seder's fifteen steps that now appears in virtually all Haggadot. *Karpas* is the third term on that list.[15]

Karpas became the object of fascinating interpretations. Chizkiah ben Manoach (France, fourteenth century) identified it with the laurel wreath worn by victorious warriors after battle, affirming Israel's ultimate victory over its enemies. He also linked *karpas* with the ornamented tunic, *k'tonet **pasim*** (Gen. 37:3), that Jacob gave to Joseph, which led to a chain of events that brought our ancestors into Egypt. The interpretation alludes to a teaching from the Talmud: "A man should never single out one son among his other sons, for on account of the two ounces of silk, which Jacob gave Joseph in excess of his other sons, his brothers became jealous of him and the matter resulted in our forefathers' descent into Egypt" (Shabbat 10b). Another approach read *karpas* backward (ספרך). Here, *samech*, the first letter, has a numerical value of sixty. *Farech*, the last three letters of the word, means "hard labor." So according to this interpretation, *karpas* reminds us of the sixty myriad (in Greek myriad means 10,000) or 600,000 Israelite males who went forth from hard labor.[16]

Matzah

Rabbi Jacob Moelin (1360?–1427), the first to comment on the arrangement of certain items on the plate, indicated that the matzot should be directly on the plate. This would ensure that when the plate is removed during the Four Questions, none of the evening's symbolic foods would be left behind.[17] Many scholars of Jewish law likewise agree that the matzot belong on the plate. Others require putting the matzot on a separate plate, shelving them beneath the plate, or bundling them in matzah holders made from cloth. Commentators have associated the three matzot with various triads: Kohen, Levi, and Israel; the three measures of choice flour that Abraham requested Sarah to bake for the three visiting angels (Gen. 18:6)—an event that the midrash sets on the night of Passover;[18] Abraham, Isaac, and Jacob, the three patriarchs; or the three types of unleavened bread offered for a thanksgiving offering (Lev. 7:12).

Just how many matzot the plate should contain—two or three—raises another argument. The Talmud comments, "All admit that on Passover one puts the broken cake in the whole one and breaks [them together].[19] What is the reason? Scripture speaks of 'Bread of poverty [Deut. 16:3].'" In those days, matzah was a pliable, flat bread, like pita or even tortillas. The Talmud describes using one-and-a-half matzot, suggesting the initial presence of two in order to end up with one broken and one whole piece. Among many others, Maimonides and the Vilna Gaon followed the tradition of two matzot.[20]

The conflict arose because it had become a custom on festivals, as on Shabbat, to bless the bread with two loaves in commemoration of the double portion of manna the Israelites gathered prior to Shabbat (Ex. 16:22). For Passover this implied three matzot—two for reciting the blessing over the bread and one to produce a broken piece over which the blessing for the matzah would be recited. The *Shulchan Arukh*, an authoritative sixteenth-century law code, affirms this practice, clearly the dominant one these days.[21]

Bitter Herbs

Questions for discussion and reflection:

- A few weeks before the Seder, ask each of your guests to bring their responses to the following question to the Seder: "One of the greatest causes of bitterness in the world today is _____." At the Seder, go around the table and share these responses with the group.

• Depending on your group, you may want to share the following with your guests prior to the Seder. You can explain that you are doing so as an aid to spiritual preparation for the holiday.

A fourteenth-century Yemenite midrash poignantly describes four sources of bitterness. "In four things there is said to be bitterness. The inability to conceive children . . . bereavement over children . . . a broken heart . . . and terrible illness. And when the Egyptians enslaved Israel, they caused all of these."[22]

• During the Seder we recall the bitterness of our ancestors' slavery in Egypt, but the holiday is also a good time to think about the sources of bitterness in our own personal lives. Yet we also dip bitter herbs in *charoset*, which takes the edge off the bitterness. What embitters you? How can you reduce that bitterness? How do you understand the difference between bitterness and sadness?

A BIT OF BACKGROUND

The origins of bitter herbs on the Seder plate reach back to that verse in Exodus (12:8) we considered earlier that describes the Passover sacrifice in Egypt: "They shall eat it roasted over fire, with unleavened bread [*matzot*] and with bitter herbs [*m'rorim*]." The book of Numbers (9:11) features a similar verse, one that we actually read at the Seder to explain the Hillel sandwich. (For more on the Hillel sandwich see pages 9–10.) The fact that both verses first refer to unleavened bread before bitter herbs accounts for the order in which we eat them at the Seder: first unleavened bread and then bitter herbs.

Along with bitter herbs, some Seder plates have a space for lettuce, in ancient times considered a form of bitter vegetable. Why? In describing the night of Passover, the Mishnah (Pesachim 10:3) mentions lettuce—*chazeret*—twice, first to be used for dipping and then as a bitter herb we are obliged to eat. Nowhere in the account do we even find the word *maror*!

Chazeret, probably a romaine-like type of lettuce, served well because it was bitter enough to fulfill the requirement of eating bitter herbs and it could also easily be dipped into condiments, like *charoset*. The first dipping evolved into the ritual of dunking *karpas* in saltwater. The second became what we call *maror*. But, over time, two customs developed in connection with the *maror*: first, *maror* was dipped in *charoset*; second, it was eaten on matzah as part of the Hillel sandwich. But the Talmud expressed hesitation about using the same vegetable more than once at the Seder and thus created room for three different vegetables.[23] Hence, some Seder plates include *karpas*, *maror* (these days, either lettuce or horseradish root), and *chazeret*, while others leave space for only *karpas* and horseradish.

Opinion divides about whether horseradish should be grated or not. Some hold that eating ungrated horseradish can be dangerous to one's health, although others argue that grating the horseradish, changing it from its natural form, renders it unfit for a blessing over a "fruit of the earth."[24] Apart from this, when it comes to dipping horseradish in *charoset*, an un-grated, spoon-like slice has clear advantages!

THE HILLEL SANDWICH

A remembrance of the Temple as was the custom of Hillel. Thus did Hillel. He made a sandwich of the Pesach offering, matzah, and bitter herbs and ate them together to perform what has been prescribed: "They shall eat it with matzot and bitter herbs" (Numbers 9:11).

—THE PASSOVER HAGGADAH

The Seder Plate also contains the ingredients for what is commonly called the "Hillel sandwich," one of so many legacies of this great sage who lived in the second half of the first century B.C.E. and the early part of the following century. Of the ten sages mentioned in the Haggadah, Hillel is the only one to have lived out his years while the Temple stood. After eating the matzah and bitter herbs separately, we combine them, as a reminder of Hillel's practice. As early as the third century, sources commented on the custom, as did the Babylonian Talmud a few hundred years later: "It was related of Hillel that he used to wrap them together. For it is said, 'They shall eat it with matzot and bitter herbs' (Numbers 9:11) . . . [One should eat] matzot and bitter herbs together without a blessing, in memory of the Temple, as Hillel [did]."[25] We don't say a blessing over the Hillel sandwich

9

because, since the destruction of the Second Temple, the sandwich has been missing the paschal sacrifice that had been its critical ingredient.

The Talmud goes on to report a disagreement about the custom. Was it permissible to fulfill the commandments of Passover by eating matzah (expressly required by the Bible) together with bitter herbs (mentioned in the Bible, but only required by rabbinic decree)? The memory of Hillel's sandwich seemed to suggest that in this case biblical and rabbinic decrees *could* be combined into a single ritual. However, out of respect for the sages who opposed such a combination, the Seder would also include the ritual of eating each separately. The compromise satisfied all sides and we have honored it on the night of Passover for more than fifteen hundred years!

As we eat a sandwich with just two of Hillel's three ingredients, we bear witness to the fact that Passover remains meaningful even without the Temple and its sacrificial rites. But at the same time the composers of the Haggadah have widened the symbolism of matzah and bitter herbs. No longer harkening back to the Exodus alone, they also serve as a remembrance of the Temple—and, by implication, of its destruction.

Through Hillel's sandwich the Haggadah transforms the symbols of the Exodus to represent all the Egypts, all the exiles in which we as a people have found ourselves over the millennia. If God brought us out of that first Egypt, then God can bring us out of other Egypts, too. If God represents the power that allows a people to find what it takes to move beyond the narrow straits, then a people that overcame that first Egypt can overcome other Egypts as well. When we eat Hillel's sandwich of matzah and bitter herbs, we express our faith in redemption as an ongoing process that can be as real for us today as it was for our ancestors.

CHAROSET

Read the following and discuss with your group.

- Ask your guests to respond to the following question: "How does *charoset* differ from other elements on the Seder plate?" See how many differences your group can discover.

- Jewish communities from different parts of the world have different recipes for *charoset*. Ask several of your guests to do some research and to bring different kinds of *charoset* to the Seder. Ask them to describe what the various ingredients symbolize.

- Consider making your *charoset* from the items mentioned below in the Song of Songs. At an appropriate time in the Seder, read or explain the following and conclude with the verses from the Song of Songs. These five verses allude to spring, which makes them a lovely reading for the Seder.

The Song of Songs has often been considered an allegory of the relationship between God and the Jewish People. As a result, the Song of Songs has many associations with Passover and the Exodus, a formative experience in the development of that relationship. According to tradition, we read the Song of Songs after the Seder has been completed and in synagogue on the Sabbath that falls during Passover. The Song of Songs also enjoys a special connection with *charoset*. A medieval commentary on the Talmud says that *charoset* should include the fruits mentioned in the Song of Songs.[26]

> Oh, give me the kisses of your mouth, for your love is sweeter than *wine* (1:2).
> The green *figs* are on the fig tree, the vines in blossom give off fragrance. Arise my darling; my fair one, come away! (2:13).
> I went down to the *nut* grove to see the budding of the vale; to see if the vines had blossomed, if the *pomegranates* were in bloom (6:11).
> I say let me climb the *date* palm, let me take hold of its branches (7:9).
> Under the *apple* tree I roused you; it was there your mother conceived you, there she bore you (8:5).
>
> —SONG OF SONGS

- Ask your guests if anyone knows why *charoset* often includes apples. If anyone knows, let them explain, if not, read the following aloud.

Rabbi Akiva credited the righteous women of that generation with the Exodus from Egypt and told the following tale. Pharaoh tried to prevent the Israelites from procreating—"the separation of husbands from wives" as we read in the Haggadah. But the women refused to go along. They furtively met their husbands out in the fields, brought them food, seduced them under the apple trees, and nine months later returned to give birth beneath the apple trees. As it says in the Song of Songs, "Under the apple tree I roused you; it was there your mother conceived you, there she bore you" (8:5). *Charoset*, says the Talmud, should be thick, "a remembrance of the clay" with which the Israelites made bricks, but it should also be tart, "a remembrance of the apple trees" and what transpired beneath them.[27]

- Make your *charoset* on the thick side and try thinning it at the table with wine or vinegar. When people ask what you're doing, tell them you're glad they asked! Share the explanation below.

Commentators discussed the ingredients of *charoset* and its texture, as well. The Jerusalem Talmud (c. 400 C.E.) cites two traditions about its texture. *Charoset* should be thick to recall the clay from which the Israelites made bricks, and it should be soft to recall the blood, perhaps the blood from the paschal sacrifice smeared on the Israelites' doorposts or the blood that turned the Nile red.[28] Many medieval commentators tried to honor both traditions. They made their *charoset* thick and thinned it with wine or vinegar at the table before eating it.[29]

ROASTED SHANK BONE AND EGG

The roasted shank bone and egg serve as silent reminders of the Temple during the time when the heart of Passover—and of so much else in Judaism—revolved around the rituals of sacrifice. We discuss them last because unlike all the other items on the plate, we generally don't eat them. But, of course (!), some claim that we *should* eat them, most often, the next day.[30] In fact, we don't mention these symbols during the Seder, and we actually seem to avoid them. For instance, when we recite Rabban Gamaliel's explanation of the paschal sacrifice, matzah and bitter herbs, we lift the Seder plate when referring to the last two items, but not when we refer to the first.[31] This reflects concern lest we create any impression that the shank bone could be a portion of the now-forbidden Passover offering.

The Mishnah's description of the night of Passover mentions a number of items that should be brought to the Seder leader: "matzah, lettuce [*chazeret*], *charoset* and two cooked dishes."[32] The Talmud explains that these two cooked dishes—and a wide variety was permitted—correspond to two distinct sacrifices associated with Passover. One recalls the Passover sacrifice. The other represents a different sacrifice, probably a special form of the *chagigah* or festival offering. This additional animal would be slaughtered if the group that one was celebrating the holiday with was too large to be sated by the Passover sacrifice alone. The extra sacrificial meat would be eaten first to ensure that the celebrants would then be able to truly savor the Passover sacrifice without being so hungry that they would wolf it down, so to speak.[33] Eventually, these two cooked dishes crystallized into our roasted shank bone and egg, roasted or boiled.

Another common explanation holds that the shank bone, *z'ro'a*, represents God's "outstretched arm" or *z'ro'a n'tuyah* (e.g. Ex. 6:6). In Aramaic, *beiyah* means egg, but the word also appears in an old Aramaic expression: "God, be willing [*b'ah*] to take us out" with the outstretched arm. Others see the egg, traditionally associated with mourning, as a doleful reminder of the lost Temple. A related custom, serving boiled eggs at the Seder, also serves as an expression of mourning for the Temple. Although eggs are a traditional food of mourning, they also symbolize spring and eternal life, all of which helps explain their connection to Passover and Easter.

Sherira Gaon (Babylonia, d.1006) noted a custom of including a third symbolic cooked food—in addition to the shank bone and egg—"in memory of Miriam, as it says, 'I brought you up from the land of Egypt, I redeemed you from the house of bondage, and I sent before you Moses, Aaron, and Miriam'" (Micah 6:4).[34] The evocation of human beings in the redemption from Egypt—reminiscent of *charoset*'s connection to Israel's righteous women in Egypt—challenges the dominant understanding of the Haggadah as attributing complete responsibility for the Exodus to God alone.

WHY DOES THIS PLATE DIFFER FROM THAT ONE?

Although there are many variations, today, the placement of the items on the Seder plate tends to follow the customs of three individuals, each of whom exerted enormous influence on Jewish practice:

- Moses Isserles (Krakow, 1530–1572), whose glosses on the *Shulchan Arukh* enabled this law code to gain acceptance among Ashkenazi Jews, making it perhaps the most authoritative of the codes.

- Isaac Luria (Safed, 1534–1572), the renowned Kabbalist whose work suffuses Jewish mysticism.

- Elijah ben Solomon Zalman (the Gaon of Vilna, 1720–1797), among the most influential scholars of Jewish law since Maimonides.

Isserles and the Vilna Gaon differed on the number of items on the plate, but they followed the same organizing principle, namely, that as the Talmud states, one should not "reach over" one commandment to fulfill another.[35] Isserles put it this way: "One should arrange the dish in front of him [the leader of the Seder] so that he will not have to reach over a mitzvah. That is, the *karpas* [which is eaten as the first "food" mitzvah] should be closest, with the vinegar or salt water [in which the *karpas* is dipped] closer than the matzah [which is eaten later] and the matzah closer than the *maror* and the *charoset* [which come only after the matzah]. The latter should be closer to him than the meat and the egg [symbols of the ancient sacrifices]."[36] But positioning the meat and the egg last might create the impression that they too were being reserved to be eaten in fulfillment of a commandment. To rectify this misimpression, the Vilna Gaon placed the meat and egg at the forefront of the plate, where they would clearly have to be passed over.

MOSES ISSERLES, 1530–1572   **THE VILNA GAON, 1720–1797**

14

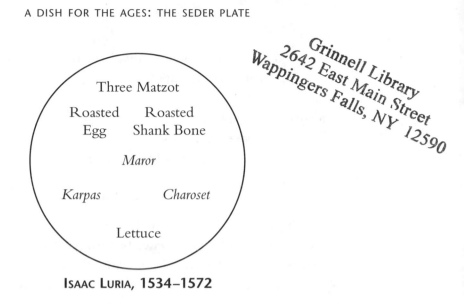

ISAAC LURIA, 1534–1572

Isaac Luria took a very different approach.[37] First, instead of just one form of bitter herbs (*maror*) he used two—adding *chazeret*, or lettuce (for the Hillel sandwich). Including the three matzot and the plate itself, Luria thus counted ten items (see below), each of which corresponds to one of the ten *sefirot*, or divine emanations through which God created and sustains the cosmos. The arrangement of the items on the plate conforms to the Kabbalistic "tree," which in turn represents a range of concepts including the mystical "body" of God and the form of the primordial Adam.

The Lurianic arrangement is not concerned with presenting items on the plate in the order in which they are used during the Seder so as to avoid "passing over a mitzvah."[38] Hayim Vital, one of Luria's principal disciples, tersely outlined the relationships between the *sefirot* and the items on the Seder plate:[39]

> The upper, middle, and third matzot correspond to the three remaining tribes—Kohen, Levi, and Israel—and to the three faculties of divine wisdom: *Chochmah* (wisdom), *Binah* (understanding), and *Da'at* (knowledge).
> Roasted shank bone: *Chesed*—kindness, God's right hand.
> Roasted egg: *Gevurah*—strength, judgment, God's left hand.

15

Maror: *Tiferet*—glory, which mediates between kindness on the right and judgment on the left.

Charoset: *Netzach*—eternity.

Karpas: *Hod*—splendor.

Lettuce: *Yesod*—foundation.

The Seder Plate which holds everything: *Malkhut*—kingdom.

FOR DISCUSSION

• You might try this on your own or with your group—depending on your guests—before the Seder begins. Rearrange the Seder plate like Moses Isserles, then the Vilna Gaon, then Isaac Luria. Explain the basic differences. Which arrangement do you and your guests like best? Why? (Since most Seder plates don't have room for the matzot, put them on another plate and cover them.)

• If you were starting from scratch, how would you organize your Seder plate?

• Ask your guests to briefly share with the group stories, if there are any, about how they came by their Seder plates.

2

The Long Road from Slavery to Freedom: From Ancient Egypt to Our Time

הָשַׁתָּא עַבְדֵי, לְשָׁנָה הַבָּאָה בְּנֵי חוֹרִין:

Now we are slaves. Next year we will be free.

—THE PASSOVER HAGGADAH

Near the beginning of the Seder we come upon this extraordinary statement. The Haggadah asks us to look within ourselves and to question how we remain enslaved by the fears that plague us or the false gods we worship. But the Haggadah also wants us to think about slavery in the physical sense, to remember what it was like, to bear in mind that, for some, those memories are not so distant, that, for too many, slavery still persists.

Scholars believe that this Aramaic passage dates from the Talmudic period, between 200 and 500 C.E. It clearly refers to a period of Jewish subjugation.[1] When this passage was composed, the fortunes of the Jewish People had fallen disastrously. In the year 70 C.E., the Romans crushed a Jewish rebellion and destroyed the Second Temple. Sixty-two years later, rebellion erupted again, this time led by Bar Kochba, a Jewish general whose followers believed him to be the Messiah. The rebellion ended with the death of hundreds of thousands of Jews and the exile of most of the Jewish population. The composers of this passage identified their fate with that of their exiled, enslaved ancestors.

"Now we are slaves. Next year we will be free." Given the tenor of their times, we can understand these words both literally and metaphorically—literally in the sense that once again the Jewish People experienced oppression and exile, and metaphorically in the sense that they interpreted their current circumstances as a *recurrence* of the familiar Exodus pattern.

This chapter explores the themes of slavery and freedom on the political plane through a series of readings and topics for discussion during your Seder.

CHOOSE ONE OF THESE SELECTIONS TO READ ALOUD DURING YOUR SEDER OR ON YOUR OWN

- Slavery in Ancient Times

- Exodus and the American Ethos

CHOOSE ONE OF THE ACTIVITIES BELOW FOR YOUR SEDER

- The Great Seal of the United States: Israelites Crossing the Red Sea versus a Pyramid

- Former Slaves Speak

- Let Freedom Ring: Historic Words on Freedom

- Jewish Values and Social Justice: American Jews in the Antebellum South

- Slavery in Our Time

QUESTIONS FOR DISCUSSION

- Consider beginning the section of the Seder called Maggid with a discussion of this passage: "Now we are here. Next year in the Land of Israel. Now we are slaves. Next year we will be free." Ask your guests to discuss what this means to them.

- To whom does this statement apply? In what ways might we, today, be enslaved?

- Imagine that you have been asked by a journalist to explain why you oppose slavery. What moral arguments might you make? Can you make a compelling moral argument without invoking religious traditions? Would you feel comfortable making your case on purely pragmatic grounds? For example, would you be willing to argue that slavery ultimately produces political instability or that slave labor is less efficient than hired labor?

SLAVERY IN ANCIENT TIMES

Either of the following selections may be read during the Maggid section of the Seder or as a reading before you sit down at the table. These short essays explore slavery in the ancient world and the role of Exodus imagery in America's founding and battle against slavery.

The road from slavery to freedom stretches back a long way. The history of slavery began with the earliest days of civilization and the discovery that one group of people was able to dominate another. Indeed, slavery may be as old as war itself: Those whom the victor did not kill were enslaved and brought home as a ready source of cheap labor.

But war was hardly the only source of slaves. They could be bought at markets in the larger cities or from traveling dealers. In times of economic distress, parents unable to care for their infants would lay them in a pit. The lucky ones might be rescued by passersby and raised as slaves. Desperate parents might also be forced to sell their children in exchange for food or clothing. If unemployment persisted or debts rose too high, fathers or mothers resorted to selling themselves in order to survive.² Kidnapping children provided another source of slaves.

Massive exploitation of slave labor actually came to Egypt rather late. Archeologists tell us that the pyramids (most were constructed between 2600 and 2300 B.C.E.) were not built by slaves, but by peasants forced into servitude for a few years and then released. But centuries later, when slavery did become widespread there, the Egyptians "perfected" it, just as they had done with everything from building and making war to cultivating crops. In its imperial heyday, Egypt became the largest consumer of slaves in the Near East.3 An Egyptian general's letter to Ramses III (1186–1154 B.C.E.) after one of Egypt's frequent victories over the Canaanites paints a graphic but typical picture:

I have brought back in great numbers those that my sword has spared, with their hands tied behind their backs before my horses, and their wives and children in tens of thousands, and their livestock in hundreds of thousands. I have imprisoned their leaders in fortresses bearing my name . . . branded and enslaved, tattooed with my name and their wives and children have been treated in the same way.[4]

As part of their homage to Egypt, Canaanite leaders regularly shipped boat-loads of slaves off to Egyptian ports.[5] Most slaves in Egypt were foreigners or Asiatics, as they were called there. But often Egyptians themselves who had fallen on hard times had no choice but to sell themselves into slavery.[6]

The demand for slaves became so great that enterprising Egyptians created special "houses of female settlement" where slaves could be conveniently bred in large numbers. For those unable to acquire their own slave, it was possible to rent one to work for just a day or two.

Egyptian law *did* include procedures for freeing slaves, as did biblical law. But the vast majority of these unfortunate people died as slaves, passing their lowly status down to their children and their children's children. In the end, Egyptian society grew increasingly dependent on slavery, more so than other ancient Near Eastern empires. Elsewhere, newly crowned kings often freed prisoners, rebels, and slaves in order to bolster their popularity: In Egypt, these freedom proclamations generally excluded slaves.[7]

Against this background, the Bible's legislation represents a significant step toward humanizing, if not eliminating, bondage. The Ten Commandments begin by invoking the Israelites' redemption from slavery: "And God spoke all these words, saying: 'I Adonai am your God who brought you out of the land of Egypt, the house of bondage'" (Ex. 20:1–2). The fourth commandment explicitly includes slaves: "But the seventh day is a sabbath of Adonai your God; you shall not do any work—you, your son or your daughter, your male or female slave, or your cattle, or the stranger within your settlements" (Ex. 20:10). And the laws given immediately after the Decalogue further regulate slavery. A Hebrew slave was to serve a maximum of six years.

But in Israel, as in Egypt, most slaves were foreigners and their lot remained bleak: "You may keep them as a possession for your children after you, for them to inherit as property for all time" (Lev. 25:46).

The laws of Hammurabi, a Babylonian king who ruled from 1792 to 1750 B.C.E., placed no limits on how a master could treat his slaves. The Bible punished cruelty toward all slaves: "When a man strikes the eye of his slave . . . and destroys it, he shall let him go free on account of his eye. If he knocks out the tooth of his slave . . . he shall let him go free on account of his tooth" (Ex. 21:26–27). And if a master struck his slave and killed him on the spot, he was guilty of murder and punished by death.

But the Bible's treatment of fugitive slaves, Hebrew or foreigner, was without a doubt its most revolutionary advance. In the Code of Hammurabi, the penalty for harboring a fugitive slave was death.[8] Compare this with Deuteronomy 23:16–17: "You shall not turn over to his master a slave who seeks refuge with you from his master. He shall live with you in any place he may choose among your settlements in your midst, wherever he pleases; you must not ill-treat him."[9]

The Bible did not outlaw slavery, but it tried to humanize the practice. And Deuteronomy's treatment of fugitive slaves represents a giant step down the road toward freedom.

EXODUS AND THE AMERICAN ETHOS

Almost three thousand years after the Israelites crossed the Red Sea in pursuit of freedom, Europeans seeking greater religious liberty sailed across the Atlantic Ocean to build a "New Israel" in the New World. In the spring of 1630, as his ship approached the shores of Massachusetts, John Winthrop preached a sermon to his Puritan disciples befitting the travails of a group who felt as if they had relived the journey from Egypt to the Promised Land:

> Now the only way to avoid this shipwreck and to provide our poster-
> ity is to follow the counsel of Micah, *to do justly, to love mercy, and to walk*
> *humbly with our God* . . . The Lord will be our God and delight to dwell
> amongst us as His own people, and will command a blessing upon us in
> all our ways . . . We shall find the God of Israel is among us, when ten
> of us shall be able to resist a thousand of our enemies . . . For we must
> consider that we shall be as a City upon a hill. The eyes of all the peo-
> ple are upon us. So that if we deal falsely with our God in this work . . .
> [we will be] consumed out of the good land where we are going.[10]

But the long arm of oppression proved difficult to escape. In their demand for freedom, the colonists identified with the struggle against Pharaoh. The English King George III and the Egyptian Pharaoh were both freedom's enemies. When the British hastily repealed the hated Stamp Act in 1766 ("No taxation without representation!") it was as if Pharaoh had been defeated. One patriotic pastor preached:

> [The colonists feared that] they should gradually be brought into a state of the most abject slavery. This it was that gave rise to the cry, which became general throughout the colonies, "We shall be made to serve as bond-servants; our lives will be bitter with hard bondage." Nor were the Jews more pleased with the royal provision in their day, which, under God, delivered them from their bondage in Egypt, than were the colonists with the repeal of that act which had so greatly alarmed their fears and troubled their hearts. It was to them as "life from the dead." They "rejoiced and were glad."[11]

Eventually, the bitterness of British tyranny led the colonists to revolt and declare independence. On July 4, 1776, the Continental Congress charged Thomas Jefferson, Benjamin Franklin, and John Adams with recommending a design for the new nation's Great Seal. Franklin proposed Moses parting the Red Sea with Pharaoh's armies drowning as their chariots were overwhelmed by the waters. Jefferson preferred an image of the children of Israel in the wilderness, led by a cloud by day, and a pillar of fire by night. As a motto they proposed, "Rebellion to tyrants is obedience to God" (see page 25).[12]

Despite their infatuation with the Exodus, America's early leaders held a wide range of opinions about slavery. Indeed Jefferson, Washington, and many others owned slaves. And ratification of the nation's Constitution rested on uneasy compromises. One provided that slaves would be counted as three-fifths of a free person when it came to apportioning seats in the House of Representatives. Another forbade harboring fugitive slaves.[13]

In the end, the Great Seal did include an image from Egypt—a pyramid, then thought to have been built by slaves—a monument to a king!

In 1790, there were fewer than 700,000 slaves in the United States. Samuel Elliot Morrison, one of America's great historians, spoke of the terrible contradiction:

The emancipation of these blacks, their becoming domestic servants, common laborers and small farmers, even the return of many to Africa, would then have been possible. But the revolutionary generation lacked the imagination to foresee the tragic consequences of perpetuating an institution which denied the very premises upon which American independence was based.[14]

Pharaoh learned the hard way that building a country on the backs of slaves is dangerous business. It cost many Egyptians their lives. Americans learned the same lesson and paid the same price.

Abolishing slavery required a civil war and the death of 600,000 Americans, more than have been killed in all our subsequent wars combined. And if ever an American president has been compared to Moses it is Abraham Lincoln. His condemnations of slavery ring out as strongly today as they did in the days of the Civil War:

This is a world of compensations; and he who would be no slave must consent to have no slave. Those who deny freedom to others deserve it not for themselves, and under a just God, cannot long retain it.[15]

More than a hundred years later, African Americans still had not fully won their freedom and rights as equal citizens. Imagery of the Exodus fueled their struggle. When he accepted the Nobel Peace Prize in 1964, Martin Luther King Jr. said, "Oppressed people cannot remain oppressed forever. The yearning for freedom eventually manifests itself. The Bible tells the thrilling story of how Moses stood in Pharaoh's court centuries ago and cried, 'Let my people go.'"[16]

Just as discrimination against African Americans did not end with the Emancipation Proclamation in 1863, it didn't end for women when they finally won the right to vote in 1920.

Changing a nation's laws is often just the first step in changing people's stubborn and unfair "habits of the heart."

The Seder is the time to explore the contradictions between the principles we preach and the realities we perpetuate.

Questions for discussion or reflection:

• Have we turned our backs on oppression when it stares us right in the face?

- Do we pretend that victims of hatred somehow deserve their plight?

- Have we treated those fairly over whom we have power?

- Among those closest to us, do we encourage the freedom to grow and change?

THE GREAT SEAL OF THE UNITED STATES: ISRAELITES CROSSING THE RED SEA VERSUS A PYRAMID

The Exodus has been a powerful symbol for many peoples engaged in the struggle for liberation. On July 4, 1776 the Continental Congress appointed a committee to make recommendations for a "Great Seal" befitting the new confederation. A small committee, it included just Thomas Jefferson, Benjamin Franklin, and John Adams! Adams described the group's emerging recommendations in a letter to his wife Abigail on August 14, 1776:

> I am put on a committee . . . to prepare devices for a Great Seal of the confederated States . . . Doctor F. proposes . . . Moses lifting up his wand, and dividing the Red Sea, and Pharaoh in his chariot overwhelmed with the waters. This motto: 'Rebellion to tyrants is obedience to God.' Mr. Jefferson proposed, the children of Israel in the wilderness, led by a cloud by day, and a pillar of fire by night. . . .[17]

In 1782, the Continental Congress finally approved the recommendations of another and far less distinguished committee. Again they chose imagery associated with the Exodus—the pyramid, a monument built to a king, then thought to have been built by slaves. You can find it on the back of a one-dollar bill. The all-seeing eye within a triangle proved to be the only image in the new seal that had been suggested by the previous committee of Jefferson, Adams, and Franklin. The eye within a triangle was to have appeared on the obverse of the seal above representations of liberty and justice.

Copy these two images for each of your guests. Discuss the differences between them, and ask your guests which they prefer and why. You might pair this activity with the earlier reading, "Exodus and the American Ethos," which also mentions the original proposal for the Great Seal.

(*Left*) The image created by Benson J. Lossing (1813–1891) to illustrate the original proposal for the reverse side of the Great Seal by Jefferson, Adams, and Franklin in 1776.[18] It depicts the Israelites, crossing the Red Sea protected by a pillar of fire, and Pharaoh's drowning army. The motto first appeared on the tombstone of John Bradshaw, head of the English court that condemned King Charles I to death in 1649. Thomas Jefferson also adopted the motto for his personal seal.

(*Left*) The seal adopted by the Continental Congress in 1782, which appears on the one-dollar bill. *Annuit Coeptis* means, "He (God) has favored our undertakings." *Novus Ordo Seclorum* means "A new order of the ages (is born)." Both Latin inscriptions paraphrase verses by the Roman poet Virgil.

25

FORMER SLAVES SPEAK

The Seder is not a time for the automatic repetition of a familiar old story. To the contrary, the Haggadah challenges us to make the remote experience of slavery in Egypt vivid and palpable. To accomplish this you might want to bring to your Seder the words of individuals who actually lived as slaves. Below you will find excerpts from three slave narratives—one from the early nineteenth century, another from the Holocaust, and a third from a man who had been a slave in Sudan and obtained his freedom in 1999. Consider the following questions before delving into the slave narratives.

- We Jews trace our ancestry back to slavery in Egypt and have suffered inordinate persecution over the ages. Some would say, "That was a long time ago," and that Jewish interests now dictate that our community's historic commitment to fighting for equality and social justice should be a lesser priority. Do you agree? Why or why not?

- To what extent, if any, do you believe that Jews have a special responsibility to the cause of social justice?

MARY PRINCE: A SLAVE IN THE NINETEENTH CENTURY

Mary Prince dictated her story to an Englishman active in the antislavery movement who published her narrative in 1831. This was the first such published work written by a woman, and it exerted a great influence on subsequent narratives. Mary was born to a family of slaves in Bermuda. She later lived in Antigua, where she married a former slave who had managed to buy his freedom. Soon afterward, her master's family moved to England, promising to free her in a few years. The separation from her husband pained Mary terribly. Increasingly arthritic, she was unable to perform heavier housework. Her master threw her out of the house penniless. Eventually she contacted the Moravian Church with which she had become active in Antigua. Moravians and Quakers gave her work and encouragement, but the story ends with Mary languishing in England, pining for her beloved husband. Here she describes her sale as a young girl.

> At length . . . the master who was to offer us for sale like sheep or cattle, arrived, and asked my mother which was the eldest. She said noth-

ing, but pointed to me. He took me by the hand, and led me out into the middle of the street, and, turning me slowly round, exposed me to the view of those who attended [the sale]. I was soon surrounded by strange men, who examined and handled me in the same manner that a butcher would a calf or a lamb he was about to purchase, and who talked about my shape and size in like words—as if I could no more understand their meanings than dumb beasts. I was then put up to sale. The bidding commenced at a few pounds, and gradually rose to thirty-eight sterling [today about $2,600] when I was knocked down to the highest bidder; and the people who stood by said that I had fetched a great sum for so young a slave. I then saw my sisters led forth, and sold to different owners; so that we had not the sad satisfaction of being partners in bondage . . . All slaves want to be free—to be free is very sweet . . . I have been a slave myself—and I know what slaves feel . . . The man that says the slave is quite happy in slavery—that they don't want to be free—is either ignorant or lying.[19]

BETTY LISSING: A SLAVE LABORER DURING THE HOLOCAUST

During World War II, slave labor contributed significantly to the German war effort. As manpower grew short and the supply of armaments began to run low, Hitler agreed to build factories in concentration camps. By 1944, more than half a million concentration camp inmates had been leased out to German companies that would in turn pay fees back to the camps.

Betty Lissing's family had lived in Holland since 1650. At age twenty-one, she arrived in Auschwitz in January of 1944. Her grandfather, parents, and two brothers had already been killed there. Until the war ended about eighteen months later, she worked in the control section of a plant, the Union, that manufactured artillery shell casings and cone-shaped metal pieces (korpers) used elsewhere in the shells. Betty's husband also survived the war and the couple eventually settled in Australia.

During my second week at the Union I came down with typhus, had a tremendously high fever and became very ill. I felt I could not go on.

27

My cousin forced me not to go to the [inmate's hospital]. She warned me that I would be gassed there. I don't remember how I survived, since I was mostly delirious. The night shift workers received an extra dish of soup at the Union, which helped us not to be completely starved. However, the work was very hazardous because everything was called sabotage; for example, stopping work a minute before the alarm went off or letting defective [parts] pass the control. As a matter of fact, I attempted to let faulty items go through on purpose as often as I was able to do so . . . I recall one incident when all girls working at a particular table were severely punished for sabotage. Then the entire work squad of the Union had to assemble in the hall. Camp commandant Hoessler screamed and whipped the girls in front of us and condemned them to be gassed. The whole work detail was in shock and I could not speak . . . The bruised and bleeding girls were taken away and we could do nothing at all to help them. Two days later, when we had assumed that they had been killed, they all suddenly returned to the block. Such things happened constantly. We were always in a state of terror. . . .[20]

FRANCIS BOK: ENSLAVED IN SUDAN, 1989–1999

Francis Bok was enslaved in Sudan for ten years. He escaped in 1999 and now works with the American Anti-Slavery Group in Boston. In September 2000 he gave this testimony before the Senate Foreign Relations Committee.

I was born in Southern Sudan, near Nyamllel. When I was seven, my mother sent me to the market to sell eggs and beans. I never saw my mother again. At the market, militia soldiers attacked. Hundreds of Arabs on horses came into the market shouting. They shot people in the head. They cut off heads with swords. The streets were a river of blood.

They took me and many children as slaves. They put me in a big basket, tied to a donkey and they took us north.

One girl had seen her parents killed, and she would not stop crying. So they shot her in the head. Her younger sister started crying. So they cut off her foot. I was quiet.

In the north, I was given as a slave to Giema Abdullah. He took me to his family, and they beat me with sticks. All of them—the women and children, too. They laughed and called me *"abeed"*—"slave." [The Arabic *abeed* is a cognate of *eved,* Hebrew for "slave."]

For ten years, they beat me every morning. They made me sleep with the animals, and they gave me very bad food. They said I was an animal. For ten years, I had no one to laugh with. For ten years, nobody loved me. But every day I prayed to God.

One day, I asked my master a question: "Why do you call me *'abeed'*? And why do you feed me bad food all the time and make me sleep with the animals? Is it because I am black?" My master was very angry. "Where did you learn to ask this question?" he said. "Never ask me this again." And he beat me and beat me. When I was 17, I decided to escape. I would rather die than be a slave.[21]

LET FREEDOM RING: HISTORIC WORDS ON FREEDOM

Below you will find a collection of historic statements on freedom spanning three thousand years. Copy this section and ask each guest to read a selection
Keep the following questions in mind and
discuss them after you've read through the selections.

• Do you think that the world is moving in the direction of greater freedom or greater oppression?

• Is the vision of a world with substantially less oppression realistic or hopelessly messianic?

• What light does the story of the Exodus from Egypt shed on this question?

• Which selection do you find to be the most personally moving and why?

• Which ones strike you as particularly relevant this year?

Thus says Adonai, the God of Israel: Let my people go. . . .

—EXODUS 5:1

Proclaim liberty throughout the land unto all the inhabitants thereof. . . .

—LEVITICUS 25:10 (INSCRIBED ON THE LIBERTY BELL IN 1752)

If liberty and equality, as is thought by some, are chiefly to be found in democracy, they will be best attained when all persons alike share in the government to the utmost.[22]

—ARISTOTLE (384–322 B.C.E.)

Those who would give up essential liberty to purchase a little temporary safety deserve neither liberty nor safety.[23]

—BENJAMIN FRANKLIN (1706–1790), 1759

We hold these truths to be self-evident, that all men are created equal; that they are endowed by their Creator with certain inalienable rights; that among these are life, liberty and the pursuit of happiness.

—THE DECLARATION OF INDEPENDENCE, 1776

Familiarize yourselves with the chains of bondage and you prepare your own limbs to wear them. Accustomed to trample on the rights of others, you have lost the genius of your own independence and become the fit subjects of the first cunning tyrant who rises among you.[24]

—ABRAHAM LINCOLN (1809–1865), 1858

It was we, the people, not we, the white male citizens, nor we the male citizens; but we, the whole people, who formed this Union. We formed it not to give the blessings of liberty but to secure them; not to the half of ourselves and the half of our posterity, but to the whole people—women as well as men. It is downright mockery to talk to women of their enjoyment of the blessings of liberty while they are denied the only means of securing them provided by this democratic-republican government—the ballot.[25]

—SUSAN B. ANTHONY (1820–1906), 1872

Give me your tired, your poor,
Your huddled masses, yearning to breathe free,
The wretched refuse of your teeming shore,
Send these, the homeless, tempest-tossed, to me:
I lift my lamp beside the golden door.
—EMMA LAZARUS (1849–1887), 1883, FROM *THE NEW COLOSSUS*,
INSCRIBED ON THE BASE OF THE STATUE OF LIBERTY

The State of Israel will be open to the immigration of Jews from all countries of their dispersion; will promote the development of the country for the benefit of all its inhabitants; will be based on the principles of liberty, justice, and peace as conceived by the Prophets of Israel; it will uphold the full social and political equality of all its citizens, without distinction of religion, race, or sex. . . .
—ISRAEL'S DECLARATION OF INDEPENDENCE, 1948

The use of force by powerful states—even when initially propelled by worthy objectives—naturally turns from a means to an end . . . Many conquerors . . . indeed provided the peoples they ruled with improved government and a higher culture . . . But history does not know of a single case where such "benign" conquest did not eventually turn to oppression and subjugation. Government by force—one which does not rest on the free will of the governed—assumes inevitably a logic of its own: maintaining government under such conditions is impossible without means of oppression, and the desire to maintain control eventually subordinates all other requirements.[26]
—DAVID BEN-GURION (1886–1973), 1964, ON THE BRITISH OCCUPATION OF PALESTINE DURING THE YEARS OF THE MANDATE, 1922–1948

There is something in the soul that cries out for freedom . . . Men cannot be satisfied with Egypt. They tried to adjust to it for a while . . . And eventually they rise up and begin to cry out for Canaan's land . . . Moses might not get to see Canaan, but his children will see it. He even got to the mountaintop enough to see it and that assured him that it was coming. But the

31

beauty of the thing is that there's always a Joshua to take up his work and take the children on in. And it's there waiting with its milk and honey, and with all of the bountiful beauty that God has in store for His children.[27]

—MARTIN LUTHER KING JR. (1929–1968), 1957

Freedom is indivisible; the chains on any one of my people were the chains on all of them, the chains on all of my people were the chains on me . . . The oppressor must be liberated just as surely as the oppressed. A man who takes away my freedom is a prisoner of hatred. He is locked behind the bars of prejudice and narrow-mindedness. I am not free if I am taking away someone else's freedom, just as surely as I am not free when my freedom is taken away from me. The oppressed and the oppressor alike are robbed of their humanity.[28]

—NELSON MANDELA (1918–), 1994

My parents shared not only an improbable love, they shared an abiding faith in the possibilities of this nation. They would give me an African name, Barack, or blessed, believing that in a tolerant America your name is no barrier to success.

If there is anyone out there who still doubts that America is a place where all things are possible; who still wonders if the dream of our founders is alive in our time; who still questions the power of our democracy, tonight is your answer.

—BARACK OBAMA (1961–)

KEYNOTE SPEECH TO DEMOCRATIC NATIONAL CONVENTION, 2004, AND VICTORY SPEECH IN U.S. PRESIDENTIAL ELECTION, 2008

JEWISH VALUES AND SOCIAL JUSTICE: AMERICAN JEWS IN THE ANTEBELLUM SOUTH

The Passover Seder ought to renew our dedication to the fight for social justice. But we know that does not always happen. Why? To probe this question, let's take a look back at the difficult question of Jewish support for slavery in the South before the Civil War. Read aloud what follows and discuss one or two of these questions:

32

- How do you feel about the fact that American Jews in the South participated in the institution of slavery?

- Can one generation judge another about what in hindsight appears to be its failure to speak out?

- What are the moral issues today about which Jews should protest more vigorously? What do you think is stopping us?

- How do you react to the two passages from the Talmud below?

Along with many passages from the prophets, the Talmud would seem to make it clear that when Jews witness social injustice, we belong on the barricades of protest.

> Whoever is able to protest against the transgressions of his own family and does not do so is punished [liable, held responsible] for the transgressions of his family. Whoever is able to protest against the transgressions of the people of his community and does not do so is punished for the transgressions of his community. Whoever is able to protest against the transgressions of the entire world and does not do so is punished for the transgressions of the entire world.
>
> —THE BABYLONIAN TALMUD, SHABBAT 54B

At the same time, the Talmud also lays down the principle of *dina demalkhuta dina,* "the law of the state is the law".[79]

> Samuel [a Babylonian sage active from 220–250 C.E.] said: "The law of the state is the law." Said Rava [a Babylonian sage active about a century later]: "You can prove this from the fact that the authorities fell palm trees [without the consent of the owners] and construct bridges [with them] and we nevertheless make use of them by passing over them." [For if the rulings of the state were not binding by religious law, it would have been a sin to make use of the bridges constructed in such a way.]
>
> —THE BABYLONIAN TALMUD, BABA KAMA 113B

Our tradition's call to justice and our history of oppression have inspired many Jews to fight for social justice. After the Second World War, American Jews played important roles in the civil rights movement. But in an earlier era, that of the Civil War for instance, few Jews opposed slavery. Jews in the South demonstrated attitudes toward slavery similar to those of their Christian neighbors. One of the pioneering studies—written by a Jewish historian—on Jewish involvement in slavery in the American South concludes: "Ante-bellum Southern Jews were more likely to quote the Talmudic maxim that 'the law of the land is the law [for Jews],' and to regard the institution of slavery as part of the law, which they were bound to uphold and follow, than they were to evaluate the failings of slavery in the light of the prophetic ethic."[30] American Jews in the South had generally risen to higher levels of social and economic status than their Northern brethren, because as whites they belonged to the dominant white "caste." In the South, blacks rather than Jews served as a ready target for prejudice. Notwithstanding how they benefited from it, Jews nonetheless played a relatively minor role in the overall institution of slavery.[31]

SLAVERY IN OUR TIME

When you've finished reading the Four Questions at your Seder, ask a participant to read the following Fifth Question. Then either summarize or lead a short discussion on the information that follows. (Much of this has been taken from *Disposable People,* by Kevin Bales and The American Anti-Slavery Group's "Modern Slavery 101.")[32]

- *A Fifth Question: Why is this night no different from all other nights?* Because on this night, millions of human beings around the world still remain enslaved, just as they do on all other nights. As we celebrate our freedom tonight, we remember those who remain enslaved.

Now either briefly summarize the information that follows or describe the four current forms of slavery and lead a discussion asking participants to define slavery, estimate how many slaves there are in the world today, define the factors that allow slavery to persist, etc.

- *Slavery, a definition:* The total control of one person by another for the purpose of economic exploitation. Slaves are controlled by violence and denied all of their personal freedom in order to make money or provide labor for someone else.

- *How many slaves are there today?* According to conservative estimates, 27 million, more than all the slaves shipped from Africa during the transatlantic slave trade.

Current forms of slavery:

- *Chattel slavery:* Closest form to the slavery practiced during the transatlantic slave trade. A person is captured, born, or sold into permanent servitude. Ownership is often asserted. Represents a small percentage of slaves. Practiced in northern and western Africa and some Arab countries.

- *Debt bondage:* The most common form of slavery. A person pledges him- or herself against a loan of money, but the length and nature of the service are not defined and the labor does not reduce the original debt. Ownership is not normally asserted, but there is complete physical control over the bonded laborer. Most common in India and Pakistan.

- *Contract slavery:* The most rapidly growing form of slavery. Contracts are offered that guarantee employment, perhaps in a workshop or factory, but when the workers are taken to their place of work they find themselves enslaved. Most often found in Southeast Asia, Brazil, some Arab states, and parts of the Indian subcontinent.

- *Sex slavery:* Girls are forced into prostitution by their own husbands, fathers, or brothers to earn money for the men in the family to pay back local money lenders. Others are lured by offers of good jobs and then beaten and forced to work in brothels. Most common in South Asia.

- *What kind of work do slaves do?* Simple, nontechnological, and traditional labor. Most slaves work in agriculture, but many also work in mining, quarrying, prostitution, and the manufacture of everything from charcoal and cloth to fireworks and chocolate.

- *Which factors allow slavery to persist?* The world's population explosion, which has produced a reservoir of poor and vulnerable people. The modernization of agriculture, which results in huge numbers of dispossessed farmers. Greed, corruption, and violence created by economic change in much of the developing world, and a breakdown of the social norms that protected potential slaves. Widespread ignorance about slavery. Generally, the kind of slavery most of us learned about in school was abolished in the nineteenth and early twentieth centuries. But we are unaware of the ways in which modern forms of slavery have evolved. Powerful nations often fear that taking a strong stand against slavery will jeopardize economic or military interests deemed to be more compelling national interests.

THREE THINGS YOU CAN DO TO HELP END SLAVERY

1. Learn more about slavery by contacting one of these organizations:

   The American Anti-Slavery Group
   198 Tremont Street #421, Boston, MA 02116
   www.iabolish.org

   Free the Slaves
   1320 19th Street NW, Suite 600
   (866) 324-FREE or www.freetheslaves.net

   Human Rights Watch
   350 Fifth Avenue 34th Floor, New York, NY 10118-3299
   (212) 290-4700 or www.hrw.org

2. Participate in ongoing social-action efforts to end slavery.

3. Encourage organizations with which you are involved to take a stand on the issue.

3

The Four "Questions": Who's Asking What and Why?

מַה נִּשְׁתַּנָּה הַלַּיְלָה הַזֶּה מִכָּל הַלֵּילוֹת?

Why is this night different from all other nights?
On all other nights we eat either leavened or unleavened bread.
On this night only unleavened bread.
On all other nights we eat all kinds of vegetables. On this night only bitter herbs.
On all other nights we don't even dip once. On this night twice.
On all other nights we eat either sitting up or reclining. On this night we all recline.
—THE PASSOVER HAGGADAH

The Four Questions are doubtless among the most familiar and beloved elements of the Seder.[1] What could be more fitting for a child to ask than what makes the night of Passover different from all other nights?

But scratch the surface just a little and you'll find a tangle of questions of another sort. How many questions are there? Four, five, or one? Really just one! *Mah nishtanah ha-lailah ha-zeh mikol ha-leilot?* (Why is this night different from all other nights?) The Four Questions are actually four answers to that single query. Take a look at your Haggadah. Some Haggadot translate these as statements. Others take a bit of license with the Hebrew and make them into questions.

37

In Hebrew, the Four Questions are known as the *Arba Kushyot,* literally the "four difficulties." In rabbinic parlance, a *kushya* refers to an observation of behavior or an idea that deviates from expectation and therefore poses a difficulty or challenge.[2]

As we'll see, the Four Questions provide an excellent window through which to take a brief look at the evolution of critical aspects of the Haggadah and the Passover Seder.

FOR SEDER LEADERS

Here's a great way to get conversation going at your Seder. A few weeks before Passover, ask each of your guests to respond to the following question: "What do you think would be a particularly important question to discuss at the Seder this year?" If you do this by e-mail, paste the responses into a document without identifying who asked which question. Make a copy for each of your guests. Before you go to the Seder table, take turns reading the questions aloud. This is an easy, non-threatening way to let the group know what's on everyone's mind. Choose a few questions for discussion throughout the Seder. You'll probably find that questions cluster around particular issues, which can guide you in choosing which questions to discuss.

ENGAGING CHILDREN DURING THE SEDER: AN ANCIENT LESSON

Read on your own.

Ancient sources stress the importance of the Seder as an educational opportunity for children and suggest introducing a bit of levity to the Seder in order to keep children involved. The Tosefta (Piskha 10:9), a law code from about the third century C.E., suggests that adults grab matzah from one another to astonish children so they won't fall asleep! The Talmud (Pesachim 109a) describes how Rabbi Akiva would distribute snacks of parched corn and nuts to children to help them stay awake.

Because matzah snatching and snacks during dinner were not regular dinner practices, these may also have been deliberate ways to provoke children to ask questions about why this night differed from others.

For instance, the Talmud (Pesachim 115b) relates a story about an old custom of suddenly removing the traylike tables before the meal had been eaten. When a child saw this and asked why, the Seder leader said, "You have exempted us from saying the *mah nishtanah!*" (A remnant of that custom survives today in some Ashkenazic Haggadot that instruct us to remove the Seder plate before the Four Questions.)

In ancient times, the goal was for children to ask their *own* questions. If for some reason the child did not or was unable to do so, the father would teach the child by asking and then answering a number of prescribed questions. The Mishnah (Pesachim 10:4) includes the oldest reference to questions—three questions, not four—during the Seder: "They mixed a second cup [of wine for the father] and here the son asks. And if the son has insufficient understanding his father instructs him. Why is this night different from all other nights? On all other nights we dip once, and on this night twice. . . ." And so on. Yes! Long ago, parents, not children, recited the *mah nishtanah*. "Why is this night different from all other nights" was the question the father posed if others had not already been asked.[3] That's why the Four Questions aren't really questions at all. They are answers to the father's rhetorical question about what distinguishes the night of Passover.

During the Middle Ages things began to change. An ambiguity in the Talmud's treatment of the questions led to different interpretations. Some scholars continued to teach that if a child asked spontaneous questions, there was no need to recite the Four Questions. Maimonides (1135–1204) instructed parents to engage in unusual behavior—matzah snatching, removing the tray that held the Seder plate before the meal, etc.—to provoke children to ask, "Why is this night different from all other nights?" But the father would still recite the *mah nishtanah*. In the thirteenth century, Ashkenazic rabbis concluded that *a young child* should ask the Four Questions. Parents should only do so if the child was unable to.[4]

Although reciting the Four Questions may have given children a special responsibility at the Seder, it also undermined the notion that the Seder should stimulate a child's spontaneous inquiry.

So what can we learn from the earliest designers of the Seder about how to engage children on the night of Passover? They hoped to create a Seder that would do at least three things, each of which relates to an important aspect of what's involved when a child asks a question. First, the elements of the Seder should involve activities that are sufficiently unusual or dramatic to evoke curiosity.

Second, the Seder must be conducted with few enough distractions so a child can pay attention to what's happening. And third, the Seder must unfold in an atmosphere in which a child feels *free* to ask occasional questions even amidst a large group of adults. That's easier said than done! Just a few minutes after the Four Questions are asked, the Haggadah tells of four children who ask entirely different questions. A "wicked" child asks such a terrible question that he's told he deserves to have been left behind in Egypt!

Unless we create an atmosphere that welcomes *all* questions, the most important ones may never make it to the table. There's nothing wrong with reciting the beloved Four Questions. But we should remember that the designers of the Seder hoped to create an experience that would stimulate children's spontaneous questions. It's our job to create a lively Seder in which that kind of spontaneity can flourish.

QUESTIONS ABOUT QUESTIONS

- Ask the children at your Seder what they think makes the Seder night most different from other nights.

- Ask adults to share their memories of learning the Four Questions and how it felt to recite them at the Seder.

- Soon after the Four Questions, three children ask three different kinds of questions and a fourth child "does not know how to ask." Why do questions play such an important role in the Seder?

- How would you compare these Four Questions to those asked by the Four Children?

THE GREEK SYMPOSIUM AND THE JEWISH SEDER

Depending on your group, read aloud or on your own.

Not long after the Four Questions, the Haggadah describes four kinds of children, three of whom also ask questions. Why are questions such an important component of the Seder? There are many reasons, but the most important one is that free people ask questions; slaves don't.

As with other elements of the Haggadah, the act of children asking their parents questions about their religious traditions fulfills an ancient biblical promise: "When, in time to come, your children ask you, 'What mean the decrees, laws, and rules that Adonai our God has enjoined upon you?' You shall say to your children, 'We were slaves to Pharaoh in Egypt . . .'" *"Avadim hayinu l'pharaoh b'mitzrayim . . ."* (Deut. 6:21). Those are the very words that follow the Four Questions.

In his commentary on the Haggadah, Abarbanel (1437–1508), the Spanish statesman and scholar, observed that these particular questions capture a certain paradox within the Seder. We simultaneously relive our enslavement and our redemption. Matzah represents both the bread of affliction and of liberation. Eating raw bitter herbs evokes the harshness of our suffering. By contrast, aristocrats dip hors d'oeuvres and recline during dinner.[5]

The Four Questions also embody the effort to adapt the Passover celebration to the loss of the Temple and the ability to perform the paschal sacrifice, the festival's central rite. Reliving the story of the Exodus and passing it down to the next generation in a lively, joyous atmosphere with questions and answers helped replace sacrifice.

The form, and to some extent even the content, of the post-Temple Passover celebration reflect what some might find a surprising influence: the Greek symposium, a structured banquet that featured a question-and-answer-style dialogue.

Typically, the symposium involved a small group of learned men who gathered to mark various occasions from birthdays to religious celebrations. The symposium began with a series of dipped hors d'oeuvres, served on small portable tables and eaten while reclining on bench-like couches. Discussion, interspersed with drinking wine, was wide ranging and touched on questions of philosophy, religion, and ancient history, and occasionally on the customs and peculiarities of various foods that had been served. Even secular symposia contained a religious component. In his *Symposium,* Plato describes a secular gathering: "Socrates took his place on the couch, and supped with the rest; and then libations were offered, and after a hymn had been sung to the god, and there had been the usual ceremonies, they were about to start drinking. . . ."[6] In Greek, *symposium* literally means "to drink with."

Plutarch (c. 45–120 C.E.), the Greek biographer, describes the interchange that followed the meal: "Even Plato did not prepare himself for the contest like a wrestler, that he may take the faster hold of his adversary . . . Questions should be easy, the problems known, the interrogations plain and familiar, not intricate and hard, so that they may neither vex the unlearned nor frighten them from disquisition . . . The discourse should be like our wine, common to all, of which everyone may equally partake."[7]

The symposium generally concluded with the inebriated guests carousing about town. To ensure that the Seder ended with appropriate dignity, the final Mishnah on Passover bans *afikomen,* often understood to mean "revelry."

Eventually, the symposium developed from an actual meal to a genre of literature structured around the dialogue accompanying a fictional meal. The Haggadah's description of the Seder of the five sages who "reclined" in B'nei B'rak seems to reflect a similar development, because it, too, was likely specially composed for the Haggadah.[8]

It's not clear whether women participated in Greek-style symposia. But we do know that the Rabbis believed women belonged at the Seder. The Tosefta (Pesachim 10:4), an ancient legal code, states that "a man is commanded to make his children and his wife happy on the holiday. With what does he make them happy? With wine. . . ." The Babylonian Talmud (Pesachim 116a) indicates that if a man's son cannot ask the questions, his wife should.

The sages who composed the earliest layers of the Haggadah worried deeply about what lay ahead for the Jewish People. To ensure a vital Jewish future, they were not afraid to borrow an approach from the broader culture with a proven track record of creating memorable evenings.

- How do you feel about the fact that the Seder reflects significant influences from Greek culture?

- What lessons can contemporary Jews learn from this example of cross-cultural influence?

WHY THESE PARTICULAR QUESTIONS?

Depending on your group, read aloud or on your own.

How these particular questions came to the Haggadah also remains a bit of a mystery.

The original three "questions" presented in the Mishnah (Pesachim 10:4) were compiled around 200 C.E. They are:

- On all other nights we dip *once*. On this night twice [i.e., once before the formal meal, and again during the meal when bitters are dipped in *charoset*].

- On all other nights we eat leavened or unleavened bread. On this night only unleavened bread.

- On all other nights we eat meat that is roasted, stewed, or boiled. On this night only roasted.

Because the Mishnah suggests that in ancient times the meal preceded the telling of the Passover story, these questions made sense. The child would have observed two rounds of dipping (first the common dipping of hors d'oeuvres and later the special dipping of mandated bitter herbs), matzah rather than bread, and roasted rather than stewed or boiled meat. These three questions correspond to Rabban Gamaliel's injunction (which we arrive at later in the Seder) to explain the meaning of three things eaten on the night of Passover during Temple times: the paschal offering, matzah, and bitter herbs.[9] Only the Mishnah's second question about matzah survived without modification.

The Mishnah's first question was changed in a subtle but revealing manner. Our current question about dipping derives from the observation of Rav Safra recorded in the Talmud (Pesachim 116a): "On all other nights we don't dip *even once*; on this night we dip twice." What had been a widespread custom of dipping hors d'oeuvres before dinner had apparently been forgotten. In earlier times, when the ways of the Greek symposium were still current, dipping a course of hors d'oeuvres—dipping once—was natural. Dipping again *during* the meal was noteworthy. The original question about dipping seems to have been divided in two, one focusing on the act of dipping and the other on the items dipped—that is, bitter herbs (nowadays often horseradish) dipped into *charoset*.

The question about how to cook meat on the night of Passover reflected the fact that in Israel (and apparently elsewhere) it remained customary to eat roasted meat at the Seder in memory of the Temple sacrifice. The yearning to eat roasted meat to recollect or substitute for the Passover sacrifice often proved irresistible. The Rabbis generally permitted this if the meat was not prepared exactly as it had been in Temple times—it could no longer be roasted whole on a metal spit or grill. But according to the Mishnah (Betzah 2:7), none other than Rabban Gamaliel himself, the leader of Jewish community between 80 and 110 C.E., ordered a whole young goat roasted on a grill for Passover!

This marks a transition in the development of the post-Temple Passover. The rituals designed to replace the paschal sacrifice had yet to become sufficiently meaningful in their own right. A more tangible link with the ancient sacrifice remained necessary.[10]

Scholars believe that, in some places, the custom of eating roasted meat on the night of Passover persisted until at least the eleventh century. In Palestine, this act was accompanied by a blessing praising God "who has commanded us to eat *matzah,* bitter herbs, and roasted meat to remember his great deeds. Blessed are You who remembers the covenant."[11] Our oldest extant Haggadah, a manuscript from the tenth or eleventh century, reflects the Palestinian rite and still includes this query.[12] By the twelfth century, Maimonides listed this question but added that it was no longer recited "for we do not have sacrifice" (*Laws of Chametz and Matzah* 8:3).

Nowadays, roasted meat on the night of Passover is widely forbidden, lest one convey the impression of consuming the paschal sacrifice, an act that would only be permitted with the rebuilding of the Temple. What began as a common practice to evoke the memory of the Temple has now become a virtual taboo.

The fourth question, about why we recline on Passover, seems to have been added between the end of the Talmudic period (500–600 C.E.) and the ninth century. It derives from the opening Mishnah (10:1) about the night of Passover: "Even a poor person in Israel may not eat unless he reclines." The Haggadah tells us that the five sages who celebrated a Seder were "reclining in B'nei B'rak." Reclining had been a standard feature of the Greek symposium and the Mishnah envisioned its incorporation into the Passover meal even for those not accustomed to such luxury. But in Mishnaic times, reclining during festive meals had been so common that it hardly distinguished Passover. Only after the custom of reclining had lapsed did the Mishnah's instruction become the basis for a question distinguishing Passover from all other nights.

4

Passover after the Temple:
From Sacrifice to Story

וַאֲפִילוּ כֻּלָּנוּ חֲכָמִים, כֻּלָּנוּ נְבוֹנִים, כֻּלָּנוּ זְקֵנִים, כֻּלָּנוּ
יוֹדְעִים אֶת־הַתּוֹרָה, מִצְוָה עָלֵינוּ לְסַפֵּר בִּיצִיאַת מִצְרָיִם.
וְכָל־הַמַּרְבֶּה לְסַפֵּר בִּיצִיאַת מִצְרָיִם, הֲרֵי זֶה מְשֻׁבָּח:

*Even if we all were wise, and perceptive, experienced, and versed in
Torah, we are commanded to tell about the Exodus from Egypt.
And all who elaborate on telling of the Exodus deserve praise.*
—THE PASSOVER HAGGADAH

A few minutes after the Seder starts, many people begin to feel lost. We make Kiddush, wash our hands, dip parsley in saltwater, break the middle matzah and set part of it aside for the *afikomen*. We continue with the Four Questions and *avadim hayinu l'pharaoh b'mitzrayim* . . . "We were slaves to Pharaoh in Egypt." So far, so good. Then the confusion begins. The Haggadah suddenly interrupts the narrative to remind us about our obligation to tell the Passover story. Five sages discuss the Exodus all through the night. Four children ask four different questions followed by what seems to be a brief retrospective of patriarchal history from the Book of Joshua. It begins with Abraham's idol-worshiping ancestors and ends with Jacob, Abraham's grandson, going down to Egypt. What's going on?

In brief, two things account for the confusion in this part of the Haggadah. First, the Haggadah is trying to accommodate the opposing views of two Talmudic sages about the meaning of enslavement. Second, the reminder about our obligation to tell the story reflects the fact that telling the story of the Exodus on Passover was a new development. The destruction of the Temple in 70 C.E. demanded a radical redefinition of Jewish practice—including the celebration of Passover—in which the sacrificial rites had been central. Telling the Passover story would take the place of the sacrifice. Was this "kosher?" Most certainly, says the Haggadah! Take a lesson from five of Israel's greatest sages.

We'll shed some light on this section of the Haggadah with a story, "Judah the Prince and the Seder." You can read it aloud to your guests before the Seder begins. It's written in fairly simple language and explains a bit about the Haggadah's early development. We follow that with an exploration of how the architects of the early Seder envisioned the experience. We also include a brief art midrash project. You'll find questions for discussion throughout. As we'll see, the transition from "disgrace" to "praise" is a motif that recurs throughout the Haggadah. When you read portions of the Haggadah, ask your guests to point out every time they see an example of this transition.

JUDAH THE PRINCE AND THE SEDER

Invite your guests to take turns reading this story about how the Haggadah developed.

Once, long, long ago—about eighteen hundred years ago—there lived a man named Judah the Prince. Judah lived in the north of Israel in a town called Tzippori, in a fancy stone house up on a hill. It was a very hard time for the Jewish People. About seventy years before Judah was born, the mighty Romans destroyed the great Temple of the Jews in Jerusalem. Near the time Judah was born, the Jewish People started a war against the Romans to try to throw them out of Israel. But the Romans won. They forced most of the Jews to leave the country. Jews moved to many different countries, near and far.

Some, like Judah's family, stayed in the hills, far from Jerusalem. Judah was called "the Prince" because he became the leader of the Jewish community that remained in Israel. He was one of the wisest rabbis in the country. Judah was afraid that without their Temple, without their country, and scattered around the world, the Jewish People would forget how to observe their traditions. He worried that they would not know how to celebrate Passover and would not remember its meanings.

The Jews *did* have their ancient Torah scrolls. But since the Torah had been written, all sorts of new traditions had grown up. For several centuries before Judah was born, great rabbis and teachers had had long conversations about what the Torah and all those new traditions meant. Besides, when it came to the holidays, the Torah mostly told you about how to celebrate them by making special sacrifices at the Temple. With the Temple then just a pile of smashed-up stones, what could Jews do to celebrate Passover?

The Rabbis who lived after the Temple's destruction finally decided that *talking* about what Passover meant—asking and trying to answer lots of questions about it—might work. Instead of sacrifices, words would have to do, and maybe they were better anyway.

So Judah decided to collect stories of the Rabbis' conversations about what they thought the Torah *really* meant and about how Jews could practice their religion without sacrifices in the Temple.

Some say Judah wrote all this down in a big book that he finished around the year 200 C.E. Others say Judah taught it to his students and they memorized his teachings. Judah's teachings were called the Mishnah, which means something like teaching and repeating. One part of Judah's teachings described the Passover Seder. It included many of the things we do at our Seders today: drinking four cups of wine, dipping, eating matzah, bitter herbs, and *charoset*, and of course asking questions and telling the Passover story.

Collecting the Passover traditions turned out to be a great idea. On this Passover night, Jews all around the world are following many of the same customs that Judah described in the Mishnah about eighteen hundred years ago. Some of the details may have changed, but the Seder remains a night of questions. And we spend a long time discussing a section from the Bible (Deut. 26:5–8) that begins, "My father was a wandering Aramean."

One difference between Judah's Seder and ours is that tonight, most of us don't focus exclusively on fathers and sons at the Seder table. Mothers and daughters can do everything that fathers and sons do.

But, of course, just as people weren't always exactly sure what the Torah meant, discussions immediately began about what Judah's Mishnah meant. In fact, some people believe that Judah wrote the Mishnah in a style that would be sure to keep the conversations about Jewish tradition going for a long time.

So it was no surprise when Rav and Shmuel, two famous Rabbis active from about 220 to 250 C.E., often disagreed with one another about what the Mishnah meant. They lived in Babylonia, not far from what is now the city of Baghdad, the capital of Iraq. Rav visited Israel, and Judah the Prince became one of his teachers. He was called "Rav," which means "master," because he was among the greatest scholars who brought the teachings from the homeland to communities living outside of Israel. Rav earned a living by making beer; he wrote many prayers and built one of the greatest centers for Jewish learning of all time. Shmuel was a wealthy farmer, an astronomer, and a doctor. Once, he sent medicine to Judah that cured him of an eye infection. Shmuel also helped create the Jewish calendar.

Both Rav and Shmuel were great teachers and leading judges in the Jewish courts. Sometimes they studied together. The two sages respected one another even though they thought about Jewish laws and customs in very different ways. Not too long after Judah finished putting together the Mishnah, Rav and Shmuel disagreed about what Judah meant about the Seder when he wrote, "He begins with disgrace and concludes with praise." The Talmud, written down between 200 and 500 C.E., records their disagreement: "What is 'with disgrace?' Rav said: *'In the beginning our ancestors worshiped idols'*; while Shmuel said: *'We were slaves.'*"[1]

Rav thought that the most disgraceful thing for the Jewish People was that our ancestors believed that statues were gods. For Rav, the most important way to be free was to know that statues made out of stone or wood or metal did not control your life. Even after God had taken the Israelites out of Egypt with a mighty hand and an outstretched arm, they soon made a statue of a Golden Calf and started praying to it as if *it* were God. They were slaves to silly ideas.

But according to Shmuel, the disgrace was slavery itself. The wicked Pharaoh treated us as if we were more like machines or animals than people. Shmuel thought that the worst thing we suffered was not to be treated like human beings created in the image of God, like real people, with feelings, fears, and hopes for a better life. To be free, we first had to escape from the tyrannical Pharaoh.

Later, the Rabbis who wrote down the Haggadah decided that Rav and

Shmuel were both right. So, one part of the Haggadah describes the Israelites' experience when *"we were slaves,"* as Shmuel said. The other part reminds us that *"in the beginning our ancestors worshiped idols,"* as Rav believed.

If you remember that the Haggadah really includes two Haggadot in one, the Seder may not seem quite as confusing as it sometimes does! Each rabbi's part of the Haggadah begins with a set of four questions that are followed by an explanation.

Shmuel's version of the Haggadah begins with the famous Four Questions. These questions all refer to elements of the Seder connected with physical enslavement. As an answer, the Haggadah says, *Avadim hayinu . . . "We were slaves* to Pharaoh in Egypt, and Adonai our God brought us forth from there with a mighty hand and an outstretched arm. . . ."

Rav's version comes next. It begins with the Four Children, who ask questions about why the Passover traditions should be important to us, so long after our ancestors left Egypt. Rav's answer begins, *"In the beginning our ancestors worshiped idols, but now the Omnipresent has brought us to God's service."* Rav tells us about our ancestors' spiritual journey from believing in idols to feeling that they had a relationship with the true God.

Tonight, we continue to celebrate Passover in the spirit of Judah the Prince, Rav, and Shmuel. We keep the conversation going about what the Exodus from Egypt means to our people and to each one of us. We try to reexperience the pain of slavery so we never take freedom for granted. We remember when we were down so we can help others up. We struggle to free ourselves from the false gods that bit by bit enslave us and lead us to forget our most important dreams. And we keep asking questions.

- Shmuel's part of the Haggadah (about redemption from slavery) comes before Rav's (about evolving beyond idolatry). Why do you think Shmuel's comes first and Rav's comes second?

- Judah's Mishnah includes a statement by Rabbi Elazar ben Azariah, one of the sages mentioned in the Haggadah, that at first might sound strange: "Where there is no flour, there is no Torah. Where there is no Torah, there is no flour" (Mishnah, Avot 3:21). How does this relate to Rav and Shmuel's opinions about the Seder?

Although the Haggadah may often seem confusing, there's one theme that recurs in many, many variations throughout: what the Mishnah called the transition from shame or disgrace to praise. As we've seen, the Mishnah (Pesachim 10:4, c. 200 C.E.) says: "And according to the son's intelligence his father instructs him. He begins with disgrace (*g'nut*) and ends with praise (*shevach*)."

- What might "disgrace" or "shame" mean? What about "praise"?

- What do you think this transition might represent and why is it so central to the Haggadah?

- Why do you think we end with "praise" rather than "joy"?

TELLING THE STORY: SOME ANCIENT ADVICE
FOR SEDER LEADERS

Read aloud the paragraph below along with the passage from the Mishnah and discuss the questions that follow. Note: The Mishnah needs very careful reading!

The Mishnah's description of the Seder includes many features that have remained more or less the same for eighteen hundred years: drinking four cups of wine, reclining, dipping, eating matzah and *charoset*, as well as explaining the meaning of the Passover offering, matzah, and bitter herbs. The Mishnah also notes how we ought to tell the story of the Exodus (in italics).

> [They] poured for him the second cup—*and here the child asks, and if the child lacks understanding, his father instructs him.* . . . How is this night different from all [other] nights? For on all the [other] nights we dip once, this night twice. For on all the [other] nights we eat leavened and unleavened bread, this night we eat only unleavened. For on all the [other] nights we eat meat roasted, steamed, or cooked [in a liquid, boiled], this night only roasted. *According to the child's understanding, his father instructs him. [He] starts with disgrace and ends with praise; and [he] expounds from, "My father was a wandering Aramean,"* until he finishes the entire portion [Deuteronomy 26:5-8].
>
> —MISHNAH, PESACHIM 10:4, CIRCA 200 C.E.

QUESTIONS FOR DISCUSSION

• What do you make of the Mishnah's concern with the level of the child's understanding? What might the implications of this concern be for how the story is told from year to year?

• What, if anything, surprises you about this excerpt from the Mishnah?

• The Mishnah refers to elements of the Seder that should be fixed and those left open for creativity and change. How do you feel about this? How does the Mishnah's approach to telling the Passover story relate to themes of the Exodus itself?

After your discussion, consider reading aloud what follows.

"THE MEDIUM IS THE MESSAGE"

The Mishnah understood that breathing life into Judaism's central story required more than rereading the eternally fixed account of the Exodus. In fact, it conceived of a radically different Seder—one that carefully balanced elements that would be fixed and those that would change from family to family, from year to year.

Fixed elements—four cups of wine, dipping, reclining, specific blessings, and so forth—would bind us together as a people, whenever and wherever we lived. But the early architects of the Seder realized that requiring each Seder to be a clone of the next would not be the best way to ensure that we'd successfully pass our central story down one generation to the next. So along with fixed rituals, they left room for creativity, especially when it came to telling the story.

The Mishnah's instructions reflect two central principles. First, telling the story of the Exodus must be geared to the level of understanding of the younger generation—and I would broaden that to include the interests of adult participants as well. Second, we are not to read a straightforward account of the story, say from the Book of Exodus. Rather, we are to tell the story through the process of expounding—*drasha*, literally "drawing out meaning," or making midrash—on a short passage about the Passover story in the Book of Deuteronomy. That midrash was to change as the level of children's understanding increased. And notice the Mishnah's

51

approach to children's questions. Rather than reciting prescribed questions, the Mishnah envisioned children asking their own questions, prompted, if none occurred to them, by their father. (For more on this, see chapter 3.) We are to make the story meaningful to those gathered around the table through an interactive, creative process.

The Mishnah implies that no two Seders should be exactly the same!

Rather than "slavishly" reading a prescribed text, the Mishnah encourages us to take liberties, using its example as a core and a guide. Back in the 1960s, Marshall McLuhan, the great critic of culture and the media, famously observed that "the medium is the message." Egypt was about productivity, not creativity. In the creativity we bring to telling the Passover story, we taste freedom and celebrate it. We experience ourselves as free, independent creators, the very antithesis of our ancestors mired in the mind-numbing pits of slavery. In so doing, we renew the divine sparks within, which mark us each as images of God, the paradigmatic free creator.

TAKING ELABORATION SERIOUSLY

Read the passage aloud, discuss the question that follows, and consider reading the paragraph below after your discussion.

"Even if we all were wise, and perceptive, experienced, and versed in Torah, we are commanded to tell about the Exodus from Egypt. And all who elaborate on telling of the Exodus deserve praise . . ."

—THE PASSOVER HAGGADAH

• Why do you think the Haggadah puts such special emphasis on telling the story of the Exodus?

The Haggadah's emphasis on telling the Passover story hints at a problem. After the Temple's destruction in 70 C.E. and the inability to carry out the ancient paschal sacrifice, it took time to develop a truly satisfying celebration of the festival. Rabban Gamaliel II, a leader of the Jewish community in the post-Temple period, advocated roasting a lamb in the same manner as had been done in Temple times.[2] He referred to it as "the Pesach," exactly as the Passover offering had been called. By the third century, the Sages forbade Gamaliel's culinary approach to the Seder.[3] Likewise, rather than telling the story of the Exodus on the night of Passover, Gamaliel studied the laws of the sacrifice. In an era when Christians began to create their own interpretations of Passover, matzah, and bitter herbs, Gamaliel required reciting precise Jewish definitions at the Seder (Mishnah Pesachim 10:5, see page 358), a far cry from storytelling. The yearning for a tangible connection to the Passover sacrifice also found expression in the ancient version of what later became the Four Questions: "On all other nights we eat meat that is roasted, stewed, or boiled, but on this night only roasted."[4] As the attachment to eating roasted meat on Passover declined, this question was eventually replaced.

Read these three passages aloud, discuss the questions that follow and consider reading the paragraph that follows after your discussion.

1. "All who elaborate on telling of the Exodus deserve praise . . ."

—THE PASSOVER HAGGADAH

2. "All [judges] who elaborate on the cross-examination [of a witness in a capital case] deserve praise."

—MISHNAH SANHEDRIN 5:2, CIRCA 200 C.E.

3. "All who elaborate on the rituals of mourning for their father or mother deserve praise [e.g. fully rending all the outer garments one wears, completely refraining from work during shiva]."

—JERUSALEM TALMUD MOED KATAN 18B, CIRCA 400 C.E.

- As far as I can tell, these are the only three examples in rabbinic literature that employ this particular language and structure—"all who elaborate . . . deserve praise."[5] What light do the second and third texts shed on the importance and meaning of the Haggadah's encouragement to elaborate on telling of the Exodus?

In both the Mishnah (2) and the Jerusalem Talmud (3), the central figures (the accused and the deceased) cannot act on their own behalf. They must trust others to preserve their life or the memory of it. Analogously, the story of the Exodus, so full of hope and promise, cannot preserve itself. In every generation, that task falls to the Jewish People—to us. Whether the story will be remembered or forgotten, whether it lives or dies, depends on the passion with which we tell it. As the Haggadah puts it, "In every generation, each individual should feel as though he or she had gone out of Egypt."

ART MIDRASH: "BEGIN WITH DISGRACE AND END WITH PRAISE"

Create an art midrash project based on the Mishnah's instructions that, when telling the story of the Exodus at the Seder, you should "begin with disgrace and end with praise." Explain that the Mishnah is a collection of teachings and laws compiled about eighteen hundred years ago. It contains the oldest directions for a Passover Seder as we have come to know it. Also mention that the transition from disgrace to praise recurs throughout the Haggadah. Ask each of your guests to make a collage that illustrates his or her feelings and ideas about beginning with disgrace and ending with praise.
See Appendix III (page 361) for general directions for art midrash projects.

CROSSING RIVERS AND TAKING RESPONSIBILITY

Now let's take a look at how the Haggagah elaborates upon Rav's interpretation of disgrace. We'll focus on the theme of taking responsibility as it relates to Passover and the imagery of crossing from one side of the river to the other. Although crossing the Red Sea certainly represents the Bible's paradigmatic story of rebirth, other less well-known tales of crossing through waters also teach important lessons about the meaning of Passover. Take turns reading the following selections. Then discuss the accompanying questions.

In the beginning our ancestors worshiped idols, but now the Omnipresent has drawn us close to His service, as it is written, "And Joshua said to all the people, 'Thus said Adonai God of Israel: Your fathers lived on the other side of the river in olden times, Terah, the father of Abraham, and the father of Nahor; and they served other gods. And I took your father Abraham from the other side of the river, and led him throughout all the land of Canaan, and multiplied his seed, and gave him Isaac. And I gave to Isaac Jacob and Esau; and I gave to Esau Mount Seir, to possess it; but Jacob and his children went down to Egypt'" (Joshua 24:2–4).[6]

—THE PASSOVER HAGGADAH

This is the beginning of the Haggadah's answer to the questions posed by the Four Children about Passover's meaning. It begins with Rav's words and concludes with Joshua's farewell speech to the Israelites just before his death, years after they had conquered the Promised Land. (Joshua was Moses' successor.) The text is well chosen. Near the beginning of the Book of Joshua, the Israelites crossed over the Jordan into the land of Canaan:

When the people set out from their encampment to cross the Jordan, the priests bearing the Ark of the Covenant were at the head of the people. Now the Jordan keeps flowing over its entire bed throughout the harvest season. But as soon as the bearers of the Ark reached the Jordan, and the feet of the priests bearing the Ark dipped into the water at its edge, the waters coming down from upstream piled up in a single heap a great way off . . . all Israel crossed over on dry land, until the entire nation had finished crossing the Jordan.

—JOSHUA 3:14–17

• The Bible first uses the term "Hebrew" (*ivri*) to identify Abraham. Five evil kings were on the warpath and they captured Lot, Abraham's nephew. Someone escaped and warned "Abraham the Hebrew" (Gen. 14:13). Abraham's army immediately set out, defeated the kings, and rescued Lot. What was Abraham doing when he learned of Lot's capture? According to the midrash, which imagined that the patriarchs fulfilled all the precepts of the Torah even before the revelation at Sinai, Abraham was baking cakes of unleavened bread to celebrate Passover. Next, the midrash explains that "Hebrew" derives from the word *ever* and means "the one who came from the other side of the river" and that *ha-ivri*, "the

Hebrew," signifies that "the whole world was on one side while he [Abraham] was on the other side."[7]

• What are some of the different meanings suggested by "crossing over" and why is it stressed in the above texts? How do these relate to the notion of moral or spiritual development?

• How does the theme of "crossing over" relate to Passover?

Immediately after crossing the Jordan into the Promised Land, Joshua oversees the reinstitution of the Passover celebration. This had apparently lapsed during the years in the desert.

Encamped at Gilgal, in the steppes of Jericho, the Israelites offered the Passover sacrifice on the fourteenth day of the month toward evening. On the day after the Passover offering, on that very day, they ate of the produce of the country, unleavened bread and parched grain. On that same day, when they ate of the produce of the land, the manna ceased. The Israelites got no more manna; that year they ate of the yield of the land of Canaan.
—JOSHUA 5:10–12 (READ IN SYNAGOGUE ON THE FIRST DAY OF PASSOVER)

• How do you interpret the fact that the celebration of Passover lapsed within a few years after the Israelites left Egypt?

• Why was it important to renew the celebration of Passover when the Israelites entered the Promised Land?

• How does Joshua 5:10–12 let you know that there are important relationships among the renewal of Passover, entering the Promised Land, the cessation of manna, and eating the "yield of the land"? What do these relationships mean? What might this text be trying to teach us by making such an explicit connection between entering the Promised Land, and assuming new responsibilities, on both the spiritual and the material levels? What are the implications of this text for contemporary Israel?

5

Five Super-Sages in B'nei B'rak

מַעֲשֶׂה בְּרַבִּי אֱלִיעֶזֶר וְרַבִּי יְהוֹשֻׁעַ
וְרַבִּי אֶלְעָזָר בֶּן־עֲזַרְיָה וְרַבִּי עֲקִיבָא וְרַבִּי טַרְפוֹן
שֶׁהָיוּ מְסֻבִּין בִּבְנֵי־בְרַק...

*A tale is told about Rabbi Eliezer, Rabbi Joshua, Rabbi Elazar ben Azariah,
Rabbi Akiva, and Rabbi Tarfon. They were reclining in B'nei B'rak, discussing the
Exodus from Egypt all through the night, until their students came to them and said,
"Masters, the time has come to recite the morning Sh'ma."*
—THE PASSOVER HAGGADAH

The Haggadah's allusion to the Seder of the five sages comes on the heels of
its injunction to tell the story of the Exodus—"Even if we all were wise,
and perceptive, experienced, and versed in Torah . . ." The gathering of sages for
an all-night discussion of the Exodus drives the point home. In the early generations of the post–Temple era, the importance of talking about the Exodus on the
night of Passover had yet to gain universal acceptance. Rabban Gamaliel, for
instance, leader of the Jewish community from 80–110 C.E., preferred a Seder that

devoted more attention to evoking the absent paschal sacrifice. Aside from the Haggadah, the B'nei B'rak Seder appears nowhere else in rabbinic literature.

In this chapter we'll explore the life and times of those gathered at the Seder in B'nei B'rak. Relations among these five sages were anything but smooth. Rabban Gamaliel, the leader of the community, is conspicuous in his absence. As we'll see, Gamaliel banned Rabbi Eliezer, and in a separate incident his colleagues deposed Gamaliel for publicly humiliating Rabbi Joshua. We'll look for fingerprints of that conflict in the Haggadah as well. If you are interested in my midrashic version of the sages' discussion at B'nei B'rak, see "Reconstructing the Conversation" at www.livelyseders.com.

Read the paragraph from the Haggadah at the beginning of the chapter and then take turns reading aloud the story beginning at the bottom of this page that is based on the Talmud and the Midrash. The story will give you a feeling for the period during which key elements of the Seder evolved and the way our tradition remembers some of the individuals who helped shape Judaism's development after the destruction of the Second Temple in 70 C.E. The story also includes a wrenching conflict among the sages that led to the banning of Rabbi Eliezer from the community. Discuss the questions that follow.

Note: This will make an excellent pre-Seder activity and is best suited for older children and adults. If you have young children at your Seder, you may want to consider inviting them to a reading of *The Last Night in Egypt* in a separate room (see page 244) while others read and discuss this section.

FIVE SUPER-SAGES: THEIR TIMES AND TEACHINGS

About nineteen hundred years ago, during some of the Jewish People's darkest days, there lived five very famous Rabbis—Eliezer, Joshua, Elazar ben Azariah, Tarfon, and Akiva.

For as long as he could remember, Eliezer had dreamed of studying with the most famous Rabbi of the time, Yochanan ben Zakkai. But his father, a wealthy farmer, insisted that he work the land and enjoy a simple, comfortable life. When he was twenty-eight years old, Eliezer ran away to Jerusalem. Nearly starving, he found Yochanan and explained his dream of studying with the great master. Yochanan took pity on Eliezer and was soon impressed by how fast he learned.

Eliezer too became a great teacher. Yochanan said, "If all the sages of Israel were on one pan of a balance scale, and Eliezer were on the other, he would outweigh them all."[1] Eliezer used to say: "Let the honor of your fellow man be as precious to you as your own. Do not be quick to anger, and repent one day before your death." His students asked, "But does a person know the day of his death?" Eliezer answered, "Let him then repent today for perhaps he will die tomorrow."[2]

Eliezer taught that three things could annul God's decrees—prayer, charity, and repentance, *tefillah, tzedakah, u-teshuvah*.[3] (Eliezer's words inspired the *Unetaneh Tokef* prayer recited during Rosh Hashanah and Yom Kippur.)

Rabbi Joshua was another of Yochanan ben Zakkai's most important disciples. His teacher compared him to a "threefold cord that cannot be easily broken" (Eccl. 4:12).[4] Despite a great knowledge of science and mathematics, Joshua lived a life of poverty and earned his living as a blacksmith making needles.

These were the days when Israel was controlled by the mighty Roman empire. Rome collected heavy taxes, and most Jews were very poor. The Jews wanted to be free. Some thought that just as they had escaped from Egypt, and as the Maccabees had defeated the Greeks, they too could win a war against Rome. Others believed such a war would be foolish. Hoping for a miracle, a group of zealots attacked the Romans in the year 66 C.E. Four years later, the Romans had almost won and demanded the surrender of Jerusalem. If the fighting continued, the Romans threatened to burn the city and destroy the great Jewish Temple.

Yochanan ben Zakkai opposed the war and pleaded with the zealots to make peace with Rome. But the zealots only fought harder, declared the rabbi a traitor, and continued killing Jews who called for peace.

Yochanan realized that if the Jews lost both their Temple in Jerusalem and all the city's great teachers, Judaism might not survive. He decided to escape and arranged for two of his disciples to smuggle him out of Jerusalem in a coffin. Eliezer carried him by the head and Joshua carried him by the feet.

When they had left Jerusalem, Joshua turned to look back at the Temple's ruins and cried to his teacher, "Woe unto us, that this, the place where the sins of Israel were atoned for, is laid waste." Yochanan said to him, "Do not grieve. We have another source of atonement as effective as this. And what is it? Acts of loving-kindness, as it is said, 'For I desire goodness, not sacrifice'" (Hosea 6:6).[5] Prayer, study, and the observance of Jewish law would also help take the place of the destroyed Temple.

The Temple was gone, but Rabbi Yochanan and his students kept Jewish tradition alive by founding a center for Jewish learning at Yavne (today a small town not far from Tel Aviv). Yavne attracted the most brilliant scholars, including Elazar ben Azariah. He came from a wealthy family and traced his lineage back almost five hundred years to Ezra, who had led the Jewish People back to Jerusalem after the Babylonian exile. At the age of eighteen, Elazar ben Azariah became the head of the Sanhedrin, the highest court in the land. Whether from anxiety about his new responsibilities or to help him look more suitable for the job, his hair turned white overnight. In the morning he said, "I am like a man of seventy."[6] (We read those very words in the Haggadah itself.)

Rabbi Tarfon also taught at Yavne. His mother, while out walking, once lost her shoe. Tarfon placed his hand under her bare foot so she would not hurt it while she walked home. Rather than benefit from his fame as a teacher, Tarfon traveled in disguise. Once he had to reveal his identity when a watchman beat him for taking grapes from his own vineyard! Rabbi Tarfon used to say, "You are not required to complete the task, but neither are you free to avoid starting it."[7] Elazar ben Azariah used to say that a court that executes a person once in seventy years is a cruel court. Tarfon and Akiva said that if *they* had been members of the court, it never would execute anyone![8]

Eliezer, Joshua, and Tarfon taught many students, but Akiva became their most important disciple. Akiva worked as a shepherd for a wealthy farmer until he was forty, and he fell in love with Rachel, his boss's daughter. They married against her father's will, but Rachel insisted that the ignorant shepherd promise to study at Yavne. Years of study kept him away from Rachel, but he finally returned—a great scholar followed by droves of students.

Akiva developed a new way of interpreting the Torah. He discovered meaning in every word. He also began to write down many of the oral traditions that had grown up over the centuries. Akiva used to say, "'Love your neighbor as yourself' is the Torah's fundamental principle" and "He who sheds blood is regarded as though he had impaired the Divine image . . . What is the reason? *'For in His image did God make man'*" (Gen. 1:27).[9]

Once Tarfon and Akiva argued before a group of sages about which was more important, study or religious observance. Tarfon said, "Observance is more important." Akiva answered, "Study is more important." The sages all agreed that study is more important because it leads to observance.[10]

Some years later, the Romans once again began to oppress the Jews in Israel. They tried to put an end to Judaism by preventing Rabbis from teaching and by banning circumcision and the observance of Shabbat. A Jewish general named Bar Kochba led another unsuccessful revolt against Rome (132–135 C.E.). Rabbi Akiva, the greatest sage of his time, refused to stop teaching and threw his support behind Bar Kochba, declaring him to be the Messiah. Other Rabbis opposed the rebellion.

Akiva was tortured and died with the *Sh'ma* on his lips. The angels asked God, "Is this the reward for studying Torah?" A Heavenly Voice declared, "Blessed are you, Rabbi Akiva, for you are destined for life in the World to Come."[11] According to legend, Elijah the Prophet carried his body for burial.

BANNING RABBI ELIEZER

The Talmud (Baba Metzia 59b) tells the story about one dispute between Eliezer and his colleagues, which led to banning him from the community. That meant that his rulings could not be taught and that except for business dealings, only his family could spend time with him. It seems that Eliezer, himself a judge in an important court, was unwilling to follow the ruling of a higher court. He also believed that human reasoning alone could not be the basis for legal decisions.

> Once Rabbi Eliezer tried to prove that a particular oven was kosher or clean. He tried every imaginable argument, but everyone still disagreed. So he said, "If halakhah [Jewish law] agrees with me, let this carob tree prove it." And the tree was torn from its roots and moved twenty-five feet. "No proof can come from a tree," they argued. "If the halakhah agrees with me, let this stream of water prove it," Eliezer said. And the stream of water flowed backwards. "No proof," they said, "can come from a stream of water." Then Eliezer said, "If the halakhah agrees with me, let the walls of this building prove it." And the walls leaned in toward each other and almost collapsed. But Joshua scolded the walls, saying: "When scholars are engaged in a halakhic dispute, why are you interfering?" Hence the walls did not fall, in honor of Joshua,

nor did they become upright in honor of Eliezer. And they are still leaning that way.

Then a heavenly voice cried out, "Why do you argue with Rabbi Eliezer, since in all matters the halakhah agrees with him!" But Rabbi Joshua arose and quoted the Torah [Deut. 30:12]: "[The Torah] is not in the heavens." What did he mean by this? That the Torah had been given at Mount Sinai. So now we pay no attention to a heavenly voice because the Torah itself says, *"One must follow the majority"* [Ex. 23:2].

Later, a rabbi met Elijah the Prophet and asked him: "What did the Holy One, Blessed be He, do in that hour?"—"He laughed [with joy]," Elijah replied, saying, "My children have defeated Me, My children have defeated Me" [since they showed such a commitment to their own creative thinking].

After they voted to ban Eliezer, Rabbi Akiva dressed in black mourning garments to bring his friend and teacher the news. "Master, it appears to me that your companions have distanced themselves from you." Then Eliezer too rent his garments, took off his shoes, got up from his chair, and sat on the earth, while tears streamed from his eyes.

The story has a perplexing conclusion. After the ban on Eliezer, "the world was then smitten: a third of the olive crop, a third of the wheat, and a third of the barley crop [withered and died]. . . ." Rabban Gamaliel, also of Seder fame, is generally thought to have initiated the action against Eliezer, his brother-in-law.

Gamaliel was traveling in a ship, when a huge wave arose to drown him. "It appears to me," he reflected, "that this is on account of none other than Rabbi Eliezer." He arose and exclaimed, "Sovereign of the Universe! You know full well that I have not acted for my honor, nor for the honor of my paternal house, but for Yours, so that strife may not multiply in Israel!" At that, the raging sea subsided.

Many years later, when Eliezer was near death, Akiva, Joshua, Elazar ben Azariah, and Tarfon went to visit him. Because of the ban they didn't enter his room. His friends praised him greatly, but Eliezer was angry that they had neither visited nor studied with him for so many years. Finally, the Rabbis asked his opinion about whether a certain item was kosher, clean or unclean. Eliezer's last word was "clean," which convinced Rabbi Joshua that Eliezer himself was "clean" and that the ban should finally be lifted.[12]

Depending on your group, you might consider assigning people to play the roles of Rabbi Joshua, Rabbi Eliezer, and God. The rest of your participants can play the role of the Sanhedrin, the court, and render a verdict. Encourage your "actors" to think freely in framing their arguments to convict or exonerate Rabbi Eliezer.

- Rabbi Joshua and Rabbi Eliezer disagreed over the ultimate source of religious authority—the "objective," direct word of God versus human interpretation of divinely inspired religious law. Which side would you take and why?

- Note, Rabbi Eliezer's punishment *(niddui)* required expulsion from the community except for purposes of business. Otherwise, his social contact was limited to his family. Beyond family, no one could greet him, eat or drink with him, or bring him any enjoyment.[13] Neither was he counted in a prayer *minyan*. Does the punishment fit the crime? Why or why not?

- How would you describe God's reaction during this dispute? Whose side does God seem to take?

- What parallels do you see between the political situation in the time of these Rabbis and Israel's situation today?

- Aside from the Haggadah, the story of the five Rabbis' Seder occurs in no other Jewish sources. Why do you think the compilers of the Haggadah created or included it?

Many interpret the five Rabbis' Seder as the meeting at which they decided to support the Bar Kochba rebellion (132–135 C.E.). It is said that they didn't realize the time had come to say the morning *Sh'ma* because the Rabbis were hiding from the Romans in a dark cave. This is unlikely, because Joshua and Eliezer died before the revolt and the ban on Eliezer would likely have excluded him from such a Seder.

Perhaps the authors of the Haggadah wanted to teach us a subtle but important lesson by fashioning a story that would reunite the five Rabbis at the Seder year after year. The compilers of the Haggadah created a scene of harmony to repair the fractured relationships among the sages, particularly between Joshua and Eliezer.

Remember, these were the two disciples of Yochanan ben Zakkai who had conspired to smuggle their master to safety outside of Jerusalem as he feigned death in a coffin. Eliezer carried the head, Joshua the feet. The compilers of the Haggadah created a text that will eternally bring Eliezer and Joshua to the same Seder table. The message is that peace and fraternity are ultimately more important than ideology or winning an argument. The Haggadah underscores the point through its placement of this passage. The story of the five sages has been sandwiched between the Four Questions and the questions asked by the wise, the wicked, and the simple children.

The Seder is a night when *all* questions are welcome. The Seder is a time for renewing sundered relationships and interrupted dialogue over the toughest questions. Even the skeptical "wicked" child and the banned Rabbi Eliezer participate in the Seder. The Seder is a table from which *none* should feel excluded.

GAMALIEL'S CONSPICUOUS ABSENCE: FINGERPRINTS ON THE HAGGADAH

Read this section aloud or on your own.

Rabban Gamaliel II, the *Nasi* or leader of the Jewish community in the fateful years between about 80 and 110 C.E., is conspicuously missing from the gathering of sages at B'nei B'rak. He was a brilliant but arrogant man whose conflicts with his colleagues reverberate through rabbinic literature. In one such clash, he gratuitously humiliated the humble Rabbi Joshua, which precipitated a virtual coup d'etat. Gamaliel's colleagues deposed him, albeit briefly. The Haggadah does not refer to the story directly, but Gamaliel's absence from the group reminds us of it, as do two other clues in the Haggadah.

First, the Haggadah quotes an excerpt from the Mishnah: "Rabbi Elazar ben Azariah said: *Behold! I am like a man of seventy*, yet I have never been worthy [to find a reason] why the Exodus should be mentioned at night, until Ben Zoma explained it . . ." (Mishnah, Berakhot 1:5).

What's the connection? After Gamaliel had been deposed, the sages of Yavne approached Elazar ben Azariah, a gifted and politically well connected eighteen-year-old, to take his place. In the Babylonian Talmud's version of the story (Berakhot 27a–b), ben Azariah asked his wife if he should accept the offer.

> His wife said, "Perhaps they will depose you later on." [Besides, she said,] "You have no white hair." He was eighteen years old that day. Eighteen rows of hair [on his beard] turned white. That is why Rabbi Elazar ben Azariah said [as we read in the Haggadah], "*Behold, I am like a man of seventy*" and he did not say simply, "[I am] seventy years old."

The compilers of the Haggadah were well aware that for the cognoscenti, a reference to Elazar ben Azariah being "like a man of seventy" would surely evoke Gamaliel's fall from power.

Second, the seating arrangement at the Seder of the five sages in B'nei B'rak yields another clue: Eliezer, Joshua, Elazar ben Azariah, Akiva, and Tarfon. The Talmud (Berakhot 46b) indicates that the individual with the highest-ranking position in the community sits in the middle. Elazar ben Azariah's position in the center hints at his brief stint as the replacement for Rabban Gamaliel as *Nasi*.[14]

Ancient rabbinic literature includes a somewhat similar story involving Rabban Gamaliel. Make a copy of both for your guests and discuss the questions that follow.

> It once happened on the first night of Passover that Rabban Gamaliel and the sages were reclining in the house of Boethus ben Zeno [a pious merchant] in Lod, and they were discussing the laws of the Passover sacrifice the entire night until the cock crowed. Then each pushed aside his table, stretched, and went along to the house of study.
>
> —TOSEFTA, PISCHA 10:12 (THIRD CENTURY C.E.)

It once happened that Rabbi Eliezer, Rabbi Joshua, Rabbi Elazar ben Azariah, Rabbi Akiva, and Rabbi Tarfon were reclining in B'nei B'rak. They were discussing the Exodus from Egypt the entire night, until their students came and said to them: Our teachers, the time has arrived for reading the morning *Sh'ma*.

—THE PASSOVER HAGGADAH

• What are the differences between these two descriptions?

• Why may the composers of the Haggadah have rejected the first?

Consider reading the concluding paragraphs aloud.

The story of five great sages who discussed the Exodus all through the night rebuffs Gamaliel's approach to the Seder, which featured a study session on the laws of the Passover sacrifice. Gamaliel had also promoted roasting a lamb on the night of Passover in exactly the same manner as had been done in the days of the Temple. After he died, the Mishnah prohibited the practice. The compilers of the Haggadah doubtless inserted—and possibly created—this passage to bolster their belief that telling the story of the Exodus represented a healthier, more adaptive approach than dwelling on the absent Passover sacrifice.[15]

Beyond these considerations, the redactors of the Haggadah seem to have preferred assembling a group of Gamaliel's opponents rather than selecting a text in which Gamaliel alone occupied center stage. On the feast of freedom, perhaps the Haggadah sought to remind future leaders of the community that treating one's colleagues with less than respect carries serious consequences. If so, maybe they had the following Talmudic dictum in mind:

Our Rabbis taught: Over three the Holy One, blessed be He, weeps every day: over him who is able to occupy himself with [the study of] the Torah and does not; and over him who is unable to occupy himself with [the study of] the Torah and does; and over a leader who domineers over the community.[16]

6

The Four Children:
A Seat at the Table for Everyone

בָּרוּךְ הַמָּקוֹם. בָּרוּךְ הוּא.

בָּרוּךְ שֶׁנָּתַן תּוֹרָה לְעַמּוֹ יִשְׂרָאֵל. בָּרוּךְ הוּא.

כְּנֶגֶד אַרְבָּעָה בָנִים דִּבְּרָה תוֹרָה.

אֶחָד חָכָם, וְאֶחָד רָשָׁע, וְאֶחָד תָּם,

וְאֶחָד שֶׁאֵינוֹ יוֹדֵעַ לִשְׁאוֹל:

*Blessed be the Omnipresent. Blessed be He. Blessed be He
who gave the Torah to His people Israel. Blessed be He.
The Torah alludes to four children: One wise, one wicked,
one simple, and one who does not know how to ask.*
—THE PASSOVER HAGGADAH

This is one of the passages of the Haggadah that contemporary interpreters have labored hard to make more attractive. The problem is, of course, the notion of "wicked" children and the pointed comparison between the "wise" and the "wicked."

The passage follows two short sections in the Haggadah: the Seder of the sages who discussed the Exodus all night long, and a rabbinic question about whether or not one should include a reference to the Exodus in the evening prayers. Then we come to the Four Children. It's as if these children had been sitting quietly at the sages' Seder and now pipe up with their reactions. These children amplify the motif of asking questions, but here their inquiries focus not on tangible symbols, as did the Four Questions, but on deeper issues of content, meaning, and their own relationship to Jewish tradition.

THE FOUR CHILDREN

Turn to your Haggadah and ask your guests to read the passage about the
Four Children aloud and discuss the following questions. I'd suggest reading each
question from the Haggadah, talking about it, and then discussing the answer and so
on. You may want to begin by reading aloud the introductory paragraph below.
(You can also make a copy for each of your guests of the section below that
includes the Haggadah's questions and answers. For the purpose of this discussion,
feel free to ignore the accompanying questions and answers from the Torah.)

The Haggadah's treatment of the Four Children seems straightforward enough. But nothing could be further from the truth. For starters, in only one case do the Haggadah's questions and answers match up with those given in the Torah. The story of the Four Children in the Haggadah is actually one of at least three ancient treatments of this parable. All of them were probably based on the Mishnah, a rabbinic text compiled around 200 C.E. It spoke about children who were able to ask questions and those who were unable to do so.[1] Over time, two children became four, generally thought to correspond to the four instances in the Torah that address the instruction of future generations about the Exodus.[2] The oldest version of our passage, from the *Mekhilta of Rabbi Ishmael,* a third-century C.E. midrash, is somewhat similar to the Haggadah, but the children are listed in a different order.[3] The Jerusalem Talmud's rendering, from the early fifth century, differs dramatically from the Haggadah. The Jerusalem Talmud gives more or less the Haggadah's answers, but to different children. There, the wise child gets the simple child's answer. And a "stupid" child gets the wise child's answer. Behind a passage that seems so simple lies a long and complicated process of evolution and very careful editing.[4]

- What might be the purpose of the blessing that introduces the Four Children?

- How do you feel about the Haggadah's comparison among the Four Children? How do you explain the order of the Four Children?

• What do you make of the answer the wise child receives and why is he told about *afikomen*?

• Some scholars believe that the Haggadah's treatment of the wise versus the wicked child reflects a response to the development of religious sects, including Christianity, which rejected many aspects of Jewish law. What kinds of questions asked at the Seder, if any, would you call "wicked"? The answer to the wicked child concludes that he rejects a major principle of faith (*kafar ba-ikar*). Comparing his question with that of the wise child and the answer given to the wicked child, what major principle(s) of faith may he have rejected?

• A twelfth-century midrash offers a fascinating observation: "If you estrange those who are distant from you, you will ultimately estrange also those who are near to you" (Numbers Rabbah 8:4). How do you understand this midrash? How might you apply it to the Haggadah's wise and wicked children?

A Note on the Questions of the Wise versus the Wicked Child: The wise child's question comes from the Book of Deuteronomy (6:20): "What mean the decrees, laws, and rules that Adonai our God has enjoined upon *you*?" Now take a look at your Haggadah. Is the pronoun at the end of this question "you" or "us"? According to the accepted text of the Bible and to standard versions of the Haggadah, the Hebrew should read *"etkhem,"* "you" in the plural. But in ancient texts, such as the Septuagint (the Greek translation of the Bible from the third century B.C.E.), and the versions of the Four Children found in the Jerusalem Talmud and the *Mekhilta,* that pronoun reads *"otanu,"* "us," instead of *"etkhem."* It's not clear whether those renderings were simply based on variant manuscripts of the Bible or whether they introduced a subtle change into the biblical text. In any case, some ancient Haggadot adopted this variant, which sharpens the difference between the wise and the wicked children. There seems to have been a concern that if the questions of both the wise and the wicked children ended with "you," some might argue that there was not such a big difference between them. Despite efforts to correct this over the centuries, you'll still find some Haggadot that use "us" in place of "you." There are also many Haggadot where the Hebrew is *"etkhem"* but the translation reads "us."[5]

• How does changing this pronoun affect your understanding of the difference between the wise and the wicked children?

A Note on Afikomen: The response to the wise child refers to the *afikomen,* the meaning of which seems to have been lost by the Talmudic era. It is now thought to mean "dessert," "dinner music," "after-dinner revelry, such as going from house to house," or "entertainment," all of which would have diverted attention from the paschal offering. However, some suggest that the *afikomen* is a messianic symbol, the reappearance of the hidden matzah representing the return of a messianic figure such as Elijah. Only the truly wise would merit such an explanation.[6] After the Temple's destruction, it was indeed traditional to conclude the meal with matzah in place of, or as a reminder of, the paschal offering. But this matzah was not called the *afikomen.* Designating the matzah eaten at the meal's conclusion as the *afikomen* seems to date back to the time of Rashi (1040–1105). He once told his students that he forgot to eat the "matzah of *afikomen*" after the meal. The expression stuck.[7]

TORAH VERSUS HAGGADAH

The Haggadah's story of the Four Children represents an interpretation, actually a midrash, on specific verses from the Torah that mention three different questions children will ask their parents about Passover and the Exodus from Egypt. The Torah also includes answers to those questions.

The contrasts between Torah and Haggadah—especially involving the "wise" (*chakham*) and the "wicked" (*rasha*) child—provide an illuminating commentary on the religious conflicts that have perennially plagued the Jewish People.

First, ask one of your Seder participants to read a question with its answer from the Torah and another to read the Haggadah's elaboration of the same exchange. After reading each pair of questions and responses, discuss the differences between them. When you have finished comparing each set, lead a discussion based on the questions at the bottom of page 72—or whatever else comes up in your group. (This will work best if you make a copy of page 71–72 for each of your guests.)

QUESTION ONE:

When, in time to come, your children ask you, "What mean the decrees, laws, and rules that Adonai our God has enjoined upon you?" you shall say to your children, "We were slaves to Pharaoh in Egypt and Adonai took us out from Egypt with a mighty hand. Adonai wrought before our eyes marvelous and destructive signs and portents in Egypt, against Pharaoh and all his household; and us He took out from there, that He might bring us and give us the land that He had promised on oath to our fathers. Then Adonai commanded us to observe all these laws, to revere Adonai our God, for our lasting good and for our survival, as is now the case. It will be therefore to our merit before Adonai our God to observe faithfully this whole instruction, as He has commanded us."

—DEUTERONOMY 6:20–25

What does the wise son say? "What mean the decrees, laws, and rules that Adonai our God has enjoined upon you?" You must tell him all the laws of Pesach, including the ruling that nothing should be eaten after the *afikomen* [the end of the Mishnah's discussion on Passover].

—THE HAGGADAH

QUESTION TWO:

And when your children ask you, "What does this service mean to you?" you shall say, "It is the Passover sacrifice to Adonai, because He passed over the houses of the Israelites in Egypt when He smote the Egyptians, but saved our houses." —EXODUS 12:26–27

What does the wicked son say? "What does this service mean to you?" To "you" and not to "him." Since he excludes himself from the community and rejects a major principle of faith, you should set his teeth on edge and say to him: "It is because of what Adonai did for me when I went free from Egypt" (Ex. 13:8). "Me" and not "him." Had he been there he would not have been redeemed.

—THE HAGGADAH

QUESTION THREE:

And when, in time to come, your son asks you, saying, "What is this?" you shall say to him, "It was with a mighty hand that Adonai brought us out from Egypt, the house of bondage."

—EXODUS 13:14

What does the simple son say? "What is this?" You shall say to him, "It was with a mighty hand that Adonai brought us out from Egypt, the house of bondage" (Ex. 13:14). [The wise child's answer according to the Jerusalem Talmud.]

—THE HAGGADAH

THE FOURTH CHILD: (BECAUSE THIS CHILD IS UNABLE TO ASK A QUESTION, WE CAN ONLY INCLUDE THE RESPONSE HE RECEIVES IN THE HAGGADAH.)

As for the son who does not know how to ask, you should prompt him, as it is said: "And you shall explain to your son on that day, 'It is because of what Adonai did for me when I went free from Egypt'" (Ex. 13:8). [The Jerusalem Talmud: "With the child who does not know how to ask, you have to begin and start with him."]

—THE HAGGADAH

• What are the major differences between the texts from the Torah and the Haggadah?

• Does the Torah appear judgmental about the three types of questions it anticipates?

• What can we learn from the contrasting messages of the Torah and the Haggadah—especially those involving the wise and the wicked children—about how we might approach conflicts within the Jewish People today?

THE WISE VERSUS THE WICKED:
A RECIPE FOR CONFLICT OR CONFLICT RESOLUTION?

This can be used as an independent reading during your Seder or
as a conclusion for either of the previous activities.

What are we to learn from the Haggadah's Four Children? Is the passage a recipe for conflict or for conflict resolution? We can read it as a harmful text, at best offering a lesson of what *not* to do when we encounter Jews with whom we sharply disagree. But we can also read it as a useful framework for containing and possibly helping to resolve conflict.

Let's begin with text's problems.

According to the Haggadah, wisdom means uncritically embracing the study of Jewish law in all its intricacies—"the decrees, laws, and rules that Adonai our God has enjoined upon you." Wickedness involves questioning the *meaning* of those injunctions.

The parable's presence in the Haggadah indicates that the clash between those who eagerly accept the framework of Jewish law and those who question the meaning of our traditions goes back a long way. In recent times, that conflict has threatened to pull us apart.

The ancient argument for the wise son, the *chakham,* and against the wicked son, the *rasha,* uses tactics familiar to anyone who has followed the recent strife along the Orthodox/non-Orthodox divide.

It begins with an attempt to commandeer tradition: "The *Torah* alludes to Four Children"—as if those asking certain kinds of questions were singled out for praise or condemnation at Sinai itself. The Torah makes no mention of wise, wicked, or simple children. The truth is that in discussing the celebration of Passover, the Torah *expects* that children will ask their parents different questions about our traditions. The Torah casts no judgment on the comparative merit of these questions. Each one seems to have its place.

The Haggadah's argument continues by labeling the protagonists. Before we even hear their questions, the Haggadah tells us who is wicked, wise, or simple. And those labels color how we hear the children's questions. Having already been introduced to the *rasha,* we hear his question—"What does this ritual mean to you?"—as if "you" were angrily written in red. And so he receives an angry response "To *you* and not to *him.*"

The next step in the polemic involves polarization, attempting to destroy any shred of commonality among the disputants.

The questions that the Haggadah takes from the Torah and ascribes to the wise and wicked children are not as different as you might think.

The wise child: "What mean the decrees, laws, and rules that Adonai our God has enjoined upon *you?*" (Deuteronomy 6:20).

The wicked child: "What does this service mean to *you?*" (Exodus 12:26).

Both can be read as expressing a certain tendency to exclude oneself from the community.

To sharpen the distinction between the *chakham* and the *rasha,* some scholars believe that about sixteen hundred years ago the Jerusalem Talmud subtly altered the wise child's question. It changed the last word in his question from "you" to "us."

So, if we look back at the Torah itself, if we can see past the labels, the questions the Haggadah attributes to the *chakham* and *rasha* end on a similar note. Of course, their questions differ, but they have something in common, too. The Haggadah, however, wants to hide even this bit of potential common ground.

At the same time, by bringing the *chakham* and *rasha* to the Seder, the Haggadah implies that Judaism needs them both. The first speaks for the concept of law, halakhah, a guide to the how and when of Jewish life. The second wonders why, a quest of the spirit identified with *aggadah*—the tales, legends, anecdotes, and aphorisms that probe reasons and illuminate meaning. Abraham Joshua Heschel wrote: "Halakhah without *aggadah* is dead. *Aggadah* without halakhah is wild . . . We must neither disparage the body, nor sacrifice the spirit. The body is the discipline, the pattern, the law; the spirit is inner devotion, spontaneity, freedom. The body without the spirit is a corpse; the spirit without the body is a ghost."[8]

Yet, as the Haggadah demonstrates, our tradition sometimes speaks with a harsh voice to those who ask the "wrong" questions. Likewise, today many don't just *question* traditional observance. With little or no real understanding, they reject it out of hand as hopelessly primitive.

What is the bottom line? We can use the Haggadah's Four Children to flatter ourselves as wise and to smugly condemn those with whom we differ. And historically that's how the Four Children have been used. Centuries of illustrated

Haggadot have depicted the wicked child as the personification of everything wrong with modernity and acculturation. But in their heart of hearts, how many Conservative, Reconstructionist, and Reform Jews equate the wise child with what they perceive to be a hyper-legalistic form of Orthodoxy that substitutes blind adherence to law in place of the search for true wisdom?

Or we can read the Four Children as a plea that we sit at the same table with the people in our community—in our own families—with whom we differ most painfully. Whatever the "wicked children" may or may not believe, they deserve a seat at the table. And our answers to their questions had better not cause them to leave.

When the Jewish People are not united against a common enemy our internal conflicts become explosive. Animosity among those certain of their own wisdom, and of others' wickedness, has become dangerous. Both sides need to stop labeling and demonizing the other. Both sides need to appreciate that each has different questions. Both sides must remember that even the questions that seem to put some of us in different camps still speak the words of Torah. That's why this contentious passage begins with a fourfold blessing of God "who gave the Torah to God's people Israel"—all God's people.

From a practical point of view, both sides should spend part of a Seder discussing a stunning insight from the midrash: "If you estrange those who are distant from you, you will ultimately estrange also those who are near to you."[9]

FOUR VOICES ON FOUR CHILDREN

Below you will find four elaborations on the Haggadah's Four Children.
Choose one or more to read aloud and react to at your Seder. Samson Raphael Hirsch's commentary may strike you as narrow-minded, especially in contrast with the other selections. Even if you reject Hirsch's message, consider how you might respond to someone expressing his position.

Four Children: the wise, the wayward, the simple, the sleeping.
Four worlds [of potential existence, according to the Kabbalists].
All are essential to the Divine Plan of Creation. Each manifests a different aspect of the Divine. All the children, all the Jewish souls, are

integral to the Jewish People. Symbolic of the four levels of Jewish Awareness. All are intrinsic to God's Plan for humanity. Each is imbued with a unique way of perceiving the Divine. Only together is the unity of the Jewish People complete . . . Rather than search in others, we must delve into ourselves. We all, to varying degrees, have aspects of the Four Children—Four Selves—within us. We must integrate the positive elements and rechannel the negative. As we hear the voices of the children, as we learn how to handle them, let us also learn how to deal with the voices of the different selves inside us. Only together is our Jewishness complete.

—THE BRESLOV HAGGADAH, BASED THE TEACHINGS OF
THE HASIDIC MASTER REBBE NACHMAN
OF BRESLOV (1772–1810), PODOLIA AND UKRAINE[10]

The wicked child: But what should be said to the members of this fallen generation who, in their apostasy, fancy themselves to be the "progressives," and deride their loyal elders as "backward"? *To them nothing should be said!* The Divine Word teaches in relation to the [three other children that their questions in the Torah are followed by the instruction that you should respond *to* your son]. But in relation to the scornful generation it does not say, "You should say *to* them" but simply, "You should say," because to *them* you have nothing to say. They expect no instruction from you. They have, indeed, "advanced" so far beyond you that they wish to instruct *you*. They wish to move you, by means of their "refined" mockery, from your stale "narrow" views, which appear to them to be burdensome encumbrances, up to their level, up to the bright, easy unrestraint of their "progressiveness." . . . The key to the hearts of the estranged generation rests in the Hands of God. Only experience can bring them back, the experience of the hollowness, the nothingness, the bleakness and emptiness of all those delusions into whose arms they have thoughtlessly thrown themselves. One day those hearts will once more be filled with yearning for the happiness of possessing the ancient Truth which was thrown away.

—SAMSON RAPHAEL HIRSCH (1808–1888), GERMANY[11]

(Hirsch led the Modern Orthodox response to the spread of Reform Judaism in Europe, though he also supported certain elements of reform within Orthodoxy, such as congregational singing, the presence of a choir, and sermons twice monthly in the vernacular.)

The *order* of the four children, with the *rasha* (the wicked one) following right after the *chacham* (the wise one), seems rather odd . . .

In the teachings of Rabbi Isaac Luria (the great sixteenth-century Kabbalist from Safed) it is stated that the four cups drunk at the Seder correspond to the four sons: the first cup relates to the *chacham;* the second cup to the *rasha;* and so forth. The principal part of the Haggadah is recited over the *second* cup [i.e., the second cup is poured just before the Four Questions and is not drunk until shortly before the meal]. Now, the *rasha* is the one of whom it is said that "If he had been there, he would not have been redeemed"; why, then, is the principal part of the Haggadah related to him? . . .

The Talmud states: "Though one sinned, one remains *Yisrael*, i.e., an Israelite." Every Jew, regardless of his personal status, is possessed of the essence of Judaism. My father-in-law, the Rebbe, thus commented on the phrase "one is wise, and one is wicked . . .": Each one is possessed of *Echad* (the One), even the *rasha*, except that in him it is concealed and one must bring it out into the open.

Yisrael is an acronym: *'Yesh Shishim Ribo Otiyot LaTorah'* (there are six hundred thousand letters to the Torah). The implication is clear: Just as the totality of the Torah depends on every single letter . . . so, too, the totality of the Jewish People depends on every single Jew. Moreover, "You are children of God, your God" (Deut. 14:1); thus even our Father in Heaven is, if one could say so, affected by every individual Jew.

The inclusion of the *rasha* in the Seder thus achieves the ultimate purpose of everything . . . The *chacham* is the only one to uncover the

Echad inherent in the *rasha* . . . This is the reason for the juxtaposition of the *rasha* with the *chacham*. The *chacham* is taught not to argue: "Why should I bother with the *rasha*? Let him be lost through his wickedness!" He must be conscious of the fact that all of Israel are surety for one another.

—MENACHEM MENDEL SCHNEERSON,
THE LUBAVITCHER REBBE (1902–1994), EUROPE AND AMERICA,
CHARISMATIC LEADER OF CHABAD HASIDISM[12]

Recent generations have witnessed the development of many feminist Haggadot that seek to create a Seder more inclusive of women. Following is a thought-provoking selection from *The Journey Continues: The 1997 Ma'yan Passover Haggadah*.

The Four Daughters

The daughter in search of a usable past. *Ma hi omeret*? What does she say?

"Why didn't the *Torah* count women among the '600,000 men on foot, aside from children' who came out of Egypt? And why did Moses say at Sinai, 'Go not near a woman,' addressing only the men, as if preparation for Revelation was not meant for us as well?"

Because she already understands that Jewish memory is essential to our identity, teach her that history is made by those who tell the tale. If *Torah* did not name and number women, it is up to her to fill the empty spaces of our holy texts.

And the daughter who wants to erase her difference. *Ma hi omeret*? What does she say?

"Can't one just be a Jew? Why must you keep pushing your women's questions into every text? And why are these women's issues so important to you?"

"To you," and not "to me." Since she so easily forgets the struggles of her mothers and sisters, you must set her teeth on edge by saying, "I thank God every morning for the blessing of being a woman."

And the daughter who does not know that she has a place at the table. *Ma hi omeret?* What does she say?

"What is this?"

Because she doesn't realize that her question is, in itself, a part of the Seder tradition, teach her that the *Haggadah* is an extended conversation about liberation, and tell her that her insights and questions are also text.

And the daughter who asks no question.

You must say to her, "Your questions, when they come, will liberate you from Egypt. This is how it is and has always been with your mothers and grandmothers. From the moment Miriam and the midwives questioned Pharaoh's edict until today, every question we ask helps us leave Egypt farther behind."[13]

7

Hardening Pharaoh's Heart:
The Toughest Part of the Story

מַה זֹּאת? וְאָמַרְתָּ אֵלָיו:
בְּחֹזֶק יָד הוֹצִיאָנוּ יְהוָה מִמִּצְרַיִם מִבֵּית עֲבָדִים:

"What is this?" You are to say to him: "By strength of hand YHWH
brought us out of Egypt, out of a house of serfs" (Ex. 13:14).
—THE PASSOVER HAGGADAH, THE "SIMPLE CHILD'S"
QUESTION AND ANSWER

The Haggadah reminds us that "whoever elaborates on the story of the Exodus deserves praise." In the spirit of elaboration and study, let's take a look at one of the most troubling aspects of the Exodus story, the hardening of Pharaoh's heart. We read in the Haggadah many times about the signs, wonders, and miracles associated with the Exodus. We recite the names of the plagues one by one and sing about the parting of the Red Sea in *Dayyenu*. Mysteriously, the Haggadah omits even a single reference to the hardening of Pharaoh's heart, though in Exodus it is mentioned in conjunction with every plague and elsewhere—twenty times in all.

Interestingly, the answer to the simple child's question includes only the passage above. Here's the verse that follows it in the Torah:

And it was when Pharaoh hardened [his heart] against sending us free, that YHWH killed every firstborn throughout the land of Egypt, from the firstborn of man to the firstborn of beast. . . .

—EXODUS 13:15[1]

One can easily imagine the debate among the Haggadah's compilers as they argued about whether or not to answer the simple child's question with a few more words. To do so would have been more faithful to the Exodus saga, as it would have brought the theme of God's hardening Pharaoh's heart into the Seder. But, given that motif's moral complexity, we can well understand the decision to avoid it by opting for a simple answer to a simple question!

THE BIBLE AND THE HARDENING OF PHARAOH'S HEART

The Bible's twenty references to the hardening of Pharaoh's heart (see pages 83–86) make for a fascinating discussion before you begin your Seder. It would be helpful to make a copy of these twenty verses from the Bible for each of your guests.

Read these questions aloud to your group before you begin reading the biblical passages that describe the hardening of Pharaoh's heart. Remind your guests that the Pharaoh of the hard heart is not the same one who earlier in Exodus ordered the killing of Jewish male infants. He is that Pharaoh's successor.

- Who appears to bear the responsibility for hardening Pharaoh's heart in each particular passage?

- Does this remain constant throughout?

- How do you feel about the notion of God hardening Pharaoh's heart? Was it justified? Was it necessary?

- What is the primary reason given in the text for hardening Pharaoh's heart?

- Why do you think the Haggadah omits this subject?

- What contemporary situations does the theme of a hard-hearted political leader conjure up for you?

You can use this material in different ways depending on the age and interests of your Seder guests. Take turns reading the biblical passages aloud.[2] Then either discuss the questions on page 82 or ask your group to divide into two groups, one defending God's hardening of Pharaoh's heart, the other opposing it.

If you have a group that enjoys text study, you might also spend some time checking out what the commentators have said, beginning on page 86.

1. After the burning bush, when Moses is about to return to Egypt. God says: "When you go to return to Egypt, see: All the portents that I have put in your hand, you are to do before Pharaoh, but I will make his heart strong-willed [*achazeik*], so that he will not send the people free" (Ex. 4:21).

2. After Moses returns to Egypt and just before he and Aaron speak to Pharaoh for the first time. God says: "But I will harden [*aksheh*] Pharaoh's heart, I will make my signs and my portents many in the land of Egypt: Pharaoh will not hearken to you, so I will set my hand against Egypt, and I will bring out my forces, my people, the Children of Israel, from the land of Egypt with great (acts of) judgment" (Ex. 7:3–4).

3. Moses' rod turns into a snake. Pharaoh's magicians perform the same trick, but Moses' snake swallows up their snakes: "Yet Pharaoh's heart remained strong-willed [*vayechezak*], and he did not hearken to them, as Adonai had spoken" (Ex. 7:13).

4. The next verse: "Adonai said to Moses, 'Pharaoh's heart is heavy-with-stubbornness [*kaveid*]—he refuses to send the people free'" (Ex. 7:14).

5. After the first plague, when the rivers turn to blood, Pharaoh's magicians also turned water to blood: "But the magicians of Egypt did thus with their occult-arts, and Pharaoh's heart remained strong-willed [*vayechezak*], and he did not hearken to them, as Adonai had spoken" (Ex. 7:22).

6. After the onset of the second plague, frogs, Pharaoh asks Moses to end the plague and says that he will let the Israelites conduct sacrifices in the desert as Moses had requested. The frogs return to the river at the appointed time: "But when Pharaoh saw that there was breathing-room, he made his heart heavy-with-stubbornness [*v'hakhbeid*], and did not hearken to them, as Adonai had spoken" (Ex. 8:11).

7. Following the onset of the third plague, lice, which Pharaoh's magicians were not able to duplicate: "The magicians said to Pharaoh: This is the finger of a god! But Pharaoh's heart remained strong-willed [*vayechezak*], and he did not hearken to them, as Adonai had spoken" (Ex. 8:15).

8. Pharaoh asks Moses to end the fourth plague, swarms of insects.[3] The plague ends and Pharaoh promises to let the people go so they can sacrifice to God in the desert: "But Pharaoh made his heart heavy-with-stubbornness [*vayakhbeid*] this time as well, and he did not send the people free" (Ex. 8:28).

9. Following the onset of the fifth plague, the death of cattle: "But Pharaoh's heart remained heavy-with-stubbornness [*vayikhbad*], and he did not send the people free" (Ex. 9:7).

10. Following the sixth plague, boils: "But Adonai made Pharaoh's heart strong-willed [*vayichazeik*], and he did not hearken to them, as Adonai had said to Moses" (Ex. 9:12).

11. After the onset of hail, the seventh plague, Pharaoh says, "This-time I have sinned! Adonai is the one-in-the-right, I and my people are the ones-in-the-wrong!" He pleads for the end of the plague: "But when Pharaoh saw that the rain and the hail and the thunder had stopped, he continued to sin: He made his heart heavy-with-stubbornness [*vayakhbeid*], his and his servants" (Ex. 9:34).

12. Next verse: "Pharaoh's heart remained strong-willed [*vayechezak*], and he did not send the Children of Israel free, as Adonai had spoken through Moses" (Ex. 9:35).

13. Next verse. Before the announcement of locusts, the eighth plague: "Adonai said to Moses: 'Come into Pharaoh! For I have made his heart and the heart of his servants heavy-with-stubbornness [*hikhbad'ti*], in order that I may put these my signs among them and in order that you may recount in the ears of your child and of your child's child how I have been capricious with Egypt, and my signs, which I have placed upon them—that you may know that I am Adonai'" (Ex. 10:1–2).

14. After the onset of the locusts, Pharaoh begs Moses to bring an end to the plague, saying that he has sinned against God and Moses. The plague

ends: "But Adonai made Pharaoh's heart strong-willed [*vayichazeik*], and he did not send the Children of Israel free" (Ex. 10:20).

15. After the onset of the ninth plague, darkness, Pharaoh is willing to let the Israelites and their children go to pray for three days in the desert as they had requested. Pharaoh insists that the Israelites leave their cattle behind. Moses says they need the cattle to make sacrifices in the desert: "But Adonai made Pharaoh's heart strong-willed [*vayichazeik*], so that he would not consent to send them free" (Ex. 10:27).

16. Moses announces the killing of the firstborn. The last plague will begin at midnight: "Adonai said to Moses: Pharaoh will not hearken to you, in order that my portents may be many in the land of Egypt. Now Moses and Aharon had done all the portents in Pharaoh's presence, but Adonai had made Pharaoh's heart strong-willed [*vayichazeik*], and he had not sent the Children of Israel free from his land" (Ex. 11:10).

17. After the Israelites leave Egypt the text includes a summary of the events and instructions about the laws of Passover: "It shall be when your child asks you on the morrow, saying: 'What is this?' You are to say to him: 'By strength of hand Adonai brought us out of Egypt, out of a house of serfs. And it was when Pharaoh hardened [*hikshah*] (his heart) against sending us free, that Adonai killed every firstborn throughout the land of Egypt, from the firstborn of man to the firstborn of beast'" (Ex. 13:14–15).

18. The Israelites are in the desert but have not yet reached the Red Sea. God says: "Now Pharaoh will say of the Children of Israel: 'They are confused in the land! The wilderness has closed them in!' I will make Pharaoh's heart strong-willed [*v'chizakti*], so that he pursues them, and I will be glorified through Pharaoh and his army, so that the Egyptians may know that I am Adonai" (Ex. 14:3–4).

19. A few verses later: "He had his chariot harnessed, his (fighting) people he took with him, and he took six hundred selected chariots and every (kind of) chariot in Egypt, teams-of-three upon them all. Now Adonai made the heart of Pharaoh king of Egypt strong-willed [*vayichazeik*], so that he pursued the Children of Israel" (Ex. 14:6–8).

20. God says to Moses He will part the sea: "But I, here, I will make Egypt's heart strong-willed [*m'chazeik*], so that they come in after them and I will be glorified through Pharaoh and all his army, his chariots and his riders; and the Egyptians shall know that I am Adonai, when I am glorified through Pharaoh, his chariots and his riders" (Ex. 14:17).

THE COMMENTATORS' STRUGGLE

Commentators have long labored to justify God's hardening of Pharaoh's heart.[4] Some have stressed the fact that initially Pharaoh seemed to harden his *own* heart. God only stepped in to strengthen the decision Pharaoh had freely made. Others see this as the exception that proves the rule that God does not interfere with human free will. But the volume of commentary on this theme points to its difficulty. Below you'll find six responses to the hardening of Pharaoh's heart. Choose one or two to read aloud and discuss.

> *For I have hardened his heart (Ex. 10:1)* . . . Rabbi Johanan said: "Does this not provide heretics with ground for arguing that he had no means of repenting, since it says, *'For I have hardened his heart?'*" To which Rabbi Simeon ben Lakish replied: "Let the mouths of the heretics be stopped up . . . When God warns a man once, twice, and even a third time and he still does not repent, then does God close his heart against repentance so He should exact vengeance from him for his sins." Thus it was for wicked Pharaoh.
>
> —EXODUS RABBAH (13:3), A COLLECTION OF ANCIENT
> MIDRASHIM COMPILED IN THE TENTH CENTURY

> *And I will harden (Ex. 7:3)* . . . Since he dealt wickedly and offered resistance against Me, and it is manifest before Me that there is no delight among the nations to set their whole heart to repentance, it is better that his heart be hardened in order to increase through him My signs, and you will recognize my might . . . Nevertheless, as regards the first five plagues it is not stated, *"And Adonai hardened the heart of Pharaoh,"* but *"And Pharaoh's heart was hardened."*
>
> —RASHI (1040–1105), FRANCE

There are some verses that lead people to fancy that God preordains and compels disobedience. This is false . . . Rather, whoever is bad is so by his own choice. If he wishes to be virtuous, he can be so; there is nothing preventing him . . . [God's] saying *"And I will harden Pharaoh's heart"*—and then punishing him and destroying him—contains a subject for discussion and a major principle stems from it . . . If Pharaoh and his followers had committed no other sin than not letting Israel go free, the matter would undoubtedly be problematic, for He had prevented them from setting Israel free . . . However, the matter is not like this, but rather Pharaoh and his followers disobeyed by choice, without force or compulsion. He oppressed the foreigners who were in their midst and treated them with sheer injustice . . . This action was due to their choice and to the evil character of their thought; there was nothing compelling them to do it. God punished them for it by preventing them from repenting so that the punishment which His justice required would befall them.

—MAIMONIDES (1135–1204), SPAIN[5]

Nowhere in the Bible is the fact of human freedom questioned, apart from the episode where God hardens Pharaoh's heart . . . But the Pharaoh episode is precisely the exception that proves the rule, for the biblical account assumes that under all normal conditions Pharaoh too would be free to release the Israelites. This is not a normal situation because God has a broader purpose to accomplish. That's why God has to intervene directly to limit Pharaoh's freedom. It takes a specific divine intervention to rob Pharaoh of his freedom—so much is freedom a natural part of the order of creation.

—NEIL GILLMAN (1933–), UNITED STATES[6]

The final decision always rests with man. At the beginning, however, man is free to choose any path of action he so desires. He is afforded equal opportunity to do good or evil. But as soon as he has made his first choice, then the opportunities are no longer so evenly balanced. The more he persists in the first path of his choosing, shall we say, the evil path, the harder will it become for him to revert to the good path, even though his essential freedom of choice is not affected. In other words, it is not the Almighty who has hampered his freedom and made the path of repentance difficult. He has, by his own choice and persistence in evil, placed obstacles in the way leading back to reformation.

—NEHAMA LEIBOWITZ (1905–1997), ISRAEL[7]

In Pharaoh's case, not listening becomes a fatal reflex, closing him to vulnerability and to growth. Nevertheless, it is based on a horror and a desire that are not alien to human experience. The process by which he moves from hardening his own heart to God's hardening his heart (in general terms, this happens after the first five plagues) is essentially a mysterious one. A stamina of endurance possesses Pharaoh: to the bystander, there is an unnatural, compulsive quality about his refusal that is . . . [as others have suggested] the idiomatic meaning of the formula: "God hardened Pharaoh's heart": where God is described as the cause of human emotional response, the effect is to suggest an *unaccountable* human reaction. On such a reading, Pharaoh increasingly strikes the reader with a kind of fascination as he compulsively resists the bombardment that should have defeated him. What demonic strength possesses him? "I shall strengthen his heart," "God made his heart impenetrable": These expressions only serve to underline the mystery of human self-destruction.

—AVIVA GOTTLIEB ZORNBERG (1944–), ISRAEL[8]

THE SOFTENING OF GOD'S HEART

Read this on your own or do so with your group after discussing the material above.

Your view of God's role in hardening Pharaoh's heart may depend on where you enter the story. If you focus just on the sequence of the plagues, it appears that Pharaoh hardens his own heart for the first five plagues, with God only stepping in for the last five. Commentators such as Maimonides and Leibowitz stress that Pharaoh's initial hard-hearted attitude foreclosed any subsequent softening. This view suggests that Pharaoh dug himself into such a hole that he *couldn't* change his mind, that he had been trapped by his own evil ways.

This interpretation tends to ignore that the first two announcements that *God* will harden Pharaoh's heart occur well before the plagues begin.

Clearly a cruel character, Pharaoh also appears to have been left with little chance for softening his position in response to the barrage of God's signs and wonders that bore down upon him. After the very first sign from God, when the snakes of Pharaoh's magicians are swallowed by those of Moses and Aaron, we read: "Yet Pharaoh's heart remained strong-willed and he did not hearken to them, *as Adonai had spoken* [emphasis mine]" (Ex. 7:13).

As Adonai had spoken? God never said anything about Pharaoh making his own heart "strong-willed." God spoke only of a divine role in making Pharaoh's heart "strong-willed." In four instances (plagues 3, 5, 6, and 7) when Pharaoh's heart becomes strong-willed or stubborn, but not explicitly on account of God, the verse ends with the same phrase *"as Adonai had spoken."* What on the surface appears to be Pharaoh's independent stubbornness upon closer inspection seems to reflect God's intervention, *"as Adonai had spoken."*

This conclusion plainly adds an uncomfortable measure of moral confusion to the Exodus story. No longer an autonomous agent of evil who brings God's wrath on his people, Pharaoh becomes a victim, a pawn in God's greater plan. The longer the story continues, the more painful the moral ambiguity becomes.

When the Egyptian army heads to the Red Sea in what will prove to be a suicidal mission of pursuit, God's strong hand and motivation both become painfully clear: "But I, here, I will make Egypt's heart strong-willed, so that they come in after them, and I will be glorified through Pharaoh and all his army, his chariots and his riders; and the Egyptians shall know that I am Adonai, when I am glorified through Pharaoh, his chariots and his riders" (Ex. 14:17). Lest there be any mistake about it, the dissonant note of divine glorification through the drowning of Pharaoh's troops strikes twice to ring down the curtain on this portion of the Exodus.

The Egyptian ruler's stubbornness and his inability to repent emerge as unmistakable props in the divine drama to teach the Egyptians that God is God and Pharaoh is not.

And we can now understand why the theme of God's hardening of Pharaoh's heart may have been excluded from the Haggadah. It paints a picture of humanity deprived of free will, and of God—not Pharaoh—as the one with a hard heart.

Add to this the fact that, as the Seder was evolving, Christianity was fast making inroads among gentiles and had reinterpreted the symbols of Passover to signify the sacrifice of Jesus. And Christians worshiped a face of God that seemed far more merciful than the God of the Exodus:

> Do you despise the riches of [God's] kindness and forbearance and patience? For do you not know that God's kindness is meant to lead you to repentance? But by your hard and impertinent heart you are storing up wrath for yourself on the day of wrath . . . ?
>
> —ROMANS 2:4–5

The God of the Exodus was plenty wrathful but allowed Pharaoh no real opportunity to repent.

We also know that during this era, the creators of what we now call Rabbinic Judaism were fearful that Jews would prove susceptible to what the Rabbis saw in Christianity—in their eyes, a religion centered on an individual rather than on God. This may be one of the reasons the Haggadah mentions Moses only once explicitly, in passing. If the Rabbis could virtually leave Moses out of the Passover story, all the easier it must have been to drop the disturbing theme of God's hardening Pharaoh's heart.

Having looked at some of the Bible's most difficult verses, let's now consider them in a broader context. The depiction of God in Genesis and Exodus differs considerably from that in later books of the Bible, particularly Prophets. In the flood, except for one family and a pair of each animal species, God destroys a morally corrupt world. No chance for repentance whatsoever! A few chapters later, God lays waste the evil cities of Sodom and Gomorrah. But the cataclysm is confined just to those two sites, and Abraham has a chance to argue for sparing the innocent. Lot and his daughters do escape. Still, the cities' residents have no opportunity to repent.

Pharaoh at least receives warnings and on the surface seems to have an opportunity to mend his ways. And the plagues are relatively contained. Only certain species of animals perish and the last plague targets the Egyptian firstborn—human and animal.

Later, after the Israelites build the Golden Calf, God threatens to wipe them out and to keep a new covenant through Moses. But God heeds Moses' plea for mercy and compassion. The Israelites repent and, in the process, mercy and compassion become central to our subsequent understanding of God.

The image of a compassionate God finds its most dramatic expression in the Book of Jonah, read on the afternoon of Yom Kippur. Here, God sends the reluctant prophet to warn the people of Nineveh of destruction unless they repent. God pleads for the innocent children and animals in "Nineveh, that great city in which there are more than 120,000 persons who cannot tell their right hand from their left hand; and also much cattle. . . ."[9] Much to the hard hearted prophet's consternation, from the king down, the Ninevites repent.

With so many raw memories of suffering under Rome, the composers of the Haggadah surely wished to call down God's wrath upon this Egypt incarnate. The God of the Exodus appealed to them. But, they were hardly willing to give up the God who saved Nineveh.

You can reconcile these contrasting images of God with the notion that the Bible reveals how the human understanding of God has evolved. Or, as Jack Miles boldly argues in *God—A Biography,* you can study the Bible as the story of how God's character has evolved through interaction with humanity.[10] Or you use creative midrash, such as the eighth-century *Pirke de Rabbi Eliezer,* to do the same thing. This midrash describes Pharaoh's repentance at the Red Sea and puts a verse from the Israelites' Song of the Sea in Pharaoh's mouth: "Who is like You, O Adonai . . . ?"

> The Holy One, blessed be He, delivered [resurrected Pharaoh] him from amongst the dead . . . He went and ruled in Nineveh . . . When God sent for Jonah to prophesy against the city's destruction, Pharaoh hearkened and arose from his throne, rent his garments and clothed himself in ashes . . . And God repented of the evil he said he would do to them and did not do it.[11]

8

The Festival of Spring:
Reconnecting Passover and Nature

יָכוֹל מֵרֹאשׁ חֹדֶשׁ, תַּלְמוּד לוֹמַר בַּיּוֹם הַהוּא...

It might have been thought that the telling should begin on the new moon [of Nisan]: therefore the text teaches us "in that day." But since it says "in that day," we might have thought that we should begin while it is day; therefore the Scripture also teaches "because of this." You could not say "because of this," if it were not referring to the time when unleavened bread and bitter herbs were lying before you.
—THE PASSOVER HAGGADAH, FROM THE MEKHILTA OF RABBI ISHMAEL,
A THIRD-CENTURY MIDRASH

Omitted from many modern Haggadot, this ancient passage takes pains to ensure that we recount the Exodus saga at the proper time: not on the new moon of Nisan, but on the date when the Israelites sacrificed the paschal offering in Egypt, the fifteenth of the month; and not during the day, but at night. This places the Seder at the most critical religious moment in the ancient Near East—the full moon after the vernal equinox![1]

The fact that Passover, *Chag HaAviv,* "the Festival of Spring," occurs when it does seems so natural that you may not have stopped to wonder why or what it means. Here we'll "unpack" the Passover-spring connection and consider what the holiday can teach us about the environment.

Why focus on spring and nature during Passover? Because humanity's survival now depends squarely on restoring our capacity to live in harmony with the environment. Jewish tradition can provide inspiration and strength for that task. Judaism evolved when humanity's dependence on the earth for sustenance was undeniable: The motif of famine runs through the Bible like a red thread. We can no longer afford to speak of *tikkun olam,* mending the world, in a metaphoric sense. We must begin repairing the earth—now. And to the extent that healing the earth brings us a little closer to nature, we'll also mend our souls.

There's not a better time for renewing our commitment to this work of *tikkun* than the Seder, when we celebrate our liberation and ponder the uses and misuses of freedom.

Sadly, our celebration of Passover gives virtually all the attention to the "what" of the Exodus and focuses very little on the "when." As a result, for many, the connections between Passover and the natural world have all but disappeared from the Seder. Those who observe the practice on the second Seder of beginning to count the *omer,* the forty-nine days from Passover to Shavuot, experience one link between Passover and the world of nature: That interval marked the period between the beginning of the barley harvest and the completion of the wheat harvest. But in Israel, where Seders are held only on the first night of Passover, even this connection fades. Those who attend synagogue on the first day of Passover will also be aware of another important link between the festival and nature. It rarely rains in Israel after Passover, so with the holiday comes a special prayer for dew, which plays an important role in sustaining crops during the hot, dry summer. In what follows, we'll try to root Passover a bit more firmly in its season and in the process develop a deeper appreciation for the festival as well as our responsibilities to the environment.

This chapter includes a range of activities for your Seder to strengthen the Passover/spring connection and build environmental awareness.

FOR DISCUSSION

- It is often said that parsley on the Seder plate reminds us of spring. The Bible instructs us to observe Passover in the month of Aviv, the month of spring. What relationships do you see between springtime and the celebration of redemption?

• Without using these particular terms, the Bible sets Passover at the full moon near the vernal equinox. This means that on Passover the periods of daylight and darkness are about equal and that the moon rises just when the sun sets and sets just when the sun rises. After this equinox, the period of daylight becomes longer than that of darkness. How might the vernal equinox or its symbolism be related to Passover?

• If Passover is a celebration of freedom, how have we used our freedom in relation to the natural environment? What do you think Jewish tradition can contribute to the environmental movement? Do you think environmental issues are a high enough priority for the Jewish community?

ON SPRING AND TIME

Depending on your group, you might read this during the Seder or on your own.

Several verses from the Book of Exodus fix the time for celebrating Passover. Everett Fox's translation of the Bible captures the ancient relationship between the festival and its season:

> YHWH said to Moshe and to Aharon in the land of Egypt saying, "Let this New-Moon be for you the beginning of New-Moons . . . [The paschal lamb or goat] shall be for you in safekeeping, until the fourteenth day after this New-Moon, and they are to slay it—the entire assembly of the community of Israel—between the setting times [twilight] . . . In the first (month), on the fourteenth day after the New-Moon, at sunset, you are to eat *matzot* until the twenty-first day of the month, at sunset" . . . Moshe said to the people, "Remember this day on which you went out from Egypt the house of serfs; for by strength of hand YHWH brought you out from here: no fermentation is to be

eaten. Today you are going out, in the New-Moon of Ripe Grain [*chodesh Aviv*] . . . You are to keep this law at its appointed-time from year-day to year-day."

—EXODUS 12:1–2, 12:6, 12:18, 13:3–4, 13:10

Aviv refers to the first stage of grain's ripening, when its "ears" are well formed but still soft and green. The stalks stand fresh and verdant in the field.[2] Later it came to mean "spring." *Aviv* was also the name of the month when the vernal equinox fell. After the Babylonian Exile, the names of the months changed and Aviv became Nisan.

Because calendars in the ancient Near East marked the beginning of each month with the appearance of the new moon, the fifteenth corresponds to the full moon. The Bible carefully sets the first Passover at the full moon near the vernal equinox. Why tell us to "keep this law at its appointed-time"? Because otherwise Passover and all the other Jewish holidays would have fallen in their appointed months, but those months and their festivals would have wandered through the seasons, just as the Muslim festival of Ramadan does. The complexity of the Jewish calendar—which reckons months by the moon and years by the sun and adds an extra month to the calendar seven out of nineteen years—derives precisely from this specification: that Passover must come "at its appointed-time," at the full moon of the vernal equinox, when the barley has just begun to ripen.

Our ancestors understood that the Bible points to a vital relationship between the season *when* the Exodus occurred and *what* the Exodus means. It is no accident, in other words, that we celebrate the freedom and birth of our people in the period that marks the rebirth of the earth itself. As the earth passes from a darker to a brighter season and renews itself, so can we: Spring embodies the potential for growth on every plane. In many ancient Near Eastern cultures, the year began on the full moon of the vernal equinox. It was a moment of the greatest imaginable awareness of the natural world, a moment of both enormous potential for regeneration and grave danger—would the standing grain yield a bountiful harvest, or would excessive heat or rain produce a devastating blight?

Feeling nature's mighty rhythms unleashes the human capacity for renewal. Disconnecting ourselves from that flow deprives us of a critical source of energy to grow, to change, to free ourselves from the narrow places where we've gotten stuck. As Rabbi Irving Greenberg notes:

> Biblical language and symbol point to spring as the proper season for deliverance. The rebirth of earth after winter is nature's indication that life overcomes death: Spring is nature's analogue to redemption. Life blossoming, breaking winter's death grip, gives great credence to the human yearning for liberation. A correct reading of the spring season would hear its message of breaking out and life reborn at the biological level simultaneously with an Exodus message of good overcoming evil, of love overpowering death, of freedom and redemption. The Bible envisions a world in which moral and physical states coincide, when nature and history, in harmony, confirm the triumph of life. The Exodus paradigm suggests that the outcome of history will be an eternal spring. Read with a historical /theological hermeneutic, spring is Exodus.[3]

The conjunction of Passover with a critical point in the lunar-solar cycle exemplifies Judaism's concept of time. Most ancient civilizations emphasized the cyclical aspect of time. The ancients watched the stars travel predictably through the heavens, the Nile flood each spring, the seasons rotate in an orderly fashion. Year after year, time returned from where it had begun. The cyclicality of nature infused life with a welcome sense of stability. Ancient religious rites embodied these cycles. They provided worshipers with a way to re-create themselves by reliving the creation of the cosmos through celebrating the birth, death, and resurrection of their gods. History, as we know it, mattered little. "Everything begins over again at its commencement every instant. The past is but a prefiguration of the future, no event is irreversible and no transformation is final . . . [Through] the repetition of paradigmatic gestures and by means of periodic ceremonies, archaic man succeeded . . . in annulling time. . . ."[4]

Against this static background, the Israelite religion made an astonishing assertion: that time could also be conceptualized as an arrow, not just an eternal cycle.[5] In proclaiming that God actively directed the course of human history, humanity now encountered God in a new realm. History became the record of God's actions and humanity's response. That record was not circular, but began with creation, moved through deliverance and revelation, and would conclude with ultimate messianic redemption. The forward march of time sweeps us away from the ancient, timeless cycles, headlong into the inexorably unfolding drama of history. (This view of time and history now dominates the secular world, which, of course, removed God from the plot, leaving the stage to humanity alone.) Archaic man might shudder, charging that we've sundered humanity from its roots, that the history we've made is pure terror. Modern man responds that at least we have the freedom to create something new![6]

If the Israelites stressed "time's arrow," they certainly had no intention of burying "time's cycle." The best evidence comes from the bond between Passover and the full moon of the vernal equinox. The Exodus from Egypt represents "time's arrow" par excellence. The full moon of the vernal equinox is the paradigmatic symbol of "time's cycle." Judaism says that we need to reckon time both ways. The cyclical aspect of time roots and strengthens us as we tap into the power of the natural world's enduring rhythms. The directional aspect of time inspires us to use that strength to change the world, to push it, however slowly, from what it is today to what it can become tomorrow. Punctuated by the weekly Sabbath, Jewish time revolves around the annual cycle of holy days, which likewise restore our capacity to repair ourselves and the world.

As did the religions of other ancient peoples, the Passover Haggadah also commands us to return to our beginning—not to the creation of the world (we do that in the fall festivals), but to our birth as a nation. "In every generation, each individual should feel as though he or she had gone out of Egypt." But the same Haggadah that bids us to remember the Exodus, when *everything* changed, calls us to go back in time, as if *nothing* had changed.

As you feast with the full moon overhead, celebrate your freedom and remember a few words from Judaism's traditional blessing for the new moon, *Kiddush Levanah:* "He told the moon to renew its crown of glory over those [He] sustained from the womb, so that like the moon, in the future, they too, will be renewed."[7] Now remember how the ancients thought about that luminous, silvery disc that graces heaven's darkened dome:

Time as governed and measured by the phases of the moon might be called "living" time. It is bound up with the reality of life and nature, rain and the tides . . . the time of sowing, the menstrual cycle . . . "Becoming" is the lunar order of things . . . The moon "divides," "spins," and "measures" or "feeds," "makes fruitful," and "blesses" . . . "initiates and purifies"—because it is living, and therefore in a perpetual state of rhythmic becoming . . .[8] [If] archaic man succeeded . . . in annulling time, he nonetheless lived in harmony with the cosmic rhythms; we might even say that he entered into these rhythms (we need only remember how "real" night and day are to him, and the seasons, the cycles of the moon, the solstices).[9]

Every spring, Passover beckons us to become free, born anew. We can begin again every year, every moment—but only if we preserve the earth, the source of our sustenance, our partner in growth, change, and renewal. The ancients may not have had much interest in history and change, but they couldn't forget their dependence on the earth for a minute. As we'll now see, that dependence gave rise to festivals —including the original Passover—dedicated to ensuring the earth's continued bounty.

THE ORIGINS OF PASSOVER: TWO VIEWS

Depending on your group, you might read this during the Seder or on your own.

As one scholar wisely observed, "A holiday is always older than the interpretation which is given to it."[10] Here we'll take a brief look at two theories of the origins of Passover. Although they differ considerably, both views emphasize the underlying ancient connection between Passover and the natural world.[11]

One school of thought holds that Passover as we know it today evolved from the fusion of two ancient festivals.[12] The first involved the annual sacrifice of a young sheep or goat firstling from the nomadic Israelites' flocks. Families carried out the sacrifice at night, in the spring under a full moon. The ritual may have begun before or after the Israelites' sojourn in Egypt. In any case, what had once been a sacrifice to ensure a healthy flock eventually became associated with the

Exodus and the legend of God's striking the firstborn of the Egyptians and sparing those of the Israelites.

Because the purity of the sacrificial victim was critical, it was essential to avoid contaminating it with the potential rot to which leavened bread was susceptible. Thus, families ate unleavened cakes with the offering. Smearing the blood of the offering on the entrance to the Israelites' tents, originally thought to ward off disease or misfortune, later acquired a historical meaning, further linking the ritual with legends of the last plague. Some maintain that the Pesach offering was initially more widely practiced in Judah, the Southern Kingdom, where seminomadic animal husbandry was more prevalent than in Israel, the agriculturally richer Northern Kingdom.

The Northern Kingdom of Israel placed greater emphasis on a spring grain holiday, the seven-day Festival of Matzot that began at the full moon before the harvest. Just after the first cereal crop—barley—had begun to ripen, farmers held a sacred feast to ensure a bountiful wheat harvest, still some weeks away. Leaven, or sourdough, a sour-smelling culture of yeast and bacteria grown from the old crop, was removed to express hope for a healthy crop and to avoid contamination of the new crop by the old. The moldy rot that leavened bread can develop was similar to what farmers feared could devastate their crops. Excessive rain and heat could destroy a barley crop with a fungal disease now known as smut.[13] Celebrated with unleavened bread from the previous year's crop, the Festival of Matzot marked the time after which the community could begin to consume grains from the new crop. It may be that this holiday developed later than the Pesach sacrifice, when formerly nomadic shepherds made the transition to sedentary agriculturists. Similar festivals occurred throughout the ancient Near East.

Because they both occurred around the same time of year, eventually the two festivals were merged. Elements of the Festival of Matzot were reinterpreted to harmonize with the Pesach offering and its ancient association with the Exodus from Egypt. What had begun as family-based rituals became centralized under King Josiah. Josiah ruled the Kingdom of Judah between 640 and 609 B.C.E. and also briefly reconquered the Northern Kingdom from Assyria. Thought to have been written not too long before Josiah's era, the Book of Deuteronomy created a national festival that combined traditions of the North and South. The single Passover ritual, including both the Festival of Matzot and the paschal offering, emerged.

Other scholars trace Passover's origin to the New Year's rituals common in the ancient Near East.[14] Rather than explicitly linking Passover to the harvest, the Bible ties it to the calendar—the full moon of the month in which the vernal equinox occurs, when many cultures in the ancient Near East observed the New Year. Indeed, the Bible specifies that the month of the Exodus shall henceforth be counted as the *first* month of the year. These ancient rituals involved feasting and offering sacrifices to propitiate the gods at a time when they were thought to make decisions concerning the fate of the community for the coming year. It was also a season when the evil spirits of the passing year were feared to be particularly dangerous. Smearing blood on their doors or bodies served to protect the faithful.

To ensure health and good fortune, it was essential to carry out New Year's rites in a state of extreme ritual purity. Leaven, associated not just with bread's rising but also more importantly with its rot and decay, had to be stringently avoided lest it contaminate the New Year's sacrificial offering and the ripening cereal crops. This underlies Passover's ban on leavened bread. (In later times, leaven was banned from the altar in the Temple.) Similarly, the biblical injunction (Ex. 12:10) to eat the offering in a single evening and to burn any remains reflects the fear of decay and ritual impurity. This theory maintains that the paschal offering and the subsequent Festival of Matzot were always elements of a single ritual.

At a season when so much hung in the balance, the fate of the firstborn aroused heightened concern. The firstborn son represented a new generation and as such was thought to be especially vulnerable at the turn of the year. Special rites of purification and dedication for the firstborn were common. The practice of sacrificing a firstborn male from the flock represented the means to ensure the firstborn son's salvation for the coming year.

Ancient New Year's rituals included several other practices that left their imprint on the development of Passover. These included the recitation of the community's version of the creation story, a tale that often involved the victory of one god over another. Passover's recounting of the creation of the Israelite people and God's triumph over Pharaoh reflects a variation on that motif. The ancient ritual also included a journey from the city to the desert in which participants dressed in costumes. This symbolized the desire to flee from the evil spirits and contamination that remained behind in the cities, as well as a wish to reestablish contact with the gods of vegetation. Although this ritual finds more concrete expression in Sukkot, it survives in Passover as we recall the flight from Egypt to the desert. The Book of Exodus (12:11) describes the appropriate costume for the journey: "This is how you shall eat it: your loins girded, your sandals on your feet, and your staff in your hand. . . ."

HISTORY TRUMPS NATURE

Depending on your group, you might read this during the Seder or on your own.

Passover is widely referred to as *Z'man Cherueinu,* "the season of our liberation," and also as *Chag HaAviv,* "the festival of spring." Why do themes associated with nature get such short shrift during the Seder? The answer is complex, but the process that produced this outcome seems to have begun in ancient times.

Over time, worship became increasingly centralized in the Temple in Jerusalem. A city grew up around the Temple; its residents, including the king and priests, could hardly carry out the agricultural feasts as people had in former times. "The movement towards Jerusalem meant a striving for uniformity, but at the same time a withdrawal from nature. The festivals no longer signified the direct sanctification of nature. The people were now sanctified by [the festivals]" through rites performed by the priesthood.[15] Over time, what had begun as agricultural festivals became "historicized."

After all, Judaism's great theological innovation was not simply that God rules the world of nature, but, more important, that God ultimately determines the shape of human history.

Downplaying the significance of nature within the Passover festival may also have represented a bulwark against the age-old tendency to worship nature, the "heavenly hosts," rather than God, who created the natural world. Deuteronomy's warning (4:19–20) could not have been more plain: "And when you look up to the sky and behold the sun and the moon and the stars, and the whole heavenly host, you must not be lured into bowing down to them or serving them. These Adonai your God allotted to other peoples everywhere under heaven; but you Adonai took and brought out of Egypt, that iron blast furnace, to be His very own people. . . ." Indeed, Ezekiel (8:16) attributes the destruction of the First Temple to sun worship by Israelites in the Temple itself.[16]

Following the commentary of Rabbenu Chananel (990–1050), some widely available Haggadot state that, "in the beginning [prior to monotheism] our ancestors worshiped the stars."[17]

The result of this evolution has produced a Passover Seder heavy with symbols that amplify the themes of redemption—political and spiritual—but relatively light on those that speak to the seasonal aspect of the holiday or the implicit relationship between the birth of a people and the rebirth of the earth.

Passover's origins seem to reach back to ancient Near Eastern agricultural and New Year's celebrations. Later it became the festival at which the Israelites expressed their gratitude through the paschal offering for redemption from Egypt. After the Temple's destruction in 70 C.E., Passover was transformed into a set of rituals to preserve the Jewish People's faith that God, who had long ago delivered the Israelites from Egypt, would once again intervene to alleviate Jewish suffering. Over the ages, Passover has been adapted to address profound spiritual needs for renewal, salvation, and hope in the face of changing external challenges. Given the festival's deep resonance with the cycles of nature and the grave environmental crisis that besets us today, it's not only appropriate but also crucial to add emphasis to these concerns during our Passover Seders.

ACTIVITIES, BLESSINGS, AND READINGS

1. *An Art Midrash Project:* Ask your guests to participate in an art midrash project by creating a collage that expresses the relationships among Passover, freedom, and spring. (See Appendix III on page 361 for art midrash directions.)

2. *Grow one of the items eaten during the Seder:* The Seder requires us to eat bitter herbs (usually either horseradish or romaine lettuce) and to dip a green vegetable (usually parsley) in saltwater. If you have access to a small garden, horseradish could not be easier to grow. Buy a horseradish root in the grocery store. Cut off the top and place it in a shallow bowl of water for several days until you see leaves begin to sprout from the top and small roots from the bottom. Plant it where it will get some sun. It requires

virtually no care beyond occasional watering. Every spring, you'll notice dark green leaves lying flat on the soil. Dig up the root below, and you're all set. Chances are you'll find more than one plant, because horseradish tends to spread quickly.

I've been growing horseradish for years. I can tell you that it adds a special zing to the Seder, and watching for the first leaves to break through the softening soil helps me keep tuned in to the coming of spring and Passover. Depending on where you live, you may also be able to winter over some parsley from the previous season. If not, you may be able to grow a bit of parsley or some romaine lettuce in a flowerpot indoors. Plant your seeds a few months before Passover. If you're more ambitious, consider planting some barley. In ancient times, Passover was associated with the ripening of the barley crop. If you plant barley seeds after Sukkot in the fall, your crop will be nearing maturity by Passover. I assure you that this is an absolutely amazing experience! I grew the plants in a few flowerpots in our greenhouse, but they will do just as well in any sunny window. A pot of barley looks great on the Seder table and will certainly prompt questions.[18] Be careful not to bring harvested barley stalks indoors during Passover because it is one of the five kinds of grain that can become *chametz*!

3. *Step outside:* Before your Seder begins, consider stepping outdoors for a few minutes. If the weather is clear, you should see a beautiful full moon overhead. Take a few deep breaths of the spring air and think about the fact that Jews have been celebrating Passover under the full moon for thousands of years.

4. *Bless the new moon:* If you have not already said the Blessing for the New Moon of Nisan, or if you've never recited the blessing, try it on the first Seder. The moon must be clearly visible. The blessing can be recited indoors or, preferably, outside. You can find the Blessing for the New Moon in Appendix IV (page 362). You may be able to read it by the light of the moon. Generally, the blessing can be recited through the fifteenth of any Hebrew month, which means it can usually be said on the first night of Passover.[19] Much of the blessing comes from the Talmud and is at

least fifteen hundred years old. Before you recite the blessing, read the following statement from the Talmud (Sanhedrin 42a): "Whoever pronounces the benediction over the new moon in its due time welcomes, as it were, the presence of the Shekhinah . . . In the school of Rabbi Ishmael it was taught: Had Israel inherited no other privilege than to greet the presence of their Heavenly Father once a month, it would have sufficed."

5. *Recite the Prayer for Dew at your second Seder:* On the first day of Passover, we begin reciting the daily Prayer for Dew and continue until the end of Sukkot, when we resume the Prayer for Rain. It rarely rains after Passover in Israel, but the quantity of dew plays an important role in the development of crops throughout the dry season. Jewish tradition, of course, imagined that God controlled the quantity of dew, which, in turn, depended on the community's worthiness in God's eyes. Whether or not you believe that in a literal sense, you may want to consider reading this excerpt from the Sephardic version of the Prayer for Dew during your second Seder.[20]

Our God, our ancestors' God:
With dewdrops of Ancient light, illuminate the earth.
With dewdrops of Blessing divine, please bless the earth.
With dewdrops of Gleeful rejoicing, give joy to the earth.
With dewdrops of Dancing exultation, enrich the earth.
With dewdrops of Heavenly splendor, give glory to the earth.
With dewdrops of Wise assembly, let the earth be gathered.
With dewdrops of Song and melody, make musk through the earth.
With dewdrops of Healing life, enable the earth to live.
With dewdrops of Timeless good, give goodness to the earth.
With dewdrops of Your saving help, redeem the earth.
With dewdrops of Care and nurturing, nourish the earth.

For you are The Abundant One, our God, who makes the wind to blow and brings down the dew.

For blessing, not for curse.
For living, not for death,
For plenty, not for dearth.

Recite the Blessings for Witnessing the Wonders of Nature

You can find these blessings at www.livelyseders.com or in most traditional prayer books. Specific blessings can be recited upon seeing fruit trees flower for the first time in the year, seeing trees of striking beauty, smelling the fragrance of plants or herbs, seeing mountains, hills, or deserts, a rainbow, the ocean, and so forth.

In Talmudic times, the Sages sought to ensure that Jews would neither take nature's wonders for granted nor lapse into the worship of nature itself. Several of the sages, for example, spoke of the virtues of praying "with the red glow of the sun."[21] More important, they developed an extensive catalog of blessings, praises to God, to be recited upon witnessing various natural phenomena. Although most of these are not explicitly tied to a particular season, many involve witnessing one or another aspect of spring's wondrous unfolding.

Here are several blessings that you might consider reciting on the appropriate occasion. You could step outdoors to recite one with your guests before the Seder begins. Whatever views you hold about God, reciting blessings of this sort has a way of adding something special to the experience of nature. They can also heighten your awareness of the world around you by giving you a moment to appreciate the wonder before your eyes. You may also find that blessings like these induce a welcome sense of humility. If these blessings don't speak to you, compose your own. But don't let wonder pass you by without marking the moment.

6. *Choose one or two of the texts below to read and discuss at your Seder. Some relate specifically to Passover; others speak to Judaism's understanding of our broader responsibility to the natural world.*

[Unleavened] bread . . . gives its name to the feast. This may be regarded from two points of view, one peculiar to the nation, referring to the migration [from Egypt] . . . the other universal, following the lead of nature, and in agreement with the general cosmic order . . . In the vernal equinox we have a kind of likeness and portraiture of that first epoch in which this world was created. The elements were then separated and placed in harmonious order with reference to themselves and each other. The heaven was donned with sun and moon and the rhythmical movements and circlings of the other stars, both fixed and planetary . . . So every year God reminds us of the creation of the world by setting before our eyes the spring when everything blooms and flowers. And therefore there is good reason for describing [Nisan] . . . as the first month because in a sense it is an image of the primal origin . . . [Food], when unleavened, is a gift of nature, when leavened is a work of art . . . [The] springtime feast . . . is a reminder of the creation of the world and its earliest inhabitants   [The ancients] wished every year to rekindle the embers of the serious and ascetic mode of faring [i.e., eating unleavened bread] and to employ the leisure of a festal assembly to confer admiration on the old-time life of frugality and economy, and as far as possible to assimilate our present day life to that of the distant past.

—PHILO OF ALEXANDRIA (FIRST CENTURY C.E.), JEWISH PHILOSOPHER.[22]

When God created the first human beings, God led them around the Garden of Eden and said: "Look at my works! See how beautiful they are—how excellent! For your sake I created them all. See to it that you do not spoil and destroy My world; For if you do, there will be no one else to repair it."

—ECCLESIASTES RABBAH 7:20
(NINTH-CENTURY-C.E. MIDRASH), LAND OF ISRAEL

How astonishing . . . is the growth of foods from seeds. A single grain that has been saved from mishaps produces a thousand grains and more. It has even been that out of one grain of wheat, as many as three hundred [stalks] will spring up, each containing over twenty grains. We also come across gigantic trees whose roots have sprung out of a single seed or a single shoot . . . Praised be the All-Wise and Gracious One who brings into existence such vast effects from causes so small and weak. . . .

—BACHYA BEN JOSEPH IBN PAQUDA
(ELEVENTH CENTURY), SPAIN, PHILOSOPHER OF MORALS[23]

Every blade of grass sings poetry to God without ulterior motives or alien thoughts—without consideration of reward. How good and lovely it is, then, when one is able to hear this song of the grasses. It is therefore a precious thing to conduct oneself with piety when strolling among them.

—REBBE NACHMAN OF BRESLOV (1772–1810),
PODOLIA, UKRAINE, HASIDIC MASTER[24]

Human beings have indeed become primarily tool-making animals, and the world is now a gigantic toolbox for the satisfaction of their needs . . . Nature as a toolbox is a world that does not point beyond itself. It is when nature is sensed as mystery and grandeur that it calls upon us to look beyond it. The awareness of grandeur and the sublime is all but gone from the modern mind. The sense of the sublime—the sign of inward greatness of the human soul and something which is potentially given to all—is now a rare gift. Yet without it, the world becomes flat and the soul a vacuum.

—RABBI ABRAHAM JOSHUA HESCHEL (1907–1972),
POLAND, GERMANY, UNITED STATES, THEOLOGIAN, SOCIAL ACTIVIST[25]

We must dare to reexamine our longstanding preference for history over nature. The celebration of "historical monotheism" . . . is a legacy of nineteenth-century Christian-Jewish polemics, a fierce attempt by Jewish thinkers to distance Judaism from the world of paganism. But the disclaimer has its downside by casting Judaism into an adversarial relationship with the natural world. Nature is faulted for the primitiveness and decadence of pagan religion, and the modern Jew is saddled with a reading of his tradition that is one-dimensional. Judaism has been made to dull our sensitivity to the awe-inspiring power of nature. Preoccupied with the ghosts of paganism, it appears indifferent and unresponsive to the supreme challenge of our age: humanity's degradation of the environment. Our planet is under siege and we as Jews are transfixed in silence.

—RABBI ISMAR SCHORSCH (1935–), UNITED STATES, FORMER CHANCELLOR OF THE JEWISH THEOLOGICAL SEMINARY OF AMERICA, "TENDING OUR COSMIC OASIS"[26]

Passover intertwines human freedom with the renewal of the earth: in the moment of spring, when new grain, new lambs and new flowers rise up against winter, not only a community of oppressed human beings but the earth itself rises up against pharaoh (in what we call the "plagues"). Today the global climate crisis threatens the whole planetary web of life, and there are some institutions—pharaohs—that make the crisis worse. They are bringing on us all the plagues of today—rivers undrinkable, frogs dying, the Great Lakes drying, hurricanes worsening, glaciers melting, polar bears drowning, seacoasts rising, droughts consuming. . . . On the Sabbath before Passover traditionally the prophetic reading in synagogue is from the Prophet Malachi. It ends with God promising to send Elijah the Prophet to turn the hearts of parents to children and the hearts of children to parents—"lest the earth be utterly destroyed." This 2,500-year-old prophetic call comes alive with new force in our generation—calling for the old and young to work together—to take on "Elijah's" mission—to heal the earth from the danger of utter destruction.

—RABBI ARTHUR WASKOW (1933–), UNITED STATES, DIRECTOR, SHALOM CENTER, "PASSOVER AS IF EARTH REALLY MATTERS"[27]

9

The Exodus as a Personal Spiritual Journey

מִתְּחִלָּה עוֹבְדֵי עֲבוֹדָה זָרה הָיוּ אֲבוֹתֵינוּ.
וְעַכְשָׁו קֵרְבָנוּ הַמָּקוֹם לַעֲבוֹדָתוֹ.

In the beginning our ancestors worshiped idols, but now the Omnipresent
has brought us close to His service.
—THE PASSOVER HAGGADAH

If you take a close look, you'll notice something special about this passage. It brims with different kinds of imagery associated with the idea of a spiritual journey—from *the beginning to now,* from *our ancestors to us,* from distance to *closeness,* from *worshiping idols* to *service* in the name of religious truth. Even this particular name of God, *HaMakom,* literally, "the Place," evokes the image of God as "destination."

After a long, arduous journey, we have drawn close to *HaMakom,* the Place of truth and insight. And that certainly merits praise and celebration.

The passage is based on the words of Rav, one of the leading sages of the early Talmudic period (Pesachim 116a). He brought not only legal traditions from

Israel to Babylonia but mysticism as well.[1] (For more on Rav and the Seder, see chapter 4.)

The Haggadah tells us that "in every generation, each individual should feel as though he or she had gone out of Egypt." On one level, that means we should relive the journey from slavery to freedom so that we neither take our freedom for granted nor lose hope in our ongoing struggles against oppression. But beneath this—and this would be Rav's view—the Haggadah cautions us to remember our ancestors' spiritual missteps so that we can better direct our own journeys.

Our journeys mark the progress of our efforts to live lives of ultimate purpose and meaning. Each stage of life presents us with particular challenges, so what feels "ultimate" at one stage of life may feel trivial at another. Phases of the journey focus on different themes: personal identity, interpersonal relationships, love, work, vulnerability. And sometimes, the journey focuses on our search for closeness to the Great One of Being.

Here we consider the story of the Exodus as a metaphor for our own spiritual journeys. We'll look at some of the milestones along the journey and at the significance of the fact that the Bible attributes humanity's first song to the Israelites after they cross the Red Sea. We conclude with a note about the spiritual journey's ultimate goal.

This chapter differs from all other chapters in this book in that it is meant to be read and digested on your own.

Before you continue, consider the following questions:

- The Haggadah tells us that "in every generation, each individual should feel as though he or she had gone out of Egypt." If you think of the Exodus as a personal journey, where are you trying to leave and where do you want to go?

- The Bible says that the paschal sacrifice was to be eaten *b'chipazon,* "hurriedly," "in a rush" (Ex. 12:11) because that was the manner in which the Israelites left Egypt (Deut. 16:3). When is it good to rush? When is it bad to rush? In your life, where and why are you rushing?[2]

- Do you think you could actually ever reach your destination? How do you know whether you are getting closer?

- How would you know whether you had arrived?

- Have you ever felt as if you had a glimpse of your destination or a taste of what it would feel like to be there?

- To what extent is your journey shared with others? Is there an element of your journey that you must experience alone?

EXODUS: THE SPIRITUAL JOURNEY

Isaiah Horowitz (c. 1565–1630), one of the great Kabbalists, began his commentary on the Haggadah with a statement that might strike you as odd: "All the aspects of freedom that we deal with during this night [of the Seder] refer to freedom of the soul. . . ."[3]

In Hebrew, *Mitzrayim,* "Egypt," can also be read *maytzarim,* "the narrows," the places of spiritual constriction or illusion. These are not only the ruts where our ancestors got stuck, but also the places where we find ourselves trapped. Read this way, the story becomes an allegory of the times when we are hopelessly mired in misery, when our lives seem to lack true purpose and we're not sure there's a way out.

Think about Moses as the part of us that struggles for positive change, for getting out of the mud.[4] Pharaoh is the aspect of ourselves that resists moving on, that finds one excuse after another for maintaining the status quo, despite its pain. God is the source of the conviction, however fleeting, that even seemingly hopeless situations *can* change for the better. Followers of the great Hasidic master Rebbe Nachman of Breslov (1772–1810) write:

> "Pharaoh" is king of *"Mitzrayim"* [Egypt]. He rules over the *maytzarim* [the narrow places]—the constrictions of the Mind, the limitations of Awareness. It is his function to restrain and repress human awareness of the Divine . . . To this aim, the king of Egypt kept us perpetually busy, our minds incessantly preoccupied with worldly illusions (Ex. 5:4–9).

113

Even today "Pharaoh" allows us to toil assiduously in the intricacies of Torah study and zealously exert ourselves in rigid stringencies of the Halakhah. He also keeps our minds troubled with the unanswerable paradoxes in Judaism . . . anything we ask for, he will grant us. With one exception. "Pharaoh" denies us the thing we need most: the time and composure to yearn for greater awareness of God. . . .[5]

We each have our own path. A student of the Seer of Lublin (Yaakov Yitzchak, d. 1815), one of the early Hasidic masters, once said, "Show me one general way to the service of God." His teacher replied, "It is impossible to tell men what way they should take. For one way to serve God is through the teachings, another through prayer, another through fasting, and still another through eating. Everyone should carefully observe what way his heart draws him to, and then choose this way with all his strength."[6]

But you can lose your way, whichever path you choose. What began as a means to a lofty end winds up becoming an end in itself. What may have been adaptive in the past now cripples you.

Arthur Green, one of our generation's great teachers, described two points of the journey this way: "Our own innermost liberation is our 'coming out of Egypt'; our own moment of truth is our 'standing before Sinai.'"[7]

MILESTONES ALONG THE ROAD

Now, let's explore some of the milestones along the road. We'll alternate among three dimensions: the Exodus story; its relevance to our personal spiritual journeys; and occasionally the way some of this finds expression in the Haggadah. That's why you'll notice a shifting focus as we survey the journey.

The journey from the mud of Egypt to the fiery revelation at Sinai, with all the doubts and backsliding along the way, represents the road that stretches forth before each of us. As we mark some of the journey's milestones, keep in mind the ancient elements of earth, water, air, and fire. The mystical tradition holds that each of these is associated with four ascending worlds of being.[8]

Mired in the brick pits of Egypt, the Israelites had lost any sense of a world beyond the muck. Pharaoh had become their God in the sense that he completely determined the scope of their consciousness. But the midwives who refused to obey Pharaoh's order to kill newborn Israelite males knew another reality. These women, who ushered new life into the world, knew something about the mysteries of creation and the miracle of birth. They could see beyond the realm that Pharaoh had built and "they feared God." They defied Pharaoh. So, too, did Moses' mother: Placing him by the water's edge, she trusted a power greater than a king of flesh and blood.

"A long time after that . . . the Israelites were groaning under the bondage and cried out; and their cry for help rose up to God" (Ex. 2:23). Sometimes it takes a long time to realize the depth of our own misery. But acknowledging our suffering and expressing it to another are the first steps in moving beyond it.

Years later, at the burning bush, Moses encountered God and learned the destination of his journey. Of course, Moses doubted his suitability for the job. How many of us ever feel fully equipped to take up the responsibilities and challenges life sets before us? Who initially assumes the mantle of leadership, at whatever level, without hesitation? Leadership means stepping out ahead with a vision, seemingly alone, with no assurance of how things will turn out. The journey from Egypt to the Promised Land would take a lot longer than Moses expected.

The power of his experience at the burning bush also convinced Moses that simply *telling* the Israelites of his encounter with God would not open their eyes to the possibilities he had envisioned. Even getting Moses' attention required a minor miracle. Remember, hundreds of years separate the narratives of Genesis and Exodus. In the stories of Genesis, the presence of God infused the lives of the patriarchs and matriarchs. Over the intervening centuries, memory of God's presence faded. So, at the burning bush, Moses asked God for signs to help rekindle the Israelites' bygone spiritual insights. There comes a point along the road when we realize that discovery is actually rediscovery.

Those signs, and later the plagues, slowly painted a picture of worlds far beyond the narrows of Egypt. Still, not all the Israelites were convinced. According to the tenth-century midrash Exodus Rabbah (14:3), even until the darkness of the ninth plague, many Israelites had no interest in leaving Egypt: "There were transgressors in Israel who had Egyptian patrons and lived in affluence and honor, and were unwilling to leave. . . ." Every Egypt offers its own seductions, its own incentives for staying put.

As the plagues unfolded, the Israelites may have increasingly sensed a power greater than Pharaoh. But nothing had been required of them. They were passive witnesses, not actors. That was about to change for those who saw, as it were, through the darkness. After the plague of darkness, the Israelites faced their first real tests of faith: the paschal sacrifice and circumcision. Both involved literally marking themselves, setting themselves apart from the Egyptians. In our lives, too, each of us must be willing to stand apart from the crowd as we further define ourselves. If we allow the fear of doing so to paralyze us, we remain in Egypt, our lives stagnant.

As the plagues approach their climax, the Israelites receive instructions about the paschal sacrifice. Earlier, Moses had asked Pharaoh to let the people go so they could sacrifice to their God in the wilderness for three days. Pharaoh offered to let them "sacrifice to your God *within* the land." But Moses refused: "If we sacrifice that which is untouchable [sacred] to the Egyptians before their very eyes, will they not stone us?" (Ex. 8:22). Facing that fear is just what God finally required. Our journeys inevitably demand overcoming our most deep-seated fears. Fear deepens the ruts that prevent us from moving on in our lives.

Participating in the paschal sacrifice constituted a test of another kind as well. The Israelites themselves revered Egyptian deities, including the sheep and goats they were ordered to slaughter. Their willingness to carry out this sacrifice would demonstrate whether or not they realized the emptiness of worshiping the gods of Egypt. As the midrash Exodus Rabbah (16:2) says:

God then said to Moses: "As long as Israel worships Egyptian gods, they will not be redeemed; go and tell them to abandon their evil ways and to reject idolatry." This is what is meant by: "Draw out lambs for your families, and slaughter the Passover offering" (Ex. 12:21). Draw out and take you lambs. That is to say: Draw away your hands from idolatry and take for yourselves lambs, thereby slaying the gods of Egypt and preparing the Passover; only through this will Adonai pass over you.

The order for circumcision came soon after: "The whole community shall offer [the paschal sacrifice] . . . but no uncircumcised person may eat of it . . . and all the Israelites did so" (Ex. 12:47–50).

The midrash suggests that the Israelites had abandoned circumcision relatively soon after settling in Egypt. "When Joseph died, they abolished the covenant of circumcision, saying: 'Let us become like the Egyptians'" (Exodus Rabbah 1:8). When the order to reinstitute circumcision came, many Israelites balked. For the Kabbalists, circumcision in Egypt symbolized removing the dross that had fallen upon the children of Israel and prevented them from sensing even the faintest glimmer of the world beyond Egypt. The same collection of midrashim (19:5) informs us that the holdouts were only persuaded when God ordered the four winds to mingle the aroma of the paschal offering with the breezes from the Garden of Eden![9]

Together, the paschal sacrifice and circumcision represent an irrevocable declaration of identity—in the most public and private realms. It's the point in the journey when we realize we are no longer trying our nascent convictions on for size.

Still, the ambivalence persisted. After the last plague, the Israelites were still not sure about leaving. In the end, "they had been *driven* out of Egypt and could not delay; nor had they prepared any provisions for themselves" (Ex. 12:39). Even when the external circumstances for change have fully ripened, the inner Pharaoh holds us back.

Moving forward requires leaving the inessentials behind. "So the people took their dough before it was leavened" (Ex. 12:34). Rabbi Yehudah Leib Alter of Ger, the nineteenth-century Hasidic master known as the Sefat Emet, described the significance of matzah:

> On every Passover a Jew becomes like a new person, like the newborn child each of us was as we came forth from Egypt. The point implanted by God within our hearts is renewed. That point is called *lechem oni* (poor people's bread), because it is totally without expansion. Matzah is just the dough itself, not having changed through fermentation. Every Jew has this inner place, the gift of God. Our task is really to expand that point, to draw all our deeds to follow it. This is our job throughout the year, for better or worse. But this holiday of matzot is the time when the point itself is renewed, purified from any defilement. Therefore, it has to be guarded from any "ferment" or change on this holiday.[10]

CROSSING THE SEA AND THE FIRST SONG

When people think back on the Seders of their childhood, they often remember with particular fondness singing the Haggadah's songs. Do you share that feeling? If so what made those that experiences so special?

All the obstacles the Israelites faced in leaving Egypt paled in comparison to what they experienced at the Red Sea. As Pharaoh's troops appear on the horizon, the children of Israel stand at the Red Sea. Now the cost of setting out on a journey to leave Egypt has risen to its ultimate price, as they realize that the journey has all been a terrible mistake, leading nowhere but to the ultimate dead end.

Every journey begins with excitement, but there's also a voice that asks, "Why are you doing this? Are you crazy? It would have been so much easier to stay home." When trouble appears, the voice says, "I told you so!" Then we look for someone to blame.

At the Red Sea, the Israelites said to Moses, "What have you done to us, taking us out of Egypt? Is this not the very thing we told you in Egypt, saying, 'Let us be, and we will serve the Egyptians, for it is better for us to serve the Egyptians than to die in the wilderness'" (Ex. 14:11–12).

Miraculously, the Israelites found a way out, a way to overcome an insurmountable obstacle. Here's the scene at the Red Sea according to a third-century midrash: "When the Israelites stood at the sea, one said: 'I do not want to go down to the sea first,' and the other said: 'I do not want to go down to the sea first . . .' While they were standing there deliberating, Nachshon, the son of Amminadav, from the tribe of Judah, jumped up first and went down to the sea and fell into the waves. . . ."[11] Nachshon acted on faith. Others may have thought he was crazy or suicidal. Sometimes we know that there is a way from here to there, though we may be the only one to see it.

The Haggadah does not explicitly mention Nachshon. But according to the Talmud, the beginning of Psalm 114 (which we recite just before blessing the second cup of wine) alludes to his willingness to take the plunge. "When Israel went forth from Egypt, the house of Jacob from a people of strange speech, Judah [the fourth son of Jacob and the ancestor of King David] became His sanctuary, Israel His dominion. The sea saw them and fled . . ." (Psalms 114:1–3). Says the Talmud, "[Because of Nachshon of the tribe of Judah] Judah was worthy to be made the ruling power in Israel, as it is said: 'Judah became His sanctuary, Israel His dominion.' Why did Judah become His sanctuary and Israel His dominion? Because the sea saw [Nachshon] and fled."[12] With Nachshon in the lead, the Israelites took a few steps into a higher world as they passed through the waters of rebirth.

Sometimes the seemingly "impossible" happens right before our eyes. The world contains possibilities neither the ancient Israelites nor we could ever imagine. What makes moments like this feel miraculous is the conviction that part of the breakthrough feels somehow to have come from *beyond* ourselves. We know we could never have done it on our own.

Such moments of "abiding astonishment," as the philosopher and theologian Martin Buber described them, call forth a profound outpouring of emotion beyond ordinary speech.[13] And so it is after crossing the Red Sea, after passing through the waters of spiritual rebirth, two breakthroughs occur: the Bible's song and its first dance.

In that awestruck moment at the Red Sea, the Israelites sang a song to God. Says Exodus Rabbah (23:4), "From the day when God created the world until the Israelites stood near the sea, no one save Israel sang unto God."[14] Many had expressed their gratitude by building altars and offering sacrifices, but until then, apparently no one in the Bible felt moved to use song for this purpose.[15] As Heschel put it: "The way to faith leads through acts of wonder and radical amazement . . . [We] sing to Him before we are able to understand Him."[16]

In song we sense more deeply the air we breathe. The Hebrew words for "breathing," *neshimah,* and "soul," *neshamah,* come from the same root and could not be closer. "Adonai God formed man from the dust of the earth. He blew into [Adam's] nostrils the breath of life (*nishmat chayyim*), and man became a living being" (Gen. 2:7). In the Song at the Sea, we discovered how to use the very breath of life to praise the One from whom it came: breath for breath. (Later in the Seder, just after Psalm 136, we recite *Nishmat kol chai,* "The breath of every living thing shall bless Your name. . . ." The Talmud refers to *Nishmat kol chai* as the "Benediction of the Song," doubtless because of its poetry and many allusions to song: "Even if our mouths were filled with song like the sea . . . we could never thank You enough.")[17]

Although the path continues on to Sinai and then Israel, we'll end our brief exploration of the Exodus as a spiritual journey at this point with a few final thoughts.

Our journey began in the muddy Egyptian brick pits. In crossing the Red Sea we moved through waters of rebirth. Filled with wonder, we breathed the air of salvation and poured forth the first song to God. We celebrate our redemption, not the drowning of the Egyptians. The fire of Sinai lies further down the road.

The Haggadah helps us to reenact our ancestors' journeys and in the process to become more conscious of our own. We taste the bitterness of the low point from which we began—the salty tears, the bitter herbs, and the muddy *charoset*. We eat matzah, the wayfarer's bread. It may not have had time to rise, but it certainly won't rot along the journey.

And we sing many, many songs of praise.

Let us sing as if we had just discovered song! Let us breathe new life into our Seder songs. Sing with the intention and fervor that we breathed into our first song on the other side of the Red Sea.

This is not easy. The followers of Rebbe Nachman of Breslov said: "Sometimes our voices are trapped. No words. No calling out. Everything caught in *maytzar hagaron,* the straits [narrows] of the throat. The voice of holiness is suppressed. We feel hampered in expressing ourselves before God. Stuck! It may be social norms or personal inhibitions. Either way, it is *Mitzrayim*. We are in 'exile.'"[18]

But don't be deterred. Ask people what they remember most fondly about the Seders of their childhood and many will tell you something about the songs. They once took us to another place; they can now, too.

The Israelites greeted their perilous escape not just with the Bible's first song, but with its first dance, as well. Having escaped the narrows of Egypt (*maytzarim*), traversing the slender passage through the waters, they emerged safe and free—finally in wide-open space. "Then Miriam the prophetess, Aaron's sister, took a timbrel in her hand, and all the women went out after her in dance with timbrels" (Ex. 15:20). Overcome the narrows that constrain you—inhibition, lack of confidence, so many doubts and hesitations. Feel the timbrel's rhythm. Move to it. Embrace the space. Dance forth fearlessly, joyously—"free at last, free at last." Rabbi Tamar Elad-Appelbaum put it this way: "Dance breaks down the apparent dichotomy between body and soul. The body, no longer an obstacle to the soul, becomes its chariot. . . . 'You have turned my dirge to a dance for me, undone my sackcloth and bound me with joy' (Psalms 30:12)."[19]

THE JOURNEY'S ULTIMATE PURPOSE

In a culture that celebrates the individual, a caution is in order, lest you conclude that from a Jewish perspective personal enlightenment constitutes the spiritual journey's ultimate goal.

Liberating the children of Israel from Egypt was an essential step in preparing the Israelites to join with God in the work of repairing the world. The midrash even asserts that the dreadful state of human affairs has forced God into exile. Heschel wrote:

> Man was the first to hide himself from God, after having eaten of the forbidden fruit, and is still hiding. The will of God is to be here, manifest and near; but when the doors of this world are slammed on Him, His truth betrayed, His will defied, He withdraws, leaving man to himself. God did not depart of His own volition; He was expelled. *God is in exile.*[20]

A world that resembled what God had intended would actually bring redemption for God and humanity alike.

From this perspective, the second sentence of the Maggid section of the Haggadah demands our attention: "*All* who are hungry, come and eat. All who are in need, come join in celebrating the festival of Passover." From the beginning, the Haggadah challenges us to take up the work of *tikkun,* "repair." Imagine if we took those words seriously. Could we ensure that on the night of Passover no one, anywhere, would be hungry? Would that be possible? Who knows? But would it bring the world one step closer to repair? Definitely. First we must do what we can to fix the world by lifting up the down and out. Then we can interpret the Haggadah metaphorically and make sure that our door remains open to those seeking spiritual nourishment.

Paradoxically, as we celebrate our liberation during Passover, we sharpen our awareness of the enslavement that reigns within and around us. At the moment we taste freedom, we remember the hungry. From a point of great light we peer through the darkness. From the heights of deliverance, we survey a shattered world crying out for healing.

You might ask, "I know I'm supposed to feed the hungry and welcome the stranger, but what is God's role in fixing the world?"

What is the source of the staggeringly audacious conviction that the present, the status quo, cannot be the end of the road? *That's* where God comes in. God speaks in a small voice within each of us, saying, "Never forget that yours is not a normal world, but a broken one, and that we can surely help fix it." At the Seder, that small voice calls a bit more audibly because with Passover we confront the reality of our freedom and how we have used it, for good or ill.

God contributes something else too. *Mitzvah goreret mitzvah.* Keeping one commandment leads to keeping another. Goodness begets goodness and unleashes a cycle of incalculable, unanticipated positive outcomes. The sum of our collective efforts to repair the world far exceeds that of our individual actions. As we take up the work of *tikkun* more earnestly, uncovering light within the darkness, God contributes all the unimaginable synergies that result from our collective efforts. God delivers as soon as we choose to treat the troubles of this earth as if they were our own leaky roof, not that of some distant stranger.

10

Enslaved in Egypt: Why?

בָּרוּךְ שׁוֹמֵר הַבְטָחָתוֹ לְיִשְׂרָאֵל. בָּרוּךְ הוּא.
שֶׁהַקָּדוֹשׁ בָּרוּךְ הוּא חִשֵּׁב אֶת־הַקֵּץ...

Blessed be He who keeps His promise to Israel. Blessed be He.
For the Holy One, blessed be He, determined the end of the bondage, thus doing that
which He said to Abraham our father in the Covenant between the Pieces.
As it is said, "He said unto Abram: Know well that your offspring shall be
strangers in a land not theirs, and they shall be enslaved and oppressed for four hundred
years; but I will execute judgment on the nation they shall serve, and in the end they
shall go out with great wealth" (GEN. 5:13–14).
—THE PASSOVER HAGGADAH

Before we look more closely at this passage, it's worth noting that commentators have long struggled to reconcile conflicts within the Bible about the duration of Israel's enslavement in Egypt. A reckoning based on the Bible's genealogical accounts does not jibe with the figure of four hundred years mentioned in the passage above. Exodus itself (12:41) states that Israel left Egypt after four hundred thirty years. Traditional commentators hold that the four hundred years refers to the span from Isaac's birth to the Exodus, while four hundred thirty years marks the time from God's announcement to Abraham that his "offspring shall be strangers in a land not theirs." The period in Egypt itself amounted to 210 years: Isaac was 60 years old when Jacob was born (Gen. 25:26) and Jacob says (Gen. 47:9) that he was 130 when he arrived in Egypt (400–[60+130]=210). An ancient rabbinic text analyzing the Bible's internal chronology concludes that the actual enslavement lasted between 86 and 116 years.[1]

But rather than concern ourselves with debates over the length of the enslavement, in this chapter we'll explore a far more fundamental question. Why were the Israelites enslaved at all?

THE COVENANT OF THE PIECES

Read the passage from the Haggadah on page 123 and the paragraphs below.
Then lead a discussion based on the questions that follow.

Soon after the Haggadah's parable of the Four Children, we arrive at our passage from the Haggadah. It includes several verses from the Book of Genesis, often referred to as the "Covenant of the Pieces."

The Seder's account of our redemption from Egypt begins with remembering God's fateful promise to Abram (his name had yet to become Abraham). The Haggadah highlights this passage not only because it foretells Israel's suffering and salvation, but also because, according to ancient midrashic tradition, the Covenant of the Pieces occurred on the fifteenth of Nisan, the first night of Passover.[2]

How did God come to make this particular promise?

God had already told Abram that he would inherit the land, and, more important, that he would sire many descendants who would become a great nation. Still childless and well into his eighties, Abram had his doubts. So far, God had given instructions and made promises. Abram had faithfully listened and obeyed. But Abram had *said* nothing to God. The more God promised, the more Abram wondered. Finally those doubts gave rise to the very first words he addressed to God—a question: "O Adonai God, what can You give me, seeing that I shall die childless . . . ?" (Gen. 15:2). God responded with yet another pledge of fruitfulness and reassurance that Abram would surely possess the land. Still unconvinced, Abram spoke a second time. Another question. "O Adonai God, how shall I know that I am to possess it?" (Gen. 15:8).

God answered by directing Abram to gather a number of animals and cut them in half. The sun began to set, Abram fell into a deep sleep, "and a great dark dread descended on him" (Gen. 15:12). That's when God told Abram that his descendants would be enslaved for four hundred years. And God added that Abram's descendants would not return for many years, "for the iniquity of the Amorites is not yet complete" (Gen. 15:16). The Amorites who inhabited Canaan had yet to become sufficiently sinful to warrant losing control of the land.

"When the sun set and it was very dark, there appeared a smoking oven, and a flaming torch that passed between those pieces [of the animals]. On that day Adonai made a covenant with Abram saying, 'To your offspring I assign this land . . .'" (Gen. 15:17–18).

Mysterious as this ritual sounds, this kind of covenant was common in the ancient Near East. When a king would promise a grant of land and a house to a loyal subject, he would take a flaming torch or a portable stove and touch it to the blood of a sacrificed animal. The gesture sealed the king's promise as if to say, "If I don't keep my promise, may I suffer the fate of this slaughtered animal."[3]

This Covenant of the Pieces represents God's eternally binding promise that Abram's descendants would return to inherit the land. And sure enough, according to the Haggadah, it all comes to pass just as God foretold. God remembers the promise of redemption, and after centuries of bitter suffering, the Exodus unfolds.

The Exodus is about more than liberation from Egypt. It's a tale of promise and fulfillment. God's promise in the passage from Genesis on page 123 includes three critical experiences the Israelites must undergo before God will redeem them: being strangers (*gerut*), being enslaved (*avdut*), and being afflicted (*inui*). We encounter the same terms again in the Haggadah's core text, which describes the ultimate fulfillment of that promise: "My father was a wandering Aramean. He went down to Egypt and 'sojourned there' (*gerut*) . . . the Egyptians 'afflicted' us (*inui*) . . . and 'they imposed heavy labor upon us' (*avdut*) . . . And Adonai brought us out of Egypt with a strong hand . . ." (Deut. 26: 5–8).

Avdut and *inui* occur repeatedly in Exodus 1:10, 11, and 13, which the Haggadah uses in its elaboration on the passage from Deuteronomy. In the book of Exodus (2:22), *ger* first appears when Moses names his son Gershom because

"I have been a stranger (*ger*) in a foreign land." Having undergone the three experiences described in the Covenant of the Pieces, God begins to honor the promise of redeeming Abraham's descendants. As we read in the Haggadah, "And their cry for help from the bondage rose up to God. God heard their moaning, and God remembered His covenant with Abraham . . ." (Ex. 2:23–24).[4]

- How do you understand what God tells Abram about the future? Is it merely a picture of what's to come or the outline of God's intentional plan that will first bring Israel to the depths of misery and then to freedom?

- How does God's statement that "the iniquity of the Amorites is not yet complete" contribute to your interpretation of God's vision of Israel's future?

ISRAEL ENSLAVED: MANY QUESTIONS, MANY ANSWERS

Read the paragraph below and lead a discussion on the questions that follow.

The Bible tersely depicts the ostensible reason for Israel's servitude in Egypt:

A new king arose over Egypt who did not know Joseph. And he said to his people, "Look, the Israelite people are much too numerous for us. Let us deal shrewdly with them, so that they may not increase; otherwise in the event of war they may join our enemies in fighting against us." So they set taskmasters over them to oppress them.
—EXODUS 1:8–11

- What might Pharaoh's fears of the dangers of a sizable Israelite minority suggest about his underlying attitude toward the Israelites or about their status in Egypt?

- If you were going to advise Pharaoh about how to prevent the Israelites from becoming a disloyal minority, what would you propose?

- What lessons might American society learn from this story about how to treat its minorities? What lessons might Israel learn about how to treat its 20-percent minority of Arab citizens?

- Did the Israelites' enslavement in Egypt serve some kind of purpose? If so, what?

- Are you more inclined to think of Israel's suffering in Egypt as a form of punishment, as a painful method of teaching an important lesson, or as a story that demonstrates that the children of Israel are somehow destined to suffer? Explain your position.

- Was the enslavement somehow necessary or could it have been avoided?

- The Talmud suggests that the new king who arose and "did not know Joseph" was in fact not a new king, but had simply begun to act as if "he did not know Joseph."[5] Is the tale of the new regime that "forgets" the contributions Jews have made to a particular society, and then turns against them, paradigmatic of the Jewish experience in Diaspora? Is aliyah, moving to Israel, the only solution, as some Zionist voices have argued?[6]

> Below you'll find a wide range of explanations for Israel's enslavement.
> Read through them and choose a few for discussion during your Seder.
> Ask your guests to discuss their reactions to these texts and to assess
> the strengths and weaknesses of each approach.

Jewish tradition has struggled for a long time to explain Israel's enslavement in Egypt.

The question has prompted so many responses because, at least on the surface, the Bible does not offer a clear answer as to why the Israelites suffered such an excruciating ordeal. These explanations fall into five categories:[7]

1. The enslavement resulted from the Egyptians' fear or wickedness.

The Bible clearly places primary culpability for Israel's enslavement upon Pharaoh. He feared that the Israelites had grown too numerous and would side with Egypt's enemies in case of war.

> 2. The enslavement punished the Israelites for a variety of sins: Abraham's lack of faith; Abraham and Sarah's mistreatment of Hagar; the Israelites' assimilationist tendencies; or their idol worship in Egypt.

In his first words addressed to God, Abraham expresses his doubts that God will deliver on the divine promise that Abraham will sire children and inherit the land (Gen. 15:2–9). The Babylonian Talmud (Nedarim 32a) suggests that Abraham's lack of trust constituted a grave sin. Rabbinic thought held that the lives of Judaism's founding ancestors were so critical in shaping the Jewish People's identity that their merits accrued to the future generations, as did guilt for their sins.

Nachmanides (1195–1270), the great Spanish philosopher and Bible scholar, believed that Abraham and Sarah's cruel treatment of Hagar helped set the stage for Israel's affliction in Egypt. Unable to conceive, Sarai—her name had yet to become Sarah—told Abraham to have a child with her handmaid, Hagar, whom the midrash says was none other than Pharaoh's daughter (generations before the time of Moses).[8] When Hagar became pregnant, Sarai became jealous. "And Sarai afflicted her and she ran away from her" (Gen. 16:7). An angel of Adonai then spoke to Hagar, saying that she will bear a son, and his "hand will be against everyone" (Gen. 16:12). Nachmanides concludes:

"Our mother transgressed by this affliction, and Abraham also by his permitting her to do so. And so, God heard [Hagar's affliction] and gave her a son . . . to afflict the seed of Abraham and Sarah with all kinds of affliction."[9]

Sarah "afflicted" Hagar. Later the Egyptians "afflicted" the Israelite strangers. (*Ger*, the Hebrew word for "stranger," is linked to the name *Hagar*.) Likewise, Hagar's fertility led to her persecution just as the Israelites' fecundity bent Pharaoh on their destruction. Bondage in Egypt is the punishment for Sarah's cruelty to Hagar.[10]

Exodus Rabbah (1:8), a tenth-century midrash, interprets the enslavement as God's punishment for the assimilationist behavior of the wayward Israelites in

Egypt. After Joseph died, the Israelites abandoned circumcision and said, "Let us become like the Egyptians . . . God converted the love with which the Egyptians loved them into hatred."

Echoing themes of the Haggadah, Ovadia Sforno (1470–1550), an Italian Bible commentator, believed that the Israelites' ordeal in Egypt resulted from the fact that they had adopted idol worship: "'Then I [God] resolved to pour out My wrath (*lishpokh chamati*) upon them, to vent all My anger upon them there, in the land of Egypt' (Ezekiel 20:8). Thus they were enslaved with hard labor until a small number repented, prayed to God and a messenger did save them."[11]

3. The enslavement was a prerequisite for accepting the Torah.

Other commentators have looked at the experience in Egypt as an essential prerequisite for accepting the Torah at Sinai. Yitzchak Arama (1420–1494, Spain) concluded, "Only this experience would make [the Israelites] see the yoke of Heaven as a relatively easy burden to bear, and they could be induced to shoulder it voluntarily, enthusiastically."[12] Others focused on Egypt as an excruciating but necessary purification. Such views often elaborate on Deuteronomy (4:20): "Adonai took you and brought you out of Egypt, that iron blast furnace, to be His very own people. . . ."

4. The enslavement embodied a difficult, but essential, educational experience.

Nehama Leibowitz (1905–1997, Russia and Israel), a modern Bible teacher, held that the bitterness of Egypt served to teach the Israelites what *not* to do to "strangers" in the society that they would build in the Promised Land. Many of the Torah's injunctions on proper treatment of the vulnerable members of society end with a coda invoking the memory of suffering in Egypt. One of numerous examples demonstrates the point: "Six days shall you labor and do all your work, but the seventh day is a Sabbath of Adonai your God; you shall not do any work—you, your son or your daughter, your male or female slave . . . or the stranger in your settlements, so that your male and female slave may rest as you do. Remember that you were a slave in the land of Egypt . . ." (Deut. 5:13–15).[13]

5. The enslavement arose as a consequence of Joseph's agrarian policies.

The Book of Genesis describes seven years of famine, during which Joseph provided the Egyptians with food and in the process enslaved them to Pharaoh. Traditional sources generally idealize Joseph, referring to him as *Yosef Hatzadik,* Joseph the Righteous.[14] Still, one can find traces of ambivalence. For example, noting that Joseph died before any of his brothers, the Babylonian Talmud (Berakhot 55a) asks, "Why did Joseph die before his brethren? Because he assumed airs of authority [i.e., haughtiness]."[15] Chaim Ibn Attar (1696– 1743, Morocco) offers an unusually frank analysis of Joseph's actions. He explains that initially Joseph only accepted payment in cash for food during the famine, and he refused to accept payment in kind (livestock) until he had drained each farmer of his money. This forced the farmers not only to buy food for themselves, but for their livestock as well, further accelerating their impoverishment. Ibn Attar uses the same verb to describe Joseph's shrewd planning (*nitchakam*) as the Bible uses to describe Pharaoh's subsequent call to deal shrewdly (*nitchakmah*) with the Israelites who had become dangerously numerous.[16]

JOSEPH AND THE ENSLAVEMENT?

Before you begin this activity, ask your guests the following question:
What is the first story in the Bible in which an entire people becomes enslaved to Pharaoh? You can read aloud this story about Joseph before or during your Seder.
Lead a discussion based on the questions that follow.

Joseph was a dreamer. As a boy he dreamed that his brothers' sheaves of wheat bowed down to him. He dreamed that the sun and the moon and eleven stars bowed down to him. When Joseph told this dream to his father and eleven brothers, his father said angrily, "What! Are we all to bow down to you?" But Joseph was his father's favorite son. That made his brothers so jealous that they threw Joseph into a pit. Slave traders found him and sold him in Egypt.

Thirteen years later, after a series of successes and setbacks, Joseph was called upon to interpret Pharaoh's troubling dreams. He dreamed that seven lean cows swallowed seven fat cows. He dreamt of seven healthy stalks of corn. Then came seven sickly stalks of corn. Joseph said the dreams meant there would be seven years of plenty followed by seven years of famine. Joseph also suggested a plan for Egypt to survive the famine. Pharaoh was impressed and appointed the thirty-year-old Joseph to be his second in command. Pharaoh gave Joseph the job of carrying out the plan to save Egypt.

Joseph naturally received all the goodies that came with his new position—the finest Egyptian linen clothing, chariots, a gold chain around his neck, Pharaoh's special ring, and of course, a beautiful Egyptian wife. "Pharaoh said to Joseph, 'I am Pharaoh; yet without you, no one shall lift up hand or foot in all the land of Egypt'" (Gen. 41:44).

During the seven years of plenty, Joseph began storing up food for the famine.

Just as Joseph predicted, seven years later, the famine began. It spread so wide that even Joseph's brothers in Canaan came down to Egypt in search of food. Eventually Joseph and his brothers were reunited. Joseph brought the whole family down to Egypt, including Jacob, his aged father. Joseph introduced them to Pharaoh.

Pharaoh told Joseph to settle them in "the best part of the land; let them stay in the region of Goshen. And if you know any capable men among them, put them in charge of my livestock" (Gen. 47:6).

As the famine grew worse, "Joseph gathered in all the money that was to be found in the land of Egypt and in the land of Canaan, as payment for the rations that were being procured, and Joseph brought the money into Pharaoh's palace. And when the money gave out in the land of Egypt and in the land of Canaan, all the Egyptians came to Joseph and said, 'Give us bread, [or we will] . . . die before your very eyes; for the money is gone!' And Joseph said, 'Bring your livestock, and I will sell to you [bread in exchange] . . . for your livestock, if the money is gone.' So they brought their livestock to Joseph, and Joseph gave them bread in exchange for the horses, for the stocks of sheep and cattle . . ." (Gen. 47:14–17).

Finally they had nothing else left to sell for food. They came to Joseph and said, "Let us not perish before your eyes, both we and our land. Take us and our land in exchange for bread, and we with our land will be slaves to Pharaoh . . . So Joseph gained possession of all the farmland of Egypt for Pharaoh, every Egyptian having sold his field because the famine was too much for them; thus the land passed over to Pharaoh. And he removed the population town by town, from one end of Egypt's border to the other" (Gen. 47:19–21).

Then Joseph said to the people, "Whereas I have this day acquired you and your land for Pharaoh, here is seed for you to sow the land. And when harvest comes, you shall give one-fifth to Pharaoh, and four-fifths shall be yours as seed for the fields and as food for you and those in your households, and as nourishment for your children." And they said, "You have saved our lives! We are grateful to my lord, and we shall be slaves to Pharaoh" (*v'hayinu avadim l'pharaoh*).[17] And Joseph made it into a land law in Egypt, which is still valid . . . Thus Israel settled in the country of Egypt, in the region of Goshen; and they acquired holdings in it, and were fertile and multiplied.

—GENESIS 47:23–27

The Egyptians sold themselves into slavery. But the Israelites prospered under Joseph's protection.

- Would you say Joseph's plan to save the Egyptians was fair, or did he take advantage of their situation? If you think Joseph was unfair, how would you explain his motives?

- Was it necessary for Joseph to *sell* grain to the Egyptians? Could he simply have given it to them?

- Faced with starvation or enslavement, the Egyptians twice said, "We shall be slaves to Pharaoh" (*v'hayinu avadim l'pharaoh*). Those words should sound familiar because they are so similar to the Haggadah's opening response to the Four Questions, *"avadim hayinu l'pharaoh,"* "We were slaves to Pharaoh." The Haggadah quotes this passage from Deuteronomy (6:21): "We were slaves to Pharaoh in Egypt and Adonai took us out from Egypt with a mighty hand." What do you make of the fact that the Bible uses virtually identical words to describe the situation of the Israelites under Pharaoh and the Egyptians under Joseph?[18]

- *Etz Hayim,* the Conservative Movement's commentary on the Five Books of Moses, offers the following note on the Egyptians' declaration, "We shall be slaves to Pharaoh" (Gen. 47:25): "A generation later, the Egyptians would take their revenge on Joseph for having reduced them to slavery, by enslaving his people."[19] This interpretation implies that the enslavement of the Israelites may have been a measure-for-measure punishment (*midah k'neged midah*) for Joseph's enslavement of the Egyptians. Do you agree? If so, what lesson might the Bible be trying to teach in its depiction of Joseph, the famine, and Israel's subsequent enslavement? How does the story of Joseph and the famine color your understanding of the meaning of Passover?

THE SELF-CRITICAL VOICE: BENEFITS AND DANGERS

Read aloud the section that follows and discuss it before your Seder.

The fact that commentators have offered such a huge number of explanations for Israel's enslavement reflects one thing: They are unwilling to accept the Bible's explanation at face value.

In part, commentators have probed beneath the surface of the biblical account from a deeply held conviction that God, and not a king of flesh and blood, ultimately directs history. Hence the many interpretations of Israel's suffering in Egypt as divinely wrought—be it punishment, purification, or preparation. But what about views that explain Israel's suffering in Egypt as flowing from the natural consequences of human rather than divine action? For example, the Talmud chides Jacob for favoring Joseph and concludes that "on account of two ounces of wool that Jacob gave Joseph [for a special coat] . . . Joseph's brothers became jealous of him, which eventually resulted in our ancestors' descent into Egypt."[20] What about the assertions that Abraham and Sarah's harsh treatment of Hagar, or Joseph's enslavement of the Egyptians, may have helped set the stage for the misery into which the Israelites would eventually fall?

These interpretations begin to blur the comfortable distinction between Israelite victim and Egyptian perpetrator. Remembering that Pharaoh's oppression of Israel included a genocidal dimension beyond mere enslavement restores that distinction. Still, reckoning Joseph's exploitation of the Egyptians among the factors contributing to Israel's oppression definitely leads to a more nuanced understanding of the Exodus story. And it certainly casts new light on Deuteronomy's injunction (23:8): "You shall not abhor an Egyptian, for you were a stranger in his land."

This line of interpretation rests on the assumption that "in the field of human destiny we reap what we sow," especially when our deeds inflict pain on others.

Two texts make this point with stunning power. First let's consider the Babylonian Talmud's (Sanhedrin 99b) astounding comment on the genealogy of Amalek, Israel's prototypical enemy, whose descendants viciously attacked the Israelites in the desert. The genealogy appears simple enough: "And Timna was the concubine of Esau's son Eliphaz; she bore Amalek to Eliphaz" (Gen. 36:12). The Talmud elaborates:

> Timna wanted to convert. She came before Abraham, Isaac and Jacob, but they did not accept her. So she went and became a concubine to Eliphaz the son of Esau. She said, "It is better to be a maidservant of this nation [i.e., the nation of Esau], and not to be a noblewoman of another nation [i.e., Israel]." Amalek issued from her, who vexed Israel. What is the reason? They should not have put her off.[21]

Here, the Talmud argues that the patriarchs' unwillingness to embrace a would-be convert literally sowed the seeds for the birth of Israel's archenemy, later personified by Haman, of Purim infamy, a descendant of Amalek.

Now let's look at the Zohar, the thirteenth-century classic text of Jewish mysticism. It elaborates on the fact that when Pharaoh's daughter opened the basket containing Moses she saw it was "a boy crying. She took pity on it . . ." (Ex. 2:6):

> Rabbi Isaac said: "The redemption of Israel depends only on weeping: When the effect of the tears of Esau ['And Esau wept aloud,' Gen. 27:38] which he shed before his father on account of the [stolen blessing] shall have been exhausted, redemption will begin for Israel." Said Rabbi Yossi: "Esau's weeping brought Israel into captivity, and when their force is exhausted, Israel, through their tears, shall be delivered from him."[22]

The Zohar implies that the deceit of Jacob brought about a fundamental rupture in the fabric of human relations, a rupture that clearly awaits repair. Esau's tears have only partially been quenched through the tears shed by the infant Moses.

Unbound by normal constraints of linear time, the midrash freely describes the Passover celebration of the patriarchs centuries before the Exodus from Egypt. The eighth-century midrash, *Pirke de Rabbi Eliezer,* supplies a fateful connection between Esau's stolen blessing and Passover. "The nightfall of the festival day of Passover came, and Isaac called unto Esau his elder son, and said, 'O my son! Tonight the heavenly ones utter songs, on this night the treasuries of dew are opened; on this day the blessing of the dews [is bestowed]. Make me savory meat whilst I am still alive, and I will bless thee. . . .'" (For more on the relationship between Passover and dew, see page 105–106.) Rebecca intervened and instructed her favored son, Jacob, to bring two goats quickly. One goat, the midrash concludes, served as the paschal offering. The other she cooked for Isaac in deceit.[23]

- What are the strengths and weaknesses of these kinds of interpretations?

- To what kinds of situations would or wouldn't you feel comfortable applying this self-critical approach?

- Sometimes the deeds of evil people may express certain realistic grievances. But evil enters the picture when the reaction to a "normal" grievance assumes vast and murderous proportions. For example, Pharaoh may have had an understandable fear of the Israelite demographic explosion. But that did not justify genocide. Do the above approaches adequately address this concern?

- What are the implications of connecting Passover with the incident of Jacob stealing the blessing from his brother Esau?

- What do you think about the difficulties placed before would-be converts by the Rabbinate in Israel in view of the Talmud's story about Timna?

11

"Strangers in a Land Not Theirs": Remembering to Treat the Strangers among Us Justly

וַיֹּאמֶר לְאַבְרָם יָדֹעַ תֵּדַע

כִּי־גֵר יִהְיֶה זַרְעֲךָ בְּאֶרֶץ לֹא לָהֶם...

He said unto Abram: "Know well that your offspring
shall be strangers in a land not theirs . . ." (GEN. 15:13).
—THE PASSOVER HAGGADAH

Although the Haggadah enjoins each of us to feel as if we had personally gone out of Egypt, it does not explicitly call on us to remember our suffering in Egypt in order to avoid imposing on others. In the Bible, the injunction to treat the "stranger" justly recurs dozens of times, more often in fact than any other positive commandment.[1] On this theme, the Haggadah remains silent, disconcertingly so to my ear. Here we'll sample the Bible's repeated exhortations that our memory of slavery in Egypt should serve as the basis for humane treatment of minorities and the weaker members of society over whom we have power. The chapter includes a blessing on this theme, which I've composed to be recited at the Seder. We'll follow with a comparison of how two Zionist leaders considered the issue of the stranger and conclude with a midrash on this theme. Questions for discussion are included throughout.

When you arrive at the passage in the Haggadah that appears on page 137—not long after the Four Children—read it aloud slowly and ask each of your guests to respond to the question that follows.

• What do you think is the most important lesson we should learn from reexperiencing our redemption from slavery in Egypt?

KNOWING THE HEART OF THE STRANGER

Read the paragraphs below and then the twelve biblical passages about the stranger.

Over the long centuries of the Haggadah's evolution, Jewish weakness, vulnerability, and exile fueled a powerful yearning for divine redemption. Oppression in Egypt became paradigmatic of later painful experiences at the hands of the Persians, Greeks, Romans, Christians, and others. The Haggadah proclaimed hope to a powerless people: "In every generation they rise up to destroy us, but the Holy One, praised be He, saves us from their hand." Understandably, the compilers of the Haggadah worried more about preserving hope for the downtrodden than about how a *strong* Jewish People would wield power.

While we certainly have our enemies, and Israel has not yet achieved peace, today the Jewish People have been blessed with a different reality than that which produced the Haggadah. Despite real setbacks in recent years, Jews throughout the world still probably enjoy greater security than at any other time in our history.

Now we must attend to another theme of the Exodus: Tonight we remember our suffering as strangers in Egypt to help us avoid imposing it on others and to renew our capacity for empathy.

Easier said than done. Once empowered, long-persecuted Christians lost no time in turning upon vulnerable Jews. Ruthless kings and colonial oppressors have been overthrown by insurgents who all too often create even more brutal, despotic regimes. We need to remember Hillel's seemingly simple words: "What is hateful to you, do not do to your neighbor. That is the meaning of the whole Torah. All the rest is commentary. Now go and study."[2]

The Haggadah speaks plainly: "In every generation, each individual should feel as though he or she had gone out of Egypt." Therefore, tonight we remember that we were strangers in the land of Egypt. Tonight we study the Bible's teachings about how we should relate to the *ger*, the stranger in our midst—the other, whom we have the power to oppress or uplift, to shun or welcome, to insult or honor, to neglect or protect. The Bible contains so many reminders to treat the stranger fairly because the experience of suffering more often leaves a thirst for vengeance rather than compassion for others: "The earth shudders . . . [when] a slave becomes king" (Proverbs 30:21–22).

Copy the passages below and the blessing that follows for each of your guests. Take turns reading the passages aloud. These are only some of the many variations on this theme.

1. There shall be one law for the citizen and for the stranger who dwells among you.

    —EXODUS 12:49

2. You shall not wrong a stranger or oppress him, for you were strangers in the land of Egypt. You shall not ill-treat any widow or orphan. If you do mistreat them, I will heed their outcry as soon as they cry out to Me, and My anger shall blaze forth and I will put you to the sword, and your own wives shall become widows and your children orphans.

    —EXODUS 22:20–23[3]

3. And you shall not oppress a stranger, for you know the feelings of the stranger, having yourselves been strangers in the land of Egypt.

    —EXODUS 23:9

4. Six days you may do your work, but on the seventh day you shall cease from labor, in order that your ox and your ass may rest, and that your bondman and the stranger may be refreshed.

    —EXODUS 23:12

5. When a stranger resides with you in your land, you shall not wrong him. The stranger who resides with you shall be to you as one of your citizens; you shall love him as yourself, for you were strangers in the land of Egypt: I, Adonai, am your God.

    —LEVITICUS 19:33–34

6. But the land must not be sold beyond reclaim, for the land is Mine; you are but strangers resident with Me.

—LEVITICUS 25:23

7. When you gather the grapes of your vineyard, do not pick it over again; that shall go to the stranger, the fatherless, and the widow. Always remember that you were a slave in the land of Egypt; therefore do I enjoin you to observe this commandment.

—DEUTERONOMY 24:17–22

8. If you really mend your ways and your actions; if you execute justice between one man and another, if you do not oppress the stranger, the orphan, and the widow; if you do not shed the blood of the innocent in this place; if you do not follow other gods, to your own hurt—then only will I let you dwell in this place, in the land that I gave to your fathers for all time.

—JEREMIAH 7:5–7

9. And the people of the land have practiced fraud and committed robbery; they have wronged the poor and needy, have defrauded the stranger without redress. And I sought a man among them to repair the wall or stand in the breach before Me in behalf of this land, that I might not destroy it, but I have found none.

—EZEKIEL 22:29–30

10. This land you shall divide for yourselves among the tribes of Israel. You shall allot it as a heritage for yourselves and for the strangers who reside among you, who have begotten children among you. You shall treat them as Israelite citizens; they shall receive allotments along with you among the tribes of Israel. You shall give the stranger an allotment within the tribe where he resides—declares Adonai God.

—EZEKIEL 47:21–23

• How do these biblical verses make you feel?

• Which passages evoke the strongest reactions?

- Who are the strangers among us today and how might you, or we as a people, act more justly toward these individuals or groups?

- Why do you think the Haggadah does not explicitly take up the theme of our relations to the stranger?

A BLESSING: TREATING STRANGERS JUSTLY

The following original blessing expresses some of Judaism's core principles.[4] You can recite it when you engage in social justice activities that advance the status of groups that suffer neglect or discrimination. Recite it after your discussion of the questions above. You can also include it regularly near the beginning of the Seder just after *Ha lachma anya*, "This is the bread of affliction," when we invite the hungry and needy to join our Passover celebration.

Blessed are You, Adonai our God, Sovereign of the universe, who sanctifies us by Your commandments and commands us to remember that we were strangers and slaves in Egypt, and are thus obligated to treat with justice the stranger who resides among us.

בָּרוּךְ אַתָּה יְיָ אֱלֹהֵינוּ מֶלֶךְ הָעוֹלָם

אֲשֶׁר קִדְּשָׁנוּ בְּמִצְוֹתָיו

וְצִוָּנוּ לִזְכּוֹר כִּי גֵרִים וַעֲבָדִים הָיִינוּ בְּמִצְרַיִם

וְעַל כֵּן חוֹבָה עָלֵינוּ לַעֲשׂוֹת צֶדֶק

עִם הַגֵּר הַגָּר בְּתוֹכֵנוּ.

Barukh Atah Adonai Eloheinu melekh ha-olam asher kid'shanu b'mitzvotav v'tzivanu lizkor ki gerim va'avadim hayinu b'Mitzrayim v'al ken chovah aleinu la'asot tzedek im ha-ger ha-gar b'tocheinu.

TWO MIDRASHIM ON THE STRANGER

Below you will find two midrashim on the stranger.
Read one or both and discuss the questions that follow.

When the Bible uses the word *ger* (plural, *gerim*), it refers to a stranger. Later, the rabbis understood *ger* to mean a convert. Sometimes the rabbis buttressed their generally favorable attitude toward converts by pointing out that key figures in the Bible applied this very term to themselves. An eighth-century midrash offers a good example.

> Beloved are *gerim*: All the prophets called themselves *gerim*. [When he bought the burial cave for his wife] Abraham said: 'I am a *ger* among you . . .' (Gen. 23:4). [When he named his son Gershom] Moses said: 'I have been a *ger* in a foreign land' (Ex. 2:22). David said: 'Hear my prayer Adonai . . . for like all my forbears, I am a *ger* resident with you (Psalms. 39:13).[5]

- What do you think might be the significance of the fact that Abraham, Moses, and David each referred to themselves as strangers? In what sense might the midrash view these individuals as converts?

- According to tradition, David is the progenitor of the Messiah. The Bible makes it clear that David's lineage was tainted, to say the least. Boaz, David's great-grandfather, descended from the forbidden union between Judah and Tamar (Genesis 38 and Ruth 4:18-22), his daughter-in-law. Ruth, David's great grandmother, descended from the forbidden union between Lot and his older daughter (Genesis 19:37).[6] What might the Bible want us to learn from David's lineage? What implications might this have for how we should relate to the stranger?

- Have you ever felt as if you were a stranger? If so, could you share the experience at the Seder? What did you learn from the experience?

A late medieval midrash offers an unusual explanation for Israel's enslavement in Egypt.

The children of Jacob's wives, Rachel and Leah, degraded the children of Jacob's maidservants, Bilhah and Zilpah. "God said, 'How can I make them accept the maidservants' children? I will send them down to Egypt and they will *all* be slaves. When I redeem them I will give them the commandments of Passover to observe—to them, and their children, and their children's children. And they will all say *avadim hayinu*, we were slaves to Pharaoh, and will discover that they are all equal.'" [7]

- How do you feel about this kind of explanation?

- What do you make of the fact that God chooses the option of enslaving the Israelites in order to teach them the lesson of equality? Does common suffering necessarily inculcate a sense of equality? Why or why not?

- If you were writing a Haggadah, how much attention would you give to the theme of the stranger?

TWO ZIONIST LEADERS ON THE STRANGER

Below you will find statements by two early Zionist leaders on the issue of how we ought to relate to the stranger. Read them aloud and discuss the questions that follow.

Chaim Weizmann (1874–1952) served as president of the World Zionist Organization for twenty-two years. He played an instrumental role in obtaining the Balfour Declaration in 1917, Britain's initial endorsement of establishing a Jewish homeland in Palestine, and in securing President Harry S. Truman's speedy recognition of Israel in 1948. Weizmann served as Israel's first president from 1949 through 1952. In *Trial and Error*, his 1949 autobiography, he wrote:

There must not be one law for the Jew and another for the Arabs. We must stand firm by the ancient principle enunciated in our Torah: 'There shall be one law for the native and for the stranger who resides in your midst.'. . . I am certain that the world will judge the Jewish State by what it will do with the Arabs, just as the Jewish People at large will be judged by what we do or fail to do in this State where we have been given such a wonderful opportunity after thousands of years of wandering and suffering.[8]

Vladimir Jabotinsky (1880–1940) led the Revisionist Movement in Zionism, a group that among other things opposed the partition of Palestine to create both a Jewish and an Arab state. Jabotinsky's ideology has played an important role in Israel's right-wing political movements. The following is an excerpt from his 1910 article, "Man is a Wolf to Man":

Sometimes we base too many rosy hopes on the fallacy that a certain people has itself suffered much and will therefore feel the agony of another people and understand it and its conscience will not allow it to inflict on the weaker people what had been earlier inflicted upon it. But in reality it appears that these are mere pretty phrases . . . Only the Bible says, "And you shall not oppress a stranger, for you know the feelings of the stranger, having yourselves been strangers in the land of Egypt." Contemporary morality has no place for such childish humanitarianism.[9]

• How do Weizmann and Jabotinsky think about the role of one's own suffering in shaping how one treats others?

• Which statement resonates with you more strongly? Why?

• Which view do you think best enhances the potential for building positive relations with the stranger?

Israel includes a 20 percent minority of Arab citizens (living within the Green Line, not in the West Bank or Gaza). Though promised equality by Israel's Declaration of Independence (see page 31), gaps between the Jewish and Arab sectors are enormous. The infant mortality rate of Arabs is more than twice that of Jews. Only 6 percent of the state's civil service employees come from the Arab community, and poverty among Arab families is more than three times more common than among Jews.[10]

• In light of the statements by Weizmann and Jabotinsky, how do you feel about the circumstances of Israel's Arab minority?

Following a tradition from the sixteenth century, some prayer books note that before beginning one's morning prayer one should recite the following: "I hereby accept the obligation of fulfilling the commandment to 'love your neighbor as yourself'" (Leviticus 19:18). (According to biblical usage, *re'a*, the word for "neighbor," can sometimes mean "the other," not necessarily an Israelite.)[11]

• How does this custom make you feel?

• How might this recitation help prepare you for prayer?

12

"In Every Generation . . ."? God's Role in History and the Jewish People's History among the Nations

וְהִיא שֶׁעָמְדָה לַאֲבוֹתֵינוּ וְלָנוּ.
שֶׁלֹּא אֶחָד בִּלְבָד עָמַד עָלֵינוּ לְכַלּוֹתֵנוּ.
אֶלָּא שֶׁבְּכָל דּוֹר וָדוֹר עוֹמְדִים עָלֵינוּ לְכַלּוֹתֵנוּ.
וְהַקָּדוֹשׁ בָּרוּךְ הוּא מַצִּילֵנוּ מִיָּדָם.

It is this [promise] that has sustained our ancestors and us, for not just one has arisen to destroy us; rather in every generation they rise up to destroy us, but the Holy One, praised be He, saves us from their hand.[1]
—THE PASSOVER HAGGADAH

With this passage, we arrive at a clear statement of one of the Haggadah's views on God's role in history and the Jewish People's history among the nations. The nations perennially seek our destruction, but God saves us. These words are often sung with such a stirring tune that you may not have paid much attention to the song's meaning. Suffice it to say, this passage raises more than a few difficult issues.

FOR SEDER LEADERS

Read the passage from the Haggadah below, paying particular attention to the portion in bold as well as the short paragraph that follows. Discuss one or several of the accompanying questions. Consider holding this conversation before you sit down at the Seder table.

Blessed be He who keeps His promise to Israel. Blessed be He. For the Holy One, blessed be He, determined the end of the bondage, thus doing that which He said to Abraham our father in the Covenant between the Pieces. As it is said, "He said to Abram, 'Know well that your offspring shall be strangers in a land not theirs, and they shall be enslaved and oppressed for four hundred years; but I will execute judgment on the nation they shall serve, and in the end they shall go out with great wealth'" (Genesis 15:13–14).

The participants lift their cups of wine and say:

It is this [promise] that has sustained our ancestors and us, for not just one has arisen to destroy us; rather in every generation they rise up to destroy us, but the Holy One, praised be He, saves us from their hand.

The cups are put back on the table.

Go out and learn what Laban the Aramean sought to do to Jacob, our father. While Pharaoh decreed death only for the male children, Laban sought to uproot all.

—THE PASSOVER HAGGADAH

This passage expresses one of the Haggadah's central ideas: that salvation from the oppression of Egypt was not the one-time event God referred to in the preceding paragraph. Rather, Egypt becomes a motif that characterizes Jewish life in every generation. Just as that motif defined Jacob's experience in the house of Laban, generations before the enslavement in Egypt, so too will it shape Jewish life in our era, millennia after the Exodus.[2]

• What emotions does this passage express? What feeling do you have when you recite these words?

- What is your reaction to the image portrayed here of God's role in the world?

- A fragment of an ancient Haggadah discovered in the Cairo Geniza, a repository for Jewish documents over many centuries, reads: "It is this that has sustained our ancestors and us, for not just one enemy has arisen to destroy us; but the Holy One, praised be He, saves us from their hand."[3] The Geniza text omits the phrase "rather in every generation they rise up to destroy us." How does adding or deleting that phrase change the tone of the passage?

- How do you feel about the image of the Jewish People reflected in the passages above?

- What do you make of the fact that the passage gives all-powerful God the credit for saving the Jewish People, but ascribes our suffering to the work of our enemies?

- The Jewish People has known political helplessness for centuries. We don't have much experience wielding political power. What are the challenges facing a people that has known the Holocaust and yet now possesses the power of the State of Israel and the American Jewish community? How well have we met these challenges?

GOD: THE ELEPHANT, AS IT WERE, AT THE SEDER

Read the following aloud and discuss it along with the questions on the next page.

God is the Haggadah's central character, an active God who rescues the innocent Israelites and punishes the wicked Egyptians. Over the ages, many have struggled to reconcile that view of God with experiences that seem to challenge it. How do we maintain faith in the God of the Exodus during the darkest times when a just, all-powerful, all-knowing God seems absent? Perhaps the interchange in the Haggadah between Rabbi Elazar ben Azariah and Ben Zoma about whether to include a reference to the Exodus in the evening prayers—times of metaphorical darkness—points to the same struggle.

According to one survey, fewer than 20 percent of American Jews definitely believe that God intervenes in the course of human events.[4] But it is precisely an interventionist God that we encounter in the Haggadah and throughout Jewish liturgy in general. The typical gap between one's beliefs about God and the representations of God in liturgy generates dissonance. And that dissonance can easily interfere with engagement in the Passover Seder and other aspects of Jewish life where liturgy plays a central role. The words on the page are hard to take literally, and yet how else should we take them?

Maybe you didn't come to the Seder to contend with God. Maybe, you came because you value the idea of celebrating freedom and talking about what that means with the people closest to you. But God is what you get—in almost every line of the Haggadah. Yet in most Seders no one talks about God. That makes God the Seder's "elephant" as it were, a big enough one to create plenty of discomfort. Rather than ignore God at the Seder, let's talk about God.

For many, the God of the Exodus is tough to accept. God saves the Israelites from a terrible ordeal, but not without virtually destroying Egypt—hardening Pharaoh's heart so he cannot let the Israelites go; raining down plagues that wipe out plants, animals, and much human life; and finally drowning a huge number of Egyptians in the Red Sea in a frightful display of divine might. What kind of God is this?

But that's not the only problem. The God of the Exodus may have been tough. But at least that God was *there,* and sooner or later everyone knew it. Our experience of God is very different, especially if we're looking for a God like the one in the Haggadah. And yet that probably *is* the God all of us carried around in our heads as children. The Seder represents a complicated, bittersweet encounter with an image of God that, on one hand, no longer seems quite realistic but, on the other, feels familiar, like an old childhood neighborhood that's no longer home. As distant as the Haggadah's God may have become, that God evokes a certain yearning.

Ana-Maria Rizzuto, a psychoanalyst, wrote a book called *The Birth of the Living God* in which she studied the development of people's concepts of God. Many individuals she interviewed began by saying that they didn't believe in

God. "Tell me," she then asked, "about the God you don't believe in." Invariably they would tell her about a god who didn't measure up to the image of an ideal god they had developed in early childhood. God now seemed too strict, punished the innocent, failed to provide comfort, appeared uninvolved, and so on.[5]

Most of us experience similar disappointment with our parents. We learn to accept their limitations and love them nonetheless. But that's a lot harder to do with God because God's not supposed to have any limitations. For many, it's easier to reject completely the idea of God than it is to develop a concept of God that can coexist with the reality of such a profoundly imperfect world and the absence of an Exodus–like, interventionist God.

And that brings us face to face with a problem that has vexed theologians and philosophers for a long time. It's a problem with a fancy name — theodicy: the attempt to reconcile God's attributes with the reality of evil and unjustified suffering. St Augustine (354–430) is credited with its earliest and most stark formulations: "Either God cannot abolish evil or He will not. If He cannot then He is not all-powerful. If He will not then He is not all-good."[6] Joseph Albo, the fifteenth-century Jewish philosopher from Spain, offered one of the most succinct responses to the problem: "If I knew Him, I would be Him."[7]

Six hundred years and a Holocaust later, with suicide bombings now commonplace and a war on terrorism raging, the enigma still haunts us. In our age, what do we mean when we sing, "the Holy One, praised be He, saves us from their hand"?

Elliot Dorff, a contemporary Conservative theologian, concluded an essay exploring the contradictions between belief in an all-good, all-powerful God and the existence of evil with this:

> Our distress will not be alleviated for long by pretending that we understand unjustified evil in our world or by divorcing God from it; denial can be beneficial for a brief time . . . but ultimately it is not healthy either psychologically or philosophically. We must instead face the ultimate ambiguity of our existence with the commitment to truth, the faith, the strength and the good sense of Jews over the ages.[8]

Dorff's conclusion deserves pondering—as much for its honesty as for its ultimate *inconclusiveness.*

Here are some questions to discuss before or duing your Seder.
You can discuss them after reading the passage above or independent of it.
Remember, the Seder should be a gathering where all
questions can safely be put on the table.

- Elliot Dorff, a contemporary Conservative theologian, highlights six assumptions about the nature of God and evil.[9] He believes that you can't hold all of these assumptions without one or more being contradicted by the others:

(1) God is one; (2) God acts in human history; (3) God is all-knowing (omniscient); (4) God is all-powerful (omnipotent); (5) God is good; and (6) there is unjustified evil [or unjustified suffering] in the world.

- Do you agree with Dorff? Does the notion that God gave human beings free will—which implies the capacity to do good or evil— allow you to hold on to all six assumptions? How do different kinds of natural disasters challenge these assumptions about God? Which of these assumptions about God are the easiest for you to accept? Which are the most difficult?

- How do you understand the following challenging verse from Isaiah (45:6–7): "I am Adonai, and there is no one else. I form the light, and create darkness; I make peace, and create evil; I Adonai do all these things." The Rabbis of the Talmud (Berakhot 11b) found this verse so disturbing that they authorized a modification for its use in the morning prayers: "I form the light, and create darkness; I make peace, and create *all things*."

- What are the kinds of events that raise questions for you about God? What are the kinds of experiences that make you feel the presence or existence of God?

- Can you imagine an event or experience that would convince you that God definitely does or does not exist? From the nature of this hypothetical event or experience what can you learn about your concept of God?

ARGUING WITH GOD

Read the paragraphs below on your own or during your Seder
and then read a few of the illustrations of arguing with God.
Discuss one or both of the questions that follow.

People have problems "believing in God" for many reasons. Many are angry with God for having "hidden His face." Others blame belief in God for many of the world's troubles. Others are disappointed when the ways of God seem so different from what they were taught to expect when they were younger. What are we to do with these feelings? Where do we express them? The matter becomes even more complicated because many also think that these very feelings put them "beyond the pale" when it comes to believing in God. The result? "I don't believe in God." The choice seems to be either being grateful to God and faithfully accepting what God sends our way or walking away from "the God proposition" entirely.

You may think that Judaism's great heroes chose the path of unending gratitude to God and faithful acceptance of their fate. But that's only on the surface. Jewish tradition contains a third approach. When God's ways appear unfair, we can argue and struggle with God.

Take a lesson from great characters such as Abraham, Jacob, Moses, Jeremiah, and Job.

God tells Abraham that God plans to destroy Sodom and Gomorrah. Abraham shoots back: "Will you sweep away the innocent with the guilty? . . . Far be it from you! Shall not the Judge of all the earth deal justly?" (Gen. 18:23, 25). God responds through a bargaining process and agrees to spare the city if it contains ten righteous people.

After wrestling a blessing out of an angel, Jacob's name is changed to Israel, meaning "he wrestled with God."

After the sin of the Golden Calf, God wants to destroy the Israelites and make a new covenant with Moses and his descendants. Moses refuses the bargain: "Alas, this people is guilty of a great sin in making for themselves a god of gold. Now, if You will forgive their sin [well and good]; but if not erase me from the record which You have written" (Ex. 32:31–32).

Jeremiah lived during the destruction of the First Temple in 587 C.E. and called God to court! Scholars have diagrammed the prophet's ancient arguments

153

with God and found them to conform to the proceedings of the ancient law courts. They include an address, an argument, a petition, and a response:[10]

[*Address:*] You will win, O Adonai, if I make claim against You, yet I shall present charges against You.

[*Argument:*] Why does the way of the wicked prosper? Why are the workers of treachery at ease? You have planted them and they have taken root, they spread, they even bear fruit. You are present in their mouths, but far from their thoughts.

[*Petition:*] Yet, You, Adonai, have noted and observed me; You have tested my heart, and found it with you. Drive them out like sheep to the slaughter, prepare them for the day of slaying!

[*Response:*] If you race with the foot-runners and they exhaust you, how then can you compare with horses? [God seems to say, "Jeremiah, you must be stronger. And wait, the contest is not yet over."]

—JEREMIAH 12:1–5

The Bible tells us that Job "was blameless and upright; he feared God and shunned evil" (Job 1:1). Unbeknownst to Job, Satan has engaged God in a little wager: that after a dose of suffering Job would curse God. So God gives Satan the right to afflict Job, kill his family, and deprive Job of every shred of comfort. Job refuses to curse God. Nor will he accept his "friends'" suggestion that somehow he must deserve his suffering. Instead, Job calls God to account:

Who can say to Him, What are You doing?
God does not restrain His anger . . .
The earth is handed over to the wicked one.
He covers the eyes of its judges.
If it is not He, then who? . . .
I insist on arguing with God.

—JOB 9:12–13, 24; 13:3

Many of the psalms also preserve the challenges to God's justice. For example, during the Seder we recite Psalm 115—the third psalm of the Hallel—which calls God to restore Israel's fortunes: "Let the nations not say, 'Where, now, is their God?' . . . The dead cannot praise Adonai. . . ."

In the spirit of their biblical forebears, the sages of the Talmud sometimes expressed their frustration with God's ways through their personal prayers. These kinds of prayers are now known as "law court prayers," because they demand justice from God, the judge. But there was a proper time and a place for these prayers. Here's how one scholar put it: "According to the vast majority of the Talmudic Sages, the 'forceful' prayer which 'hurls accusations at heaven' and demands the rights of the petitioner is definitely considered to be out of place in the statutory public prayer. This pattern is strictly reserved for emergencies only, when all other means of petition have not availed, and is most appropriately used by pious men who are interceding for the community."[11] The Mishnah's account of Honi the Circle Drawer, a miracle worker who lived in the first century B.C.E., represents the classic example. When rain had not fallen he drew a circle around himself and told God he would not move from it until God showed mercy "upon his children" by ending the drought. It worked![12]

- How do you feel about the concept of arguing with God?

- If you were going to argue with God, what kinds of things would you say? Try to answer this question whatever your beliefs about God.

THE SAGES ON INNOCENT SUFFERING

Below you'll find six examples of how the sages of ancient times struggled with the question of why "bad things happen to good people." Before your Seder begins (perhaps in your living room) explain that you'll be having a conversation on this issue based on a number of views held by the Rabbis of ancient times. Depending on your group, you might read all six responses and take a few minutes of discussion after each.

Begin by reading aloud the paragraph below.

The Rabbis of ancient times felt free to argue with God when they felt God's actions were unjust. But this did not exhaust their struggle to justify their belief in an all-just, all-powerful God in the face of the undeserved suffering they witnessed at every turn. Here are six classic rabbinic approaches to the question of why "bad things happen to good people." The fact that many of these explanations are followed by rebuttals (not included here) demonstrates how unwilling the sages were to accept simple answers to difficult questions.[13] The Rabbis offered so many solutions to the problem because in the end none was truly satisfying. Despite, or perhaps because of, their questions, the Rabbis instituted a blessing upon receiving bad news: "Blessed is the true Judge."[14] The Rabbis concluded that faith must be affirmed at the very moment it is most likely to waver.

1. *Innocent on the outside, guilty within:* "There is no suffering without sin" (Babylonian Talmud, Shabbat 55a).

2. *Suffering is a sign of God's love:* Afflictions should lead to introspection and in turn to more virtuous behavior. "If the Holy One, blessed be He, is pleased with a man, he crushes him with painful sufferings . . . Rabbi Hiyya bar Abba fell ill and Rabbi Yochanan went in to visit him. He said to him: 'Are your sufferings welcome to you?' He replied: 'Neither they nor their reward'" (Babylonian Talmud, Berakhot 5a-b).

3. *Wait for the world to come:* Only in the world to come will the righteous receive their just desserts. "Rabbi Akiva said: 'He deals strictly with the righteous, calling them to account for the few wrongs which they commit in this world, in order to lavish bliss upon and give them a goodly reward in the world to come'" (Genesis Rabbah 33:1).

4. *Human beings possess free will, for good or ill:* God endowed humanity with both a good and an evil inclination (*yetzer ha-tov* and *yetzer ha-ra*). God also provided the Torah as an "antidote" to the evil inclination. Straying from its teachings allows evil to invade the world. "The sword comes to the world from the delay of justice, from the perversion of justice, and from interpreting the Torah in opposition to Jewish law" (Mishnah, Avot 5:11).

5. *God's ways are simply inscrutable:* Once, God granted Moses the privilege of looking into the future and seeing that Rabbi Akiva taught the same Torah that had been revealed to Moses. "Then said Moses, 'Master of the Universe, You have shown me his Torah, now

show me his reward.' 'Turn around,' said He; and Moses turned round and saw them weighing out Akiva's flesh at the market-stalls [after his martyrdom in 135 C.E.]. 'Master of the Universe,' cried Moses, 'such Torah, and such a reward!' He replied, 'Be silent, for such is My decree'" (Babylonian Talmud, Menachot 29b).

6. *God suffers along with us:* We may not know why we suffer, but we don't suffer alone. "God said to Moses: 'Do you not realize that I live in trouble just as Israel lives in trouble? Know from the place whence I speak unto you—from a thorn-bush—that I am, as it were, a partner in their trouble'" (Exodus Rabbah 2:5). When the Temple was destroyed, God "wept and said, 'Woe is Me for My house! My children, where are you? My priests, where are you? My lovers, where are you?'" (Lamentations Rabbah, Prologue 24).

• Which, if any, of these positions, expresses a view that you can accept? Which is most problematic? Why?

MODERN VOICES

Choose one or more of these passages to read aloud and discuss before or during your Seder. If you do so during the Seder, relate the conversation to the passage from the Haggadah at the beginning of this chapter. Argue with these readings! But don't forget that in the end, Judaism worries more about our actions than those of God. As you'll see, a number of these selections refer to God's hidden face, an image that recurs frequently in the Bible.

Whenever Rabbi Levi Yitzhak came to that passage in the Haggadah of Passover which deals with the four sons, and in it read about the fourth son ... who "knows not how to ask," he said: "'The one who knows not how to ask,' that is myself, Levi Yitzhak of Berditchev. I do not know how to ask you, Master of the World, and even if I did know, I could not bear to do it. How could I venture to ask you why everything happens

157

as it does, why we are driven from one exile into another, why our foes are allowed to torment us so. But in the Haggadah, the father of him 'who does knows not how to ask,' is told: 'It is for you to disclose it to him.' And the Haggadah refers to the Scriptures in which it is written: 'And you shall tell your son.' And, Master of the World, am I not your son? I do not beg you to reveal to me the secret of your ways—I could not bear it! But show me one thing; show it to me more clearly and more deeply: show me what this, which is happening at this very moment means to me, what it demands of me, what You, Master of the World, are telling me by way of it. Ah, it is not why I suffer, that I wish to know, but only whether I suffer for your sake."[15]

—LEVI YITZHAK OF BERDITCHEV (1740–1810),
POLAND AND RUSSIA, HASIDIC MASTER

If God lived on earth, people would break the windows in God's house.

—YIDDISH PROVERB[16]

On the road that leads to the one and only God, there is a way station without God. True monotheism must frame answers to the legitimate demands of atheism. An adult person's God reveals himself precisely in the emptiness of the child's heaven . . . But only the person who recognized the veiled God can demand his revelation.

—EMMANUEL LEVINAS (1905–1995), LITHUANIA AND FRANCE,
JEWISH EXISTENTIALIST PHILOSOPHER[17]

Does not history look like a stage for the dance of might and evil—with man's wits too feeble to separate the two and God either directing the play or indifferent to it? The major folly of this view seems to lie in its shifting the responsibility for man's plight from man to God . . . God was thought of as a watchman hired to prevent us from using our loaded guns. Having failed us in this, He is now thought of as the ultimate Scapegoat.

—ABRAHAM JOSHUA HESCHEL (1907–1972), POLAND, GERMANY,
AND UNITED STATES, THEOLOGIAN[18]

When I say we live in the time of the death of God, I mean that the thread uniting God and man, heaven and earth, has been broken. We stand in a cold, silent, unfeeling cosmos, unaided by any purposeful power beyond our own resources. After Auschwitz what else can a Jew say about God? . . . The time of the death of God does not mean the end of all gods. It means the demise of the God who was the ultimate actor in history . . . In a world devoid of God we need Torah, tradition, and the religious community far more than in a world where God's presence was meaningfully experienced.

—RICHARD RUBENSTEIN (1924–),
UNITED STATES, THEOLOGIAN[19]

When the sound of the closing of the door, after the first child was shoved into the crematorium, reached heaven, Michael, the most beneficent of angels, could not contain himself and angrily approached God. Michael asked, "Do You now pour out Your wrath upon children? In the past, children were indirectly caught up in the slaughter. This time they are the chief target of destruction. Have pity on the little ones, O Adonai." God, piqued by Michael's insolence, shouted back at him, "I am Lord of the Universe. If you are displeased with the way I conduct the world, I will return it to void and null." Hearing these words, Michael knew that there was to be no reversal. He had heard these words once before in connection with the Ten Martyrs. He knew their effect. He went back to his place, ashen and dejected, but could not resist looking back sheepishly at God and saw a huge tear rolling down His face, destined for the legendary cup which collects tears and which, when full, will bring the redemption of the world. Alas to Michael's horror, instead of entering the cup the tear hit its rim, most of it spilling on the ground—and the fire of the crematorium continued to burn.

—DAVID WEISS HALIVNI (1927–), ROMANIA AND UNITED STATES, SCHOLAR
OF RABBINIC THOUGHT AND LITERATURE,
HOLOCAUST SURVIVOR[20]

Evil, which can neither be explained nor comprehended, does exist. Only if man could grasp the world as a whole would he be able to gain a perspective on the essential nature of evil. However, as long as man's apprehension is limited and distorted, as long as he perceives only isolated fragments of the cosmic drama and the mighty epic of history, he remains unable to penetrate into the secret lair of suffering and evil. To what may the matter be compared? To a person gazing at a beautiful rug, a true work of art, one into which an exquisite design has been woven— but looking at it from its reverse side. Can such a viewing give rise to a sublime aesthetic experience? We, alas, view the world from its reverse side. We are, therefore, unable to grasp the all-encompassing framework of being. And it is only within that framework that it is possible to discern the divine plan, the essential nature of the divine actions.

—JOSEPH B. SOLOVEITCHIK (1903–1992) RUSSIA AND UNITED STATES, CENTRIST ORTHODOX SCHOLAR AND LEADER[21]

An engine bolt breaks on flight 205 instead of on flight 209, inflicting tragedy on one random group of families rather than another. There is no message in all of that. There is no reason for those particular people to be afflicted rather than others. These events do not reflect God's choices. They happen at random, and randomness is another name for chaos, in those corners of the universe where God's creative light has not yet penetrated.

—HAROLD S. KUSHNER (1935–), UNITED STATES, CONSERVATIVE RABBI AND BEST-SELLING AUTHOR[22]

Examining the world scene, a Jew can see nowhere the presence of God in the history of the nations or religions—unless it be in the history of Israel and only through it also in the history of man . . . Only the reality of Israel resists explanation on the level of man-made history alone. Because of Israel the Jew knows that history is messianism, that God's guidance—however impenetrably wrapped in mystery—is never absent from the life of the nations.

—ELIEZER BERKOVITZ (1908–1992), UNITED STATES, ORTHODOX THEOLOGIAN[23]

[God] is the liberator of men and their societies. God is the Power working within individuals that will not permit them to acquiesce in servitude, their own or that of others. He is the spark that kindles them into rebellion and the iron that makes them stubborn for freedom's sake. And simultaneously He hardens the heart of tyrants, until, lost to reason, incapable of either learning or forgetting, they destroy themselves.

—MILTON STEINBERG (1903–1950), UNITED STATES,
CONSERVATIVE RABBI[24]

If a person who cynically refused to believe in God could observe everything a congregation said and did whenever its members gathered for prayer, study, and communal meetings, by the end of a year or two he would know a lot about what God does, even if God never showed up. For, while God does not have hands, we do. Our hands are God's. And when people behave as if their hands were the hands of God, then God "acts" in history.

—LAWRENCE KUSHNER, (1943–), UNITED STATES,
REFORM RABBI AND AUTHOR[25]

From biblical times to the present day, the Jews have wandered the uncertain terrain between power and powerlessness, never quite achieving the power necessary to guarantee long-term security, but equally avoiding, with a number of disastrous exceptions, the abyss of absolute impotence. They developed the consummate political art of living with uncertainty and insecurity; their long survival owes much to this extraordinary achievement. Jews today must struggle to come to terms with this history in light of their present power, to see both past and present through a realistic lens, neither inflating their power nor exaggerating their powerlessness.

—DAVID BIALE (1949–), UNITED STATES,
PROFESSOR OF JEWISH HISTORY[26]

13

"Go Out and Learn . . .": How the Haggadah Tells the Story of the Exodus

צֵא וּלְמַד,

מַה בִּקֵּשׁ לָבָן הָאֲרַמִּי לַעֲשׂוֹת לְיַעֲקֹב אָבִינוּ.

שֶׁפַּרְעֹה לֹא גָזַר אֶלָּא עַל הַזְּכָרִים

וְלָבָן בִּקֵּשׁ לַעֲקֹר אֶת־הַכֹּל

שֶׁנֶּאֱמַר: אֲרַמִּי אֹבֵד אָבִי,

וַיֵּרֶד מִצְרַיְמָה, וַיָּגָר שָׁם בִּמְתֵי מְעָט.

וַיְהִי שָׁם לְגוֹי גָּדוֹל, עָצוּם וָרָב:

Go out and learn what Laban the Aramean planned to do to Jacob,
our father. While Pharaoh decreed death only for the male children,
Laban sought to uproot all. As it is said: "An Aramean sought to destroy
my father. He went down to Egypt with few in numbers and sojourned there;
but there he became a great and very populous nation . . ." (Deut. 26:5).
—THE PASSOVER HAGGADAH

You'll find this passage in your Haggadah in the Maggid section, just after *v'hi she-amdah la-avoteinu,* "And it is this that has stood by our ancestors and us...."

Every year many people come to the Seder expecting to hear the story of the Exodus. They leave with a certain frustration: "I sort of heard the story, but it was confusing and all broken up!" Here we'll look at one of the central ways that the Haggadah "tells" the story—midrash—and why it chose that approach. We'll also explore a biblical passage, often called the Pilgrims' Prayer, on which the Haggadah based its midrash. As we'll see, the Haggadah framed the opening of its midrash in two ways. First, it provided an introduction asserting that Laban, Jacob's uncle, was worse than Pharaoh. Next, it chose a particular way of understanding *arami oved avi,* the first three words of the Pilgrims' Prayer. Rather than reading these words as "My father was a wandering Aramean," as we find in most translations of the Bible, the Haggadah read them to mean "An Aramean sought to destroy my father," a rendering also found in many ancient midrashic sources.

HOW THE HAGGADAH TELLS THE STORY

This will make a good pre-Seder activity. Read aloud what follows.

About eighteen hundred years ago, the Mishnah's instructions for the Seder said we should "begin with disgrace and conclude with praise and . . . expound upon *arami oved avi,* 'My father was a wandering Aramean' . . . until [finishing] the whole section" (Pesachim 10:4). The Mishnah refers to a passage from the twenty-sixth chapter of the Book of Deuteronomy known as the Pilgrims' Prayer. Farmers would recite it when they brought their first ripe fruits to the Temple beginning in the early summer and continuing through the fall. Originally, the prayer was not connected with Passover, but with the festival of Shavuot, in ancient times also known as *Yom Habikurim,* "the day of first fruits." Later, when the Rabbis reinterpreted the ancient agricultural festivals in historical terms, Shavuot came to commemorate receiving the Torah at Sinai. Some scholars believe that the Pilgrims' Prayer was also recited as part of the Passover celebration during the time of the Second Temple until it was destroyed in 70

C.E.[1] The Mishnah indicates that this was one of relatively few prayers that had to be recited in Hebrew. Since many pilgrims spoke dialects of Aramaic, priests prompted those who couldn't manage the Hebrew. Gradually, embarrassed non-Hebrew speakers stopped bringing offerings to the Temple. So a new custom evolved: *Everyone* recited the prayer phrase by phrase following a priest.[2]

A little background on the Book of Deuteronomy sheds a good deal of light on the Pilgrims' Prayer. Most scholars agree that the Book of Deuteronomy was composed either shortly before or during the reign of King Josiah, ruler of the Kingdom of Judah between 640 and 609 B.C.E. Josiah introduced far-reaching religious reforms, including the centralization of sacrifice at the Temple in Jerusalem, to strengthen monotheism against the inroads of idol worship. In the process, Passover evolved into a national festival. Josiah also briefly succeeded in wresting the Northern Kingdom of Israel from Assyrian domination. Jeremiah, who lived during Josiah's reign, evoked powerful imagery of the redemption from Egypt to fortify support for the king's military campaigns: "'In that day,' declares Adonai of Hosts, 'I will break the yoke from off your neck and I will rip off your bonds. Strangers shall no longer make slaves of them; instead they shall serve Adonai their God . . .'" (Jeremiah 30:8–9).

The Pilgrims' Prayer represents one of only three examples of a prescribed prayer in the Five Books of Moses, all of them found in Deuteronomy.[3] Given Josiah's interest in ridding his nation of alien religious practices, the development of fixed prayers makes perfect sense.

> Following the instructions below, you'll find the passage from Deuteronomy upon which the Haggadah builds its midrash. The nonitalicized verses provide important context for understanding the Pilgrims' Prayer, Deuteronomy 26:3–10. (The Haggadah includes only the italicized verses.) Read the entire passage aloud. Then try either of these activities.

- Discuss the questions below.

- Read the passage from Deuteronomy through once aloud. Then ask your guests to take turns reading a phrase or two of the italicized verses and adding a few sentences of elaboration, including details, their own interpretations, comments about contemporary parallels, etc.

Use these few verses as a framework around which to weave the tale of Israel's sojourn and departure from Egypt. Make your own midrash!

THE PILGRIMS' PRAYER

[1]When you enter the land that Adonai your God is giving you as a heritage, and you possess it and settle in it, [2]you shall take some of every first fruit of the soil, which you harvest from the land that Adonai your God is giving you, put it in a basket and go to the place where Adonai your God will choose to establish His name. [3]You shall go to the priest in charge at that time and say to him, "I acknowledge (*higad'ti*) this day before Adonai your God that I have entered the land that Adonai swore to our fathers to assign us." [4]The priest shall take the basket from your hand and set it down in front of the altar of Adonai your God. [5]You shall then recite as follows before Adonai your God:

"My father was a wandering Aramean. He went down to Egypt few in numbers and sojourned there; but there he became a great and very populous nation. [6]*The Egyptians dealt harshly with us and oppressed us; they imposed heavy labor upon us.* [7]*We cried to Adonai, the God of our fathers, and Adonai heard our plea and saw our plight, our misery, and our oppression.* [8]*Adonai took us out from Egypt by a mighty hand, by an outstretched arm and awesome power, and by signs and portents.*

[9]He brought us to this place and gave us this land, a land flowing with milk and honey. [10]Wherefore I have now brought the first fruits of the soil which You, O Adonai, have given me.

—DEUTERONOMY 26:1–10

- Why do you think the Mishnah wants us to tell the story by elaborating on these italicized verses, rather than giving us a number of verses to read from the Book of Exodus, which tell the story in a more direct way?

- What makes this passage particularly suitable for telling the Passover story? What seems to be missing from this brief review of Israelite history? What might account for these omissions?

- Why do you think the Rabbis who compiled the Mishnah, about 130 years after the Temple's destruction, would have chosen a declaration so strongly associated with the Temple for the Haggadah's central text?

- Does this passage place more emphasis on God as author of history or ruler of the natural world? Why might the passage have taken this position?

THE PILGRIMS' PRAYER AND THE HAGGADAH

Read this on your own, or depending on your group,
do so following the discussion above.

Now let's look at why the compilers of the Haggadah may have chosen this passage as a basis for telling the story of the Exodus and how it functions within the Haggadah. First, remember that Deuteronomy prescribed the recitation of this passage when farmers brought their offerings of first fruits to the Temple. As such, for centuries it would have been one of the most familiar of all biblical texts. Beyond this, it's important to consider four additional aspects of this passage.

The language of family history: The Book of Exodus enjoins us to tell the Passover story to our children as we would the history of our family. With that tone in mind, our passage begins "My *father* was a wandering Aramean." Most of the narration that follows occurs in the first person plural. *We, us,* and *our* are the operative pronouns, and their presence helps erase the long years that separate the pilgrim from his ancestors who suffered and escaped from Egypt. "The Egyptians dealt harshly with *us* and oppressed *us; they* imposed heavy labor upon *us. We* cried out to Adonai, the God of *our* fathers, and Adonai heard *our* plea and saw *our* plight, *our* misery, and *our* oppression. Adonai took *us* out . . ." For the Jew, this is *our* story, *our* family history—not a tale about other people who lived long ago or far away. If the pilgrim bringing his first fruits to the Temple centuries after the Exodus could find meaning in the story of redemption from Egypt, so can we today.

The language of promise and fulfillment: Within the sequence of the Haggadah, the story of the "wandering Aramean" occupies a critical place. Shortly before we come to our passage, we bless God, "who keeps His promise to Israel." Then we read several verses from Genesis (15:13–14) in which God foretells Abraham of his descendants' enslavement and redemption from Egypt. Then we recite, *v'hi she-amdah la-avoteinu,* "and it is this [usually thought to mean 'this promise'] that has stood by our ancestors and us." Now we come to the story of the "wandering Aramean."

Structurally, the passage serves to demonstrate that God kept the promise to Abraham. God redeemed Abraham's ancestors and brought them to the Promised Land. But more than that, our passage from Deuteronomy repeats the precise terms of God's covenantal promise to Abraham. God tells Abraham that his descendants must experience three things before they will be redeemed: being strangers (*gerut*), being enslaved (*avdut*), and being oppressed (or afflicted, *inui*). We find all three terms (the roots of each word) in two verses from our passage: "My father was a wandering Aramean. He went down to Egypt with few in number and sojourned there (*gerut*); but there he became a great and very populous nation. The Egyptians dealt harshly with us and oppressed us (*inui*); they imposed heavy labor (*avdut*) upon us." These three terms occur in close proximity only twice in the Five Books of Moses, and the Haggadah includes them both: first in God's promise to Abraham in Genesis (15:13–14) and again in our passage from Deuteronomy![4]

"Not by a messenger . . .": The fact that the Pilgrims' Prayer leaves Moses out of the story may have further added to its suitability for the Haggadah. At a time when nascent Christianity was constructing a religion that revolved around Jesus as the redeeming intermediary—in the Gospel of John (14:6), Jesus says, "No one comes to the Father but through Me"—Judaism emphasized redemption through an unmediated relationship between God and humanity.[5] But the absence of Moses in this passage may also point to an even older concern. The Book of Deuteronomy tells us that the great leader's burial place remains unknown "to this day" (Deut. 34:6). Why the secret? As the philosopher Gersonides (1288–1344) put it, "So that generations to come should not go astray and worship him as a deity."[6] (For more on Moses and the Haggadah, see chapter 16).

The meaning of making midrash: With all these explanations in mind, a question still remains. Why does the Mishnah (Pesachim 10:4) say "he expounds" on a passage from Deuteronomy rather than simply recounting the Passover story as it unfolds in the Book of Exodus?

"He expounds," *hu doreish,* means "he makes midrash," "draws out meaning," "studies." Indeed, the Haggadah prefaces its midrash with these words: "Go out and learn. . . ." The injunction to "expound" or "go out and learn" constitutes a theme that runs throughout the Haggadah. The Seder table includes objects and rituals designed to prompt questions. After a short general answer to questions about the differences between the night of the Seder and other nights—"We were slaves in Egypt"—the Haggadah says, "Whoever elaborates on the story of the Exodus is praiseworthy." Then five sages discuss the Exodus all through the night. Then the Four Children present additional questions. Then we "expound" on "my father was a wandering Aramean." After recounting the plagues, three sages again expound on the location and number of the plagues. Rabbi Akiva "proves" there were not ten, but three hundred plagues!

All of this points to the Haggadah's conviction that the Seder should embody *expounding, learning,* and *teaching* about the meaning of the Exodus. A dry, mechanical reading of the same text year in and year out is the antithesis of what a Seder should be.

We can fully appreciate the significance of this instruction to "expound" and make meaning, and to "go out and learn," only when we remember what had been Passover's central rite when the Temple stood: sacrifice. The loss of the Temple, and with it the central ritual of Passover, posed an enormous challenge to Judaism's future and demanded a far-reaching reinterpretation of Passover, the very holiday associated with the Jewish People's birth.[7] At the same time, the Temple's destruction rendered Passover's celebration of redemption all the more crucial. In a move both radical and adaptive, the Rabbis of the post-Temple era resolved that sacrifice would be replaced by acts of kindness, prayer, and observing the commandments, and particularly by study. In fact, the seeds for such a development had begun to sprout among the Pharisees while the Temple stood, but they only came into full flower after the Temple had fallen. In the words of the Talmud, "whoever occupies himself with the study of the Torah needs neither burnt-offering, nor meal-offering, nor sin-offering, nor guilt-offering."[8]

In one sense, the instruction to "expound" on the Pilgrims' Prayer embodied the rabbinic ideal of combining the written Torah with the beloved oral tradition (all the legends and lore passed down through the generations).[9] It also expressed the daring freedom to midrashically re-create what had previously been a hallowed, but frozen, declaration.

The Rabbis resolved to encounter God, to join God as a creator through the medium of midrash, drawing out meaning from what they knew to be God's words and discovering new connections among them. It's not just that the mode of "expounding" breathed new life into an old text. At its best, the midrashic method actually gives birth to new texts—the Haggadah, for example—an act of creation and freedom that for the Rabbis epitomized the meaning of redemption from Egypt, if not godliness itself.

A MUCH-INTERPRETED PHRASE

Read the following indented paragraph aloud and discuss the questions below with your guests.

The Mishnah's instructions for the Seder tell us to "expound" on the passage from Deuteronomy that begins with the Hebrew phrase *Arami oved avi*. The Haggadah also gives the passage the following introduction:

> Go out and learn what Laban the Aramean planned to do to Jacob, our father. While Pharaoh decreed death only for the male children, Laban sought to uproot all. As it is said: *Arami oved avi,* "An Aramean sought to destroy my father. . . ."

Most translations of the Bible render *Arami oved avi* as "My father was a wandering Aramean." Interpreters such as Rashi and others have claimed that the phrase's grammatical structure supports a very different reading: "An Aramean sought to destroy my father." Suffice it say, despite centuries of debate, the latter became standard for all traditional renderings of the Haggadah.[10]

• What are the major differences between the two readings of *Arami oved avi:* "My father was a wandering Aramean" versus "the Aramean sought to destroy my father"? Which reading do you prefer and why? Why do you think the Haggadah wanted to suggest that Laban, the Aramean, was a greater threat to the Jewish future than Pharaoh?

• Commentators have long differed on how to understand *Arami oved avi*. Today, Haggadot reflect those differences.[11] Why do you think that some modern Haggadot are more comfortable with "My father was a wandering Aramean" than "The Aramean sought to destroy my father?"

Following are four interpretations of *Arami oved avi*.
Choose one or two to discuss at your Seder. Depending on your group,
you might want to provide the following background on Laban.

Laban the Aramean was Jacob's uncle (the brother of his mother, Rebecca). After stealing his brother Esau's blessing, Jacob fled to Laban, who took him in, gave him two daughters in marriage, Leah and Rachel, and employed him for twenty years. Following a series of disputes over property and wages, Jacob sensed Laban's mounting hostility. God told Jacob to "return to the land of your fathers" (Gen. 31:3). When Jacob furtively fled, Laban pursued him. But God appeared to Laban in a dream, saying, "Beware of attempting anything with Jacob, good or bad" (Gen. 31:24). In the end, they swore a covenant of mutual nonaggression.

An Aramean sought to destroy my father. Laban sought to uproot all when he pursued Jacob. [And because he contemplated doing so] the Omni-present charges him as though he had done it; for [as regards] the heathen peoples, the Holy One, blessed be He considers . . . a thought to be the equivalent of a deed.

—RASHI (RABBI SHLOMO BEN YITZHAK), 1040–1105, FRANCE, THE MOST FAMOUS BIBLE AND TALMUD COMMENTATOR[12]

"Go and learn what Laban the Aramean planned to do to Jacob, our father." [The Haggadah begins] to recount from the first of the evildoers who plotted against us to destroy us [*aleinu l'khaloteinu*, as in the foregoing passage in the Haggadah, "In every generation they rise up to destroy us . . ."]. And this is Laban. In order to continue this recounting, those who bring the first fruits also recall the going out of Egypt. And we expound on these verses in the Passover

Haggadah, as the Mishnah says, "from *Arami oved avi* to the end of the portion."

—RASHBETZ (RABBI SHIMON BEN TZEMACH DURAN), 1361–1444, SPAIN AND NORTH AFRICA, RABBINIC AUTHORITY, PHILOSOPHER, AND SCIENTIST[13]

Arami, that is the evil inclination [*yetzer ha-ra*] because it is a great deceiver [*ramai,* a play on *Arami*]. This is the meaning of "Now the serpent was the shrewdest [*arum*] of all . . ." (Gen. 3:1). He deceived the creatures [Adam and Eve] in order to destroy them. That is the meaning of "destroyed my father" (*oved avi*). It means the first human being [Adam]. This is the meaning of "Your earliest ancestor sinned" (Isaiah 43:27). And [the serpent, the evil inclination] destroyed him and brought death to him and to the generations coming after him. And he implanted in every soul a part of that evil.

—RABBI CHAYIM BEN MOSHE ATTAR (1696–1743), MOROCCO AND ISRAEL, TORAH COMMENTATOR, ALSO KNOWN AS *OHR HACHAYIM,* THE TITLE OF HIS MAJOR COMMENTARY, KABBALIST, AND LEADER OF THE EARLY MOROCCAN COMMUNITY IN ISRAEL[14]

[The claim that Laban was worse than Pharaoh] is trying to show us two things about Pharaoh [and the Egyptians] that deserve praise . . . First . . . that we ate their food for a long time, as it says, "We remember the fish that we used to eat free in Egypt, the cucumbers, the melons, the leeks, the onions, and the garlic" (Num. 11:5). And we also know that Jacob went down to Egypt with seventy people and [hundreds of thousands] left with great wealth. From this we must clearly recognize the goodness of the Egyptians, hence "You shall not abhor an Egyptian, for you were a stranger in his land" (Deut. 23:8). Second, the Torah does not suggest that Pharaoh forced the Israelites to worship idols and caused them to sin. He just afflicted them with physical labor. By contrast, Laban wanted Jacob to assimilate . . . And this is what the compilers of the Haggadah wanted . . . to stress on the night of Passover—that we have faced evildoers worse than Pharaoh, evildoers who wanted us to assimilate and thereby uproot and eradicate the people of Israel . . . And evildoers of this kind are sometimes more dangerous to us than those like Pharaoh.

—MENACHEM KASHER (1895–1983), POLAND AND ISRAEL,
RABBI AND HALAKHIST, DISTINGUISHED FOR
HIS RESEARCH IN RABBINIC LITERATURE[15]

LABAN AND PHARAOH

Not many of us would begin a narrative of the Exodus with Laban, Jacob's uncle, father-in-law, and employer for some twenty years. In the Bible Laban was hardly a saint, but neither was he anything like the arch-villain the Haggadah depicts.

Indeed, many scholars have tried to explain the Haggadah's demonic rendering of Laban, a view that it shares with many other midrashic sources.[16] Some have suggested that the Haggadah's charge that Laban was worse than Pharaoh arose as a means of placating the Egyptian regime that ruled Palestine in the third century B.C.E. and deprecating its rival Syria, which was called, in Hebrew, Aram. Others have argued that the pejorative treatment of Laban represents a veiled expression of animus toward Rome. The Hebrew words for Aramean, ארמי, and Roman, רמאי, contain the same letters. A dictionary of rabbinic literature defines ארמי, Aramean, as "gentile" or "Roman."[17] Alas, each of these approaches contains weaknesses.

A close reading of the Bible helps explain the Haggadah's link between Laban and Pharaoh. The Bible uses some of the same words in both stories. Here's Laban's pursuit of Jacob (Gen. 31:22–23): "On the third day, Laban was told [*vayugad*] that Jacob had fled [*ki barach*]. So he took [*vayikach*] his kinsmen with him and pursued him [*vayirdof*]. . ." Now here's Pharaoh's pursuit of Jacob's descendants, "the children of Israel" (Ex. 14:5, 7–8): "When the king of Egypt was told [*vayugad*] that the people had fled [*ki barach*]. . . . He ordered his chariot and took [*vayikach*] his men. . . . and he pursued [*vayirdof*] the Israelites." No wonder that the midrash finds hostility in Laban's pursuit of Jacob.[18]

The story of Jacob's travails with Laban also employs the same three terms— *avdut* (enslavement), *inui* (affliction), and *gerut* (being strangers)—found in God's covenantal promise to Abraham.[19] As we've seen (pages 125, 168), these three terms appear prominently in the Exodus story as well as in the Pilgrims' Prayer.

Some believe that the story of Laban was actually retouched to include parallels with the Exodus. Those parallels darkened Laban and cast Jacob, a flawed character to say the least, in a better light.

This brings us to the opening of the Haggadah's extended midrash on the Exodus. Grammatically, the beginning of Deuteronomy 26:5 can be read "My father was a wandering Aramean" or "The Aramean sought to destroy my father," as the Haggadah and many other early sources read it. What helped the second reading gain such a foothold? First, it would have been odd for the Sages of old to identify Jacob as an Aramean, because the Bible never identifies him that way. By contrast, five of the Bible's six references to Arameans refer to Laban or his father. Then we have the linguistic parallels between both tales including Laban's hostile pursuit of Jacob. To an astute reader, those parallels, combined with the oddity of identifying Jacob as an Aramean, may have been enough to favor the second reading: "The Aramean sought to destroy my father."

Laban thus became a prototype of Pharaoh. And this accords with the rabbinic view that the lives of the patriarchs prefigure those of their descendants. Jacob/Israel survived the clutches of Laban; the children of Israel endured the house of bondage. In both cases, God's redemptive hand intervened. The parallels between Laban and Pharaoh affirm the Haggadah's conclusion: "In every generation they rise up to destroy us, but the Holy One . . . saves us from their hand."

DEUTERONOMY'S ISRAELITE HISTORY WITHOUT SINAI

Read the following passage aloud during your Seder.

Deuteronomy's understanding of God and revelation may help explain a glaring omission from the Pilgrims' Prayer—the absence of any reference to receiving the law at Sinai. Deuteronomy depicts God in far more abstract terms than does Exodus. In Deuteronomy's brief account of the revelation (4:36), the people hear God's voice from heaven amidst divine fire. In Exodus (19), God actually descends upon Sinai, and the people need to keep their distance lest they *see* God and die. In Deuteronomy, revelation is almost cerebral; in Exodus, it's physical—frighteningly so.[20] In fact, Deuteronomy envisions an understanding of God's will that transcends the need for a Sinai-like revelation. Not long before his death,

Moses speaks pointedly of the contrast. "Surely this Instruction which I enjoin upon you this day is not too baffling for you, nor is it beyond reach. It is not in the heavens, that you should say, 'Who among us can go up to the heavens and get it for us and impart it to us, that we may observe it?' . . . No, the thing is very close to you, in your mouth and in your heart, to observe it" (Deut. 30:12–14).[21]

In addition, for the Deuteronomist, Sinai represented only one version of the covenant: "These are the terms of the covenant which Adonai commanded Moses to conclude with the Israelites in the land of Moab, in addition to the covenant which He had made with them at Horeb [Sinai]" (Deut. 28:69). A reference to both covenants would have complicated an otherwise simple declaration; the exclusion of either may have offended those closer to one tradition or the other.

The absence of any reference to received law in the Pilgrims' Prayer allows the declaration to speak fully in terms of reciprocity rather than commandment. Instead of bringing his first fruits because the law commands it (which, of course, it does), the pilgrim's actual declaration states that I brought (*heiveiti*) this offering to God because God "brought us" (*vayivi'einu*) to the Land of Israel. This roots ritual in personal experience, not abstract legal obligation. Moses told the Israelites that the Torah was in their mouths and hearts, not in heaven. The absence of any reference to revelation in the Pilgrims' Prayer affirms that point.

Our celebration of Passover should likewise feel as if it comes from our heart rather than from imposed laws.

14

Women of the Exodus: Redeemed
by Their Righteousness

גָּדוֹל עָצוּם, כְּמָה שֶׁנֶּאֱמַר:
וּבְנֵי יִשְׂרָאֵל פָּרוּ וַיִּשְׁרְצוּ וַיִּרְבּוּ
וַיַּעַצְמוּ בִּמְאֹד מְאֹד
וַתִּמָּלֵא הָאָרֶץ אֹתָם...
וַיַּרְא אֶת־עָנְיֵנוּ, זוֹ פְּרִישׁוּת דֶּרֶךְ אֶרֶץ...

" . . . *Great and very populous . . ." (Deut. 26:5): "But the Israelites were fertile and
prolific; they multiplied and increased very greatly, so that the land
was filled with them" (Ex. 1:7).*

*"And [God] saw our affliction . . ." (Deut. 26:7):
that is the enforced separation of husband and wife. . . .*
—THE PASSOVER HAGGADAH

Much of the Haggadah can be read as an extended midrash on the biblical Exodus. But the Haggadah's rendering curiously differs from that
of the Bible and the midrash in its virtual omission of women. In fact, the
Haggadah mentions only one woman by name—in a song toward the end of the

Seder. This becomes all the more striking in light of a teaching by Rabbi Akiva from the Talmud: "The Israelites were delivered from Egypt as a reward for the righteous women who lived in that generation."[1] The Haggadah alludes to Pharaoh's plan to destroy the Israelites by preventing them from procreating—"the enforced separation of husband and wife." Akiva credits women with thwarting Pharaoh's scheme by defiantly meeting their weary husbands in the fields under the apple trees, feeding them warm food, anointing them with oil, seducing them, and later stealing off to deliver their children. Akiva's allusion to the apple tree finds its way onto the Seder plate. The Talmud explains that *charoset*—in many traditions made with apples—must be thick as a reminder of the clay from which the Israelites made bricks. But it must also be "tart to commemorate the apple trees" and the events that transpired beneath them.[2] For Akiva, women's unwillingness to forsake love and sensuality in the midst of degradation was the critical ingredient that human beings contributed to their redemption from Egypt. Women brought life into a world where Pharaoh had decreed death. But as we'll see, even this hardly gives full credence to the many roles women played in the Exodus.

In this chapter, we'll explore the contributions of women to the Exodus through readings and rituals you can include in your Seder.

Before you begin your Seder, ask your guests to try to list the names of as many of the biblical and rabbinic figures mentioned in the Haggadah as they can. A reference of any significance in any part of the Haggadah counts. But we're not counting God. What do you notice about this list? Unless your group is unusual, you probably won't get them all. The traditional Ashkenazic Haggadah includes more than twenty such figures. When you begin your Seder, ask your guests to let you know whenever a name appears. With a little imagination, you can easily make this into a game.

PASSOVER IN AN UPSIDE-DOWN WORLD

Read the following passage aloud during your Seder.

In these trying times, what can we learn from the story of the Exodus about how to repair our world? According to the Passover Haggadah, God is the main character in the drama of the Exodus. Seemingly alone, God's strong arm and outstretched hand bring us from sorrow to joy.

This message does not help at a time when the world so desperately needs fixing. It leads both to passivity and alienation as a result of God's seeming absence precisely when evil struts so brazenly about.

Alas, while the Haggadah provides a deep reservoir of hope, it may not be the best guide to fixing the world. Today, we also need a powerful reminder that righting our upside-down world depends on *human* action.

We don't have to look far for this lesson. The beginning of the Book of Exodus contains the inspiring, but often overlooked, story of five women whose actions ultimately play a decisive role in the Exodus. Pharaoh has turned the Israelites' world upside down. He decrees that birth shall not mean life, but death. Pharaoh speaks to Shiphrah and Puah, two midwives of the Hebrews, and orders them to kill all newborn Hebrew males. "The midwives, fearing God, did not do as the king had told them; they let the boys live" (Ex. 1:17). Yocheved, Moses' mother, hides the baby for three months as Egyptians scour the country for newborn Hebrew boys to drown. Unable to hide her son any longer, Yocheved cooks up a risky plan. She builds a miniature ark to float the baby to safety. Pharaoh's daughter brashly defies her father's call for the murder of Hebrew male infants. Hearing Moses' cry from the basket along the banks of the Nile, "She took pity on it and said, 'This must be a Hebrew child'" (Ex. 2:6). Miriam, Moses' sister, the spy in the tale, then steps in and arranges for Moses' mother to nurse him. Raised in Pharaoh's palace, Moses grows up as both an insider and an outsider—the essential experience for a leader who must shepherd his people from one world to another, from slavery to freedom.

The heroic deeds of these five women should speak volumes to us about what it takes to fix our world. They display the courage for decisive action, but they act in concert with others. They take risks because they know there are never guarantees. They don't wait for signs and miracles. They also demonstrate the capacity for maintaining concern about the welfare of others in circumstances when it might seem smarter to save your own skin.

Through these women's actions, Moses becomes the leader God chooses to confront Pharaoh. The rest, so to speak, is history. God plays a role in the story, but only well after human beings have acted decisively to transform their world.[3]

WOMEN AND THE HAGGADAH: MISSING IN ACTION

Depending on your group, read this on your own or aloud.

Over the past generation, we've seen many additions to the Seder highlighting the role of women, particularly Miriam, in the story of the Exodus. Some have opposed this development on the grounds that it violates a central theme of the Haggadah: God's exclusive responsibility for the Exodus from Egypt. That's why the Haggadah "stars" God, not Moses. Leaving aside the question of God's ultimate authorship of history, let's explore other reasons why it makes sense to weave female Jewish figures into the Seder's ritual.

First, the Haggadah tells us that "whoever elaborates on the story of the Exodus deserves praise." As a result, even the "traditional" Haggadah represents a liturgy that has evolved over more than a thousand years. The beloved Ashkenazic ritual of Elijah's Cup seems to have first appeared in Seders in the Middle Ages. If a cup for Elijah could be added to the Seder, why not one for Miriam?

The Haggadah's vision of history doesn't exclude human actors—only women. Although it certainly considers God the director of history, it also features a huge cast of exclusively male characters, with the single exception of Hadassah (Esther), who is mentioned in a song for the second Seder.[4] The cast includes ten rabbinic sages (not uncoincidentally the traditional number for a prayer *minyan*), Abraham, his brother Nahor, and their father Terah; Isaac, Jacob, his brother Esau, and their uncle, Laban; Aaron, Pharaoh, David, and his father Jesse; Elijah; Haman; Daniel; Moses; and a few more depending on which songs you include. (For more on Moses and the human role in redemption, see chapter 16.)

The Haggadah clearly envisions a place for human actors on the stage of Jewish history because, like the Bible, it understands that God acts through human beings—men *and* women. That's why there is no good theological reason why the Haggadah's human actors should exclude females. Rather, women's absence from the Haggadah reflects the particular cultural milieu of its compilers.

In recent times, scholars have studied the declining public role of women from the biblical era through the Second Temple era (538 B.C.E.–70 C.E.) and into rabbinic times. One view holds that in their earlier, more revolutionary days, the

Pharisees were more open to public roles for women. When they became the "rabbinic establishment," they adopted the more "misogynistic" views that they expressed in the Mishnah.[5] The absence of women in the Haggadah may also reflect the inexorable influence of the Hellenistic world in which women were clearly consigned to the private rather than the public domain.[6]

The Passover Seder serves as a perfect illustration of the profound Hellenistic influence on developing Jewish practice. The Seder was modeled after the Greek symposium, a banquet, to which a learned man would invite a few of his colleagues for a meal followed by a stylized intellectual discussion over successive glasses of wine. If women were present, they remained "socially invisible."[7]

The traditional Haggadah provides unhappy confirmation of Judith Plaskow's penetrating observation: "The need for a feminist Judaism begins with hearing silence. It begins with noting the absence of women's history and experiences as shaping forces in the Jewish tradition."[8] The Seder ought not perpetuate that silence.

THE WOMEN OF THE EXODUS IN MIDRASH

Although the Haggadah represents a wonderful specimen of rabbinic midrash, it overlooks the enormous role of women in the Exodus. Yet other midrashim hardly remain silent on this matter. Below you'll find a collection of biblical and midrashic texts recounting the early events of the Exodus story. Passages in italics indicate verses from the Bible. Selections from various midrashim and Talmudic *aggadah* (i.e., stories from the Talmud) have occasionally been reworked to make them more accessible.

Read the story below and discuss the questions that follow. You might consider using the story to supplement a portion of the Maggid section of the Haggadah.[9]

The midwives, fearing God, did not do as the king of Egypt had told them; they let the boys live . . . And God dealt well with the midwives; and the people multiplied and increased (Ex. 1:17 and 20). The midwives modeled their conduct after Abraham, of whom God said, *"For now I know that you fear God"* (Gen. 22:12). They said: "Abraham, our ancestor, peace be upon him, opened an inn where he fed travelers belonging to many different religions. As for us, not only have we nothing to feed the babies we deliver, but we have even been ordered to slay them! No, we will keep them alive." But the midwives went further than this. They performed deeds of kindness. When poor women came to them, the midwives would go to the houses of the rich to collect water and food and give them to the poor and thus keep alive their children.

Then Pharaoh charged all his people, saying, "Every boy that is born you shall throw into the Nile, but let every girl live" (Ex. 1:22). "Amram was the greatest man of his generation; when he saw that the wicked Pharaoh had decreed, *'Every boy that is born you shall throw into the Nile,'* he said: 'We labor in vain. Why should we continue to have children?' He arose and divorced his wife. So all [the Israelites] divorced their wives. His daughter, Miriam, said to him, 'Father, your decree is more severe than Pharaoh's. Pharaoh decreed only against the males whereas you have decreed against the males and females . . . In the case of the wicked Pharaoh there is a doubt whether his decree will be fulfilled or not, but in your case, you are righteous. It is certain that your decree will be fulfilled . . .' He arose and took his wife back; and they all took their wives back."

Yocheved became pregnant. Miriam, the prophetess, said, "My mother will bear a son who will be the savior of Israel." When Moses was born, the whole house was filled with light. Her father arose and kissed her upon her head, saying, "My daughter, your prophecy has been fulfilled."

[Yocheved, Moses' mother,] *hid him for three months. When she could hide him no longer, she got a wicker basket for him and caulked it with bitumen and pitch. She put the child into it and placed it among the reeds by the bank of the Nile* (Ex. 2:2–4). When they cast Moses into the river, Miriam's father arose and smacked her on the head, saying: "Where is your prophecy now?" . . . But she still believed her prophecy. And that is why we read *"And his sister stationed herself at a distance, to learn what would befall Moses"* (Ex. 2:4).

The daughter of Pharaoh came down to bathe in the Nile, while her maidens walked along the Nile. She spied the basket among the reeds and sent her slave girl to fetch it. When she opened it, she saw that it was a child, a boy crying. She took pity on it and said, "This must be a Hebrew child." . . . She named him Moses, explaining, "I drew him out of the water" (Ex. 2:5–10).

Why did Pharaoh's daughter, known in the midrash as Bitya, go down to the Nile? The midrash says it was to cleanse herself of her father's idols. "When [the maidens] saw that she wished to rescue Moses, they said to her, 'Mistress, it is the custom of the world that when a human king makes a decree, though everybody else does not obey it, at least his children and the members of his household obey it; but you transgress your father's decree!' The angel Gabriel came and beat them to the ground."

Pharaoh's daughter called him Moses, because she had "drawn" him out of the water, and because he would "draw" the children of Israel out of the land of Egypt in a day to come. From this you can learn how great the reward is for those who perform kind acts. Although Moses had many names, the name by which he is known throughout the Torah is the one that Bitya, the daughter of Pharaoh, called him, and even God called him by no other name.

God said to Bitya, the daughter of Pharaoh: "Moses was not your son, yet you called him your son. You, too, are not My daughter, yet I will call you My daughter, Bat-Ya, the daughter of God."

Bitya enjoyed an unusual life. Because of her special relationship with Moses, she was the only firstborn Egyptian that God spared during the last terrible plague. Bitya left Egypt with the Israelites and later married Caleb, an Israelite. Along with Joshua, Caleb was one of the two spies who gave truthful reports about what he saw in the Land of Israel.

Why, of all people, did Bitya marry Caleb? Because they were both rebels: He rebelled against the counsel of the spies and she rebelled against her father's decree to kill newborn Israelite boys. Some say that they were well suited because Caleb helped prevent Israel, the sheep, from wandering back to Egypt and Bitya helped deliver Moses, their shepherd.

According to legend, Bitya never died. She joined a small and celebrated group who ascended to heaven while still alive.

- What do you make of the fact that the Bible identifies the midwives by name, but not Pharaoh?

- The Bible is ambiguous about whether the midwives are actually Hebrew or not. Pharaoh addresses *"la-meyaldot ha-ivriyot,"* a phrase that can imply either the "Hebrew midwives" or the "midwives of the Hebrews." The midrash resolves this ambiguity in identifying the midwives as Yocheved and Miriam. What difference does it make if the midwives are Egyptian or Israelite?

• Suzanne Scholz, a feminist Bible scholar, offers the following assessment of the roles occupied by the women of the Exodus. Do you agree with this critique?

"Many feminists have cherished [Exodus] 1:22–2:10 as a prototype story because it teaches women to live in solidarity with each other. Overcoming ethnic, religious, and social differences, mother, sister and pharaoh's daughter care for the infant who eventually escapes the cruel order of the king. However, the characterization of these women as heroines is problematic. The women stay within traditional gender boundaries that are never challenged or subverted by the narrative."[10]

• In these midrashim, women accomplish their aims without force. In contrast, Amram hits his daughter and Gabriel strikes down Pharaoh's handmaidens. What might these stories be suggesting about a male and female approach to bringing about redemption? Remember, of course, that Moses' first act involves striking and killing an Egyptian taskmaster and that God accomplishes the redemption through ten blows against the Egyptians. The Bible certainly does not describe women as universally nonviolent. Witness Yael's killing of the enemy general Sisera (Judges 4:21) or Jezebel's slaying of God's prophets (I Kings 18:13). Might the Bible be offering the women of the Exodus as a model of nonviolence, albeit one that neither men nor women always manage to follow?

EDEN AND EGYPT: TWO TALES OF EXODUS

Read this on your own or aloud at your Seder.

You'll understand the role that women play in the Exodus better—and the story of the Exodus itself—if you take a look back at the beginning of the Book of Genesis.

Just as children must outgrow childhood, Eve understood that human destiny could not be fulfilled in Eden, a comfortable, but limiting, garden. Nachmanides (1195–1270), the great Spanish Bible commentator, offers an astounding interpretation of life in Eden, comparing human behavior to the predetermined motion of the moon:

> Man's original nature was that he did whatever was proper for him to do naturally, just as the heavens and all their hosts do, "faithful workers whose work is truth, and who do not change from their prescribed course" [a phrase from the Talmud's blessing for the new moon] and in whose deeds there is no love or hatred . . . But after he ate of the tree of knowledge, he possessed the power of choice; he could now do evil or good to himself or to others.
>
> —NACHMANIDES' COMMENTARY ON GENESIS 2:9[11]

Without knowledge of good and evil, precisely what God denied Adam and Eve, humanity's moral development would have been stillborn. As Buber wrote, "The curse [of expulsion] conceals a blessing."[12] So Eve, *Chavah* ("mother of all the living," according to Genesis 3:20), defied the masculine God's decree, and in humanity's first test of free will, she ate from the tree of knowledge of good and evil. God sent Adam and Eve out to begin their journey.

As the Book of Exodus begins, women receive another decree from a different male authority figure. Armed with the knowledge of good and evil, they defy Pharaoh. Eventually, he too sends the people out.

Eden and Egypt (*Mitzrayim*) both ultimately represent narrow places (*maytzarim*). The Bible points to a connection between the two. When Abraham's nephew, Lot, surveys the land, he looks over a well-watered plain "like the garden of Adonai [i.e., Eden], like the land of Egypt" (Gen. 13:10). The midrash explains that as a reward for Egypt's honorable treatment of Joseph and Jacob, God said, "I will call [Egypt] by the name of the Garden of Eden." God knows that just as humanity had to leave the Garden, so Israel must eventually leave Egypt.[13]

Although not often reflected in translation, the operative verbs describing the departures from Eden and Egypt are the same. Everett Fox's translation captures the similarity. "So YHWH, God, sent (*vayeshalcheihu*) him away from the Garden of Eden . . . He drove (*vayegaresh*) the human out . . ." (Gen. 3:23–24). "YHWH said to Moshe: I will cause one more blow to come upon Pharaoh . . . When he sends (*k'sholcho*) you free, it is finished—he will drive, yes drive (*yigaresh*) you out from here" (Ex. 11:1). What awaits humanity upon leaving Eden is "to work (*la'avod*) the soil" (Gen. 3:23). What awaits Israel after the Exodus is "to serve (*la'avod*) YHWH our God" (Ex. 10:26).[14]

Eden and Egypt: each an Exodus. To fulfill its destiny, humanity must leave the first. Israel's destiny requires going forth from the second. That women should be central in pushing humanity and then Israel through those narrows should come as no great shock. It's what giving birth is all about.[15]

SERAKH BAT ASHER AND THE EXODUS

Read the following story about the amazing Serakh and discuss the questions that follow. Consider substituting this for a portion of the Maggid section of the Haggadah.

A word of background: The Bible includes three genealogies listing Serakh, the adopted daughter of Asher, the eighth son of Jacob. Genesis 46:17 mentions her among those who went down into Egypt. Numbers 26:46 counts her among those who departed. I Chronicles 7:30 enumerates her as one of Jacob's descendants. In all three cases she is the only granddaughter of Jacob mentioned. That she is listed among those who went into Egypt and those who left, a period of several hundred years, suggests unusual longevity. (Moses lived to 120.) Other than her tantalizing presence in these genealogies, Serakh is nowhere else mentioned in the Bible. Midrash filled the void, and then some.[16]

In the Bible, Shiphrah and Puah, two midwives, refused to obey Pharaoh's command to kill all the Israelite boys they delivered. Yocheved, Moses' mother, saved her son by floating him down the Nile River in a basket. Miriam watched out for her brother as he drifted to the spot where Pharaoh's daughter, Bitya, bathed. Bitya took pity on the baby and pulled him from the water. Miriam offered to find a Hebrew nurse for Moses—his mother. As a result of her goodness, Bitya was the only Egyptian who did not suffer from the plagues. According to legend, she never died, but was taken up to heaven while she was still alive.

(The same happened to Elijah the Prophet, for whom we will open our doors near the end of the Seder.)

But there is one story that may top even these, the legend of Serakh bat Asher.

Joseph's brothers were jealous because their father, Jacob, favored him. They hated Joseph and decided to throw him into a pit in the desert to die. They told their father that a wild beast had killed Joseph, and Jacob never stopped mourning for his lost son.

But Joseph survived. Traders pulled Joseph from the pit and sold him. He became a slave in Egypt. Many years later, when his brothers went down to Egypt to buy food during a famine, they discovered that Joseph had risen to become Pharaoh's top advisor. When Jacob's sons returned from Egypt to tell their father the good news about Joseph, they were afraid that the depressed and fragile old man would die from shock. Rather than tell him directly, they found Serakh, who was wise and skilled at playing the harp, and she played a song for Jacob over and over again with these words: "Joseph is in Egypt. There have been born on his knees Menashe and Ephraim." (In Hebrew the phrases rhyme: *Yosef b'Mitzrayim/yuldo lo al birkayim/Menashe v'Ephrayim*.) Gradually the words began to penetrate, and Jacob's heart filled with joy. "My daughter," he said to Serakh, "May death never have power over you, for you revived my spirit." As a result of Jacob's wish, Serakh lived a long life and instead of dying she became one of the few people taken up to heaven while she was still alive. Because she never really died, Serakh returned over the ages to help her people at critical moments when they needed her.

Serakh went down to Egypt with Jacob's family. Eventually, a new Pharaoh arose who did not know Joseph. He enslaved the Israelites. Hundreds of years later, Moses came to liberate them, but the Israelites did not believe that God had really chosen him to lead them out of Egypt. At the burning bush, God told Moses what to tell the Israelites in order to convince them. God said to tell them, "I have surely remembered you, *pakod pakadti*. . . ." The people heard these words and saw the special signs God had given Moses. But they still refused to believe him. Only Serakh could convince the Israelites that Moses was indeed God's chosen leader.

Long before, God had told Jacob that when the redeemer of Israel came to Egypt he would utter special words. Jacob handed down this secret to Joseph, who later told his brothers. Asher, one of Joseph's older brothers, handed down the secret to his daughter Serakh. When Moses called on the people to leave Egypt, Serakh was the only person still alive who had heard the secret words. Serakh recognized them. *Pakod pakadti,* "I have surely remembered. . . ." She told the Israelites that Moses had truly been sent by God.

Finally, when the Israelites were about to leave Egypt, Moses realized that they could not depart until they honored a request that Joseph had made generations earlier, just before he died. Joseph made the children of Israel promise to take his bones with them when they left Egypt for the land God had sworn to Abraham, Isaac, and Jacob. He wanted to be buried in Israel.

But only Serakh remembered where Joseph had been laid to rest in Egypt. She told Moses, "The Egyptians made a metal coffin for [Joseph] which they put in the river Nile so that its waters would be blessed." Moses went and stood on the bank of the Nile and cried, "Joseph, Joseph! The time of God's promise to redeem you has arrived. If you appear we'll take you with us. If you don't, we are free of our promise to you." Joseph's coffin immediately floated to the surface of the Nile.

Serakh's people needed her again, many years later, during the reign of King David. An evil man tried to start a rebellion against the king. David's general rushed off to destroy the entire city where the man lived. He had already begun to batter down the walls when he heard a woman shouting to him. "Listen! Listen," she cried, "there's another way." Serakh persuaded him to wait and then convinced the townspeople to turn over the evil fellow. The city was saved. Serakh taught everyone an important lesson. "Wisdom is more valuable than weapons of war" (Eccl. 9:18).[17]

More than a thousand years later, in the first century C.E., Yochanan ben Zakkai, one of the most famous rabbis of the time, was teaching his students about the Israelites crossing the Red Sea. "When the sea parted," he said, "the wall of water was like a lattice." A woman in the back of the class disagreed. "I was there and it was only like a window opened for illumination." It was Serakh.

Tonight, we remember Serakh. Without her help, we might still be in Egypt!

- How would you compare the roles of the women of the Exodus in the beginning of the story (Shiphrah and Puah, the two midwives;

Miriam, Moses' sister; Yocheved, his mother; and Bitya, Pharaoh's daughter) with those played by Serakh?

- Why was it so important to take Joseph's bones out of Egypt? What does the story about Joseph and Serakh have to tell us about the importance of memory?

- Serakh taught her people that "wisdom is more valuable than the weapons of war." What can we learn from that today?

- What meanings might there be in the difference between the way Rabbi Yochanan ben Zakkai and Serakh described what the Israelites saw when they crossed the Red Sea: a lattice as opposed to a window opened for illumination?

THE LEGEND OF MIRIAM'S WELL

Here we explore the legend of Miriam's Well and her complex relationship with Moses, her brother. You may want to read this yourself or read it aloud during your Seder in connection with Miriam's Cup. Questions for discussion follow.

The legend of Miriam's Well developed from the juxtaposition of two biblical verses. The first mentions Miriam's death; the next, a sudden absence of water, a problem that had not occurred since the Israelites' early days in the desert. "The Israelites arrived in a body at the wilderness of Zin on the first new moon [of the fortieth year] and the people stayed at Kadesh. Miriam died there and was buried there. The community was without water . . ." (Num. 20:1–2).

Phyllis Trible offers a moving interpretation of this passage. "Nature's response to Miriam's death is immediate and severe. It mourns, and the community suffers. Miriam, protector of her brother at the river's bank and leader in the victory at the sea, symbolized life. How appropriate, then, that waters of life should reverence her death."[18]

The midrash describes the well as a "rock, shaped like a kind of beehive, and wherever they journeyed it rolled along and came with them. When the standards [under which the tribes journeyed] halted and the tabernacle was set up, that same rock would come and settle down in the court of the Tent of Meeting and the princes would come and stand upon it and say, 'Spring up, O well' (Num. 21:17), and it would rise" (Numbers Rabbah 1:2). Another midrash holds that from the well came "most of the Israelites' enjoyments . . . The well used to produce for them various kinds of herbs, vegetables, and trees. The proof of this is that when Miriam died and the well ceased to give its waters to them they said, 'Why did you make us leave Egypt to bring us to this wretched place, a place with no grain or figs or vines or pomegranates? There is not even water to drink!'" (Num. 20:5; Song of Songs Rabbah 4:27).

The imagery of water is also crucial in the complex relationship between Miriam and Moses, binding them together throughout their lives. Miriam's name may mean "bitter sea" (*mar*: bitter, and *yam*: sea). The midrash attributes the link with bitterness to the fact that her birth occurred when Pharaoh's oppression of the Israelites began.

Later, Miriam watched over her infant brother as he floated down the Nile in a basket. When Pharaoh's daughter took him from the river, she named him Moshe, meaning, "I drew him from the water." After crossing the Red Sea, Moses led the people in song. When his song was finished, "Then Miriam the prophetess, Aaron's sister, took a timbrel in her hand, and all the women went out after her in dance with timbrels" (Ex. 15:20). Two years later, "Miriam and Aaron spoke against Moses because of the Cushite [Ethiopian] woman he had married . . . They said, 'Has Adonai spoken [prophesied] only through Moses? Has he not spoken through us as well?' Adonai heard it" (Num. 12:1–2).

As punishment for their challenge to Moses, God afflicted Miriam—only Miriam—with leprosy. Moses successfully prayed for her healing. Miriam is not mentioned again until her death, thirty-eight years later, not long before the Israelites entered the Promised Land. Just after Moses lost his sister, a figure so deeply linked with water and all it represented, he lost his temper when God told him to "order the rock to yield its water. Thus you shall produce water for them from the rock . . ." (Num. 20:8). Instead, Moses angrily struck the miraculous, water-bearing rock (a rock that is reminiscent of the above description of Miriam's Well itself). After that lapse, God barred Moses from entering the Promised Land.

- For Moses, Miriam represented both protection and nurturing despite her one-time challenge to his authority. To what extent do you think Moses' wrath toward the water-giving rock may have expressed his anger and anxiety over the loss of his older sister?

- If the complexities of his relationship with Miriam ultimately prevented Moses from entering the Promised Land, what may the Bible be suggesting about family relationships?

THE RITUAL OF MIRIAM'S CUP

The ritual of Miriam's Cup that has developed over the past thirty or so years represents a wonderful example of the Seder's continuing evolution. It evokes not only Miriam's critical role in the story of the Exodus but also that of the Israelite women in general. As Rabbi Akiva taught, "The Israelites were delivered from Egypt as a reward for the righteous women who lived in that generation."

When you set the table, place a large, empty glass goblet or wine glass beside the Cup of Elijah. This will serve as Miriam's Cup. After reciting the blessing for candlelighting, read the following paragraphs aloud. If everyone has a copy of this material, follow the directions as to who reads what. If not, pass the book around and ask several guests to read a few paragraphs each. Tell your guests that you will be returning to Miriam's Cup toward the conclusion of the Seder.

The following excerpt from *The 1997 Ma'yan Passover Haggadah: The Journey Continues* can be used at your Seder to help integrate the women of the Exodus into your celebration.

All: Miriam's Cup. Legend tells of a mysterious well filled with *mayim chayim,* living waters that followed the Israelites though their wandering in the desert while Miriam was alive.

Reader: Miriam's Well was said to hold divine power to heal and renew. Its fresh waters sustained our people as we were transformed from a generation shaped by slavery into a free nation. Throughout our subsequent journeys, we have sought to rediscover these living waters.

[When the Seder falls on a Saturday night, add the following: In the sixteenth century, this is what Moses Isserles, one of the greatest rabbis of his era, said about Miriam's Well: "Some make it a practice to draw fresh water after the Sabbath. They say that every Saturday night Miriam's Well encircles all the wells of the world and those who are ill and drink of these waters will be healed."[19]]

All: Tonight at our Seder, let us remember that we are still on the journey. Just as the Holy One delivered Miriam and her people, just as they were sustained in the desert and transformed into a new people, so may we be delivered, sustained and transformed on our journey to a stronger sense of ourselves, both as individuals and as one people. May the Cup of Miriam refresh and inspire us as we embark on our journey through the Haggadah.

Miriam's Cup is now filled. Each individual pours water from her or his own water glass into Miriam's Cup. Return Miriam's Cup beside the Cup of Elijah. You will drink from it later.

זֹאת כּוֹס מִרְיָם, כּוֹס מַיִם חַיִּים.
זֵכֶר לִיצִיאַת מִצְרָיִם.

All: Zot Kos Miryam, kos mayim chayim. Zeicher l'ytzi-at Mitzrayim.

Reader: This is the Cup of Miriam, the cup of living waters. Let us remember the Exodus from Egypt. These are the living waters, God's gift to Miriam, which gave new life to Israel as we struggled in the wilderness.

All: Blessed are You, God, Who brings us from the narrows into the wilderness, sustains us with endless possibilities, and enables us to reach a new place.

When it is time to open the door for Elijah the Prophet,
return to this section and continue reading.

Reader: At this point in the Seder, Jewish communities, beset by persecution during the Crusades, opened their doors and recited the angry plea, *"Sh'fokh chamat'kha . . ."* ("Pour out Your wrath upon the nations who do not know You").

All: In other communities during the same period, the hope for redemption was so intense that they sang to invoke the Prophet Elijah, who, according to legend, would herald an era of messianic peace, justice, and healing.

Reader: We open our doors now with the need to act on both impulses. The crimes of humanity that we continue to see—the rape and torture of innocents, ethnic cleansing, the destruction of entire cities and cultures—cry out for just retribution beyond our limited capacity. And our longing for peace, for healing of earth, body, and spirit, still brings the hope-drenched melody of *"Eliyahu Hanavi"* to our lips.

All: Elijah the Prophet, come to us soon, for you herald messianic days. Miriam the Prophet, strength and song are in her hand. Miriam will dance with us to strengthen the world's song. Miriam will dance with us to heal the world. Soon, and in our time, she will lead us to the waters of salvation.

All sing the familiar tune of *"Eliyahu Hanavi,"* adding the verses about Miriam.

אֵלִיָּהוּ הַנָּבִיא, אֵלִיָּהוּ הַתִּשְׁבִּי, אֵלִיָּהוּ הַגִּלְעָדִי

בִּמְהֵרָה בְיָמֵינוּ, יָבוֹא אֵלֵינוּ עִם מָשִׁיחַ בֶּן דָּוִד.

מִרְיָם הַנְּבִיאָה, עֹז וְזִמְרָה בְּיָדָהּ.

מִרְיָם תִּרְקוֹד אִתָּנוּ, לְהַגְדִּיל זִמְרַת עוֹלָם.

מִרְיָם תִּרְקוֹד אִתָּנוּ, לְתַקֵּן אֶת הָעוֹלָם.

בִּמְהֵרָה בְיָמֵנוּ הִיא תְּבִיאֵנוּ,

אֶל מֵי הַיְשׁוּעָה, אֶל מֵי הַיְשׁוּעָה.

Eliyahu ha-navi, Eliyahu ha-tishbi,
Eliyahu ha-giladi.
Bimheirah v'yameinu, yavo eileinu,
im Mashiach ben David.
Miryam ha-nevi'ah, oz v'zimrah b'yadah.
Miryam tirkod itanu,
l'hagdil zimrat olam.
Miryam tirkod itanu, l'takein et ha-olam.

193

Bimheirah v'yameinu, hi t'vi-einu.
El mei ha-yeshu'ah, el mei ha-yeshu'ah.[20]

Now each person takes a sip from the Cup of Miriam and all continue with the Seder.

REDEEMED THROUGH BLOOD AND WATER: BALANCING ELIJAH'S CUP WITH MIRIAM'S CUP

Here we explore water and blood as mediums for redemption. You can read this yourself or read it aloud during your Seder in connection with Miriam's Cup.
Questions for discussion follow.

According to the Mishnah (Avot 5:8), Miriam's well was one of ten things God
fashioned on the eve of the Sabbath just before completing the work of creation.
Deuteronomy Rabbah (3:8), a collection of midrashim compiled between 450 and
800 C.E., recounts six miraculous instances in the story of the Exodus when salvation came through water. Each comes with its own biblical "prooftext."

> The Rabbis say: Come and see how all the miracles that God wrought
> for Israel He wrought only through water. How? While they were still
> in Egypt, He wrought miracles for them through the river. Rabbi Isaac
> said: The Egyptians and the Israelites went to drink from the river; the
> Egyptians drank blood, but the Israelites drank water. And when Israel
> came out of Egypt He wrought miracles for them only through water.
> How so? For it is said, "The sea saw it, and fled" (Psalms 114:3). What
> did it see? Rabbi Nehorai said: It saw the name of God engraved upon
> [Moses'] staff and it parted . . . After the Israelites crossed through the
> Red Sea they arrived at Marah where the waters were bitter, and He
> wrought for them miracles. How so? For it is said, [Moses threw a
> branch] "into the water and the water became sweet" (Ex. 15:25). At the
> Rock he wrought miracles for them through water. How so? For it is
> said, "Order the rock to yield its water. Thus you shall produce water for
> them from the rock . . ." (Num. 20:8). At the well He wrought miracles
> for them and they sang a song, as it is said, "Then Israel sang this song"

194

(Num. 21:17). Moses said to Israel: "Know that all the miracles which God wrought for you, He wrought only through water. And also when you pass over the Jordan to take possession of the land God will also work miracles for you through the waters of the Jordan."

Beyond honoring the role of women in the Exodus, Miriam's Cup restores to the Seder an element of the Jewish tradition's appreciation of water as a symbolic source of salvation, as the above midrash amply demonstrates. By contrast, the Haggadah gives that role to blood alone. After the ninth plague, the Israelites received two essential commandments, both involving blood. The Passover sacrifice should forever commemorate that God saw the blood of the lamb smeared on the Israelites' doorposts, passed over their homes, and spared their firstborn. And for men, in ancient times, eating the paschal offering would require circumcision, a covenant, as it were, of blood.

A common addition to many Sephardic and Ashkenazic Haggadot evokes these commandments in a quotation from Ezekiel 16:6, a passage that also figures prominently in the ritual of circumcision: "Then I passed you and saw you wallowing in your blood [literally, 'bloods'] I said to you, 'In your [two] bloods you shall live'; and I said to you, 'In your [two] bloods shall you live.'"[21] The Seder's invocation of Elijah the Prophet further reinforces the theme of redemption through blood. Elijah not only heralds the Messiah, but, according to tradition, he also witnesses every circumcision!

Against this backdrop, the water of Miriam's Cup adds an important balance to the wine/blood of Elijah's. The Jewish ritual for conversion reflects a similar balance: immersion in "living waters" for both men and women, and circumcision for men.[22]

- What do you think blood and water might symbolize?

- How do you feel about adding Miriam's Cup to the Seder ritual?

- Women have gradually found their voice in Western society. What are other groups that remain silenced?

15

The Ten Plagues: Who Suffered and Why?

אֵלוּ עֶשֶׂר מַכּוֹת שֶׁהֵבִיא הַקָּדוֹשׁ בָּרוּךְ הוּא
עַל־הַמִּצְרִים בְּמִצְרַיִם, וְאֵלוּ הֵן:
דָּם. צְפַרְדֵּעַ. כִּנִּים. עָרוֹב. דֶּבֶר. שְׁחִין.
בָּרָד. אַרְבֶּה. חֹשֶׁךְ. מַכַּת בְּכוֹרוֹת:

These are the ten plagues which the Holy One, blessed be He,
brought upon the Egyptians: blood, frogs, lice, insects, cattle blight, boils,
hail, locusts, darkness, the slaying of the firstborn.
—THE PASSOVER HAGGADAH

Near the conclusion of the Haggadah's lengthy account of the Israelites' suffering in Egypt, we arrive at the point in the Seder when we recount the ten plagues.[1] We do so briefly, first reciting "blood and fire and pillars of smoke," a passage from the prophet Joel (3:3), then naming each plague, and concluding with Rabbi Yehuda's ten-letter acronym, *"Detzakh, Adash, B'achav."*[2] With each word, we spill a drop of wine from our cups. Traditional texts of the Haggadah follow this with a much longer elaboration of the number of plagues the Egyptians suffered in Egypt and at the Red Sea. Of note, this extended midrashic treatment of the plagues includes different methods of enumerating the plagues, but it does not actually mention what a single one of these plagues involved. And many modern Haggadot omit this elaboration entirely.

What's interesting about this is that in the Book of Exodus, the plague narrative occupies the bulk of the story, extending through more than five chapters, while details of the Israelites' suffering in Egypt involves relatively few verses. The Haggadah reverses this, expounding on suffering and skimming over the plagues. Why? Because the Haggadah's purpose is to renew our faith in redemption, not to whet our appetite for our enemy's defeat. But as we'll see, the plagues raise a number of uncomfortable issues, of which the compilers of the Haggadah were doubtless aware. The tendency to consign the ten plagues to a supporting rather than starring role in the Haggadah may reflect those discomforts as well.

- If you had the same amount of power that God displayed through the plagues, how might you have tried to bring about the Exodus?

- Why did God's plan to redeem the Israelites require such a lengthy series of plagues? And why these kinds of plagues?

- Toward the end of the Book of Deuteronomy (28:49), Moses tells the people of Israel that if they defy God's will, "Adonai will bring a nation against you from afar, from the end of the earth, which will swoop down like the eagle" to punish the wayward Israelites. Why didn't God do the same with the Egyptians?

- Whom do the plagues seek to influence and to what end?

PLAGUES AGAINST THE ISRAELITES?

Read the following paragraphs and discuss the question on the next page.

A plain reading of the Bible suggests something surprising: that the Israelites themselves suffered through the first three plagues—blood, frogs, and lice. God expressly spares the Israelites and afflicts the Egyptians in five of the remaining plagues—insects (4), cattle blight (5), hail (7), darkness (9), and slaying of the firstborn (10).

While less clear-cut, the language of the sixth (boils) and eighth (locusts) plagues also can be taken to mean that only the Egyptians were targeted.

Two great medieval Spanish commentators differed on whether the first three plagues struck the Egyptians alone.

Ibn Ezra (1089–1164) argues that the first three plagues struck both the Israelites and the Egyptians. "Many say that the water near the Egyptians turned red like blood, but in the hands of the Israelites it became clear. If so, why wasn't this sign (*ot*) written in the Torah? And according to my opinion, the plagues of blood, frogs and lice included the Egyptians and the Hebrews, because we must follow what is written in the Torah. These three plagues did but little damage. Only starting with the plague of insects, which was severe, did God distinguish between the Egyptians and Israel."[3]

Nachmanides (1195–1270) asserts that none of the plagues fell upon the Israelites. "Due to the fact that the first [three] plagues were not migratory in nature, [there was no need for the Bible to mention that] that they were confined to the land of Egypt and were not to be in the land of Goshen [Israel's habitation]. But this [the fourth plague, swarms of insects] was a migratory plague . . . Therefore it was necessary for God to say, 'I will set apart the region of Goshen.'"[4]

- What difference does it make in your understanding of the story if the Israelites were completely spared the plagues or suffered the first three? Why do you think God may have visited the first three plagues on the Israelites as well as the Egyptians? Or, alternatively, why would one want to argue that Israel escaped all the plagues?

WHY SPILL WINE FROM OUR CUPS?

Read aloud and discuss the following section.

Traditional Haggadot prescribe spilling a total of sixteen drops of wine from our cups: one for each of the three wonders mentioned by the prophet Joel (3:3), "blood and fire and pillars of smoke"; one for each of the ten plagues; and one for each of the three terms of Rabbi Yehuda's acronym—*Detzakh, Adash, B'achav.* Why sixteen drops? Some say because there are sixteen individuals called to the Torah each week and the Torah is a "tree of life" (*etz chayim hi*). The numerical value for the last word in this expression (in Hebrew spelled *hey, yod, alef*) is sixteen.[5]

But why spill any wine from our cups in connection with the plagues? Following are two explanations. Discuss which explanation you prefer and why.

> It is as if to say we were saved from all this [i.e., the plagues]. And it will be brought upon those who hate us. These very cups [now symbolically purged of ill fortune] represent the success of Israel.
>
> —JACOB BEN MOSES MOELLIN (CIRCA 1360–1427), GERMANY[6]

> A drop of wine is spilled from each cup at the mention of each plague to indicate that the joy of our redemption is not complete. Even though the plagues were deserved, our redemption was brought about through the suffering meted out to the Egyptians. "When your enemy falls, do not exult" (Proverbs 24:17).
>
> —WIDELY (BUT QUESTIONABLY) ATTRIBUTED TO ISAAC ABARBANEL (1437–1508), SPAIN[7]

WHEN OUR ENEMIES FALL

Read the following section aloud or on your own.

The aversion to celebrating the suffering of our enemies is hardly new to Jewish ethical sensibilities.

The Talmud (Megillah 10b) asks, "What is the meaning of the verse, 'And one came not near the other all the night?' (Ex. 14:20). The ministering angels wanted to chant their hymns, but the Holy One, blessed be He, said, 'The work of my hands is being drowned in the sea, and you are chanting hymns?'"

An eleventh-century midrash elaborates, imagining a dialogue between God and various angels, including Uzza, the angel of the Egyptians. Uzza finally persuades God to deal "with [the Egyptians] according to Your attribute of mercy, and take pity upon the work of your hands . . . Adonai had almost yielded to Uzza's entreaties, when [the angel] Michael gave a sign to Gabriel that made him fly to Egypt swiftly and fetch thence a brick for which a Hebrew child had been used as mortar. Holding this incriminating object in his hand, Gabriel stepped into the presence of God, and said: 'O Master of the World! Will You have compassion upon the accursed nation that has slaughtered Your children cruelly?' Then Adonai turned Himself away from His attribute of mercy, and seating Himself upon His throne of justice He resolved to drown the Egyptians in the sea.''[8]

An early-fourteenth-century midrash, *Yalkut Shimoni,* observes that, with reference to Sukkot, the Bible instructs us to rejoice—in three passages. We find no such command with respect to Passover. Why does Scripture give not even one command to rejoice on Passover? "Because the Egyptians died during the Passover. Therefore you find that, though we read the entire Hallel on each of the seven days of Sukkot, on Passover we read the entire Hallel only on the first day and the night preceding it. Why not on the other days of the festival? 'If your enemy falls, do not exult; if he trips, let not your heart rejoice'" (Prov. 24:17).[9]

In the end, we must recognize that, as wonderful as it was, the redemption from Egypt was not, as it were, complete or ideal. To use Franz Rosenzweig's distinction, the Exodus may be better understood as a temporary deliverance rather than an ultimate redemption.[10] The human cost of our deliverance was enormous, and deliverance from Egypt did not inoculate the children of Israel from subsequent oppression. We can only pray that if an ultimate redemption awaits us, it will be brought about through peace, not suffering.

THE PLAGUES AND KNOWING GOD

Read aloud the passage below and discuss the questions that follow.

We can understand the story of the plagues from many points of view—as a punishment to Pharaoh and the Egyptians, as a demonstration of God's superiority over the gods of Egypt, or as a difficult but important opportunity for the Israelites and the Egyptians to come to know God in a new way. Here we'll concentrate on the last approach.[11]

Nehama Leibowitz (1905–1997), one of our generation's great Bible teachers, notes the significance of Pharaoh's opening response in what will prove a lengthy dialogue with Moses.[12]

> Afterward Moses and Aaron went and said to Pharaoh, "Thus says Adonai, God of Israel: Let my people go that they may celebrate a festival for Me in the wilderness." But Pharaoh said, "Who is Adonai that I should heed Him and let Israel go? I do not know Adonai, nor will I let Israel go."
>
> —EXODUS 5:1–2

Leibowitz notes that the theme of "knowing God" recurs ten times during the plague narrative and the events at the Red Sea. Consistent with her view, the Book of Exodus generally refers to the plagues as "signs" (*otot*) and "wonders" (*moftim*). Only three times does the narrative refer to these afflictions as a form of punishment or judgment (*sh'fatim*) against the Egyptians (Ex. 6:6, 7:4, and 12:12).

It's worth noting what the Bible seems to want the Israelites and the Egyptians to "know" about God.

After Moses and Aaron's first meeting with Pharaoh, the king orders the Israelites to gather their own straw to make bricks:

> [God instructs Moses to tell the Israelites] I am Adonai . . . I will redeem you with an outstretched arm and through extraordinary chastisements. And I will take you to be My people, and I will be your God. And you shall *know* that I, Adonai, am your God who freed you from the labors of the Egyptians.
>
> —EXODUS 6:6–7[13]

Before the first plague, God announces that "the Egyptians shall *know* that I am Adonai when I stretch My hand over Egypt and bring out the Israelites from their midst" (Ex. 7:5). After this simple statement, we find a gradual elaboration of what God wants the Egyptians to know: "that there is none like Adonai our God," "that I Adonai am in the midst of the land," "that there is none like Me in all the world," "that the earth is Adonai's."[14]

- Do you tend to think of the plagues more in terms of punishing the Egyptians or of teaching them something about God?

- If you think of the plagues as an educational strategy, is it successful? Who learns what?

SIGNS, WONDERS, AND FAITH:
OR DID THE PLAGUES FAIL?

Read the following section on your own or aloud,
perhaps as a conclusion to your discussion above.

And you [the Israelites] shall *know* that I, Adonai, am your God who freed you from the labors of the Egyptians . . . But when Moses told this to the Israelites, they would not listen to Moses, their spirits crushed by cruel bondage.

—EXODUS 6:7–9

Do the Israelites come to "know God" through the plagues? Before the cycle of signs and wonders, the Israelites seem a sullen bunch. Since Moses' first visit to Pharaoh, the Israelites' plight has only grown more desperate. The foremen of the Israelites angrily confront Moses. "May Adonai look upon you and punish you for making us loathsome to Pharaoh and his courtiers—putting a sword in their hands to slay us" (Ex. 5:21).

Throughout the plagues, the Israelites remain mute. They neither complain when the first three plagues strike them along with the Egyptians nor rejoice when the subsequent afflictions spare them. All we hear of them is that by the time the last blow falls upon the Egyptians they've begun to follow orders. Moses tells the Israelites how they should sacrifice the paschal offering: "The people then bowed low in homage. And the Israelites went and did so, just as Adonai had commanded Moses and Aaron, so they did" (Ex. 12:27–28).

Their faithful posture doesn't last long. With the Egyptians in hot pursuit, the Israelites speak at the Red Sea for the first time since the plagues began. "And they said to Moses, 'Was it for want of graves in Egypt that you brought us to die in the wilderness?'" (Ex. 14:11).

After the sea parts, the children of Israel seem to have changed their tune. They sing: "Adonai is my strength and might; He is become my deliverance" (Ex. 15:2). But how enduring is their faith now?

Soon enough—three days later—they are grumbling about a lack of water and whining about the food. Manna from heaven was not sufficient. Three months later they worshiped the Golden Calf. Despite the mighty signs and wonders they witnessed, the Israelites do not come to "know God" in a lasting way.

We can explain this in several ways. Perhaps their spirits had been destroyed to the point that "knowing God" in any enduring way was impossible. Or maybe awesome signs and wonders didn't make quite the impression that God imagined they would.

Sensational acts of this sort actually represent an innovation in God's modus operandi. Prior to the Exodus, God's communication with the characters of Genesis was far more intimate. Even Moses' encounter with the miraculous burning bush involved a comparatively "low-key" manifestation of divine power. Maybe God thought that a crowd demanded an earthshaking display. If so, it would seem that God miscalculated.

Or maybe God was really more interested in punishing the Egyptians and humiliating their gods than in using the plagues to teach anyone anything. Maybe the goal was simply to instill fear. Perhaps God equated fear with faith. Another miscalculation.

Strange as it sounds, the Bible is full of such divine "miscalculations." God "regrets" creating the world and destroys it in a flood. Having redeemed the Israelites from Egypt, God nearly destroys them when they worship the Golden Calf. God then turns to plan B—to establish a new covenant with Moses, a deal that Moses flatly refuses. And the idea of sending forth spies to reconnoiter the Promised Land also comes from God. It too backfires: "And Adonai said to Moses, 'How long will this people spurn Me, and how long will they have no faith in Me despite all the signs that I have performed in their midst?'" (Num. 14:11).

Here God painfully acknowledges the limits of trying to build a relationship based on signs and wonders. Eventually God will discover, as it were, that human faith arises not from impressing us with awesome gestures, but from touching us during quiet, intimate moments of openness. And even after countless fleeting glimpses and whispering intuitions—often overlooked, forgotten, or misunder-stood—the sense of God's presence consolidates only slowly.

Like the Israelites of the Exodus, how often do we find ourselves blind to the very insights that yesterday seemed so compelling? In the end, God discovers a cornerstone of rabbinic thought: "Everything is in the hand of heaven except the fear of heaven" (Babylonian Talmud, Berakhot 33b).[15]

MEASURE FOR MEASURE

Read aloud what follows and discuss the questions below.

Most of us probably think of the plagues as God's punishment of the Egyptians. Indeed, toward the beginning of the Haggadah (just before the section about the wandering Aramean) we read a passage from Genesis that raises this theme. God says to Abram (his name has not yet been changed to Abraham): "Know well that your offspring shall be strangers in a land not theirs, and they shall be enslaved and oppressed for four hundred years; but I will execute judgment on the nation they shall serve, and in the end they shall go out with great wealth" (Gen. 15:14).

Although the Book of Exodus does not stress this interpretation of the plagues, it refers to judgments (*sh'fatim*) against the Egyptians on three occasions, twice before the plagues begin and once in connection with the slaying of the firstborn. The midrash elaborates on the theme of punishment, measure for meas-ure, and attempts to link each blow against Egypt with a particular aspect of its oppression of the Israelites. The tenth-century midrash Exodus Rabbah (3:8) jus-tifies the drowning of Pharaoh and his armies at the Red Sea: "[God] would drown [the Egyptians] in the sea, to exact from them measure for measure, because the [Egyptians] had said: 'Every boy that is born you shall throw into the Nile . . . '" (Ex. 1:22).

The problem is that the Pharaoh who had ordered the drowning of all new-born Israelite males had long since died when the plagues begin to unfold. The Pharaoh of the plagues is not the Pharaoh whose orders nearly resulted in the murder of Moses in his infancy and of so many other Israelite male infants. Before Moses returns from Midian with God's charge to lead the Israelites out of Egypt, the Bible tells us that "the king of Egypt died" (Ex. 2:23).

The last plague, the slaying of the Egyptian firstborn, becomes even more morally dubious in light of the fact that it seems to have included the firstborn of Egyptians in prison. "In the middle of the night Adonai struck down all the firstborn in the land of Egypt, from the firstborn of Pharaoh who sat on the throne to the firstborn of the captive who was in the dungeon, and all the firstborn of the cattle" (Ex. 12:29).

Exodus Rabbah (18:10) offers the following explanation:

God made a day of rejoicing for Israel when He redeemed them and He proclaimed: "All who love My sons may come and rejoice with them." The virtuous among the Egyptians came, celebrated the Passover with Israel, and went up with them, for it says: "And a mixed multitude went up with them" (Ex. 12:38), but those who did not desire the redemption of the Israelites died with the firstborn. . . .

• This midrash illustrates a measure of moral discomfort with the plagues. Does this explanation satisfy you? Why or why not?

• One of the questions the plague narrative raises is whether the entire Egyptian population deserves the suffering that befalls it. Pharaoh makes all the decisions. But the entire Egyptian people, the land, the plants, and the animals all suffer as a result of a mighty king who refuses to accept limitations on his power. Are the Egyptian people also guilty? Should they be punished for the policies of their despotic ruler, a ruler whom they probably had little chance to influence or oppose? What contemporary issues does this story raise?

REVEALING THE CREATOR THROUGH ANTI-CREATION

Read this on your own.

If, through the plagues, God wished to become known to the Israelites, the Egyptians, and indeed the whole world, what were they to learn about God? God is all-powerful; even a casual reader of Exodus could not miss that. Some scholars believe that the story contains a related, but more pointed, lesson—that God is not only powerful but also the creator of all.

If you read the tale of the plagues carefully, you find a surprising number of allusions to the creation story. This makes sense, because Exodus marks the creation or birth of a people. It also makes sense because, as we've seen, the festival of Passover shares many attributes of other ancient Near Eastern spring New Year's celebrations, a major feature of which included recounting myths of the creation. Recitation of the myth brought renewal of the year and with it revival of nature and fertility. During their spring festival, the Israelites recounted the story of their creation as a people, while the fall festivals related the story of the world's creation.

In the ancient Near East, creation myths revolved around the transition from watery chaos to order. Kings were expected to perpetuate the fundamental order of creation. Whether the king violated or maintained the created order determined whether his land would be blessed with plenty or afflicted with famine, drought, disease, and so forth. In this view, "law, nature, and politics are only aspects of one comprehensive order of creation."[16] In Israelite culture, the ruler and populace shared the responsibilities of maintaining the rules of God's created order. But the consequences remained:

> Now if you obey Adonai your God, to observe faithfully all His commandments . . . Blessed shall be the issue of your womb, the produce of your soil, the offspring of your cattle, the calving of your herd and the lambing of your flock . . . Adonai will open for you His bounteous store, the heavens, to provide rain for your land in season and to bless all your undertakings . . . But if you do not obey Adonai your God to observe faithfully all His commandments and laws . . . Adonai will make the rain of your land dust, and sand shall drop on you from the sky . . . Adonai will inflict extraordinary plagues upon you and your offspring, strange and lasting plagues, malignant and chronic diseases. He will bring back up all the sickness of Egypt that you dreaded so . . . You shall be left a scant few, after having been as numerous as the stars in the skies, because you did not heed the command of Adonai your God.
>
> —DEUTERONOMY 28:1, 4, 12, 15, 24, 59–62

The Talmud (Shabbat 88a) made the point more succinctly: "The Holy One, blessed be He, stipulated with the works of creation and said to them, 'If Israel accepts the Torah, you shall exist; but if not, I will turn you back into *emptiness and formlessness*'" (Gen. 1:1).

Pharaoh's treatment of the Israelites flouted the very concept of God as the ultimate creator and ruler of all.

God promised Abraham that his descendants would be "as numerous as the stars of heaven and the sands on the seashore" (Gen. 22:17). That promise reached fulfillment in Egypt. "The Israelites were fertile and prolific; they multiplied and increased very greatly, so that the land was filled with them" (Ex. 1:7). God also promised that "all the families of the earth shall bless themselves by you" (Gen. 12:3). But instead of Pharaoh feeling blessed by Abraham's descendants, he feels cursed by them and seeks their destruction. God creates life, and Pharaoh destroys it. In response, God strikes back, selectively undoing the general order of the natural world. In Pharaoh's Egypt, nature loses one of its chief characteristics: predictability.[17]

The prophet Ezekiel (29:3) captures this aspect of the conflict between God and Pharaoh. "Thus said Adonai God: I am going to deal with you, O Pharaoh king of Egypt, mighty monster, sprawling in your channels, who said, 'My Nile is my own: I made if for myself.'" (This reading from Ezekiel serves as the haftarah for the portion in Exodus that describes the plagues.)

The general theme of "de-creation" becomes obvious as soon as you look at the parallel between God's destruction of the world through the flood and the significance of water in God's battle with Pharaoh. Water, a source of life, but also the prime symbol of primordial chaos, frames the contest. The first plague turns the Nile to blood. The last blow falls at the Red Sea with the drowning of Pharaoh and his army.

The events at the Red Sea evoke dramatic symbols of creation and de-creation. Ancient Near Eastern creation stories regularly began with a god subduing a watery, chaotic void and establishing a dry home for humanity. When humanity sinned against the gods, the world returned to watery formlessness. The Egyptian Book of the Dead (1550–1350 B.C.E.) describes a threat by the enraged god Atun. "I shall destroy all that I have made, and this land will return unto Nun, into the floodwaters, as [in] its first state."[18] God's splitting the Red Sea so the Israelites could walk on dry land, then allowing the "waters to turn back" upon the Egyptians, recapitulates creation and the flood.

The midrash, of course, notes the parallel:

> Let us [say the Egyptians] deal cunningly with Israel and plan such a scrfdom for thcm that thcir God will not be able to punish us in the same coin. For if we persecute them with the sword, He can visit us with the sword, and if with fire, He can bring fire upon us. We know that He swore that He would no longer bring a flood on the world, let us, therefore, persecute them with water, which He cannot bring upon us. God then said to them: "Wretches! True I have sworn that I will not bring a flood into the world, but I will do this to you; I will drag each onc of you to his own flood."[19]

Some have also pointed to a relationship between the ten plagues and the ten utterances, through which the Mishnah states that God created the world: "With ten [divine] pronouncements was the world created. Now what is this meant to teach us? . . . It is but to [make clear that God will] exact punishment from the wicked who destroy the world that was created by ten pronouncements."[20]

Beyond these general parallels, the creation and plague narratives share a number of common expressions that serve to link the themes of creation and anti-creation. Following are three of many other examples:[21]

- *Blood:* In delivering this plague, God tells Moses that Aaron should hold his rod over the waters of Egypt, literally, "over the gathering of its waters" (*v'al kol mikveih meimeihem*, Ex. 7:19). On the third day, God separates the waters. "God called the dry land Earth, and the gathering of waters He called Seas" (*u'l'mikveih ha'mayim;* Gen. 1:10).

- *Frogs:* "The Nile shall swarm (*v'sharatz*) with frogs" (Ex. 7:28). On the fifth day, God creates "the living creatures of every kind that creep which the waters brought forth in swarms . . ." (*shartzu,* Gen. 1:21). In Egypt, the frogs come up and cover the land. In Genesis, God tells the creatures of the waters to fill the sea, to be fruitful and multiply. In Egypt, the frogs exceed the boundaries of creation. The creator seems to have rewritten the rules. (On the fifth day, God also creates the great sea monsters, *ha-taninim ha-gedolim*. When Aaron casts down the rod before Pharaoh it becomes a serpent, *tanin*. In Ezekiel 29:3, when Pharaoh says he has created the Nile, God calls Pharaoh the great sea monster, *ha-tanim ha-gadol*. Not infrequently, the Bible depicts God's battle against Israel's enemies as a clash with sea monsters, which are symbolic of the uncontrollable and, hence, of evil.)[22]

• *Darkness:* "People could not see one another, and for three days no one could get up from where he was; but all the Israelites enjoyed light in their dwellings" (Ex. 10:23). On the first day of creation, "God saw that the light was good, and God separated the light from the darkness" (Gen. 1:4). On the fourth day. God creates "lights in the expanse of the sky to separate day from night . . ." (Gen. 1:14). In Egypt, light and darkness have been separated geographically and the cycle of day and night has come to a halt.

So what does this mean? Why bother to link the plagues and creation?

Exodus offers us two paradigms of faith. The first represents the relationship between a people and their liberator, a relationship that with time may cool. Besides, human beings can also bring about liberation. The second represents the connection between humanity and its creator, a more fundamental relationship that may well enjoy greater durability. Creation, on the cosmic scale at least, still remains beyond human reach. Hence the redactors of the Exodus story may have been reluctant to leave the stage solely to God as liberator.

The justifications for the Sabbath given in the Torah's two versions of the Ten Commandments illustrate both paradigms. The fourth commandment of Exodus (20:11) instructs us to remember the Sabbath because "in six days Adonai made the heaven and earth and sea, and all that is in them, and He rested on the seventh day." Deuteronomy's fourth commandment (5:15) tells us to keep the Sabbath in remembrance of the fact that "you were a slave in the land of Egypt and Adonai your God freed you from there with a mighty hand and an out-stretched arm. . . ."

As reflected in the daily liturgy, Jewish tradition has clearly chosen to harmonize both paradigms. Certain prayers speak to God as creator, while others give greater weight to God as liberator. The Kiddush for Shabbat may represent the perfect balance: "You have graciously given us Your holy Sabbath as a heritage in remembrance of the creation. The Sabbath is the first among the holy festivals which recall the Exodus from Egypt."

16

Moses in the Haggadah:
The Human Role in Redemption

וַיּוֹצִאֵנוּ יְיָ מִמִּצְרַיִם בְּיָד חֲזָקָה וּבִזְרֹעַ נְטוּיָה וּבְמֹרָא גָּדֹל וּבְאֹתוֹת
וּבְמֹפְתִים. . . . וּבְאֹתוֹת. זֶה הַמַּטֶּה. כְּמָה שֶׁנֶּאֱמַר: וְאֶת־הַמַּטֶּה הַזֶּה תִּקַּח
בְּיָדְךָ אֲשֶׁר תַּעֲשֶׂה־בּוֹ אֶת־הָאֹתֹת: . . . וַיַּרְא יִשְׂרָאֵל אֶת־הַיָּד הַגְּדֹלָה אֲשֶׁר
עָשָׂה יְיָ בְּמִצְרַיִם וַיִּירְאוּ הָעָם אֶת־יְיָ וַיַּאֲמִינוּ בַּיְיָ וּבְמֹשֶׁה עַבְדּוֹ:

Adonai took us out from Egypt by a mighty hand, by an outstretched arm and awesome
power, and by signs and portents (Deut. 26:8). . . . "And by signs": This is the staff, as it
is said, "And take with you this staff in your hand, with which you shall perform the
signs" (Ex. 4:17). . . . Israel saw the great hand which Adonai laid upon the
Egyptians, and the people revered Adonai and they believed in Adonai
and in His servant Moses (Ex. 14:31).
—THE PASSOVER HAGGADAH

A curious myth has grown up about Moses' complete absence from the traditional Haggadah.[1] Search the Internet with the words "Moses" and
"Haggadah" and you'll find no shortage of such observations. Sometimes even
scholarly works make the same claim. As one very important study on the

Haggadah put it, "in the entire Haggadah Moses' name is not mentioned."[2] The most common interpretation suggests that in completely erasing Moses, the compilers of the Haggadah wanted to teach us that credit for Israel's redemption from Egypt belongs exclusively to God. After all, the Haggadah itself says, "Adonai brought us out from Egypt not by an angel, not by a seraph, not by a messenger, but by the Holy One, blessed be He, Himself." There are two problems with this. First, at least since the fourteenth century, Haggadot have referred to Moses— twice, once by name and once implicitly. Second, the Haggadah goes on to explain that "not by an angel, not by a seraph, not by a messenger" refers to slaying the Egyptian firstborn, not to Exodus more generally.

In this chapter we'll explore the traditional Haggadah's two references to Moses and why the Haggadah minimized his presence in its recounting of the Exodus. Finding Moses in the Haggadah will set the stage for taking a fresh look at the Haggadah's understanding of the human role in the redemption from Egypt. We conclude with five midrashic perspectives on roles of God and humanity in the process of redemption.

Before continuing, you might have noticed references in the previous paragraphs to the *traditional* Haggadah. What is a traditional Haggadah? It is a version of the text that reached its "final" development—in the Ashkenazic, Sephardic, or Yemenite traditions—by the sixteenth or seventeenth century. The Maxwell House Haggadah, for example, contains the traditional Ashkenazic text. The most recent Haggadot published by the Conservative, Reconstructionist, and Reform Movements, all fine Haggadot, omit sections of the traditional text and add other material as well. If you look for Moses in something other than a traditional Haggadah, you might find an abundance of references or none at all.

FOR DISCUSSION

- Ask one or more of your guests to look through some nontraditional Haggadot to see how they treat Moses. Ask them to share their findings at the Seder.

- Ask your guests how many of them have heard that Moses is completely absent from the traditional Haggadah.

- Although the Haggadah does in fact refer to Moses twice, it certainly minimizes him. Why do think that is the case? (You can find these two references on page 213.)

- If you were writing a Haggadah today, what role would you give Moses? Are there other figures in the biblical Exodus to whom you feel the Haggadah should have given a more prominent role? If so, who? Why?

- The Haggadah puts God in a starring role and in contrast to the biblical Exodus, it tends to minimize the human contribution to the story. Why do you think the Haggadah might have taken this view? What are the strengths and weaknesses of this approach?

In discussing the Seder, Maimonides (1135–1204) wrote:

It is a mitzvah to inform one's sons even though they do not ask, as Ex. 13:8 states: "You shall tell your son." A father should teach his son according to the son's knowledge: How is this applied? If the son is young or foolish, he should tell him: "My son, in Egypt, we were all slaves like this maidservant or this slave. On this night, the Holy One, Blessed be He, redeemed us and took us out to freedom. If the son is older and wise, he should inform him what happened to us in Egypt and the miracles wrought for us by Moses, our teacher; everything according to the son's knowledge.[3]

- How might you explain Maimonides' approach? How do you feel about it?

WHERE'S MOSES?

Below are the Haggadah's two references to Moses. Both have appeared in Haggadot since at least the fourteenth century. Read both passages aloud and discuss the questions that follow. The numbered paragraphs that correspond to these two passages contain background information that you may wish to share with your guests.

1. Adonai took us out from Egypt by a mighty hand, by an outstretched arm and awesome power, and by signs and portents (Deut. 26:8). . . . "And by signs": This is the staff, as it is said, "And take with you this staff in your hand, with which you shall perform the signs" (Ex. 4:17).

—THE PASSOVER HAGGADAH

These are God's last words to Moses at the burning bush. "You" refers to Moses. In the Haggadah, this passage appears a bit before we recite the names of the ten plagues. In some traditional Haggadot the translation reads, "This is the rod *of Moses*," adding his name, although it does not appear in the Hebrew.

2. Israel saw the great hand which Adonai laid upon the Egyptians, and the people revered Adonai and they believed in Adonai and in His servant Moses.

—THE PASSOVER HAGGADAH, QUOTING EX. 14:31.

In Exodus this verse appears just after the Israelites cross the Red Sea and witness the drowning of Pharaoh's army. In the Haggadah it comes just after we spill wine from our cups as we recite the names of the plagues. It occurs in a midrash on the number of plagues the Egyptians suffered at the Red Sea.[4] As is often the case in rabbinic literature, in its original source the midrash only quotes the beginning of the verse from Exodus and therefore excludes the name of Moses. Haggadot of the Geonim from Babylonia in the ninth and tenth centuries include this midrash with its partial quotation from Exodus. By the fourteenth century, European Haggadot routinely included the full verse from Exodus and with it Moses' name. (See the illustration from the Sarajevo Haggadah on page 217).

FOR DISCUSSION

- What do you make of the fact that God tells Moses to bring the staff before Pharaoh?

- What similarity do you notice between Exodus 4:17 and 14:31?

- What might these verses say about the relationship between the divine and the human roles in redemption?

Dating from the early decades of the fourteenth century, the Sarajevo Haggadah is thought to have been created in Spain. It is the most celebrated and perhaps the oldest surviving illuminated manuscript of a Haggadah. This page includes the verse in Exodus (14:31): "And when Israel saw the great hand which Adonai had wielded against the Egyptians, the people feared Adonai; they had faith in Adonai and in Moses His servant." The last word on the left above the illumination is *u'v'moshe,* "and in Moses." Traditional Haggadot still include this single mention of Moses' name as well as an allusion to Moses' rod (Ex. 4:17).

Read on your own, or after your discussion, consider reading
the paragraphs below aloud.

Though diminished, the *presence* of Moses in the Haggadah challenges the idea of deliverance from Egypt as the work of God alone. According to legend, Moses' staff had miraculous properties. It was among the final ten objects God fashioned just before the first Sabbath began.[5] Doubtless, God could have instructed the staff to walk into Pharaoh's palace on its own and to stand by Moses' side as he addressed Pharaoh. That would have gotten Pharaoh's attention! But God chose a human being to bring the staff to Pharaoh.

Moses' staff in the Haggadah reminds us that we each hold unique gifts in our hand—our talents, passions, wisdom, and creativity—that can help redeem the world. And like Moses, we too are hesitant to use our gifts. The question is whether we can overcome our reluctance, as Moses eventually did, and fully embrace the work of redeeming our world. If we do, the world inches closer to redemption. If we don't, the world drifts downhill. The Haggadah invokes the hands of both God and Moses. God *and* humanity share responsibility for redeeming the world. We cannot forget the human contribution to the task—and the importance of leadership—even as we celebrate God's "strong hand and out-stretched arm."

"NOT BY AN ANGEL . . ."

If you have a group that enjoys text study, consider copying these two selections, reading the short paragraph below, and then discussing the accompanying questions.

The passage on the left comes from the Passover Haggadah. The one on the right comes from the *Mekhilta of Rabbi Ishmael*, a third-century midrash from which the Haggadah borrowed extensively. The passage from the *Mekhilta* may well have influenced the second passage from the Haggadah. Note: Italics indicate biblical quotations.

THE PASSOVER HAGGADAH

1. *And saw our oppression*, that is, the conjugal separation of husband and wife, as it is written: *God saw the children of Israel and God knew* (Ex. 2:25). *Our misery* refers to the drowning of the sons, as it is written: *Every son that is born you shall cast into the river, but you shall let every daughter live* (Ex. 1:22). *Our oppression* means the pressure used upon them, as it is written: *I have also seen how the Egyptians are oppressing them* (Ex. 3:9).

2. *Adonai brought us out from Egypt by a mighty hand, by an outstretched arm and awesome power, and by signs and portents* (Deut. 26:8). *Adonai brought us out from Egypt* not by an angel, not by a seraph, not by a messenger, but by the Holy One, blessed be He, Himself, as it is written: *I will pass through the land of Egypt on that night; I will smite all the firstborn in the land of Egypt from man unto beast; on all the gods of Egypt I will execute judgments; I am Adonai* (Ex. 12:12). *I will pass through the land of Egypt on that night*, I and not an angel; *I will smite all the firstborn in the land of Egypt*, I and not a seraph; *On all the gods of Egypt I will execute judgments*, I and not the messenger; *I am He*, I and no other.[6]

THE MEKHILTA OF RABBI ISHMAEL, THIRD-CENTURY MIDRASH[7]

1. *I will pass through the land of Egypt on that night; I will smite all the firstborn in the land of Egypt....* (Ex. 12:12). *I will smite:* I might understand this to mean by an angel or by a messenger. But it says that *Adonai smote all the firstborn* (Ex. 12:29)—not by an angel, not by a messenger....

2. *I am Adonai your God* (Ex. 20:2). Why is it said? For this reason. At the Red Sea He appeared to them as a mighty hero doing battle. . . . At Sinai He appeared to them as an old man full of mercy. . . . Scripture, therefore, would not let the nations of the world have an excuse for saying that there are two Powers, but declares: *I am Adonai your God*. I am He who was in Egypt and I am He who was at the sea. I am He who is in this world and I am He who will be in the world to come. As it is said, *See, then, that I, I am He; there is no god beside Me. I deal death and give life . . .* (Deut. 32:39) . . . . *I am Adonai, the first and last, I am He* (Isaiah 41:4).

FOR DISCUSSION

• Do you sense any difference in tone between the first and second passages from the Haggadah? If so, how would you characterize that difference?

• Does the second paragraph from the Haggadah seem to make a point about God's role in the Exodus in general or about who was responsible for the last plague? Is there a difference between the two?

• The first paragraph of the midrash proves its point by citing Exodus 12:29, which says that God "smote all the firstborn." How does this phrase support the idea that God acted alone?

• The second paragraph in the midrash begins with the words: "I am Adonai your God," *Anokhi Adonai elohecha*. These are the first words of the Ten Commandments. What about this phrase might stimulate the midrash to argue against "two Powers?" The same issue might also come up in the *Sh'ma*: "Hear O Israel! Adonai our God, Adonai is one" (Deut. 6:4). The *Sh'ma* uses the phrase "Adonai our God," *Adonai eloheinu*.

WHY MINIMIZE MOSES?

Read this on your own, or depending on your group, you might
want to read it aloud before your Seder.

'*Adonai brought us out from Egypt*'—not by an angel, not by a seraph, not by a messenger, but by the Holy One, blessed be He, Himself . . ."

—THE PASSOVER HAGGADAH

With this passage from the Haggadah's midrash on the Exodus, the tone abruptly switches from storytelling to polemic. As we shift from Pharaoh's oppression of the Israelites to God's slaying of the Egyptian firstborn, the Haggadah suddenly takes pains to deny any role for supernatural figures aside from God. What lies behind this strident repudiation? The Haggadah's denial reflects prominent concerns about the concept of monotheism in the centuries that followed the Temple's destruction. It was an era when many religious groups, including some Jews, believed that God worked with or through a wide array of quasi-independent supernatural beings.

Elements of the Bible itself could be marshaled to support such views. Some identified God's many names in the Bible with different divine attributes. They identified Adonai with God's mercy and Elohim with divine judgment. (Note that Elohim is in the plural.) But others identified a multiplicity of divine figures with those distinct names. The same argument ensued over contrasting images of God: the kindly father or the man of war. As one scholar described it, the argument was between modalism—one God with different attributes—versus binitarianism—different gods with different attributes.[8] Leaving aside different names or images of God, what are we to make of texts like this: "God [Elohim] stands in the divine assembly among the divine beings [Elohim]" (Psalms 82:1)? And in the Book of Exodus, an additional supernatural figure *does* play a role in slaying the Egyptian firstborn, contrary to the Haggadah's claim, "Not by an angel."

> For when Adonai goes through to smite the Egyptians, He will see the blood on the lintel and two doorposts, and Adonai will pass over the door and not let the Destroyer (*ha'mashchit*) enter and smite your home.
>
> —EXODUS 12:23

The Book of Numbers seems to speak a similar language: "We cried to Adonai and He heard our plea, and He sent a *malach* [an angel or messenger] who freed us from Egypt . . ." (Numbers 20:16).

Many centuries later, these kinds of figures came to life in the Book of Jubilees (135–105 B.C.E.), a Jewish text that was not included in the Bible. There, a character called Mastema carried out the last plague.[9] Mastema (in Hebrew, "the prince of enmity") was a supernatural being, an object of human worship, to whom God had given special powers. Mastema does battle with the Angel of the Presence, God's ally in saving the Israelites.

> For on this night—the beginning of the festival and the beginning of the joy—you were eating the Passover [sacrifice] in Egypt, when all the powers of Mastema had been let loose to slay all the first-born in

the land of Egypt, from the first-born of Pharaoh to the first-born of the captive maid-servant in the mill, and to the cattle. . . . [After the Israelites left Egypt, Mastema] took courage and cried to the Egyptians to pursue you with all the powers of the Egyptians, with their chariots, and with their horses, and with all the hosts of the peoples of Egypt. And I [the Angel of the Presence] stood between the Egyptians and Israel, and we delivered Israel out of his hand . . . and Adonai brought them through the midst of the sea as if it were dry land.

—THE BOOK OF JUBILEES, 49:2-3, 48:12-13

By the third century C.E., early midrashic texts argued against the notion that two independent powers in heaven bore responsibility for critical events in Israelite history such as the redemption from Egypt and the revelation at Sinai. (See the passage from the *Mekhilta* on page 219 for a classic example.) Gnostics, Samaritans, Christians, and some Jews as well held those beliefs. (Believing in angels was fine, so long as you didn't worship them and didn't claim that they acted independently of God.) When the Haggadah says "not by an angel, not by a seraph, not by a messenger," it does not deny *human* participation in the Exodus. It is arguing against the existence of more than one autonomous *supernatural* figure.

The story becomes more complicated precisely because some thought—again, Jews among them—that Moses was quasi-divine and may have merited worship. A third-century midrash, for example, comments on a verse contained in the second paragraph of the *Sh'ma*. Keep in mind that the speaker is Moses: "If, then, you obey the commandments that I enjoin upon you this day, loving Adonai your God and serving Him with all your heart and soul, I will grant the rain for your land in season . . ." (Deut. 11:13-14). The midrash comments:

I will grant: I [God], not by an angel, not by a messenger.[10]

The midrash wanted to quash a literal reading of the verse, lest it give aid and comfort to those who believed in Moses as a supernatural figure who controlled the rains.[11]

Another midrash comments on the Bible's description of Moses as "a man of God," *ish ha'elohim* (Deut. 33:1), which can also be read "man, the God."

> What is the meaning of "man, the God"? His lower half was "man," but his upper half was "God."[12]

An eleventh-century midrash asks why the grave of Moses remains unknown and answers flatly, "So that Israel would not go there and put up a sanctuary (*beit ha'mikdash*) and make sacrifices and offer incense."[13]

To sum up, the Haggadah downplays Moses not because it subscribes to a theology in which human beings play no part in the redemption from Egypt, but as a rejection of those who believed in the existence of more than one power in heaven and in related tendencies to deify Moses. To those so inclined, the Haggadah offers a sharp rebuke. Their quasi-divine hero *almost* disappears from the story. But for those seeking a role in the redemption played by human beings—the *human* Moses and the Israelites—the Haggadah, as we will now see, speaks in a friendlier tone.

FRESH READINGS: THE HAGGADAH AND THE HUMAN ROLE IN THE EXODUS
THE COVENANTAL CONTEXT OF REDEMPTION

Read aloud the material below and discuss the questions that follow.

The Haggadah sets the Exodus in the context of a covenantal relationship that began between God and Abraham and continued with his descendants. Near the beginning of its narrative, the Haggadah quotes a passage from Genesis known as the Covenant of the Pieces. God says to Abraham:

> Know well that your offspring shall be strangers in a land not theirs and they shall be enslaved and oppressed for four hundred years; but I [God] will execute judgment on the nation they shall serve, and in the end they shall go out with great wealth.
> —THE PASSOVER HAGGADAH, QUOTING GENESIS 15:13-14

Later the Haggadah says:

> We cried to Adonai, the God of our ancestors (Deut. 26:7). . . . God heard their groaning; God remembered His covenant with Abraham, with Isaac, and with Jacob (Ex. 2:24).

- Why do you think the Haggadah stresses the role of the covenant in the way it tells the story of Passover?

- If a covenant implies responsibilities of both partners, how would you think about the covenantal responsibilities of God and of the Israelites in the context of the Exodus?

After your discussion, consider reading the paragraph below aloud.

God and the Israelites each had a role to play in fulfilling their covenant—including the divine promise of redemption from Egypt. The Israelites needed a sufficient collective identity so that God could deliver "one nation from the midst of another" (Deut. 4:34), as the Haggadah puts it. And God had to remember the covenantal promises to Abraham and his descendants. The Haggadah tells us that both partners fulfilled their parts of the bargain. It points out that Israel became a nation in Egypt, which "means that they became a distinct people in Egypt." Had they assimilated, as did many foreign groups in Egypt, God would not have had a people to redeem.[14] A bit further on, we come to God's side of the agreement. The Haggadah relates that the Israelites cried out to God from the pain of oppression. Note what follows: "God heard their groaning; God remembered His covenant with Abraham, with Isaac, and with Jacob" (Ex. 2:24). God and the Israelites both proved faithful to the covenant. The rest is history.

RIGHTEOUS WOMEN, APPLE TREES AND *CHAROSET*

The Haggadah alludes to Pharaoh's plan to destroy the Israelites by preventing them from procreating—"And [God] saw our affliction—the enforced separation of husband and wife." As we've seen in our discussion of *charoset* (see page 12), according to a legend recounted by Rabbi Akiva, the Israelite women thwarted

Pharaoh's plan by furtively meeting their husbands out in the fields and seducing them under the apple trees. Nine months later they returned to give birth under those trees. As a result, Akiva argues, "Israel merited redemption because of the righteousness of the women of that generation."[15] Had women allowed the separation between man and wife to stand, the Israelites would have disappeared. End of story. No Exodus. So *charoset*—which the Talmud says should be tart to recall the apple tree—reminds us of oppression, but also of human defiance, without which the Exodus would have been impossible.

PURIM IN THE HAGGADAH

Read aloud the paragraphs below and discuss the questions that follow.

Just before the first two psalms of Hallel we come to one of the Ashkenazic Haggadah's most poetic passages:

> We praise . . . the One who has brought us forth from slavery to freedom, from sorrow to joy, from mourning to a festival, from darkness to great light and from bondage to redemption.[16]

The phrase "from sorrow to joy, from mourning to a festival" comes near the end of the Book of Esther (9:22) when Mordecai institutes the festival of Purim. The Jews have just been saved from Haman's genocidal plan, and Mordecai sends out instructions to observe Purim annually on "the same days on which the Jews enjoyed relief from their foes and the same month which had been transformed for them from one of "sorrow to joy and from mourning to a festival [*yom tov*]."[17]

- Why do you think the compilers of the Haggadah might have wanted to bring a reference to Purim into the Seder?

- What do Purim and Passover share in common? How do they differ?

After discussing the questions above, consider reading aloud what follows.

225

Purim and Passover both celebrate redemption from a genocidal tyrant. Purim sadly affirms the Haggadah's claim that "in every generation they rise up to destroy us." Indeed, a careful reading of various dates in the Book of Esther reveals that the climax of the Purim story actually takes place during Passover![18]

But the Haggadah's reference to Purim stands out for an even more important reason. Passover falls in Nisan, counted as the first month in the Jewish calendar. Purim falls in Adar, the last month. God's active presence defines the Exodus. Purim draws the starkest contrast: not only do human beings redeem the Jews of Shushan, but the Book of Esther is the only book in the Bible that does not mention God.[19] The cycle of the Jewish year traces the course of God's *decreasing intervention* on the one hand and humanity's *maturing responsibility* on the other. Passover demonstrates the potentiality of redemption and of God's role as redeemer. Purim reminds us that in a world where God's hand remains hidden, redemption lies in our hands.[20] In placing an allusion to Purim at the heart of the Seder, the compilers of the Haggadah call us, albeit subtly, to remember humanity's responsibility for the work of redemption at the very moment we celebrate God's role in the process.

IN EVERY GENERATION

Discuss the following questions, then read the paragraph below aloud.

The phrase "in every generation" occurs twice in the Haggadah.

1. In every generation they rise up to destroy us, but the Holy One, blessed be He, saves us from their hand.

2. In every generation, each individual should feel as though he or she has gone out of Egypt.

- What similarities and contrasts do you find between these two passages?

- How would you compare the roles of God and the Jewish People in each passage?

- What are the differences between feeling as though you were taken
  out of Egypt and feeling as though you went under your own steam?

In the first passage, and throughout much of the Haggadah, God acts; we are acted upon. "Had not God *taken our ancestors out* of Egypt, we . . . would still be enslaved to Pharaoh in Egypt." But in the second passage, when the Haggadah expresses its core goal, we find very different language. We must see ourselves as though we went out of Egypt under our own steam, as independent actors in the story. The differences in language highlight the point that God and humanity both participate in the redemptive process: "You can't have one without the other."

We are hardly the first generation to live in times when the active hand of a redeeming God seems to have withdrawn from the stage. The compilers of the oldest parts of the Haggadah lived at one of the darkest times of Jewish history. The Temple lay in ruins and most Jews had been exiled from the land. The longing for God to return to the stage of history to visit justice upon those who oppressed the Jews is palpable throughout the Haggadah.

But the Haggadah also reminds us that the responsibility for redemption cannot be left to God alone. Our job is not merely to practice personal piety in the hope that God will reward us with a magically repaired world. Our job is to ensure that the celebration of Passover, along with every other sacred moment of the Jewish calendar, revives our strength to join with others to redeem our world, day by day, brick by brick.

FIVE MIDRASHIC VOICES ON REDEMPTION

Although the Haggadah speaks quietly about the human contribution to redemption, other midrashic sources take a much bolder approach. Here are just a few examples. Choose one or more and discuss the questions that follow.

The last example speaks of the resurrection of the dead.
This is an ancient Jewish belief, one that traditional Jews share with Christians.

"Or has any god ventured to go and take for himself one nation from the midst of another nation. . . .?" [Deut. 4:34, a verse which appears in the Haggadah]. There is no point in saying "from the midst of another nation" except to suggest that it was like a man who draws out the young calf from the cow's womb.

—MEKHILTA OF RABBI ISHMAEL, THIRD-CENTURY MIDRASH[21]

Rabbi Judah the Prince says, "Through the alertness/strength [*zrizut*] of God, Israel went out of Egypt." Another opinion, "With an alertness/strength of their own Israel went out of Egypt."

—MEKHILTA OF RABBI ISHMAEL, THIRD-CENTURY MIDRASH[22]

God said to Israel, "The time of My redemption is in your hand, and the time of your redemption is in My hand."

—*PESIKTA DE-RAV KAHANA* (17:5),
FIFTH- OR SIXTH-CENTURY MIDRASH[23]

God says, "My Torah is in your hands, and the time of redemption is in My hands. Each of us has need of the other. If you need Me to bring the time of redemption, I need you to keep My Torah and bring about sooner the rebuilding of My house and of Jerusalem."

—PESIKTA RABBATI (31:5), SIXTH- OR SEVENTH-CENTURY MIDRASH[24]

God says to the righteous, "Behold, you are My equals. . . . 'If you produce what is noble out of the worthless, you shall be as My mouth' (Jeremiah 15:19). Even as I create worlds and resurrect the dead, so shall you."

—MIDRASH ON PSALMS (116:8), THIRD THROUGH
THIRTEENTH CENTURY[25]

FOR DISCUSSION

• The first midrash expresses a view of redemption that most would associate with that of the Haggadah. How would you characterize the role of God and the Israelites in that midrash? How do you feel about that approach to redemption?

• Several of these sources refer to the idea that God in some sense needs to be redeemed. What does this mean to you?

• How do you feel about the notion that God and the Jewish People have a role in redeeming one another? Does it surprise you?

• How would you feel about a Haggadah that emphasized the mutual redemption of God and Israel? Do you think that would be an appropriate theme for the Passover Seder? What might you title such a Haggadah?

17

Dayyenu: It Would Have Sufficed

אִלּוּ הוֹצִיאָנוּ מִמִּצְרַיִם
וְלֹא עָשָׂה בָהֶם שְׁפָטִים, דַּיֵּנוּ:

*If He had brought us out of Egypt and not brought judgment
upon them, it would have sufficed.*
—THE PASSOVER HAGGADAH

Singing has long been central to the Seder. Indeed, the Ashkenazic Haggadah twice calls us to sing "a new song" to God.[1] This little phrase hints at something very significant. The feeling of having been redeemed unleashes an urge to sing something new—or maybe to sing an old song as if it were new. Sometimes ordinary words just won't do. The Haggadah's emphasis on song reminds me of what St. Augustine (354–430) said: "One who sings, prays twice."[2] In this chapter we'll explore *Dayyenu*, one of the Seder's most beloved songs. We'll review its development, meaning, and some of the difficulties the song raises. We'll also consider *Dayyenu* as a microcosm of some of the Haggadah's most important underlying themes.

SUGGESTIONS FOR SEDER LEADERS

- Ask a few of your guests to share their recollections about singing the songs of the Seder.

- Ask your guests to bring drums, tambourines, maracas, or other suitable musical instruments. You might want to pick up a few extras just in case. We use these for a spirited accompaniment to the Seder's songs.[3]

FOR DISCUSSION

- Why do you think that singing plays such a special role in the Seder?

- What connections might you make between singing and the Exodus?

- The midrash includes two traditions about when the first song was sung—in Egypt, on the night before the Exodus or after crossing the Red Sea.[4] What point might underlie this disagreement? Based on your understanding of the Israelites throughout the Exodus, where do you think it more likely that the Israelites would first have sung? In Egypt, before they left, or after they crossed the Red Sea? Why?

FIRST SONGS: THE SONG AT THE SEA AND *DAYYENU*
Read on your own or consider reading aloud.

Dayyenu is the Haggadah's first major song, complete with a refrain. It comes at a most appropriate moment in the Seder—just after we recite the ten plagues and a midrash that multiplies the numbers of the plagues that the Egyptians suffered in Egypt and at the Red Sea. Its placement parallels the Bible's first song, the Song at the Sea, which the Israelites chanted after they had successfully crossed the Red Sea and witnessed the drowning of Pharaoh's army. Moses and the Israelites sang the complete song. Then Miriam led the Israelite women with timbrels and dancing: "Sing to Adonai, for He has triumphed gloriously; horse and rider He has hurled into the sea" (Exodus 15:21).

These two songs share something else as well: both begin with events connected with the Exodus and end with the references to the Temple in Jerusalem. The Song at the Sea concludes: "You will bring [Your people] and

232

plant them in Your own mountain, the place You made to dwell in, Adonai, the sanctuary, Adonai, which Your hands have established" (Exodus 15:17). *Dayyenu* ends this way: "If He had brought us into the Land of Israel and had not built us the Temple, *Dayyenu*" Both songs reveal an understanding of the Exodus that may be more expansive than ours. These songs see the Exodus as a process of redemption—first physical and then spiritual—that begins with leaving Egypt and ends with the ability to serve God in the Temple.[5] Finally, as we will soon discuss more fully, *Dayyenu* refers to fifteen acts of divine favor, and ancient midrashic tradition suggested that the Song at the Sea included fifteen praises of God.[6]

The act of singing at this point in the Exodus—and in the Haggadah's narrative—not only expresses gratitude, but releases the tension of having experienced, or relived, such a harrowing escape. So the Haggadah's first song recapitulates the Bible's first song. The parallel provides a good example of what the Haggadah means when it says, "In every generation, each individual should feel as though he or she had gone out of Egypt."

SUGGESTIONS FOR SEDER LEADERS

- A few weeks before the Seder, ask your guests to do a little spiritual preparation. Ask them to write down fifteen things for which they feel particularly grateful. Consider asking a few of your guests to share their lists during the Seder.

- Compose your own group's *Dayyenu*. Ask each of your guests to compose a simple verse to *Dayyenu* by filling in the blanks. If _____ and not _____, it would have sufficed! *Dayyenu*! Go around the table and ask each guest to share his or her verse with everyone joining in for the chorus.

- Ask a few of your guests to do some online research and find different versions of *Dayyenu* to share and sing at the Seder.

Below are the fifteen divine favors *Dayyenu* recounts. You might want to consider copying them for your guests and discussing the questions that follow.

1. brought us out of Egypt
2. executed judgments against the Egyptians
3. smote their gods
4. slew their firstborn
5. gave us their wealth
6. split the Sea for us
7. led us through it on dry land
8. sank our foes in it
9. sustained us in the desert for forty years
10. fed us with the manna
11. gave us the Sabbath
12. brought us to Mount Sinai
13. gave us the Torah
14. brought us to Israel
15. built the Temple for us

• How might you categorize these fifteen degrees of divine goodness?
What kind of progressions might the categories make?

• How does it make you feel to be singing a cheery tune to a verse
that speaks of drowning the Egyptians in the sea? Some versions of
Dayyenu in contemporary Haggadot omit this verse. How do you
feel about that approach?

• How do you feel about the fact that the degrees of divine goodness
end with the Temple in Jerusalem? What events might you bring
into the song to extend it up to our time?

ROOTS?

The origins of *Dayyenu* remain obscure. Because the song concluded with a reference to the Temple, it was long thought to have been composed in the period of the

Second Temple.[7] Modern scholars attribute the song to a much later period. Our oldest source containing the song comes from the prayer book of Saadiah Gaon (Babylonia, 882–942), where it appears as an acceptable addition to the Haggadah. It can regularly be found in European illuminated Haggadot of the Middle Ages.

As for biblical influences on the song's development, *Dayyenu* reflects what has been called an "Exodus review," generally a succinct summary of Israel's history featuring the events of the Exodus, but occasionally also including events that preceded or followed it. Toward the end of the Seder, the Haggadah actually includes one such review, Psalm 136. Although this psalm recounts God's beneficence from the creation to Israel's entry into the Land of Israel, almost a third of it addresses the Exodus. Psalm 136 refers to God striking the Egyptian firstborn, bringing Israel out of Egypt with a strong hand and outstretched arm, splitting the Red Sea, taking Israel through it and drowning the Egyptians. As *Dayyenu*, Psalm 136 also includes a refrain—"His steadfast love is eternal."

The fact that *Dayyenu's* refrain—"It would have sufficed!"—stresses Israel's gratitude may be a response to a number of biblical Exodus reviews that emphasize ingratitude. For example, Psalm 106 weaves together highlights of the Exodus with condemnations of Israel: "They forgot God who saved them, who performed great deeds in Egypt.... They rejected the desirable land, and put no faith in His promise. They grumbled in their tents and disobeyed Adonai" (Psalms 106:21, 24, 25). Insofar as the Passover Seder embodies the fulfillment of so many divine commandments and seeks to bolster hope in God's unfailing love of Israel, a denunciation of Israel's shortcomings would hardly strike the proper note.[8]

Below you will find three midrashic sources that may have contributed to the inspiration of *Dayyenu*. Read one or more aloud and discuss the questions that follow.

The Sifre on Deuteronomy, a midrash compiled by the third century, describes the Israelites' anxiety lest they become separated from Moses:

> [T]he man who brought us out of Egypt (*hotzianu mi'mitzrayim*), split the sea for us, brought down manna for us, supplied us with the quail [in the desert] and performed miracles and wonders for us . . .[9]

- What do you make of the fact that the midrash ascribes these miracles to Moses while *Dayyenu* attributes them to God?

The *Mekhilta*, a third-century midrash from which the Haggadah drew heavily, presents an Egyptian *Dayyenu* of sorts.

> The Egyptians said, "If we had been plagued without letting them go, it would have sufficed [*k'die hu*]. Or if we had been plagued and let them go without our money being taken, it would have sufficed. But we were plagued, let them go, and our money was taken."[10] . . . Pharaoh said, "It would not be worth our while [*lo Dayyenu*] to pursue the Israelites [just to get *them*] but for the sake of the silver and gold they have taken from us, it is enough [*k'die hu*]."[11]

- If you were composing a *Dayyenu* from the Egyptian point of view, what might you include in it?

- Does your understanding of *Dayyenu* change in light of the fact that its composer may have been inspired by an ancient litany of Egyptian complaints? If so, how?

Leviticus Rabbah, a midrash from the fifth or sixth century, comments on a verse from the prophet Malachi that now happens to be read in synagogue on Shabbat HaGadol, the Sabbath prior to Passover. God says, "Bring the full tithe into the storehouse [of the Temple] and let there be food in My house, and thus put Me to the test—said Adonai of hosts. I will surely open the floodgates of the sky for you and pour down upon you blessings immeasurable" (Malachi 3:10). What, asks the midrash, is the meaning of "immeasurable," *ad b'li die*? "Until your lips shall wear away from saying, "*Dayyenu*," explains the midrash. As if to say, God's blessings will be so abundant that your lips will wear out from expressing gratitude or *Dayyenu*, "enough," "it would suffice."[12]

- Do you feel you've received "blessings immeasurable"? If so, in what sense?

- What are the experiences that make you feel blessed?

- How might you deepen your sense of being blessed?

• The midrash suggests that "your lips shall wear away from saying *Dayyenu*." In your rendition, how many times do you repeat the word *Dayyenu*?

WHY FIFTEEN DIVINE FAVORS?

Read on your own or consider reading aloud.

Dayyenu comprises an introduction—"How many degrees, *ma'a lot*, of goodness God has bestowed upon us!"—and fourteen stanzas, which include fifteen divine favors. Why fifteen? First we should note that many Jewish prayers feature fifteen praises of God, among others *Kaddish, Birkot Hashachar,* and *Yishtabach* (which appears in the Haggadah as well as in the daily liturgy). The Priestly Blessing (Numbers 6:24–27) also includes fifteen words. Thus, it is often said that as God instructed the priests to bless the people of Israel with fifteen words, when we praise God in prayer we should reciprocate with fifteen tributes. It's also worth remembering that fifteen is the numerical value of one of God's names—*Yah,* as in Halleluyah, or "Praise God." Commentators have made many other connections as well: some assert that Isaiah 26:4 alludes to fifteen divine saving acts; Ezekiel recounts fifteen acts of kindness done by God for the Israelites in Egypt; the number fifteen occurs twice in the dimensions of the tabernacle in the desert; and so forth.[13] The most common interpretation notes that the Hebrew word "degrees," *ma'alot,* can also mean "steps." In fact, this is the same word the Mishnah uses in a key passage describing the path traversed by a pilgrim in the course of bringing an offering to the Temple.

> Fifteen steps, *ma'alot,* led [from the Court of the Women] to the Court of the Israelites, corresponding to the fifteen Psalms which begin "A psalm of ascent," and upon which the Levites used to sing.[14]

So when we sing *Dayyenu,* it's as if we are traversing our history from the depths of exile to the heights of the Temple in Jerusalem. Deuteronomy (26:5) tells us that Jacob "*went down* to Egypt." When the exiles returned from Babylonia, "all whose spirit had been roused by God, got ready to *go up* to build the House of

Adonai that is in Jerusalem" (Ezra 1:5). We're also following in the footsteps, as it were, of our ancestors as they ascended the fifteen steps toward the Temple's altar.

DAYENNU AS MICROCOSM

If you are looking for something quite concise to illustrate the essence of the Haggadah, *Dayyenu* would suffice!

THE HAGGADAH	DAYYENU
1. The Seder developed as a substitute for sacrifice in the Temple.	1. *Dayyenu*'s fifteen divine favors evoke the fifteen steps in the Temple that pilgrims would climb en route to slaughtering the paschal sacrifice.
2. The Mishnah (Pesachim 10:4) tells us to make a midrash on Deuteronomy 26:5–9. The passage begins with the Exodus and ends with the Temple.	2. *Dayyenu* can be thought of as such a midrash. It begins with the Exodus and ends with the Temple.
3. The same Mishnah says we should "begin with degradation and end with glory."	3. *Dayyenu* begins with the events of Egypt (degradation) and ends with entering the Land of Israel and building the Temple (glory).
4. The Talmud debates whether "degradation" refers to slavery or idol worship. The Haggadah includes both options.	4. *Dayyenu* first deals with the liberation from Egypt and then with matters of spiritual elevation.
5. After crossing the Red Sea, the Israelites burst into their first song. The Haggadah tells us that we should feel as if we had left Egypt.	5. After we read about the plagues the Egyptians suffered at the Red Sea, we burst into *Dayyenu*, the Haggadah's first song.

SINAI WITHOUT TORAH: WOULD IT HAVE SUFFICED?
FOR DISCUSSION

- How might you explain the verse in *Dayyenu* that says, "If He had brought us to Mount Sinai and not given us the Torah, it would have sufficed!" What reason could there have been for going to Sinai without receiving the Torah?

- What other problems does the song raise? How might you explain them?

Read on your own or consider reading aloud.

Dayyenu clearly wants us to count our blessings, to see the glass as half full. Nonetheless, the song has presented commentators with many difficulties. Some involve the apparent abrogation of divine promises. For example, how could God not have given the Israelites the Egyptians' wealth when God told Abraham that his descendants would leave Egypt with great wealth (Gen. 15:14)?

Well, says a commentary attributed to Rabbi Shmuel ben Meir, Rashbam (c. 1085–1158), *Dayyenu* is not referring to what the Egyptians gave the Israelites in Egypt, but to additional booty—according to the midrash—that they received at the Red Sea.[15] A different issue arises when the song says, "If God had not sustained us in the desert for forty years, *Dayyenu!*" Wouldn't the Israelites have perished? No, says Rashbam. They had their flocks, and with all that wealth from the Egyptians, they could have bought whatever they needed from neighboring nations.

These challenges pale when compared to *Dayyenu*'s assertion that had we been at Sinai and not received the Torah, it would have sufficed! Given the Torah's absolute centrality in traditional Judaism, how can this be? Rashbam argued that the verse means this: Had we received the Ten Commandments from God directly and the rest of Torah from Moses, it would have sufficed. Or if God had revealed only part of the Torah at Sinai and the rest on another occasion, it would have sufficed. Others resolved the problem by referring to a strange passage in the Talmud about Eve's sin in the Garden of Eden. The Talmud claims that Israel's presence at Sinai cleansed it of the residual sinfulness brought about by Eve's reputedly having consorted with the snake before she tempted Adam to eat of the

forbidden fruit.[16] Others asserted that by commanding Israel to observe the
Sabbath, God had already given the people something as valuable as the entire
Torah. As the midrash says, "Observing the Sabbath is equal to all the commandments in the Torah."[17] Rabbi Yosef Shalom Eliashiv, a leading contemporary sage
among the ultra-Orthodox in Israel, takes yet a different tack. He focuses on the
fact that *Dayyenu* says that God gave *us* the Torah, meaning that *we*, not God, have
the responsibility of interpreting it. Thus the Talmud teaches that in disputes of
Jewish law, the majority opinion of judges even trumps a *bat kol*, an undisputed
divine voice from heaven![18]

18

Reliving the Exodus:
The Story of the Last Night in Egypt

... זֶבַח פֶּסַח הוּא לַיהֹוָה
אֲשֶׁר פָּסַח עַל בָּתֵּי בְנֵי יִשְׂרָאֵל בְּמִצְרַיִם,
בְּנָגְפּוֹ אֶת־מִצְרַיִם וְאֶת־בָּתֵּינוּ הִצִּיל...

... It is the Passover sacrifice to Adonai because He passed over the houses of the Israelites in Egypt when He struck the Egyptians, but saved our houses ... (Ex. 12:27).
—THE PASSOVER HAGGADAH

Ever since the compilation of the Mishnah eighteen hundred years ago, the Seder has required us to *explain* the meaning of three of Passover's central symbols—the ancient paschal offering, matzah, and bitter herbs. The passage above serves as the Haggadah's explanation of the ancient paschal sacrifice. But the Haggadah challenges us to go further than mere explanation. It calls us to reexperience the pain of slavery and the joy of freedom, reliving the journey from one state to the other: "In every generation, each individual should feel as though he or she had gone out of Egypt." How can we achieve this? The Haggadah contains the answer in a simple phrase: "Moreover, whoever elaborates upon the story of the Exodus deserves praise." In that spirit, here is a set of pre-Seder activities designed to bring the saga of the Exodus to life. As you'll see, this chapter involves a number of "reenactments" of the Exodus that will prove particularly engaging when children and adults participate together.

These activities have been designed to take place before your Seder actually begins (unless you intend to begin early), so you may want to ask guests to arrive earlier than usual. If you are adding a number of pre-Seder activities, you may want to keep this in mind when planning your formal Seder.

We begin with a review of what you'll need to prepare before your guests arrive and continue with suggestions for how to present the activities included. *The Last Night in Egypt,* the story of the Exodus, has been written for reading aloud with children.

SETTING THE STAGE

What you'll need:

- A small, wrapped sandwich of horseradish and matzah and a back-pack, shopping bag, or small suitcase for each Seder participant

- Several yards of red ribbon or several sheets of red construction paper, cut or torn into shapes resembling blood smeared on a doorpost

- Several yards of blue ribbon or blue construction paper, torn, cut or folded to resemble the parted Red Sea

- Scotch tape

- Copies of the Wayfarer's Prayer (see page 251) for each of your guests

Before your guests arrive, take a few pieces of red ribbon, fabric, or construction paper and fashion them to represent the lamb's blood smeared upon the Israelites' doorposts on their last night in Egypt. Tape these around the doorway

242

of the room where you will conduct the activities that follow. (You can also ask younger participants to help with this.) This room will represent Egypt. Later, you can explain to the group that this blood served as a sign for God to pass over the houses of the Israelites as God slew the Egyptian firstborn (Ex. 12:21–23). This will help set the mood for getting back to Egypt. Prepare strips of blue ribbon, fabric, or construction paper to represent the Red Sea. Have these ready so you can later place them at the exit of this room when you head out of Egypt.

Place a small piece of matzah and a slice of horseradish in aluminum foil, plastic wrap, or a waxed paper bag. If you are using chopped horseradish, make a sandwich. Make enough packages for each Seder participant. Bring these along with the backpacks, etc. into your "Egypt" room.

When your guests arrive, if possible, gather them together in a room other than the room where you will be eating the Passover meal. This will enhance the feeling of departure from Egypt and arrival in the Promised Land. (In our house, we sit in the living room.)

Now you are ready to begin.

Explain that you will be engaging in a variety of activities designed to help achieve the goal of the Haggadah: "In every generation, each individual should feel as though he or she had gone out of Egypt."

If you haven't already done so, explain the meaning of the red ribbon construction paper on the doorpost. Tell your guests that you'll be reading a story about the Exodus from Egypt, *The Last Night in Egypt,* and then taking up one or two questions it raises:

- Should the Israelites let Egyptians who are seeking to escape from God's final plague into their homes?

- Should the Israelites risk leaving Egypt for an unknown destination?

Following the story below, you'll find suggestions for using these questions as the basis of a short bibliodrama that your Seder participants will be sure to remember. If you prefer, you can simply discuss these questions after you read the story and skip the bibliodrama. As a third option, you might include an activity based on the Wayfarer's Prayer, described on pages 250–251.

THE LAST NIGHT IN EGYPT

Read *The Last Night in Egypt* aloud. Depending on your group, you might ask one
individual to read the entire story or let everyone read a few paragraphs.
This works best if you have a copy for everyone. The story sets the stage for addressing
the two questions described earlier, but you can also use it on its own.
Italics indicate quotations from the Book of Exodus.

Once, more than three thousand springtimes ago, near the very beginning of the
Jewish People's history, there lived a very rich and mighty Egyptian king. He was
also super stubborn. Everyone called the king "Pharaoh." Many kinds of people
lived in his kingdom—Egyptians, Africans, and many Israelites (that's what they
called Jews in the olden days. Jews were also sometimes called "Hebrews").

Kings who are very mighty sometimes get scared that someone else will try
to take away some of their power. That happened to Pharaoh. He always worried
that someone would rise up against him. He was afraid his enemies would attack
him. He was even afraid his friends would attack him. He was so afraid that he
became meaner and meaner.

The Israelites had come to Egypt several hundred years before. They had
grown from about seventy people to more than a million. Pharaoh began to fear
that maybe the Israelites would side with his enemies. That made him really scared
and even meaner than usual. Pharaoh enslaved the Israelites. He also gave orders
to the midwives who delivered the Israelite babies to kill all the boys. That would
be the end of them! But the midwives feared God and disobeyed Pharaoh's order.

So Pharaoh gave an order to the Egyptian people saying, *"Every [Hebrew] boy
that is born you shall throw into the Nile, but let every girl live"* (Ex. 1:22).

One mother named Yocheved decided to help her baby son escape. She
lined a wicker basket with waterproof tar, put her son inside, and placed it in the
reeds along the riverbank. She kissed him. "Good-bye, my sweet little boy," she
called sadly. "I pray that an Egyptian mother will see your cradle and save you."
Miriam, the baby's sister, hid nearby to see what would happen to her brother.

Soon, Pharaoh's daughter came down to bathe in the Nile. Guess what she
found! *She spied the basket among the reeds and sent her slave to get it. When she opened
it, she saw it was a child, a boy crying. She took pity on it and said, "This must be a
Hebrew child"* (Ex. 2:5–6).

She wondered how her own father could be so mean.

Just then Miriam popped out of the bushes. Moses' sister *said to Pharaoh's daughter, "Shall I get you a Hebrew woman to nurse the child for you?"*

And Pharaoh's daughter answered, "Yes."

So the girl went and called the child's mother.

And Pharaoh's daughter said to her, "Take this child and nurse it for me, and I will pay your wages."

So the woman took the child and nursed it. When the child grew up, she brought him to Pharaoh's daughter, who made him her son. She named him Moses, explaining, "I drew him out of the water" (Ex. 2:7–10).

Only a few people knew that Moses was an Israelite, and they kept it a big secret from Pharaoh.

But Pharaoh was still afraid and mean. He forced the Israelites to become his slaves. They built huge buildings. They built whole cities. The weather in Egypt was boiling hot, especially in the summer. Hotter than 100 degrees. But Pharaoh hardly gave them any water. They weren't even allowed to ask any questions. When his slaves complained or sat down in the shade, his soldiers beat them with whips.

Meanwhile, Prince Moses grew up in Pharaoh's palace. One day, he took a walk to watch a new city being built. That was very exciting. Huge blocks of stone that weighed tons were being rolled along on round logs. Using long ropes, Israelite slaves dragged these stones for miles. As Moses came closer, he saw some soldiers whipping a Hebrew slave.

"Why is he doing that?" Moses wondered. "That slave is so weak, he couldn't hurt anyone."

"I may be a prince of Egypt," Moses said to himself, "but these are still my people." Moses looked this way and that way. He saw no one. He punched the soldier so hard that the soldier died. Moses buried him in the sand.

When Moses came back the next day, the Israelite slaves were afraid of him. One said, *"Do you mean to kill us like you killed the Egyptian?"*(Ex. 2:14). Moses knew he had to leave Egypt. Soon Pharaoh would hear what Moses had done. Pharaoh would finally learn that he had been tricked. Soon he would know that Moses was not really an Egyptian, but an Israelite.

So Moses set off into the desert to escape from his adopted father. He came to the land of Midian, where he became a shepherd. He got married and had two sons. Many years went by. The old Pharaoh died, but a new one took his place who was just as mean, and even more stubborn.

One day, while tending his flocks, Moses saw a strange light in the mountains. It was a bush on fire. Instead of burning up, it kept on burning and burning. Moses wondered, *"Why doesn't the bush burn up?"* (Ex. 3:3).

Suddenly Moses heard a voice. *"Do not come closer. Remove your sandals from your feet, for the place where you stand is holy ground. I am,"* He said, *"the God of your father, the God of Abraham, the God of Isaac, and the God of Jacob." And Moses hid his face for he was afraid to look at God* (Ex. 3:5–6).

Moses had heard about this God from his mother. She told him that the God of the Israelites was invisible and even stronger than Pharaoh. God knew everything, even exactly what was going to happen in the future. The voice told Moses that God knew about how mean Pharaoh had been to his Israelite slaves. God heard their cries of pain and wanted to take them out of Egypt and set them free.

"But Moses, you must be their leader," said God. "Go tell Pharaoh to let my people go. I know that mean Pharaoh won't want to let the Israelites go. I will harden his heart so I, the mighty and awesome God, will show him who is boss. I'll send ten plagues to Egypt and then Pharaoh will let my people go."

Moses heard all this and grew more and more afraid. "What if no one believes you?" Moses asked God. "And why should the Israelites listen to me. I have a lisp and can't even speak clearly. And forget about Pharaoh! He doesn't listen to anybody anyway!"

"Your brother Aaron will help you," said God. And God gave Moses special signs to convince the Israelites and the Egyptians that God meant business. God gave Moses three mysterious signs to show when he got back to Egypt—turning a rod into a snake, making the skin on his hand change from very smooth to very rough, and making water turn red like blood. God gave Moses a special rod to help create these signs.

Moses was right! No one listened. Pharaoh just made his Israelite slaves work even harder! He even took away the straw they needed to make bricks. That made their work so hard it was almost impossible.

So God told Moses to warn Pharaoh about the plagues, one at a time. First the rivers all turned to blood. But Pharaoh didn't care. Then frogs started jumping out of the river until the whole country smelled of frogs. Pharaoh pleaded with Moses to make the frogs go away. But when they did, he still wouldn't let the children of Israel leave Egypt.

Then lice came and made everyone itch. Then insects covered everything. Then all the cattle that belonged to the Egyptians started to get sick. Then all the Egyptians started to get big sores all over their bodies. Then huge hailstones fell all over Egypt. The hailstones were so big they made holes in the roof. Then swarms of crickets came and ate all the plants. Then the sun didn't come out for three whole days. And the darkness was so thick you could touch it.

Each time a plague came Pharaoh agreed to let the Israelites go. But as soon as the plague ended he changed his mind. Pharaoh's heart grew harder and harder. So God sent another plague. Pharaoh told Moses never to come back. But he still wouldn't let the Israelites go.

God told Moses to get ready for the last and worst plague of all. This one would finally convince Pharaoh to let the Israelites go free. God was going to kill all the firstborn Egyptian males—people and even animals. God spoke to Moses, saying, "Tell the Israelites to paint their doorposts with the blood of a lamb as a sign so I will *pass over* their homes. They should roast the lamb and eat it with bitter herbs and matzah. And tell them to stay inside their homes."

God also told Moses this: "Tell the Israelites that every spring they should have a holiday to remember what happened on this last night in Egypt. For seven days they should eat matzah but no bread. When your children ask what this holiday is all about you shall tell them, *'It is the Passover sacrifice to Adonai because God passed over the houses of the Israelites in Egypt when God struck the Egyptians, but saved our houses'"* (Ex. 12:27).

That was a long, scary, and very sad night for everyone in Egypt. Many Egyptians died. The Israelites were safe. But Egyptian mothers trying to save their children kept knocking on the doors of Israelite homes. And the Israelites did not know what to do.

Should they let these Egyptians in or not?

That was one thing the Israelites were thinking about that night. But they were also wondering about leaving Egypt the next morning. Life was bad in

Egypt, but it was still home. And where would they go? Out into the desert, following orders that Moses got from the mighty and invisible God? And what would they take with them? And what would they eat and drink in the desert? Maybe it would be better to stay in Egypt?

But by the time morning came, stubborn Pharaoh had finally decided to send the Israelites out of Egypt. And the children of Israel had finally decided it was time to leave Egypt. It was time to learn how to be a free people. "Maybe," they thought, "we can make a country that is a better place for people to live than Egypt." And that is what we, the Jewish People, are still trying to do.

> B'khol dor vador chayav adam lirot et atzmo k'ilu hu yatza mimitzrayim.
> In every generation, each individual should feel as though he or she had gone out of Egypt.

BIBLIODRAMA: KNOCKING IN THE NIGHT

In the middle of the last plague, Egyptian mothers seeking to save their firstborn sons knock frantically on the doors of the Israelites' homes. Should the Israelites let them in?

This works very well as a simple drama. Choose someone to be a door. He or she simply stands in the middle of the room with arms outstretched parallel to the floor. Ask a few people to stand on one side of the door and play the part of Egyptians trying to seek refuge. Ask a few other people to be on the other side of the door and play the role of Israelites. Some should argue for letting in the Egyptians and others should oppose this. If you have many people at your Seder, you can either let people participate in the drama from the "audience" or ask people who have something to say to join the drama on one side of the door or the other. Feel free to allow questions about the morality of this last plague.

After the "drama" has reached an end, share the following midrash (Exodus Rabbah 18:2) with the group. It was written down about a thousand years ago, but it is probably based on a more ancient source:

When the Egyptians heard that God would strike down their firstborn, some were afraid and some were not. Those who were afraid brought their firstborn to an Israelite and said: "Do please allow him to pass with you this night." When midnight struck, God smote all the first-born. As for those who took asylum in the houses of the Israelites, God passed between the Israelites and the Egyptians, killing the Egyptians and leaving the Israelites alive. When the Jews awoke at midnight, they found the Egyptians dead among their surviving firstborn.

Now ask the group to reflect on what contemporary situations the "drama" and midrash evoke for them. The theme of rescue, from the Holocaust to September 11, should be fairly close to the surface.

- Have we acted as our "brothers' keepers"?

- The Seder begins with an invitation to the hungry and poor to join us. Should we invite a homeless person to our Seders? Why or why not?

- Have we stood "idly by the blood" of our neighbors (Lev. 19:16)?

- Have we remembered to "know the heart of the stranger because [we] were strangers in Egypt" (Ex. 23:9)?

- Have we used our memories of suffering and persecution—in Egypt and elsewhere—to nurture vengeance or to affirm our responsibility to create a better world?

BIBLIODRAMA: TO STAY OR TO LEAVE?

Should the Israelites risk leaving Egypt for promises of a better life in their own land?

Set the stage by giving your guests the following background:

Life in Egypt was difficult, but maybe heading out into the unknown desert would be even worse. The text in Exodus tells us that God was not very trusting of the Israelites' loyalty to their new destination:

Now when Pharaoh let the people go, God did not lead them by way of the land of the Philistines, although it was nearer; for God said, "The people may have a change of heart when they see war and return to Egypt" (Ex. 13:17).

A bit later, Pharaoh changes his mind and sets out for the Red Sea to capture his fleeing slaves. The Israelites too have a change of heart.

Greatly frightened, the Israelites cried out to Adonai. And they said to Moses, "Was it for want of graves in Egypt that you brought us to die in the wilderness? What have you done to us, taking us out of Egypt? Is this not the very thing we told you in Egypt, saying, 'Let us be, and we will serve the Egyptians, for it is better for us to serve the Egyptians than to die in the wilderness'?" (Ex. 14:10–12).

Ask some members of your group to defend leaving and others to defend staying. After arguing the pros and cons of leaving Egypt, you may want to try broadening the discussion to include contemporary events or personal situations that involve the plight of refugees. The road to freedom always requires risks. The responsibility for building a just society is daunting because it never ends.

As individuals and a community, here and in Israel, how well have we done this year? What are the habits or the empty values that keep us enslaved and prevent us from moving on in our lives?

A PRAYER FOR THE JOURNEY

The Exodus from Egypt represents one of *the* paradigmatic journeys of all time. Before you prepare to set off for the Promised Land, ask your group this question:

> If you were setting out on a journey as momentous as the Israelites' departure from Egypt, and you wanted to offer a prayer before you left, what would be the main ideas you'd include in your prayer?

Briefly summarize the themes that emerge in your guests' answers. When you've finished this, hand out a copy of the Wayfarer's Prayer to each guest. Read it aloud and ask for a few very brief comments on the differences and similarities between the themes included in this prayer and those raised by your guests.[1]

With only a few modifications, the Wayfarer's Prayer—*Tefilat Ha-derekh*—comes from the Babylonian Talmud (Berakhot 29b), which was completed in about the year 500.

In the Talmud, the prayer is in the singular, while the traditional version recited today is always in the plural, even if the journey involves only a single individual. One who sets out on a journey should recite the following prayer upon leaving the city limits:

The Wayfarer's Prayer

May it be Your will, our God, and God of our ancestors, that You lead us toward peace, cause us to take steps toward peace, and guide us toward peace. And bring us to our desired destination—life, joy, and peace. Save us from the hand of every enemy or ambush on the road and from every kind of disaster that could ever threaten the world. May You bless the work of our hands and grant us grace, kindness, and mercy—in Your eyes and in the eyes of all who see us. Hear the voice of our supplication, because You are a God who hears prayer and supplication. Blessed are You, God, who hears prayer.

MARCHING FROM EGYPT TO THE PROMISED LAND

Now you are ready to begin the march from Egypt, through the Red Sea, to the Promised Land—the Seder table. Jews from some Islamic countries still practice the custom of symbolically re-creating the Exodus by walking around the Seder table while carrying matzah wrapped in napkins slung over their back. We conclude with a variation on that wonderful tradition. Give everyone a plastic bag with a piece of matzah and a slice of horseradish (or a sandwich of chopped horseradish). Everyone should take his or her bag of bitterness and load it into a backpack, suitcase, or shopping bag. We must never forget our oppression in Egypt even when we Jews are a free people, and especially when we have power. Before you leave Egypt don't forget to lay down the blue fabric or construction paper that represents the Red Sea.

When everyone is ready, form a line, with children at the head, and wind your way from Egypt, where you've been, across the Red Sea, through the desert to the Promised Land. Remember that the journey from Egypt to the Promised Land took a long time and the route was circuitous. Walk in circles, up and down stairs, etc., until you reach the Seder table!

Just before you start your journey, read the following ancient midrash:[2]

The only edibles the Israelites took were the remains of the unleavened bread and the bitter herbs, and these not to satisfy their hunger, but because they were unwilling to separate themselves from what they had prepared lovingly at the command of God. These possessions were so dear to them that they would not entrust them to their beasts of burden; they carried them on their own shoulders.

On your journey, sing *Let My People Go* with gusto!

When Israel was in Egypt's land
Let my people go
Oppressed so hard they could not stand
Let my people go
Go down, Moses, way down in Egypt land
Tell ole Pharaoh
To let my people go

Unpack your suitcases and save your sandwich of matzah and bitter herbs for the appropriate point in the Seder.

19

Israel and the Haggadah

וְאוֹתָנוּ הוֹצִיא מִשָּׁם לְמַעַן הָבִיא אֹתָנוּ
לָתֶת לָנוּ אֶת־הָאָרֶץ אֲשֶׁר נִשְׁבַּע לַאֲבֹתֵינוּ.

And us He took out from there, that He might bring us and give us the
land that He promised on oath to our ancestors (Deut. 6:23).
—THE PASSOVER HAGGADAH

Based on many of the biblical passages quoted in the Haggadah, you might expect references to the Land of Israel to appear throughout the Seder. But, as we'll see, that's hardly the case. In this chapter, we'll consider how the Haggadah relates to Israel as well as some broader questions concerning the relationship between Passover and the State of Israel.

As you make your way through your Seder, ask your guests to let you know every time they notice a reference to the Land of Israel, Zion, Jerusalem, the Temple, and the land of Canaan. See whether you notice any parts of the Seder where these references occur more or less often. Ask your guests to discuss why this might be the case.

THE FRUITS OF ISRAEL AND EGYPT: A PUZZLE

This activity requires a trip to the grocery store. Pick up a head of garlic, a cucumber, a leek, an onion, a melon, grapes, figs, and a pomegranate (if you can't find a pomegranate, make one out of red paper). Put the garlic, cucumber, leek, onion, and melon in one basket (or bowl) and the remaining items in another.

Before your Seder begins, gather your guests and show them both baskets. Explain that you'll be solving a puzzle based on two passages in the Bible in which these groups of fruits and vegetables appear. Read the paragraphs below and the question that comes after. After you've concluded your discussion, you may want to read one or both of the "solutions" that follow.

Following the Exodus from Egypt, the Israelites camped near Mount Sinai for almost a year. After having received the Torah and dedicated the Mishkan (the portable sanctuary for the Ark of the Covenant), they finally began their march to the Promised Land, a distance of only several months' (or maybe less) travel. Three days into the journey, they complained bitterly, longing to return to Egypt:

> The riffraff in their midst felt a gluttonous craving; and then the Israelites wept and said, "If only we had meat to eat! We remember the fish that we used to eat free in Egypt, the cucumbers, the melons, the leeks, the onions, and the garlic. Now our gullets are shriveled. There is nothing at all! Nothing but this manna to look to."
>
> —NUMBERS 11:4–6

A few chapters later, twelve spies are sent to scout out the land of Canaan. All except Joshua and Caleb spread evil reports about the land in order to persuade the Israelites to return to Egypt. After the ensuing rebellion against Moses and Aaron, God condemns the people to thirty-nine more years in the desert. What did the spies bring back from Canaan?

> They reached wadi Eshcol, and there they cut down a branch with a single cluster of grapes—it had to be borne on a carrying frame by two of them—and some pomegranates and figs.
>
> —NUMBERS 13:23

- Why do you think garlic, cucumbers, leeks, onions, and melons are associated with Egypt, while grapes, figs, and pomegranates are connected with Israel? There is more than one satisfying answer to this puzzle! Deuteronomy 8:8 notes the seven choice species of the Land of Israel—wheat, barley, grapes, figs, pomegranates, olives, and honey. Here we are just concerned with those mentioned in Numbers 13:23.

Following are two solutions to the puzzle that you might share with your group.

From the Depths to the Heights: Garlic, onions, leeks, melons, and cucumbers mature under or upon the soil. When harvested, they bear the signs of their habitat: they are fully or partially covered with dirt. These crops shared their earthen realm with the Israelites, who were so long mired in the muddy clay of Egypt's brick pits. Grapes, figs, and pomegranates grow on trees or vines, which elevate them above the ground. This difference represents the journey from degradation to redemption on both the physical and the spiritual plane.

Israel's descent begins with Jacob's journey down to Egypt. As we read in the Haggadah, "My father was a wandering Aramean. He went down few in numbers to sojourn there . . ." (Deut. 26:5).

> The Egyptians ruthlessly imposed upon the Israelites the various labors that they made them perform. Ruthlessly they made life bitter for them with harsh labor at mortar and bricks and with all sorts of tasks in the field.
> —EXODUS 1:13

Redeeming the Israelites first meant literally lifting them out of the mud, then bringing them to Sinai, and later up to Israel, as in Psalms 40:3–4: "He lifted me out of the miry pit, the slimy clay, and set my feet on a rock, steadied my legs. He put a new song into my mouth, a song of praise to our God." The produce of Egypt represents the lowly state to which Israel had fallen and to which they had sadly grown accustomed. The fruits of Israel embody the promise of ascent. "And God spoke to Israel in the visions of the night . . . I myself will go down with you to Egypt; and I will also surely bring you up again" (Gen. 46: 2–4). If you move to Israel, you make *aliya*, which means "going up." Emigrating from Israel is (somewhat derogatorily) called *yerida*, "going down." And remember that huge cluster of grapes the spies carried back on two poles? A few thousand years later, it became the official logo of Israel's Ministry of Tourism!

The yearning for the crops of *Mitzrayim* suggests that it is easier to take the slaves out of Egypt than to take Egypt out of the slaves. After almost forty years of wandering in the desert, those who had lived in Egypt as adults died. Alas, as did their forebears, the new generation also grumbled. They cried to Moses and Aaron: "Now why did you make us go up from Egypt to bring us to this evil place, not a place of seeds and figs, vines, and pomegranates—and water [there is] none to drink!" (Numbers 20:5).[1] The generation of former slaves craved the produce of Egypt. Their offspring yearned for the fruits of Israel that the spies had brought back thirty-eight years earlier. Both generations complained—but one wanted to head backward, the other forward.

Roots and Responsibilities: Cucumbers, leeks, garlic, onions, and melons are all annuals—they have to be replanted each year. Grapes, figs and pomegranates are perennials—plant them once and they produce for many, many years. They also take several years before they mature and bear fruit. Now, although the Israelites stayed in Egypt for several hundred years, it was never truly their home. When God promises the land to Abraham, God also says this to Abraham: "Know well that your offspring shall be strangers in a land not theirs . . ." (Gen. 15:13).

The land of Egypt does not belong to the Israelites, despite how long they have resided in it. Later, when Joseph brings his father Jacob to meet Pharaoh, Jacob says he has come to "sojourn in this land." The stay may be long, but it is ultimately temporary. So the Israelites put down shallow roots in Egypt, like the plants for which they yearn. For the Israelites, the Promised Land is their ultimate destination, home in the deepest sense. And that is where one really puts down roots. That is where one is sure to be long enough to justify plantings that will take time to bear fruit.

The issue of roots—shallow or deep—also relates to the type of care required by these different kinds of plants. The plants associated with Egypt need people to water them, and fairly frequently. That takes work. These particular fruits of Israel draw their own water from the soil's depths. But that water only comes if the Israelites obey the laws they have received in the desert after leaving Egypt. That too takes work, but of a different kind:

For the land that you are about to enter and possess is not like the land of Egypt from which you have come. There the grain you sowed had to be watered by your own labors, like a vegetable garden; but the land you are about to cross into and possess, a land of hills and valleys, soaks up its water from the rains of heaven. It is a land which Adonai your God looks after, on which Adonai your God always keeps His eye, from year's beginning to year's end. If, then, you obey the commandments that I enjoin upon you this day, loving Adonai your God and serving Him with all your heart and soul, I will grant the rain for your land in season, the early rain and the late.

—DEUTERONOMY 11:10–14

When given the choice between serving Pharaoh and God, between the familiar land of Egypt and the strange land of promise, the Israelites who had come of age in *Mitzrayim* preferred Pharaoh and Egypt. As a result, they wandered for forty years in the desert and never made it to the Promised Land. In Hebrew, *avodah* can mean ordinary "work" or "service of God." Passover is a good time to consider the balance in our lives of both kinds of *avodah*. If you are all about work, you may lack connection with the One of Ultimate Purpose. If you pursue only matters of the spirit, you may be cut off from the material world that cries out to be mended. Have you struck a healthy balance?

ISRAEL'S ABSENCE FROM THE HEART OF THE HAGGADAH

Take turns reading the following paragraphs aloud and then lead a discussion on any or all of the questions at the end of this section.

Where were the Israelites headed after leaving Egypt? Doesn't the Haggadah lead us on a journey from slavery to redemption, from Egypt to Israel, albeit an Israel from which we were exiled for so many long centuries? Reading only the beginning and the conclusion of the Haggadah, that would seem to be the case.

Near the beginning of the Haggadah we read:

This is the bread of affliction that our ancestors ate in the land of Egypt. Whoever is hungry, let him come and eat; whoever is in need let him come join in celebrating the Pesach festival. This year we are here, next year may it be in the Land of Israel! This year, slaves; next year, free people!

At the Haggadah's conclusion we read:

The order of the Pesach service is now completed in accordance with all its laws, its ordinances and statutes. Just as we were found worthy to perform it, so may we be worthy to do it in the future. O Pure One who dwells on high, raise up the congregation which is without number! Soon, and with rejoicing, lead the offshoots of the stock that you have planted redeemed to Zion.

L'shanah ha-ba'ah birushalayim!
Next year in Jerusalem!

So far, so good. But now let's look more closely at some of the Haggadah's core texts, where Israel literally drops off the page.[2]

The Haggadah answers the Four Questions with the following quotation from Deuteronomy 6:21: "*Avadim hayinu* . . . We were Pharaoh's slaves in Egypt; and Adonai took us out of Egypt with a mighty hand. . . ."

But the next verses from Deuteronomy read: "Adonai wrought before our eyes marvelous and destructive signs and portents in Egypt, against Pharaoh and all his household; and us he took out from there that He might bring us and give us the land that He had promised on oath to our ancestors" (Deut. 6:22–23).

A bit later, the Haggadah describes God's covenant with Abraham:

Blessed be He who keeps His promise to Israel. Blessed be He. For the Holy One, blessed be He, determined the end of the bondage, thus doing that which He said to Abraham our father in the Covenant between the Pieces. As it is said, "He said unto Abram: 'Know well that your offspring shall be strangers in a land not theirs, and they shall be enslaved and oppressed for four hundred years; but I will execute judgment on the nation they shall serve, and in the end they shall go out with great wealth'" (Gen. 15:13–14).

God's promise to Abram went further, but the Haggadah omits the rest of it: "And they shall return here . . . To your offspring I assign this land . . ." (Gen. 15:16, 18).

Eighteen hundred years ago, the Mishnah described many of the Seder's essentials, instructing us to expound on the following passage from the Book of Deuteronomy *"until [we] complete the whole section"*:

My father was a wandering Aramean. He went down to Egypt few in numbers and sojourned there; but there he became a great and very populous nation. The Egyptians dealt harshly with us and oppressed us; they imposed heavy labor upon us. We cried to Adonai, the God of our fathers, and Adonai heard our plea and saw our plight, our misery, and our oppression. Adonai took us out from Egypt by a mighty hand, by an outstretched arm and awesome power, and by signs and portents.

—DEUTERONOMY 26:5–8

Despite the Mishnah's clear instructions to complete the section, the Haggadah stops short and omits the next verse: "And he has brought us to this place and has given us this land, a land flowing with milk and honey" (Deut. 26:9).

Let's consider one more example of Israel's diminished presence in the Haggadah. According to the most common explanation, the Seder's four cups of wine each correspond to an aspect of God's fourfold redemptive promise:

Say, therefore, to the Israelite people: I am Adonai. I will [1] take you out from the labors of the Egyptians and [2] deliver you from their bondage. I will [3] redeem you with an outstretched arm and through extraordinary chastisements. And I will [4] take you to be My people and I will be your God. . . .

—EXODUS 6:6–7

But the next verse includes a fifth promise: "I will [5] bring you into the land which I swore to give to Abraham, Isaac, and Jacob, and I will give it to you for a possession, I Adonai" (Ex. 6:8).

The fifth aspect of redemption relates to Israel.

So shouldn't we drink five cups of wine instead of four? Some used to. Today, standard versions of the Talmud (Pesachim 118a) read: "Over the fourth cup one recites the Hallel and the Great Hallel (Psalm 136)." But other manuscripts of the Talmud read: "Over the *fifth* cup one completes the Hallel and the Great Hallel. These are the words of Rabbi Tarfon." Rashi preferred the text that specified only four cups and, for most, his view held sway.[3]

- Why do you think the compilers of the Haggadah downplayed the presence of Israel?

- If you were writing a Haggadah today, what role would you assign Israel?

- How do you feel when you say, "Next year in Jerusalem"? What do you mean when you say it?

- Do you think a people can be truly free without a connection to a particular land? Can the Jewish People be free without Israel?

WHITHER ISRAEL?

You may want to read this on your own or, depending on your group,
after discussing the questions in the previous section.

Had not Bar Kochba's disastrous rebellion (132–135 C.E.) led to the exile of most Jews from Israel, Jewish history and Judaism itself would surely have evolved differently. Rabbinic Judaism developed after the Second Temple's destruction, and its task was to create a portable Judaism, independent of both the Temple and the Land of Israel. Building on earlier examples in the Bible, Rabbinic Judaism consolidated the transformation of the Exodus from Egypt into a symbol of hope in God's future redemption of the Jewish People. The

Jew would encounter God in the world of sacred time and commandments instead of sacred space and sacrifice.

At Passover, the celebration of faith in God's ultimate redemption of Israel, a people in exile, could hardly give repeated emphasis to passages promising that Abraham's descendants would inherit the land. Of course, the hope of restoration to Israel remained. But exile must have imposed its own reading upon the Haggadah's injunction: "In every generation, each individual should feel as though he or she had gone out of Egypt." Gone *out* of Egypt; not necessarily *into* the Promised Land. That's another story and one that required a good many years to complete.

The Sages, of course, continued to extol the beauties of Zion. But it didn't take long for the idea of a heavenly Jerusalem to take root, a city whose mythic radiance far outshone that of the earthly city.[4] Likewise, they also lauded the virtues of living in Israel, while at the same time putting the brakes on any messianic impulse to retake the land. Thus, Rabbi Helbo, a sage active in Israel during the early fourth century C.E. interpreted a verse from the Song of Songs (8:4)—"Do not wake or rouse love until it please"—as God's warning to the Jewish People "that they should not attempt to go up from the Diaspora by force."[5] The Jewish People should not force God's redemptive hand.

The references to Israel in the beginning and at the end of the Seder (as well as in its various psalms and songs) were not necessarily to the Israel of this world, but to the Israel of an idealized, messianic future. As Benjamin Segal writes:

> If one's eyes were set Zionward, they were also primarily set toward the future. The "city of the kings, the royal city" was such in *potential,* but in the present she could only be called on . . . to "arise, come forth from the rubble." On the Sabbath in particular, but in all other prayer cycles as well, the "Israel" of note is a future, ideal, rebuilt, perfected Zion—in short, messianic Jerusalem.[6]

Although there were many differences of opinion about the significance of living in Israel, rabbinic Judaism succeeded so well that Maimonides no longer counted returning to Israel among his enumeration of the 613 *mitzvot,* or commandments.[7]

Remember, too, that between the third and tenth centuries, when much was added to the Haggadah's Mishnaic core, the community in Babylonia increasingly became the intellectual center of the Jewish world. In 922, rivalry between the communities of Israel and Babylonia turned bitter over whose calendar would determine the date of Passover. Unable to resolve the dispute, each community followed its own calendar for a year. Ultimately, Saadiah Gaon, the chief Babylonian protagonist, proved victorious. It's probably not accidental that Saadiah's Haggadah omitted the following passage included in the Haggadot of his predecessors and those of today:[8] "And us He took out from there, that He might bring us and give us the land that He had promised on oath to our ancestors" (Deut. 6:23). Even before Saadiah, the Babylonian drive for dominance over Israel may have left its fingerprints on the Haggadah in Israel's rather muted presence.

The compilers of the Haggadah may also have downplayed Israel because they did not want it to overshadow what they felt to be the ultimate purpose of the redemption from Egypt, namely the revelation at Sinai with the gift of Torah. In fact, at the end of the second Seder we begin counting the *omer,* marking the forty-nine days between Passover and Shavuot when, according to tradition, we received the Torah. Joseph B. Soloveitchik explained it this way:

[A]lthough the Jewish People did enter into the Land of Israel subsequent to the Exodus from Egypt this was not the primary goal of *Yitziat Mitzrayim* [the Exodus from Egypt]. It was their destination but not their destiny. The direct goal of *Yitziat Mitzrayim* was the revelation at Sinai. The goal was the transformation of a subjugated people into "a kingdom of priests and a holy nation" [Exodus 19:6]. It was not just to grant them political and economic freedom, but also to create a sacred people.[9]

There's one more factor that may contribute to the way compilers of the Haggadah treated Israel. First, it's important to note that the elimination of allusions to "the land" occurs in the part of the Haggadah that addresses the enslavement in Egypt. To bring Israel into the Seder at that point would be to undermine one of the Haggadah's central injunctions: to reexperience not just the suffering but also the hopelessness that our ancestors endured in Egypt. The notion of a homeland in which the children of Israel would one day enjoy sovereignty could not have been further from the consciousness of those mercilessly enslaved for generations in Egypt. Reminders of Israel in this part of the Haggadah would undercut the intended dramatic tension, giving away, as it were, the story's ending.

That's why Israel begins to appear after the Haggadah's treatment of the plagues, with the singing of *Dayyenu,* which concludes: "Had He taken us to the Land of Israel without building the Temple for us—it would have sufficed."

We noted earlier that the passage from Deuteronomy (6:21) that provides the answer to the Four Questions (*Avadim hayinu . . .* We were slaves) continued with a reference to God's promise of the land to Abraham's forebears. That reference was omitted at the beginning of the Seder. It appears after *Dayyenu,* just before we recite the first two psalms of the Hallel (literally, "praise"): "And us He took out from there, that He might bring us and give us the land that He had promised on oath to our ancestors" (Deuteronomy 6:23).

THE FIFTH CUP

Read the following paragraphs aloud. Then either discuss with your
Seder participants whether or not they would like to celebrate the fifth cup
or explain why you've decided to do so. You can decide where it would be
most appropriate to insert the fifth cup. Some have suggested doing so after *Dayyenu,*
because its conclusion refers to Israel. A somewhat more traditional view
would suggest inserting an extra cup after completing the *Yehalelukha*
passage that follows the conclusion of the Hallel. According to this tradition,
the fourth cup would be drunk without a blessing. The fifth and final cup
would then be drunk with a blessing as described for the former fourth
cup. To accompany the fifth cup, you may wish to read one of the
selections that follow this reading.[10]

Say, therefore, to the Israelite people: I am Adonai. I will [1] take you out from the labors of the Egyptians and [2] deliver you from their bondage. I will [3] redeem you with an outstretched arm and through extraordinary chastisements. And I will [4] take you to be My people and I will be your God . . . I will [5] bring you into the land which I swore to give to Abraham, Isaac, and Jacob, and I will give it to you for a possession, I Adonai.

—EXODUS 6:6–8

If the cups of wine we drink at the Seder correspond to the number of God's redemptive promises, we should enjoy five cups of wine. Indeed, by the twelfth century, commentators noted interpretations that linked a fifth cup to the fifth promise of redemption.[11] A long list of Judaism's greatest sages—Rashi, Maimonides, the Maharal of Prague, and many others—added a fifth cup to their Seders. They all recognized that the Haggadah required only four cups, but they deemed a fifth cup to be "an excellent work of piety."[12] Still, the fifth cup has remained a debated question of Jewish law.[13] In the eighteenth century, the Vilna Gaon offered what has become a well-known response to the question: Because we are unable to answer this question with certainty, we shall leave the fifth cup for Elijah and await his return to settle the matter.

With the establishment of the State of Israel, the rationale for a fifth cup corresponding to the fifth redemptive promise becomes even more compelling. In our era, the Seder *should* be a time for marking Israel's rebirth and expressing our hopes for the country and its citizens. From the early days of Zionism, the dreams for a Jewish state resonated with the ancient themes of the Passover Seder. In a passage from *Altneuland* ("Old-New Land"), Theodore Herzl's 1902 novel about life in the Jewish state, we read:

It was one of the happy moments when one realizes the progress of civilization. For a time we even considered doing business by wire, quite a marvel. And so it was. At that time we had not got the power from the Dead Sea Canal. Today we no longer need English coal for ploughing the soil of Palestine. Even the locomotive standing at the edge of the field has become outmoded in our eyes. We now have the cables bringing power to our fields from the falls of the Jordan, from the Dead Sea Canal, and the brooks of the Hermon and Lebanon. Instead of coal we have water . . . It was a new version of *Chad Gadya* ["one kid"] . . . [It] is the story of the plough which is first dragged by man, then by oxen, then by a locomotive driven by coal, then by a petrol-motor, then by power taken from water . . . And above it all is God—down to the one kid, the one kid.[14]

Not long after the State of Israel's establishment, Rabbi Menachem Kasher, one of the last century's greatest scholars of rabbinic literature, approached the Rabbinate in Israel to request that they institute the fifth cup. They refused. Nonetheless, the custom has begun to catch on.[15]

READINGS FOR THE FIFTH CUP

Soon after the birth of the State of Israel in 1948, the Rabbinate of Israel and S.Y. Agnon, the Israeli writer and scholar who won the Nobel Prize for Literature in 1966, composed this prayer for Israel. It is included in many prayer books.

A Prayer for the State of Israel

Our Father in heaven [*avinu she-bashamayim*], Rock and Redeemer of the people Israel: Bless the State of Israel, the first flowering of our redemption. Shield it with Your love; spread over it the shelter of Your peace. Guide its leaders and advisers with Your light and Your truth. Help them with Your good counsel. Strengthen the hands of those who defend our Holy Land. Deliver them; crown their efforts with triumph. Bless the land with peace, and its inhabitants with lasting joy. And let us say: Amen.

Rabbi Shlomo Riskin notes that the additional cup is traditionally drunk after the words *Ki mei'olam v'ad olam atah Eil,* "For from eternity to eternity You are God." This endows it with universal redemptive significance that extends beyond the matter of the Jewish People and their land.[16] In that spirit, the reading below focuses on world peace.

A Prayer for Peace

May we see the day when war and bloodshed cease, when a great peace will embrace the whole world. Then nation will not threaten nation, and mankind will not again know war. For all who live on earth shall realize we have not come into being to hate or to destroy. We have come into being to praise, to labor, and to love. Compassionate God, bless the leaders of all nations with the power of compassion. Fulfill the promise conveyed in Scripture: I will bring peace to the land, and you shall lie down and no one shall terrify you. I will rid the land of vicious beasts and it shall not be ravaged by war. Let love and justice flow like a mighty stream. Let peace fill the earth as the waters fill the sea. And let us say: Amen.[17]

Rabbi Menachem Kasher (1895–1983) composed this not long after Israel's birth.

The Fifth Cup: We Are Commanded to Give Thanks for a Miracle
Now, in our time . . . we have been privileged to behold the mercies of the Holy Name . . . and His salvation over us in the establishment of the State of Israel, which is the beginning of redemption and salvation from . . . exile . . . Even as it is written, *"And I shall bring you* into the land, the same which I have lifted my hand to give unto Abraham, unto Isaac, and unto Jacob, and I have given it unto you as an inheritance. I am the Eternal"—it is fitting and proper that we observe this pious act, the drinking of the fifth cup, as a form of thanksgiving . . .

Just as we have been privileged to see the first realization of "And I shall bring them," so may we be worthy of witnessing the perfect and complete redemption, the coming of the Messiah. May we witness fulfillment of the vision of the prophets, that "evil shall disappear as smoke in the wind, and that all the earth shall be filled with the knowledge of God."[18]

PASSOVER, MESSIANISM, AND ISRAEL

This is a reading for discussion before or during your Seder. Tragically, Israel has known little peace in its short life. While the country has perpetually struggled to contend with dangers from without, it has also faced threats from within. A fervent

strain of messianism has flourished in Israel that has exacerbated the
conflicts between Israel and its Arab neighbors.

Read the short essay below. Depending on your group, you may wish
to discuss how serious a danger Jewish messianism poses to
Israel and the Jewish People today.

Shortly before his death, Theodore Herzl (1860–1904) told a close friend about
a dream he had in his twelfth year. The "King Messiah" appeared to Herzl and
took him "on the wings of heaven" on an ascent where he met Moses:

> The Messiah called out to Moses, "For this child I have prayed." To me
> he said, "Go and announce to the Jews that I shall soon come and per-
> form great and wondrous deeds for my people and for all mankind!"[19]

After the Holocaust and two homeless millennia of reciting a liturgy laden
with a longing for Zion, the redemptive significance of statehood loomed large.
In 1946, David Ben-Gurion testified before the Anglo-American Committee of
Inquiry, one of the numerous postwar commissions charged with deliberating
Palestine's fate:

> [M]ore than 3,300 years ago the Jews left Egypt. It was more than
> 3,000 years before the *Mayflower,* and every Jew in the world knows
> exactly the date when we left. It was on the 15th of Nisan. The bread
> they ate was matzot. Up till today all the Jews throughout the world
> . . . on the 15th of Nisan eat the same matzot, and tell the story of the
> exile to Egypt; they tell what happened, all the sufferings that happened
> to the Jews since they went into exile. They [begin] with these two sen-
> tences: "This year we are slaves; next year we shall be free. This year we
> are here; next year we shall be in the Land of Israel." Jews are like that.[20]

Yet the Haggadah dreams not only of returning to Israel but of rebuilding
the Temple as well. The blessing over the second cup of wine, the core of which
the Mishnah attributes to Rabbi Akiva, gives voice to that yearning.[21] (See chapter 23.)

Adonai our God and God of our ancestors, bring us in peace to other holy days and festivals that are approaching that we might be happy as we rebuild your city and joyful as we serve You. There we will eat from the sacrifices and Passover offerings, the blood from which will reach the wall of Your altar and please You.

And Akiva was not merely imagining a Temple in the "heavenly Jerusalem." In 132 C.E., he threw his support behind the Bar Kochba rebellion, convinced that its leader was the Messiah himself.

The exile and devastation that followed Bar Kochba's failed rebellion went a long way to dampening the messianic strivings that have nonetheless erupted at different times and places throughout Jewish history.

Israel's birth gave concrete expression to messianic yearnings that had long lain dormant.

Soon after 1948, Israel's Rabbinate composed a prayer for the new state, celebrating its birth as "the first flowering of our redemption." Israel's stunning victory in 1967 unleashed a powerful movement to hasten the coming of the Messiah and rebuilding of the Temple.

Masquerading as Swiss tourists, Rabbi Moshe Levinger and friends booked rooms in Hebron's Park Hotel one day before the first Seder in 1968. After the Seder, they refused to leave. Thus began the first attempt to redeem Israel and bring the Messiah by settling the territories conquered during the Six-Day War. The Jewish settlement in Kiryat Arba, just outside of Hebron, was the child of Levinger's Seder.

In 1984, Israeli police arrested a group of Jewish terrorists planning to blow up the Dome of the Rock in Jerusalem, an act that would almost certainly have precipitated a devastating Arab response. The abortive plot hardly extinguished hopes to rebuild the Temple. An organization called the Temple Mount Faithful regularly engages in provocative deeds, including repeated efforts to lay a cornerstone for the Third Temple. Posters depicting the Third Temple in place of the Dome of the Rock are widely available in Israel. In 2003, one group proudly announced in the *New York Times* that it had built a replica of the Temple's altar and awaits a sufficiently chaotic moment to sneak it onto the Temple Mount and resume animal sacrifice.[22]

In the Spring of 2010 hopes for rebuilding the Temple reached new heights based on a prophecy attributed to the Vilna Gaon (1720–1797). The Vilna Gaon reputedly predicted that the construction of the Third Temple would begin when the Churvah Synagogue in Jerusalem had been rebuilt twice. (The word *churvah* means "destroyed.") The first reconstruction occurred in 1864 and the second was completed on March 15, 2010. According to the prophecy, this meant that construction of the Third Temple should have begun on March 16, or the first of Nisan.[23]

What can we learn from this?

First, that Jewish messianism taps deep into the core of Judaism's commitment to hope, not in itself a bad thing. The capacity to produce messianic offshoots attests to a religion's vitality. But those offshoots are not always benign. The ancient notion "of the birth pangs of the Messiah"—that things must get worse before they get better—coupled with the messianist's proclivity to disregard the law, create an explosive mixture.

One may, of course, ask, "Why worry about internal dangers of this kind at a moment when the Jewish People find themselves beset with so many real external enemies?" Alas, history suggests that messianic movements often arise precisely at such moments of vulnerability. We dangerously flatter ourselves if we imagine that we are immune from producing messianic zealots similar to those bred by other religious traditions.

20

The Restoration of Wonder:
The Miracles of Egypt and Our Day

לְפִיכָךְ אֲנַחְנוּ חַיָּבִים לְהוֹדוֹת...
לְמִי שֶׁעָשָׂה לַאֲבוֹתֵינוּ וְלָנוּ אֶת־כָּל־הַנִּסִּים הָאֵלּוּ.

Therefore it is our duty to thank . . . the One who performed
all these miracles for our ancestors and for us.
—THE PASSOVER HAGGADAH, QUOTING THE MISHNAH, PESACHIM 10:5 (CIRCA 200 C.E.)

It's hard to read the Haggadah without feeling that it is trying to convince you to believe in miracles. The question is, "What's a miracle?"

The passage above from the Haggadah is followed by this statement: "He has brought us forth from slavery to freedom, from sorrow to joy, from mourning to festivity, from darkness to great light and from bondage to redemption. Let us then recite before Him a new song; Hallelujah." In one sense, these are the Haggadah's miracles—once we were idol-worshiping slaves and now we are free to worship the true God.

But of course, the Haggadah points to wonders of another kind as well. After recounting the suffering of the Israelites, the Haggadah turns to the Book of Deuteronomy (26:8) to describe God's mighty deeds of redemption. The words are among the Seder's most memorable. "Adonai took us out from Egypt by a mighty hand, by an outstretched arm and awesome power, and by signs and wonders (*b'otot u-v'moftim*)."[1] After elaborating on this passage, the Haggadah cites another from Deuteronomy (4:34) that seeks to remove any lingering doubts: "Has any god ventured to go and take for himself one nation from the midst of another by prodigious acts, by signs and wonders, by war, by a mighty hand and an outstretched arm and awesome power (*mora'im gedolim*), as Adonai your God did for you in Egypt before your very eyes?"

These are just a few of the Haggadah's references to the miraculous.

As you proceed through the Haggadah, ask your guests to interrupt and let you know whenever they notice a reference to miracles.

In this chapter, we'll consider "the miraculous," a subject that leaps out from the Haggadah, but one that you may never have discussed at your Seder.

THE BIBLE AND THE DICTIONARY

Read the following section aloud or on your own.

The Bible uses many different terms to describe what we might call miraculous phenomena: *mora'im gedolim* (great deeds), *nifla'ot* (wondrous deeds), *pele* (from the same root as *nifla'ot*), *ot* ("sign"; plural, *otot*), *mofeit* ("wonder" or "portent"; plural, *moftim*), and many more. The last two appear frequently in passages the Haggadah quotes from Deuteronomy.

The final verses of Deuteronomy (34:10–12) provide a beautiful illustration of how the Bible uses many of these terms:

> Never again did there arise in Israel a prophet like Moses—whom Adonai singled out, face to face for the various signs and wonders (*ha-otot v'hamoftim*) that Adonai sent him to display in the land of Egypt, against Pharaoh and all his courtiers and his whole country, and for all the great might and awesome power (*ha-mora ha-gadol*) that Moses displayed before all Israel.[2]

272

Sometimes these expressions appear in surprising contexts. For example, *ot*, "sign," refers both to the sign of a rainbow (Gen. 9: 12, 17) and to the sign of circumcision (Gen. 17:11).[3]

The most familiar term in modern Hebrew for "miracle," *nes* (as in the dreidel's *nes gadol hayah sham*, a great miracle—*nes*—happened there), appears only once in the Bible in the context of a wondrous sign. In the Book of Numbers (26:10), the followers of Korach who rebelled against Moses were swallowed up by the earth and "became an example" [or a "sign," *l'nes*]. As a term for miracle, *nes* only became common in rabbinic parlance.

In the Bible, *nes* generally means a banner, ensign, or pole used to communicate a particular message. The copper serpent that Moses makes to cure snake bites (Num. 21:8–9) is mounted on a standard or pole, a *nes*. As one scholar notes, "In certain scriptures, the pole serves as a symbol of freedom, its function being to inform captives, exiles and imprisoned people of their 'liberation' and return to their homes . . . Indeed, the primary purpose of 'freedom' [in ancient Near Eastern cultures] is the restoration of the individual to his home and to his inheritance."[4] For example, in the haftarah for the eighth day of Passover we read: "He will hold up a signal (*nes*) to the nations and assemble the banished of Israel, and gather the dispersed of Judah from the four corners of the earth" (Isaiah 11:12).

In many translations of the Bible you won't even find the word "miracle." That's because the Torah speaks about "signs," "wonders," or "portents" rather than outright miracles. These phenomena refer to events that point beyond themselves to something greater, to the creator of nature and the author of human destiny. The Bible's miracles are meant to inculcate faith.

The crossing of the Red Sea and the sight of drowned Egyptians on the shore provide a perfect example: "And when Israel saw the wondrous power [literally, the "great hand"] that Adonai had wielded against the Egyptians, the people feared Adonai; they had faith in Adonai and in His servant Moses" (Ex. 14:31). Note that this is the traditional Haggadah's only explicit reference to Moses. (See chapter 16.)

The Bible does describe some great wonders that would seem to lie *beyond* the laws of nature. For instance, the sun stands still to provide extra daylight to facilitate Joshua's victory over the Amorites (Jos. 10:13). But even here, later commentators disagreed about whether this meant the battle went so quickly that the sun seemed not to move or the sun actually stood still.[5] Generally, the Bible's wonders involve events that are highly unlikely or unexpected rather than impossible. For example, the earth swallows Korach and his followers, who have rebelled against Moses (Num. 26:10).

Most often, however, the Bible finds the wondrous *within* nature: "When I behold Your heavens, the work of Your fingers, the moon and stars that You set in place . . ." (Psalms 8:4). "Let abundant grain be in the land, to the tops of the mountains . . . and let men sprout up in towns like country grass . . . Blessed is Adonai God, God of Israel, who alone does wondrous things [*nifla'ot*]" (Psalms 72:16, 18). Even in parting the Red Sea, God works through nature: "Adonai drove back the sea with a *strong east wind* all that night, and turned the sea into dry ground" (Ex. 14:21).

Still, if hearing about miracles makes us feel uncomfortable, part of that discomfort may derive from how we define them.

Most likely, we have embraced the definition of miracles developed by the British philosopher David Hume (1711–1776). Hume wrote, "A miracle is a violation of nature. A miracle may be accurately defined as a transgression of a law of nature by a particular volition of the Deity, or by the interposition of some invisible agent."[6] Indeed, Hume's definition comes very close to the first one listed in the dictionary: "An effect or extraordinary event in the physical world that surpasses all known or natural powers and is ascribed to a supernatural cause."[7]

The dictionary includes another definition. "A wonder, a marvel." Here we find the ancient Latin root of the word: *mirari,* "to wonder," *mirus,* "wonderful." And this definition brings us a lot closer to what the Bible had in mind. Skepticism about miracles *beyond* nature blinds us to the truly miraculous *within* nature.

THE SAGES ON MIRACLES

Read the paragraphs that follow. Then choose one or more of the
three selections from ancient rabbinic literature to read aloud and discuss.
Questions follow each selection.

What did the sages who lived in the era of the Haggadah's early development think about miracles? Of course, they held different opinions. They accepted the notion of God's infinite power and the possibility of miracles, but they were generally reluctant to rely on them. For example, Rabbi Yannai (active in Palestine between 220 and 250 C.E.) said, "A man should never stand in a place of danger and say that a miracle will be wrought for him, lest it is not."[8] Many of the sages believed that the miraculous was best evidenced in God's creation of the natural world, hence the dictum, "The day of rain is greater than that of the resurrection of the dead."[9] At the same time, the Mishnah prescribes a special blessing to be recited if a person sees "a place where miracles had been wrought for Israel . . . : Blessed is He that wrought miracles for our ancestors in this place."[10]

Since ancient times, the daily liturgy (*Modim anachnu lakh*) has expressed thanks "for Your miracles which are daily with us." The sages also included references to miracles in other prayers. Still, the concept of miracles aroused a certain ambivalence, because it implied that God's original creation may have been less than perfect. Why would a "violation of nature" be required if God's creation had been perfect in the beginning? Hence, the sages taught that God fashioned the conditions or instruments for the Bible's miracles during creation. (In this, the Rabbis expressed greater comfort with the notion of miracles within rather than beyond nature.)

The sages knew well that most of us remain oblivious to the wonders around us. Rabbi Eliezer, one of the rabbis we encounter in the Haggadah, taught that "even the person for whom a miracle is performed is unaware of the miracle."[11]

And, of course, the Rabbis understood that occasionally even the Torah's claims could not be taken literally. Sometimes, says the Talmud, "the Torah spoke in exaggerated terms."[12]

Choose one or two of the following selections to read aloud and discuss during your Seder.

Rabbi Johanan [late second century C.E.] said: The Holy One, blessed be He, made a stipulation with the sea that it should divide before Israel; thus it is written, "And the sea returned to its strength" (*l'eitano*, Ex. 14:27): that is, in accordance with its agreement (*l'tenao*, a wordplay on *l'eitano*). Rabbi Jeremiah ben Eliezer [early fourth century C.E.] said: Not with the sea alone did God make a stipulation, but with everything which was created in the six days of creation, as it is written, "My own hands stretched out the heavens, and I marshaled all their host . . ." (Isaiah 45:12). "I commanded the sea to divide. . . ."

—GENESIS RABBAH 5:5, FIFTH-CENTURY-C.E. MIDRASH

• Which is easier to believe—that God might simply contravene a law of nature or that at creation God had anticipated all the historical circumstances that might require "miraculous" intervention? What about human free will in determining historical events?

Said Rav Papa to Abaye [active 278–338 C.E.]: How is it that for the former generations miracles were performed and for us miracles are not performed?

—BABYLONIAN TALMUD, BERAKHOT 20A

• How might you respond to this question?

The Rabbis were inclined to find "miracles" in the seemingly commonplace. The following midrash picks up on Psalm 136, which we read toward the end of the Seder. The Psalm includes these verses: "Who alone works great marvels" and "Who split apart [sundered] the Red Sea."

Many miracles and wonders do You perform for us every day and no man knows. Then who does know? You, O Adonai. Rabbi Eliezer ben Pedat [active 290–320 C.E.] said: See what is written: Who alone works great wonders. He alone knows. And what is written thereafter? "Who split apart the Red Sea"—the piece of bread [literally, "the divided bread," i.e., livelihood] is equal in importance to the sea which was divided in two. Just as the world cannot do without the piece of bread, so it is not possible for the world to do without miracles and wonders. How are we to envisage this? A man is lying on a bed, and a serpent is on the ground before him. When he seeks to rise, the serpent becomes aware of him. When he is about to put his feet on it, the serpent flees from him. And the man does not know what wonders the Holy One, blessed be He, performs for him. . . .

—MIDRASH ON THE PSALMS, COMPILED
BETWEEN THE THIRD AND THIRTEENTH CENTURIES C.E.[13]

• Are there particular times when you've felt as though you've witnessed a miracle or have had a strong sense of the miraculous? In the grind of "earning bread" what can you do to retain awareness of the wonders around you?

THE RESTORATION OF WONDER

Read this on your own or aloud at your Seder.

It's hard to ignore miracles in the Haggadah. The Haggadah takes us through the Red Sea three times.

• "Had He split the Sea for us, but not led us through on dry land, it would have sufficed! *Dayyenu!*"

• "The sea saw them [the Israelites] and fled . . . What alarmed you, O sea, that you fled . . . ?" (Psalms 114:3, 5).

• "Praise Adonai . . . Who split the Red Sea . . ." (Psalms 136:1, 13).

How are we to understand these allusions to the miraculous? The plagues and miracles of the Exodus were supposed to provide the Israelites with firsthand experience of God. But the experience didn't last very long:

They did not keep God's covenant; they refused to follow His instruction; they forgot His deeds and the wonders that He showed them. He performed marvels in the sight of their fathers, in the land of Egypt . . . He split the sea and took them through it; He made the waters stand still like a wall.

—PSALMS 78:11–13

Maybe the wonders and miracles were aiming at something more modest: the restoration of the capacity for wonder. Maybe the wonders of Egypt just helped the children of Israel open their eyes. To be aware of God, you must first open your eyes.

Think of Egypt as the paradigmatic experience that destroys the ability to experience wonder. You keep your nose so close to the grindstone that all else begins to fade. The tedium of work and the fear of the taskmaster's lash cripple your curiosity. Nothing can surprise you. One day is exactly like the next. The months blur together. The seasons slide by unnoticed. Beauty becomes imperceptible. Nothing shimmers or sparkles. Egypt, "the narrow place," blunts the acuity of your senses: Your eyes don't see, your ears don't hear.

During the Seder, we read the psalmist's description of idols. It applies just as well to the Israelites enslaved in Egypt: "They have mouths but cannot speak, eyes but cannot see; they have ears, but cannot hear, noses but cannot smell. . . ." (Psalms 115:5). Oppression deadens awareness, and with it, the capacity for wonder. Without wonder, life becomes routine, dull, joyless. The spirit has become enslaved. Hasidic master Rabbi Chanokh said, "The real exile of Israel in Egypt was that they had learned to endure it."[14]

The Haggadah's recounting of the miracles of Egypt reminds us that we, like our ancestors, may have lost the ability to glimpse the extraordinary that breathes behind the commonplace. We remain slaves, trapped in a monotonous, gray existence where everything seems oppressively ordinary. References to color in the Book of Exodus only begin to appear with the plagues and the disintegration of routine life in Egypt. The Nile turns to blood and the locusts leave not a green thing uneaten. Color appears more vividly with the building of the Mishkan, in which blue, purple, and scarlet dominate the decor. In Genesis, the sign—*ot*—of God's covenant with Noah is the rainbow.

God sends mighty wonders precisely because the Israelites have become trapped in a colorless, wonderless world. Suddenly, nothing can be taken for granted. The miraculous takes center stage in both the Exodus story and the Haggadah because both understand the relationship between "knowing God" and wonder. Heschel said it best: "Awareness of the divine begins with wonder."[15]

"Why is this night different from all other nights?" asks the Haggadah. Because the Seder seeks to arouse our dormant sense of curiosity. The Talmud says that Rabbi Akiva used to "distribute parched ears of corn and nuts to children on the eve of Passover, so that they might not fall asleep but ask [the 'questions']."[16]

The children at the table may literally close their eyes. But the rest of us may be even more asleep to the Seder's call to rekindle our sense of wonder.

JEWISH VOICES ON MIRACLES

Here you'll find a sampling of Jewish thought on miracles
over the past thousand years. Choose one or more to read aloud
and discuss the questions that follow each.

How great is the blindness of ignorance and how harmful. If you told a man . . . that God sends an angel who enters the womb of a woman and forms a fetus there, he would be pleased with this assertion and would accept it and should regard it as a manifestation of greatness and power on the part of the deity, and also of His wisdom . . . Nevertheless he would also believe at the same time that the angel is a body formed of burning fire and that his size is equal to that of a third part of the whole world. He would regard all this as possible with respect to God. But if you tell him that God has placed in the sperm a formative force shaping the limbs and giving them their configuration and that this force is the angel . . . he would shrink from this opinion. For he does not understand the notion of the true greatness and power that consists in the bringing into existence of forces active in a thing, forces that cannot be apprehended by any sense.

—MAIMONIDES (1135–1204), *THE GUIDE OF THE PERPLEXED*[17]

- Because Maimonides acknowledged God's creation of the cosmos, he admitted the possibility of miracles that *seem* to contravene natural law, but he preferred to explain such events in terms of natural causes. He also had a deep appreciation for the "miraculous" within nature. Do you tend to think of life itself as a miracle? Is there anything more miraculous?

It follows that the great signs and wonders constitute faithful witnesses to the truth of the belief in the existence of the Creator and the truth of the whole Torah. And because the Holy One, blessed be He, will not make signs and wonders in every generation for the eyes of some wicked man or heretic, He therefore commanded us that we should always make a memorial or a sign of that which we have seen with our eyes, and that we should transmit the matter to our children, and their children, to the generations to come . . . Through the great open miracles, one comes to admit the hidden miracles. . . .

—NACHMANIDES (1195–1270), SPANISH BIBLE COMMENTATOR AND PHILOSOPHER[18]

• Nachmanides is alluding to the Passover Seder, an important occasion for transmitting the story of the Exodus to our children. How do you explain "miraculous" stories, such as the parting of the Red Sea, to children? Ask some of the children seated around the Seder table to share their ideas about the story of the Red Sea. (Please urge all to listen with great respect.) What might the difference be between open and hidden miracles?

By a similar Divine mandate the sea opened a way for the Jews, namely by an east wind which blew strongly all night . . . Although the circumstances attending miracles are not related always in full detail, yet a miracle was never performed without them. This is confirmed in Exodus 14:27, where it is simply stated that "Moses stretched forth his hand, and that waters of the sea returned to their strength in the morning," no mention being made of a wind; but in the Song of Moses (Ex. 15:10) we read, "You made Your wind (i.e., with a very strong wind) blow, the sea covered them." Thus the attendant circumstance is omitted in the history and the miracle is thereby enhanced.

—BARUCH SPINOZA, DUTCH PHILOSOPHER (1632–1677)[19]

The Amsterdam rabbinical authorities excommunicated Baruch Spinoza in 1656 in part because he concluded that God and nature were essentially indistinguishable. With reference to miracles, he argued that because natural laws are divine decrees, to think that God would act contrary to God's own laws would be absurd. Spinoza therefore sought natural explanations for all miracles.

- Imagine that you saw Moses stretch out his rod and witnessed the sea split exactly as the Bible describes. What effect would it have on your belief in God? How long do you think that effect would last? If you told others who had not seen what you did, how do you think they would react?

The following phenomenon is a common occurrence in the region of the Suez: at high tide, the waters of the Red Sea penetrate that sand from under the surface, and suddenly that water begins to ooze up out of the sand, which had hitherto been dry; within a short time the sand turns to mud, but the water continues to rise and ultimately a deep layer of water is formed above the sand, the whole area becoming flooded . . . This sometimes happens when the Red Sea is at low tide; the water covering the sand gradually diminishes and finally disappears, and in the part that, several hours earlier, was covered by water suddenly dry land appears . . . I have no wish whatsoever to rationalize the biblical story . . . The miracle consisted in the fact that at the very moment when it was necessary, in just the manner conducive to the achievement of the desired goal, and on a scale that was abnormal, there occurred, in accordance with Adonai's will, phenomena that brought about Israel's salvation.
—UMBERTO CASSUTO (1883–1951), ITALIAN BIBLE SCHOLAR WHO BECAME CHAIR OF BIBLE STUDIES AT HEBREW UNIVERSITY IN 1939[20]

- Does Cassuto's attempt to explain the miracle in natural terms work for you? From this point of view, what is the relationship between a miracle and good luck? Is the Torah's intent supported by such explanations or undermined by them?

A scientific theory, once it is announced and accepted does not have to be repeated twice a day. The insights of wonder must be constantly kept alive, since there is a need for daily wonder, there is a need for daily worship. This is one of the goals of the Jewish way of living: to experience commonplace deeds as spiritual adventures, to feel the hidden love and wisdom in all things. In the Song of the Sea [when the Israelites celebrate having crossed the Red Sea] we read:

> Who is like Thee, O Adonai, among the gods?
> Who is like Thee, majestic in holiness,
> Sublime in glorious deeds, doing wonders.
>
> —EXODUS 15:11

The Rabbis remarked: It is not written here: *Who did wonders,* but *Who does wonders* . . . He did and still does wonders for us in every generation. . . .

—ABRAHAM JOSHUA HESCHEL (1907–1972), SCHOLAR, THEOLOGIAN, AND SOCIAL ACTIVIST[21]

• What are the principal wonders that you experience? What enhances your sense of wonder? Is your sense of wonder enhanced by prayer? What is the relationship between wonder and the story of the Exodus?

You find it strange that I consider the comprehensibility of the world . . . as a miracle or an eternal mystery. Well, *a priori* one should expect a chaotic world which cannot be grasped by the mind in any way. One could (yes *one should*) expect the world to be subjected to law only to the extent that we order it through our intelligence. Ordering of this kind would be like the alphabetical ordering of the words of a language. By contrast, the kind of order created by Newton's theory of gravitation, for instance, is wholly different. Even if the axioms of the theory are proposed by man, the success of such a project presupposes a high degree of ordering of the objective world, and this could not be expected *a priori*. That is the "miracle" which is being constantly reinforced as our knowledge expands.

—ALBERT EINSTEIN (1879–1955), FROM A 1952 LETTER TO A FRIEND[22]

- Does the underlying order of which Einstein speaks stir your sense of wonder? Does it affect your opinion of this viewpoint to know that these are Einstein's words rather than those of a religious figure?

The Egyptians, who were situated in strongly fortified positions, shot everything they had at the Israeli [amphibious landing craft] crossing the canal. You could see tracer bullets and the tails of rockets flashing over the canal. We could not really see the boats, and were slightly puzzled why the Egyptians were wasting such firepower. But, when the boats landed, the Egyptians fled their positions. The next day a pontoon bridge was built and Israeli soldiers crossed the canal on this bridge relatively safe from the enemy fire. My unit made its way to Fuad, an Egyptian air base. We arrived *erev* Shabbat and took over a building for sleeping quarters and set up for Shabbat. In the building next to us were the [boat] drivers and their vehicles. They were still totally exhausted and were resting under the vehicles. It was from them that I heard the story of their crossing of the Canal. One of them said, "I saw God's hand push the missiles away from my [boat]." All of the others nodded in agreement, indicating that they too had seen it. I asked him what he meant by that. He said simply, "I saw a hand, like a big hand, the palm of a hand, and as the shell approached my boat this hand pushed it aside." . . . That night at Kabbalat Shabbat, as we sang *Lekha Dodi,* when we came to the verse which says, "Those who despoil you shall become a spoil, and all who would devour you shall be far away," I myself felt the presence of a giant hand in the room, the same hand I am sure that had removed those who wanted to swallow us up. At dinner others recounted having the same feeling; it was as if we also had been protected by the hand.

> —RABBI MICHAEL GRAETZ, WHOSE ISRAEL DEFENSE FORCES
> UNIT OVERLOOKED THE SUEZ CANAL,
> A PASSAGE BETWEEN THE MEDITERRANEAN
> AND RED SEAS, DURING THE 1973 WAR[23]

• How do you react to this story? Have you ever had a similar feeling? How do you relate to this story in light of the following observation by Abraham Joshua Heschel: "The God of Israel is also the God of her enemies. . . ."[24]

When the people of Israel crossed through the Red Sea, they witnessed a great miracle. Some say it was the greatest miracle that ever happened. On that day they saw a sight more awesome than all the visions of the prophets combined. The sea split and the waters stood like great walls, while Israel escaped to freedom on the distant shore. Awesome. But not for everyone.

Two people, Reuven and Shimon, hurried along among the crowd crossing through the sea. They never once looked up. They noticed only that the ground under their feet was still a little muddy— like a beach at low tide.

> "Yucch!" said Reuven, "there's mud all over this place!"
> "Blecch!" said Shimon, "I have mud all over my feet!"
> "This is terrible," answered Reuven. "When we were slaves in Egypt, we had to make our bricks out of mud, just like this!"
> "Yeah," said Shimon. "There's no difference between being a slave in Egypt and being free here."

And so it went, Reuven and Shimon whining and complaining all the way to freedom. For them there was no miracle. Only mud. Their eyes were closed. They might as well have been asleep (Exodus Rabbah 24:1).

People see only what they understand, not necessarily what lies in front of them. For example, if you saw a television set, you would know what it was and how to operate it. But imagine someone who had never seen a television. To such a person it would be just a strange and useless box. Imagine being in a video store, filled with movies and stories and music, and not even knowing it. How sad when something is right before your eyes, but you are asleep to it. It is like that with our own world too.

—RABBI LAWRENCE KUSHNER (1943–), AUTHOR OF
OVER A DOZEN BOOKS ON JEWISH SPIRITUALITY AND MYSTICISM[25]

• What might you pay more attention to so you can better appreciate the wonders that surround you? What makes it hard for Reuven and Shimon to open their eyes? What makes it hard for you to open yours?

AT THE RED SEA: THE HORSE AND DRIVER

You might want to consider discussing the midrash below in small groups
before you sit down at the Seder table. Or you can take a few minutes
to talk about it before singing *Dayyenu* (which mentions the parting of the Red Sea).
Depending on your group, you may want to read aloud Appendix II,
"What Is Midrash?"

The scene is as follows: The Red Sea has miraculously parted and the Israelites have safely passed through. "The waters turned back and covered the chariots and the horseman—Pharaoh's entire army that followed them into the sea; not one of them remained . . . Then Moses and the Israelites sang this song to Adonai. They said: 'I will sing to Adonai, for He has triumphed gloriously; Horse and driver He has hurled into the sea . . .'" (Ex. 14:28; 15:1).

The midrash expounds:

The Holy One, blessed be He, would bring the horse and his driver and make them stand trial. He would say to the horse, "Why did you run after My children?" The horse would answer, "The Egyptian drove me against my will, as it is said: 'And the Egyptians pursued . . .'" (Ex. 14:9). God would then say to the Egyptian, "Why did you pursue My children?" And he would answer, "It was the horse that ran away with me against my will, as it is said, 'For the horses of Pharaoh went in . . .'" (Ex. 15:19). What would God do? He would make the man ride upon the horse and thus judge them together. As it is said, "The horse and driver He has hurled into the sea" (Ex. 15:1).

—MEKHILTA OF RABBI ISHMAEL, SHIRATA 2:120–127[26]

• What contemporary situations does this midrash make you think about?

• What might the midrash be saying about human nature?

• Earlier in the Book of Exodus, God says, "And I will stiffen the hearts of the Egyptians so that they go in after them; and I will gain glory through Pharaoh and all his warriors, his chariots and his horsemen" (Ex. 14:17). With this in mind, what is your reaction to the midrash?

21

"Blessed Are You . . . Who Redeemed Us": The Seder of Redemption

בָּרוּךְ אַתָּה יְיָ אֱלֹהֵינוּ מֶלֶךְ הָעוֹלָם,
אֲשֶׁר גְּאָלָנוּ וְגָאַל אֶת־אֲבוֹתֵינוּ מִמִּצְרַיִם
וְהִגִּיעָנוּ לַלַּיְלָה הַזֶּה,
לֶאֱכָל־בּוֹ מַצָּה וּמָרוֹר.

*Blessed are You, Adonai our God, King of the Universe, who has redeemed us
and our ancestors from Egypt and enabled us to reach this
night that we may eat matzah and maror.*
—FROM THE HAGGADAH'S BLESSING OVER THE SECOND CUP OF WINE

When you sit down for your Passover Seder, remember that you are doing
so at what was and probably remains one of Judaism's most fertile
moments for redemption.

Ever since the Exodus from Egypt, the month of Nisan, with its festival of
Passover, has shimmered with the alluring promise of redemption. As the Talmud
(Rosh Hashanah 11a) taught, "In Nisan they *were* redeemed and in Nisan they *will
be* redeemed in the time to come." Unable to bear constraint, redemptive yearnings

have periodically erupted—sometimes in connection with the season of Passover. It's no accident that the climax of Jesus' ministry unfolded during Passover.

More than a millennium later, Maimonides railed against an early-twelfth-century messianist in Yemen who preached that the Messiah would reveal himself on Passover.[1] Amidst the fervor surrounding the brief messianic career of Shabbetai Zevi (1626–1676), the resonance with Passover continued. The Jews of Yemen had concluded that for them the Messiah would arrive on Passover: Their only question was whether it would be in 1666 or 1667.[2] Marvelous tales also spread about Shabbetai Zevi's "innovations" in Jewish law. For example, on the evening of Passover in 1666 he sacrificed a lamb and roasted it with its fat—both major transgressions. He accompanied the deed with the following blessing: "Blessed art Thou, O God, who permits that which is forbidden."[3]

According to legend, the Ba'al Shem Tov (1700–1760), founder of Hasidism, set out during Passover on an abortive journey to Israel "to prepare for the hour of deliverance."[4] When World War II broke out in 1939 (5699 in the Hebrew calendar), large numbers of religious Jews in Europe were convinced that the war would be short-lived. Numerous arcane sources predicted the Messiah's arrival in 5700. One popular speculation was based on "deciphering" a verse from the Song of the Sea, sung by the Israelites after they crossed the Red Sea. The "decoded" verse contained this message: "On the day after the festival in the month of Nisan [i.e., Passover] in the year 5700, the Jews will be redeemed."[5]

This chapter explores the concept of redemption, undoubtedly the Haggadah's primary theme.

THE SEDER OF HOPE: TUNING IN TO THEMES OF REDEMPTION

Before you begin your Seder, perhaps in the living room,
read the following paragraphs aloud. Discuss the questions that follow.

A single word captures the concern of the entire Passover Haggadah: redemption.

The story of the Exodus recounts Israel's redemption from Egypt and we relive it every Passover. "In Nisan they were redeemed," the Talmud teaches, "and in Nisan they will be redeemed in the time to come." So whatever darkness this Nisan may hold, the next one promises to dispel it with great light.

Symbols of salvation permeate the Seder. Matzah may be called the bread of affliction, but it's equally the bread of liberation. As the Seder begins, we uncover the matzah, invite the poor to join us, and declare, "Now we are here; next year may we be in the Land of Israel. Now we are slaves; next year we will be free."

The four cups of wine (as we saw earlier) are traditionally associated with God's fourfold promise of redemption in the Book of Exodus. Some believe we should drink a fifth cup of wine corresponding to the fulfillment of a fifth redemptive promise, "I will bring you into the land [of Israel]." And a special cup belongs to the Prophet Elijah, herald of the Messiah, for whom we open our door near the Seder's conclusion.

The text of the Haggadah refers to many different dimensions of redemption, for example:

- (*Prior to the Four Children*): The sages define the requirement to "remember the day you left Egypt all the days of your life." "The days of your life" means the present world, and "all the days" includes the messianic era.

- (*After the Four Children*): "At first our forefathers worshiped idols, but now the Omnipresent has brought us near to His service. . . ."

- (*Traditionally recited before the Seder's concluding songs, but placed at the Seder's conclusion in some Haggadot*): "Soon, and with rejoicing, lead the offshoots of the stock that You have planted, redeemed to Zion. Next year in Jerusalem."

- (*The last verse of* Chad Gadya, *the final words of most traditional Haggadot*): "Then came the Holy One, blessed be He, and slew the angel of death. . . ."

The *Encyclopedia Judaica* defines *redemption* as "salvation from the states or circumstances that destroy the value of human existence or human existence itself."[6]

Redemption can apply both to individuals and to groups, to the body and to the soul. Redemption from physical forms of oppression may be easier to understand. But human beings who seem to be relatively free often wind up living empty lives, trapped by the pursuit of goals that they themselves find relatively unimportant. Some see redemption as an evolving process of change or progress, the result of human efforts to repair the world. Others see it in more messianic terms, as a radically new era ushered in by God or by the bold actions of particular individuals.

Before you begin the Seder, ask your guests to let you know every time they come across something in the Haggadah that relates to the theme of redemption. Also ask your group to pay close attention to biblical and rabbinic figures as they are mentioned in the Haggadah. Invite your guests to comment about what role these figures play in the redemptive drama. Then discuss the following questions.

- What does redemption mean to you in terms of your own life? Do you believe that humanity's lot will change for the better? Do you believe that anti-Semitism will someday end? Do you believe that eventually Israel will live in peace with its neighbors?

- What is the relationship between the Haggadah's treatment of redemption and the question of hope?

- Is the yearning for redemption a response to the bitterness of Jewish history? If so, is it an adequate response?

- How might the Jewish People be different today had our commitment to the concept of redemption been weaker or had it been replaced by something else? What might have replaced it?

- Do you think the Haggadah represents Judaism as a fundamentally optimistic religion? If so, in your experience, does today's Jewish community reflect that optimism?

REDEMPTION IN THE BIBLE
AND THE ANCIENT NEAR EAST

You may want to read this aloud at your Seder, asking participants to share their reactions to each passage. This would be suitable for a short conversation before or after one of the four cups of wine.

290

The theme of redemption lies at the heart of the Haggadah. But it is a concept that many find confusing or maybe even alienating. In part, that's because the idea is so multifaceted.

In the Bible it is God who redeems the Israelites from Egypt. But in other contexts, the Bible places the responsibility for redemption squarely upon human shoulders: "And you must redeem every firstborn male among your children" (Ex. 13:13). If desperation leads an individual to become a slave, "one of his kinsman shall redeem him" (Lev. 25:48). "If your kinsman is in [dire] straits and has to sell part of his holding, his nearest redeemer [kinsman] shall come and redeem what his kinsman has sold" (Lev. 25:25). A murderer was to be killed by the victim's next of kin, literally known as a "blood redeemer" (Num. 35:19).

But the biblical view of redemption extends far beyond this. "Zion shall be redeemed in judgment and its inhabitants with righteousness" (Isaiah 1:27). God "will redeem Israel from all their iniquities" (Psalms 130:8). "In famine He will redeem you from death, in war from the sword" (Job 5:20). "I [God] will save them, redeem them from very Death" (Hosea 13:14) The list goes on and on.

In the context of the ancient Near East, redemption figures prominently in "proclamations of freedom" from virtually all ancient civilizations in the region. Ramses IV issued the following freedom proclamation when he became pharaoh of Egypt in 1154 B.C.E.:

> It is a good day. Heaven and earth rejoice, because you are the great lord of Egypt. Fugitives have returned to their cities, those in hiding have come out. The hungry are sated and rejoice, the thirsty are satisfied, the naked are clothed with good linen clothing . . . the chained are released, those who are bound now rejoice. The houses of the widows have been opened, the exiles return. . . .[7]

Another common kind of proclamation freed forced laborers from a particular area and assigned them to serve in the local temple. A Mesopotamian king from the twenty-second century B.C.E. issued the following order:

> [The god] opened up for the path of justice . . . thirty-eight cities were liberated for Shamash (the god), indeed, I sought no forced labor from

them, I drafted them not into military service. They shall serve (Shamash) in the temple alone.[8]

Although the terms of these royal proclamations differed, they included a number of common elements. Prisoners and slaves were permitted to return home, and various special signs announcing their impending freedom accompanied their release. In Mesopotamia, for instance, it was customary to raise a torch signifying the liberation. Ancient texts compare the torch to a light that illuminates the country or to the sun. In other civilizations, it was common to raise a special pole or banner for the occasion. Often the king issued such proclamations to inculcate loyalty among his people, but another motive also came into play—the notion that enslaving the servants of a god could bring destruction upon the oppressor's kingdom.[9]

Although brief, even this small bit of background sheds enormous light on the cultural milieu of the Exodus story. In the role of liberator, God takes the Israelites from captivity, enabling and fully expecting them to serve God instead of Pharaoh. The biblical laws (Lev. 25:42–43) forbidding the permanent enslavement of one Israelite by another sharpen the point. "For they are my servants [avadai, "my servants" or "my slaves"], whom I freed from the land of Egypt; they may not give themselves over into servitude. You shall not rule over them ruthlessly [b'farekh, the same word that appears in Exodus to describe Pharaoh's oppression of the Israelites]." As one scholar observed, the events of the Exodus conform to an ancient Near Eastern practice, when a slave undergoes "a change of master."[10] Pharaoh's refusal to "let My people go that they may serve Me," the refrain that runs throughout the plague narrative, brings ruin upon his country.

When the Israelites finally do leave, the Egyptians give them silver and gold, and also clothing (Ex. 12:36), as one might expect in light of Ramses IV's freedom proclamation. The Bible connects political and economic aspects of redemption.

The various signs that precede the Exodus go further than mere poles and banners, though Isaiah (11:11–12) uses the same imagery. "In that day, Adonai will apply His hand again to redeeming the other part of His people from Assyria—as also from Egypt . . . He will hold up a signal [nes] to the nations and assemble the banished of Israel." The word *nes* also means "miracle," though this word is not used in the Book of Exodus. The pillar of fire that gives the departing Israelites light by night is reminiscent of the Mesopotamian sunlike torch that heralds the dawn of freedom.

There is, of course, one enormous difference between ancient Near Eastern freedom proclamations and the biblical account of Israel's redemption from Egypt. The beneficiaries of royal freedom proclamations owed loyalty to the king, not to any superior god. When God freed the Israelites from Pharaoh, they owed service and loyalty to God alone.[11]

AN AGE-OLD QUESTION: WHY DID GOD REDEEM THE ISRAELITES FROM EGYPT?

This question echoes throughout the Midrash, that vast body of literature that seeks answers to the deepest questions raised by our ancient texts. Some say that the children of Israel merited redemption because of their own virtues or those of their ancestors. Others claim that Israel was essentially undeserving and only merited redemption after accepting the Torah at Sinai. A third view holds that prior to the Exodus, God gave the Israelites two specific commandments to follow; the Passover sacrifice and circumcision. Only observance of these commandments rendered them worthy of leaving Egypt.

> Copy one or both of the following texts and distribute them
> to your guests. This will make for an interesting discussion for small groups
> before the Seder. Ask each group to focus on one of these midrashim.
> During the Seder, ask each group to report briefly on its discussion.
> Each text is accompanied by a few questions, but don't let them limit
> the discussion. Depending on your group, you may want to
> introduce this with Appendix II, "What Is Midrash?"

Rabbi Eliezer ha-Kappar [active in Israel between 170 and 200 C.E.] says: Did not Israel possess four virtues more worthy than anything else in the whole world? They were above suspicion in regard to their sexual behavior [i.e., they refrained from sexual relations with those whom they could not marry, presumably Egyptians] and tale bearing [gossiping, *lashon ha-ra*]. They did not change their names and they did not change their language.

—THE MEKHILTA OF RABBI ISHMAEL, A COLLECTION OF MIDRASHIM
COMPILED IN THE THIRD CENTURY C.E.[12]

• Must a slave possess particular merits to deserve redemption? Which of these four virtues is the most surprising to you? What is the relationship among these qualities, and what role might they have played in the Exodus from Egypt? What other virtues might you have expected to be included in this list? How do these factors strike you in terms of current concerns about the Jewish future?

"These are the records of the Tabernacle . . ." (Ex. 38:21). When Israel toiled under harsh labor in Egypt, it was decreed that the men could not return at night to sleep in their homes. Rabbi Shimon bar Chalafta [active in Israel c. 200 C.E.] said: What would the daughters of Israel do? They went down to draw water from the Nile and the Holy One, blessed be He, filled their jugs with small fish. Some they sold to buy wine. Some they cooked and brought with the wine to their husbands in the fields. As it says, *"with all sorts of tasks in the field"* (Ex. 1:14). When they had eaten and drunk they would take [copper] mirrors and look into them with their husbands. She said, "I am more fair than you." And he said, "I am more fair than you." And this led to arousing their appetite for each other and they were fruitful and multiplied. And the Holy One, blessed be He, took note of them immediately. [They bore many children . . .] and all this resulted from the mirrors. As it says, *"The land was filled with them"* (Ex. 1:7). *"And the more they were afflicted the more they multiplied"* (Ex. 1:12). From the merit of those mirrors that they would show to their husbands and which would arouse them, they raised up all the hosts, as it says, *"All the hosts of Adonai departed from the land of Egypt . . . and Adonai brought the Israelites from the land troop by troop"* (literally in their "hosts," Ex. 12:41, 51).

When the Holy One, blessed be He, told Moses to build the Mishkan (the Tabernacle in the desert) all Israel donated. He who had silver or gold or copper . . . or other treasures, brought it all immediately. Said the women, "What have we to donate?" They stood up and brought the mirrors to Moses. When Moses saw them, he flew into a rage. He said to the men of Israel, "Take rods and break their thighs. These mirrors! Why are they necessary?" The Holy One, blessed be He, said to Moses, "Moses, these you despise? These mirrors raised up these hosts in Egypt. Take them and make a copper basin with a copper stand for the priests to sanctify themselves. As it says, *'He made the basin of copper and its stand of copper, from the mirrors of the women who performed tasks at the entrance of the Tent of Meeting'"* [or midrashically, *"from the mirrors of the women who created hosts"*] (Ex. 38:8).

—MIDRASH TANCHUMA, COMPILED BETWEEN
THE FIFTH AND NINTH CENTURIES C.E.[13]

• What is the relationship between the actions of women and of God in this midrash? What is the significance of the fact that procreation in the face of oppression is associated with redemption? How would you relate the women's actions to the concept in Genesis (1:27) that human beings, "male and female," are created in God's image? What do you make of the fact that Moses shows so little understanding of the significance of the women's mirrors?

THE FOUR CUPS OF REDEMPTION

Wine clearly plays an important role in the Seder. We spill sixteen drops of wine from our cups (see page 199), pour a special cup for Elijah (see page 319), raise our cups when reciting particular passages in the Haggadah, and, of course, we drink at least four cups.[14]

Two factors help explain why drinking wine at the Seder became so important. First, during the period of the Seder's early development, the Sages were particularly fond of wine. The Babylonian Talmud put it this way: "A person in whose house wine does not flow like water has not reached the ultimate stage of blessedness!" (Eruvin 65a). Second, according to the Talmud, wine served as a substitute for the missing paschal offering in the post–Temple era: "Now that the Temple no longer exists there is no rejoicing except with wine" (Pesachim 109a). The latter, in particular, may shed light on why the Mishnah (Pesachim 10:1) takes the drinking of wine on the night of Passover so seriously: You must drink not less than four cups even if you have to borrow from the "pauper's dish" to buy the wine. On Shabbat you can substitute other drinks for wine, but not on Passover. The Babylonian Talmud (Pesachim 117b) explains: "Our Rabbis instituted four cups as symbolizing freedom." But why four cups? For that we must turn to the Jerusalem Talmud, compiled in the Land of Israel between 200 and 400 C.E. Below are several of the Jerusalem Talmud's explanations.

Read the first interpretation and discuss the questions that follow. You may want to contrast this with the text that follows the questions.

> Whence four cups? Rabbi Yochanan said in the name of Rabbi Benaiah: [They] correspond to the four redemptions [or acts of redemption, mentioned in reference to Egypt]: "Say, therefore, to the Israelite people; 'I am Adonai. I will take you out [*v'hotzeiti*] from under the suffering of the Egyptians and deliver you [*v'hitzalti*] from their bondage. I will redeem you [*v'ga'alti*] with an outstretched arm and through extraordinary chastisements [i.e., judgments against the Egyptians]. And I will take you [*v'lakachti*] to be My people . . .'" (Ex. 6:6–7).
>
> —JERUSALEM TALMUD, PESACHIM 10:1

- How would you explain the relationship among the four promises or aspects of redemption mentioned in the above passage from the Jerusalem Talmud?

- Jacob Neusner, one of the great authorities on rabbinic literature, suggests that these four elements of redemption involve: "God's redeeming Israel from (1) Egyptian oppression; (2) subjugation to others; (3) a psychological slave mentality—by openly vanquishing their oppressor—and (4) their old identity, giving Israel a new identity as God's people."[15] How do you feel about Neusner's interpretation?

- What respective roles do you think God and human beings play in redemption?

- The same passage in Exodus that refers to the four promises of redemption includes a fifth pledge: "I will bring you [*v'heveiti*] into the land that I swore to give Abraham, Isaac, and Jacob, and I will give it to you for a possession, I Adonai" (Ex. 6:8). This has prompted some to argue for drinking a fifth cup of wine at the Seder. The ancient link between redemption and return to the Land of Israel took on renewed meaning with the advent of Zionism. Now recited in many synagogues on the Sabbath, the Prayer for the State of Israel refers to Israel as *reishit tzemichat ge'ulateinu,* "the first flowering of our redemption." In your understanding of redemption, what role does or should the State of Israel play?

The Jerusalem Talmud also includes several less familiar explanations of the four cups. The tone of the interpretation below may remind you of the passage "Pour out Your wrath," which appears in traditional Haggadot and is read prior to completing the Hallel.

> And Rabbis say, [They] correspond to the four cups of retribution that the Holy One Praised be He, will give the nations of the world to drink: For thus said Adonai, the God of Israel to me: "Take from My hand this cup of wine—of wrath—[and make all the nations to whom I send you drink of it]" (Jer. 25:15); "[Flee from the midst of Babylon. . . . For this is a time of vengeance for Adonai, He will deal retribution to her]. Babylon was a golden cup in Adonai's hand, it makes the whole earth drunk" (Jer. 51:6-7); "For in Adonai's hand there is a cup [with foaming wine fully mixed in; from this He pours; all the wicked of the earth drink, draining it to the very dregs]" (Psalms 75:9); "He will rain down upon the wicked blazing coals and sulfur, a scorching wind shall be the portion of their cup" (Psalms 11:6).
>
> —JERUSALEM TALMUD, PESACHIM 10:1

• How would you contrast this interpretation with the one above? What are the potential dangers of such texts? How do Jewish texts of this kind make you feel?

A QUARTET OF TWENTIETH-CENTURY JEWISH VOICES ON REDEMPTION

Even more than Judaism remembers the past redemption from Egypt, it finds evidence of redemption in the present and yearns for more to come in the future. Here are four twentieth-century voices on redemption.
Choose one or two to read aloud and discuss the questions that follow. Or you may want to read a selection to accompany each of the four cups of wine.

• Which of these statements speaks most powerfully to you and why?

• Do you think you would have responded similarly five or ten years ago? Why?

• Do you agree that redemption of the individual and society are inextricably linked?

The salvation that modern man seeks in this world, like that which his fathers sought in the world to come, has both a personal and a social significance. In its personal aspect it represents the faith in the possibility of achieving an integrated personality . . . In its social aspect, salvation means the ultimate achievement of a social order in which all men shall collaborate in the pursuit of common ends in a manner which shall afford each the maximum opportunity for creative self expression. There can be no personal salvation so long as injustice and strife exist in the social order; there can be no social salvation so long as the greed for gain and the lust for dominance are permitted to inhibit the hunger for human fellowship and sympathy in the hearts of men . . . The God of salvation . . . is the Power that makes for the fulfillment of all valid ideas.

—MORDECAI M. KAPLAN (1881–1983)[16]

Mordecai Kaplan was born in Lithuania. His family moved to the United States in 1890. Kaplan was a rabbi, teacher, theologian, and spiritual father of the Reconstructionist Movement. He rejected most supernatural ideas in Judaism and defined God as the power that made possible the pursuit of fundamental values, such as freedom and improving the world.

The lived moment leads directly to knowledge of revelation, and thinking about birth leads indirectly to the knowledge of creation. But in his personal life probably not one of us will taste the essence of redemption before his last hour. And yet here, too, there is an approach. It is dark and silent and cannot be indicated by any means, save by my asking you to recall your own dark and silent hours. I mean those hours in the lowest depths when our soul hovers over the frail trap door which, at the very next instant, may send us down into destruction, madness, and suicide at our own verdict. Indeed, we are astonished that it has not opened up until now. But suddenly we feel the touch of a hand. It reaches down to us, it wishes to be grasped—and yet what incredible courage is needed to take that hand, to let it draw us up out of the darkness! This is redemption. We must realize the true nature of the experience proffered us: It is that "our redeemer lives" (Job 19:25), that He wishes to redeem us—but only by our own acceptance of His redemption with the turning of our whole being.

—MARTIN BUBER (1878–1965)[17]

Martin Buber was born in Vienna and immigrated to Palestine in 1938. A philosopher, Zionist leader, and scholar of biblical and Hasidic literature, Buber thought of God as an "Eternal Thou," always available to be experienced by those fully willing to open themselves to the encounter.

The destiny of man is to be a partner of God and a mitzvah is an act in which man is present, an act of participation; while sin is an act in which God is alone; an act of alienation. Such acts of man's revelations of the divine are acts of redemption. The meaning of redemption is to reveal the holy that is concealed, to disclose the divine that is suppressed. Every man is called upon to be a redeemer, and redemption takes place every moment, every day. . . . The world is in need of redemption, but the redemption must not be expected to happen as an act of sheer grace. Man's task is to make the world worthy of redemption. His faith and his works are preparations for *ultimate redemption.*

—ABRAHAM JOSHUA HESCHEL (1907–1972)[18]

Abraham Joshua Heschel, a descendant of great Hasidic masters on both sides of his family, was born in Warsaw and lived in Poland and Germany. He immigrated to the United States in 1940. A theologian and philosopher, Heschel was Professor of Jewish Ethics and Mysticism at The Jewish Theological Seminary of America and a social activist who marched with Martin Luther King Jr. during the civil rights era.

The hope for Redemption is the force that sustains Judaism in the Diaspora; the Judaism of Israel is the very Redemption . . . Redemption is continuous. The Redemption from Egypt and the Final Redemption are part of the same process, "of the mighty hand and outstretched arm," which began in Egypt and is evident in all of history. Moses and Elijah belong to the same redemptive act; one represents its beginning and the other its culmination, so that together they fulfill its purpose. The spirit of Israel is attuned to the hum of the redemptive process, to the sound waves of its labors which will end only with the coming of the days of the Messiah.

—RABBI ABRAHAM ISAAC KOOK (1865–1935)[19]

Rabbi Abraham Isaac Kook was an early religious Zionist leader. Deeply steeped in mysticism, Rav Kook immigrated to Israel in 1904 and from 1921 until his death he served as Chief Ashkenazic Rabbi of Palestine under the British Mandate. He revived the ancient notion that the ultimate Messiah would be preceded by the Messiah ben Joseph, a figure who would die in battle and lay the groundwork for the final redemption. In fact, when Kook eulogized Theodore Herzl in 1904, he likened the Zionist leader to Messiah ben Joseph. Kook believed that even secular Jews played a critical role in the redemptive process, and he built strong relationships among Jews from all religious back-grounds. Rav Kook's thinking has become central to Israel's settler movement.

ON FAITH IN REDEMPTION

Read the following passage aloud during your Seder.[20]

A single word captures the concern of the entire Passover Haggadah: redemption.

At its core lies a relatively simple idea: that the future will be better than the present. Not just a little brighter—eventually it will be more like the difference between night and day. Maimonides put it simply: "In that era there will be neither famine nor war, neither jealousy nor strife."[21]

Redemption is about the potential for positive change, ultimately dramatic change, even if it comes about slowly.

"Now we are slaves. Next year we will be free." Whether you interpret that statement in terms of political oppression or spiritual enslavement to false gods, how can you say those words if you don't believe in the possibility of change?

Maybe that's what the Haggadah's "wicked" child represents: a cynical voice calling Passover a charade, arguing that *nothing* really changes. Why study all the laws and customs of Passover? They're all about making Passover different from the rest of the year. Why bother to make one night different from all others if the fundamental reality points to an eternal status quo rather than a world we can improve, however slowly? During the Seder we recline like kings and queens. We ask questions, as free people are wont to do. The Seder promises that we *can* make one night different, and that's a start.

The fact that Jews held Seders in concentration camps provides an infinitely poignant illustration of Judaism's unshakable faith in redemption. For some inexplicable reason, the Germans permitted Jews in Bergen-Belsen to bake matzah one Passover. Rabbi Israel Spira of Bluzhov (1881–1981) led the Seder. In the midst of unspeakable degradation (metaphorically in the word *avadim,* Hebrew for "slaves"), Rabbi Spira searched and found hope. Here's part of what he said:

Tonight we have only matzah, we have no moments of relief, not a moment of respite for our humiliated spirits . . . But do not despair, my

301

young friends . . . For this is also the beginning of our redemption. We are slaves who served Pharaoh in Egypt. Slaves in Hebrew are *avadim;* the Hebrew letters of the word *avadim [ayin, bet, dalet, yod, mem]* form an acronym for the Hebrew phrase: David, the son of Jesse, your servant, your Messiah [*David: dalet; ben: bet; Yishai: yod; avdekha: ayin; meshichekha: mem*— a phrase that appears in the morning liturgy for the Sabbath and festivals as well as in the Haggadah]. Thus, even in our state of slavery we find intimations of our eventual freedom through the coming of the Messiah. We who are witnessing the darkest night in history, the lowest moment of civilization, will also witness the great light of redemption. . . .[22]

Perhaps faith in redemption would not have become such a prominent feature in the Jewish psyche had our history been less traumatic.

And that's the rub.

The very experiences that nurture faith in redemption can also spawn unbridled hopelessness. It's not hard to look back and agree that "in every generation they rise up to destroy us," to quote the Haggadah's powerful, but uncharacteristically embittered take on Jewish history. The good news is that "the Holy One, blessed be He, saves us from their hand." But that's hardly an end to the oppression and persecution that have stalked our people over the ages.

On the whole, however, the Haggadah wants us to choose hope over despair. The last verse of *Chad Gadya,* in many traditions the Seder's conclusion, leaves us with a glimmer of the ultimate hope—the triumph of life over death: "Then came the Holy One, blessed be He, and slew the angel of death."

We cannot know when our travails will end. We can only *know*—or have faith, if you prefer—that the future need not be as bleak as the past. To believe otherwise is to reject the promise of hope that animates the entire story of the Exodus and the Haggadah. To choose despair and cynicism is to endorse *Mitzrayim* as the end of the road, the ultimate truth. To have faith in redemption is to believe that suffering, exile, and oppression will end—someday. However distant that day may be, those who can envision it muster the strength to bring it closer.

Belief in redemption stands as one of those fundamental human divides. It's the difference between those who believe we're in a tunnel, though we sometimes can't see the light at the end, and those who think there is no tunnel, just a world that's unalterably dark. Those who believe in redemption retain a degree of optimism and energy to repair a world plagued by evil, even if they know they won't finish the task. Those who don't believe in redemption see an ever-broken world and surround themselves with walls that only further shut out the light of hope.

The compilers of the Haggadah certainly knew the dark times of Jewish history. But they chose to bequeath us a book that defiantly celebrates hope. Tonight we hold their shining gift in our hands. May we guard it with love and tenacity. May our Passover Seders fortify our faith in redemption. May we pass that faith down to our children. May we strengthen one another to build a world redeemed.

22

Passover Without a Seder? The Paschal Sacrifice

כֵּן יְיָ אֱלֹהֵינוּ וֵאלֹהֵי אֲבוֹתֵינוּ הַגִּיעֵנוּ
לְמוֹעֲדִים וְלִרְגָלִים אֲחֵרִים הַבָּאִים לִקְרָאתֵנוּ
לְשָׁלוֹם שְׂמֵחִים בְּבִנְיַן עִירֶךָ וְשָׂשִׂים בַּעֲבוֹדָתֶךָ.
וְנֹאכַל שָׁם מִן הַזְּבָחִים וּמִן הַפְּסָחִים אֲשֶׁר יַגִּיעַ
דָּמָם עַל קִיר מִזְבַּחֲךָ לְרָצוֹן.

Adonai our God and God of our ancestors, bring us in peace to other holy days and fes-
tivals that are approaching that we might be happy as we rebuild your city and joyful as
we serve You. There we will eat from the sacrifices and Passover offerings, the blood from
which will reach the wall of Your altar and please You.
—FROM THE PASSOVER HAGGADAH'S BLESSING OVER THE SECOND CUP OF WINE

Rabbi Akiva proposed these words for the blessing over the second cup of wine more than eighteen hundred years ago.[1] His prayer reflects the biblical mandate that the blood from sacrificed animals must be sprinkled or poured on the altar. Akiva lived in the shadow of the Second Temple's destruction and died at the hand of Roman executioners in 135 C.E. His words convey a deep yearning—and near certainty—that the Temple would soon be rebuilt so that the annual Passover sacrifice, along with the rest of the sacrificial rites, could resume once again.

This prayer also highlights the striking difference between the Passover celebration before and after the Temple's destruction. In Temple times Passover revolved around a sacrifice. We have no evidence that telling the story of the Exodus played any role in the festival. Without the Temple, the festival increasingly focused on a slowly evolving liturgy that integrated various approaches to recounting the Exodus.

The Haggadah often refers to the Temple, but Akiva's prayer embodies its most vivid reference to the ancient sacrificial rite. This chapter will explore the ritual sacrifice that defined Passover before the Seder developed.

Here's what we'll consider:

• the first Passover in Egypt;

• the Passover celebration in Temple times;

• Jewish sources on sacrifice;

• the role of sacrifice—broadly understood—in our lives today.

You'll find questions for discussion throughout.

A few words may help frame this chapter. Why is it worth devoting a chapter to the subject of animal sacrifice, a practice that seems primitive, and one that, in any case, Jews have given up for two thousand years? The subject deserves attention for three reasons. First, animal sacrifice was ubiquitous throughout most of human history and was central to Jewish practice until the destruction of the Temple in 70 C.E. Some religious communities still practice it today. On the day before Passover the Samaritan community in Israel still sacrifices lambs on Mount Gerizim, a place of blessing described in the Book of Deuteronomy.[2] And Muslims complete the *haj* (a cognate of the Hebrew *hag*, "pilgrimage festival") with *Eid al-Adha*, the Festival of Sacrifice, with the sacrificial slaughter of a sheep, goat, or camel. The rite commemorates the trials of Abraham and his willingness to sacrifice his son.[3]

Second, the Passover Seder—among many other elements of Judaism—evolved as a substitute for the sacrificial rites carried out in the Temple. In that light, it makes sense to develop some understanding of the original practices for which our Seders became a replacement. Third, a better understanding of animal sacrifice in ancient times may clarify the role that the concept of sacrifice ought to play in our lives today.

> As you read the Haggadah, ask your guests to point out references
> to the Temple and consider this question:

• Why would the Haggadah want to remind us of the Temple?

PASSOVER IN EGYPT

Consider copying the paragraph below and the following passage from Exodus for your guests, or simply read it aloud. Discuss the questions that follow.

The Book of Exodus describes what has come to be called *Pesach Mitzrayim*, "the Passover of Egypt," as opposed to *Pesach Dorot*, "the Passover of the Ages" or Passover as it was to be celebrated by later generations. The distinction highlights the fact that the festival evolved considerably over the millennia. For example, a number of features are unique to the Passover of Egypt: selecting the animal to be sacrificed four days before Passover; daubing the doorposts with blood; eating the meal in a particular garb and doing so hurriedly.

> [God says to Moses] [3]Speak to the whole community of Israel and say that on the tenth of this month each of them shall take a lamb to a family, a lamb to a household. [4]But if the household is too small for a lamb, let him share one with a neighbor who dwells nearby, in proportion to the number of persons: you shall contribute for the lamb according to what each household shall eat. [5]Your lamb shall be

without blemish, a yearling male; you may take it from the sheep or from the goats. ⁶You shall keep watch over it until the fourteenth day of this month; and all the assembled congregation of the Israelites shall slaughter it at twilight. ⁷They shall take some of the blood and put it on the two doorposts and the lintel of the houses in which they are to eat it. ⁸They shall eat the flesh that same night; they shall eat it roasted over the fire, with unleavened bread and with bitter herbs. ⁹Do not eat any of it raw, or cooked in any way with water, but roasted—head, legs, and entrails—over the fire. ¹⁰You shall not leave any of it over until morning; if any of it is left until morning, you shall burn it. ¹¹This is how you shall eat it; your loins girded, your sandals on your feet, and your staff in your hand; and you shall eat it hurriedly: it is a Passover offering to Adonai. ¹²For that night I will go through the land of Egypt and strike down every first-born in the land of Egypt, both man and beast; and I will mete out punishments to all the gods of Egypt, I Adonai. ¹³And the blood on the houses where you are staying shall be a sign for you: when I see the blood I will pass over you, so that no plague will destroy you when I strike the land of Egypt.

—EXODUS 12:3–13

- Obviously there are many differences between this first Seder and ours, but there are also some important similarities. What are some of the similarities?

- What questions does this account of the festival raise for you?

- We usually connect the story of the binding of Isaac (Genesis 22) with Rosh Hashanah, but many ancient sources link it to Passover. A third-century midrash comments on the last verse in the passage above. According to this source, when God says, "when I see the blood" (Exodus 12:13), God is referring to the "blood of the binding of Isaac."⁴ (The midrash follows a tradition that a small amount of Isaac's blood was indeed shed when he was bound for sacrifice.)⁵ Other ancient texts claim that the binding of Isaac actually occurred on the fifteenth of Nisan, the date on which Passover begins.[6] What parallels can you see between the stories of the binding of Isaac and Passover? What messages might these ancient sources wish to convey?

IN TEMPLE TIMES

FOR DISCUSSION

- Try to imagine yourself as a farmer about two thousand years ago making the pilgrimage to the sacred Temple in Jerusalem. How do you think you might feel?

- In the days of the Temple, you might have brought a lamb or a goat you had raised for the Passover sacrifice, or you could have purchased one in Jerusalem. Imagine that you were about to sacrifice your animal. What might be some of the feelings you'd experience at that moment?

- *Korban*, one of the biblical terms for sacrifice, shares the same root as the word *kareiv*, which means "to approach or draw close." In what ways might sacrifice have created a feeling of drawing close to God?

IF YOU WILL BE A GUEST AT A SEDER

The Seder developed as a substitute for the Passover sacrifice. The term for the last of the Seder's fifteen steps, *nirtzah*, "acceptance," provides a quiet reminder of this. A rare word in the Bible, *nirtzah* appears in this form in conjunction with sacrifice: "He shall lay his hand upon the head of the burnt offering, that it may be acceptable [*nirtzah*] in his behalf, in expiation for him" (Leviticus 1:4).

In ancient times, celebrating Passover entailed bringing an offering to the house of God and hoping it would be accepted. As guests at a Seder, we should consider bringing an offering, of sorts, to our hosts. We might contribute to the meal or bring something special to the discussion.[7]

THE PASSOVER RITE

Read this on your own.

Dramatic changes in the celebration of Passover took place in the seventh century B.C.E. King Josiah, a religious reformer who reigned between 640–609 B.C.E., sought to eradicate the vestiges of idol worship. To do so, he destroyed local sacrificial altars and centralized all such rites in the Temple in Jerusalem. With this, Passover—along with Shavuot and Sukkot—evolved from an annual, home-based ritual with a celebration at a local altar, to a nationwide pilgrimage to Jerusalem.[8]

Josephus (c. 38–100 C.E.), Jewish historian and priest, describes the impression made on pilgrims by the Temple Herod had rebuilt in about 20 B.C.E.:

> Viewed from without, the [Temple] had everything that could amaze either mind or eyes. Overlaid all round with stout plates of gold, in the first rays of the sun it reflected so fierce a blaze of fire that those who endeavored to look at it were forced to turn away as if they had looked straight at the sun. To strangers as they approached it seemed in the distance like a mountain covered with snow; for any part not covered with gold was dazzling white.[9]

Celebrants made their arrangements for eating the festival meal in advance. Josephus notes that "it is not permissible to feast alone, a sort of fraternity group is formed round each victim, consisting of at least ten adult males, while many groups have twenty members."[10] (*Chavurah*, the Hebrew term for this "fraternity," nowadays denotes a small religious community that gathers for prayer, holidays, and so forth.)

Entering the Temple required a state of ritual purity as defined by Leviticus—the absence of various skin diseases and illnesses, menstruation, or contact with the dead. Even those who met these standards immersed themselves in a ritual bath, often dressed in white, and remained barefoot.[11]

The sacrifice took place between three and five o'clock in the afternoon.[12] Men (with their lamb or goat in tow) and women entered the Women's Court. Women remained in an upper gallery, and men proceeded up fifteen rounded stairs to the Court of the Israelites and then to the Temple Court itself, where they carried out the sacrifice.

The Mishnah, another important source on the Second Temple period, notes that participants entered in three successive groups.[13] As each group entered, the Temple Gates were closed and the shofar sounded a sustained blast, followed by a quavering note, then another sustained blast. Levites chanted the Hallel, likely the very psalms we recite at the Seder. As prescribed in Exodus, men sacrificed their animals themselves.[14] Philo of Alexandria (c. 20 B.C.E.–50 C.E.) observed, "On this occasion the whole nation performs the sacred rites and acts as priest."[15]

The sacrifice followed the basic principles of kosher slaughter, namely that a sharp knife was required to cut the animal's throat in such a way as to make death as quick and painless as possible.[16]

Priests stood in two rows. Those in one row held gold basins, those in the other, silver. As the animal was slaughtered, a priest caught its blood in a basin, and passed the basin from one priest to the next until it reached the priest closest to the altar. He then threw the blood against the base of the altar. The empty basins were returned down the next row of priests. The design of these basins conveys a sense of the importance attached to the blood reaching the altar. they did not have a flat base, "lest the priests should set them down and the blood congeal."[17] (Holes in the floor near the base of the altar directed the blood through a channel under the floor that ran from the Temple to a nearby stream.)

The next job involved flaying the animal, removing the skin and the sacrificial portions— the fat surrounding the entrails and organs as well as the kidneys and liver—as specified by Leviticus.[18] Again, the people carried this out themselves and seem to have been quite familiar with the process. The animal was suspended from iron hooks fixed to the walls and pillars of the courtyard. If all of these were in use, a supply of wooden staves stood ready, "which a man could put on his own and his fellow's shoulder."[19] A priest collected the sacrificial portions on a tray and carried them up a ramp to the fire on the altar.

Having completed the sacrifice, the pilgrim wrapped the carcass in its skin, swung it over his shoulder—like a traveler carries his bag, says the Talmud—and headed home or to one of the communal roasting ovens.[20] Great care was taken to comply with the direction in Exodus that the meat should be cooked solely by roasting it over a fire. Metal spits or grills were forbidden lest the heat from the metal, rather than flame alone, contribute to the cooking process. To avoid this, celebrants used skewers of pomegranate wood.[21]

It was also essential to consume the meat from the actual animal for which your company had registered, from the animal that had, in a sense, been slaughtered in your name. You could withdraw from one group and join another, but only prior to the time that the animal had been slaughtered.[22]

What about the festival meal? Some of it will be quite familiar. The Book of Jubilees, a Jewish source from the second century B.C.E., tells us that it included wine.[23] The Haggadah notes that Hillel, born in the middle of the first century B.C.E., combined the Passover offering in a sandwich of matzah and bitter herbs. Rabbi Eliezer ben Zadok, a priest who served in the Temple during the first century, suggested that *charoset* was also required.[24] The Talmud recalls the joy of the celebration: "Even though there was only as much as an olive's bulk of the Passover-offering to eat, the sound of the Hallel split the roofs!"[25]

Read on your own or consider reading aloud.

What may the sacrifice have meant to those who performed it? A study of the origins of sacrifice sheds light on the meaning behind these ancient rites.

"Because the victim is distinct from [those offering up the sacrifice] and the god, it separates them while uniting them: they draw close to each other, without giving themselves to each other entirely."[26] Participants in the rite must be set apart or specially purified. Without an intermediary, the individual carrying out the sacrifice "would find death, not life. The victim takes his place. It alone penetrates into the perilous domain of sacrifice, it dies there, and indeed it is there in order to die. The [one carrying out the sacrifice] remains protected: the gods take the victim instead of him. *The victim redeems him.* . . . There is no sacrifice into which some idea of redemption does not enter."[27]

However alien or abhorrent you may find these ancient sacrificial rites, they tangibly bound religion to the realm of ultimate concerns—your life, your death, and the welfare of your community. Those bonds were visceral, so powerful that by comparison, today's religious rituals may seem abstract, perhaps even pale.

Slitting an animal's throat, its blood spattering upon you, feeling the life ebb from its body: all this underscored the fragility of life, and rendered the importance of securing divine favor all the more crucial. The ascending column of smoke from the altar—a "pleasing odor to Adonai," says Leviticus—assured a measure of well-being as it visibly connected this world to the abode of "God who dwells on high" (Psalms 113:5).[28] At the Seder we recite Hallel, some of the very psalms the Levites intoned during the Passover sacrifice. The sacrifice nears completion. In heaven and on earth all seems right:

> I shall not die but live . . . [God] harshly chastised me but to death did not deliver me. . . . We beseech You, Adonai, pray, rescue. We beseech you, Adonai, make us prosper . . . Adonai is God and He shines upon us. Bind the festive offering with ropes all the way to the horns of the altar. You are my God, and I acclaim You, my God, and I exalt You. Acclaim Adonai, for He is good, forever is his kindness.
>
> —PSALMS 118:17–27 (FROM THE PSALMS OF
> HALLEL THAT WE READ AT THE SEDER)

SOURCES ON SACRIFICE

Below you will find twelve sources on sacrifice spanning roughly three thousand years.
Scholars disagree about the dating of the biblical sources. I've followed the
Jewish Study Bible for the dates below.[29] You might want to copy these texts
and ask your guests to take turns reading some or all of them aloud.
Discuss the questions that follow.

1. "What need have I for all your sacrifices?" says Adonai . . . "I cannot endure them. . . . Your hands are stained with crime. Wash yourselves clean; put your evil doings away from my sight. Cease to do evil; learn to do good. Devote yourselves to justice; aid the wronged, uphold the rights of the orphan, defend the cause of the widow."
   —ISAIAH 1:11–17, EIGHTH CENTURY B.C.E.

313

2. For the life of the flesh is in the blood, and I have assigned it to you for making expiation for your lives upon the altar; it is the blood, as life, that effects expiation.

—LEVITICUS 17:11, SIXTH CENTURY B.C.E.

3. May Adonai answer you on the day of distress . . . May He recall all your grain offerings, and your burnt offerings may He relish.

—PSALMS 20:2–4, DATE UNCERTAIN

4. Were I hungry, I would not tell you, for Mine is the world and all it holds. Do I eat the flesh of bulls, or drink the blood of he-goats?

—PSALMS 50:12, DATE UNCERTAIN

5. Adonai, open my lips, and let my mouth declare Your praise. You do not want me to bring sacrifices; you do not desire burnt offerings; true sacrifice to God is a contrite spirit; God, You will not despise a contrite and crushed heart.

—PSALMS 51:17–19, DATE UNCERTAIN

6. Be favorable Adonai, our God, toward Your people Israel and their prayer and restore the service to the sanctuary of the Holy of Holies of Your Temple. The fire-offerings of Israel and their prayer accept with love and favor, and may the service of Your people Israel always be favorable to You.

—THE TRADITIONAL JEWISH PRAYER BOOK, FROM
THE *AMIDAH*, RECITED THRICE DAILY. PART OF THE PRAYER
PREDATES THE DESTRUCTION OF THE SECOND TEMPLE IN 70 C.E.[30]

7. "I will bring them to My sacred mount and let them rejoice in My house of prayer . . ." (Isaiah 56:7). "And when prayer has come, the Temple service will come, as it says, 'Their burnt offerings and sacrifices shall be welcome on My altar'" (Isaiah 56:7).

—BABYLONIAN TALMUD, MEGILLAH 18A, 550–650 C.E.

8. Prayer is more efficacious than offerings. As it says, "What need have I [God] for all your sacrifices?" (Isaiah 1:11).

—BABYLONIAN TALMUD, BERAKHOT 32B, 550–650 C.E.

9. God revealed the laws of sacrifice at a time when humanity was accustomed to offering various species of living beings in temples. This was the nature of pagan worship. God's requirement of sacrifice was a ruse of sorts, based on the needs of humanity at the time. Religion without sacrifice would have been as difficult to accept in those days as religion would be in our day without prayer, fasting, or calling on God for help in times of misfortune. Therefore God allowed sacrifice to continue, but directed it to serve God rather than the objects of pagan worship.

—MAIMONIDES (1135–1204), SPAIN (PARAPHRASED)[31]

10. May He soon rebuild His house. Quickly, quickly, soon, in our days God, rebuild God, rebuild, soon rebuild Your house.

—THE PASSOVER HAGGADAH, THE REFRAIN FROM *ADIR HU*, "HE IS MIGHTY," FOURTEENTH CENTURY. (REBUILDING GOD'S HOUSE, THE TEMPLE, IMPLICITLY ANTICIPATES THE RESUMPTION OF SACRIFICE.)

11. In ironic contrast to our mechanized, mass-produced society, where the killing of animals for food takes place at a remove from our consciousness and from our direct participation, the sacrificial system in fact involved worshipper and priest alike, and the symbolic value of its operation, whatever it may have been in specific cases, lay in its directness, in its consciousness of the taking of life.

—EVERETT FOX (1947–), UNITED STATES, SCHOLAR AND TRANSLATOR OF THE BIBLE[32]

12. I prefer to look at sacrifice as a cultural language which once opened all sorts of possibilities for meaning, just as every other cultural language does. . . . The first thing that the symbolic system of Leviticus conveys to me—and conveys better than any other discipline or art I know—is that everyday life, ordered in keeping with God's command,

can be wonderfully rich and good *despite* the very real terror that haunts us (or me, at least) every day of life: the knowledge that one day death will take all we love from us, including life itself. In sacrifice, I stand in front of the altar, my hand on the body of a throbbing animal about to die. I hear its scream and see its blood and smell its death, and I cannot but think: there but for the grace of God go I, today. One day it *will* be me. I scream too when I realize this, not cognitively but in my *kishkes*, my guts, from the depths.

—ARNOLD EISEN (1951–), UNITED STATES, CHANCELLOR OF THE JEWISH THEOLOGICAL SEMINARY OF AMERICA[33]

FOR DISCUSSION

• Which of these do you find particularly interesting or surprising? Why?

• How do you understand prayers that call on God to rebuild the Temple? How do you feel about reciting those kinds of prayers?

• The last two sources suggest that the rituals of sacrifice created a heightened awareness of life and death. Do you agree? Why or why not?

• Can you make an argument for resuming animal sacrifice? If so, on what grounds?

SACRIFICE IN OUR LIVES TODAY

Consider reading the following aloud and discussing the
questions that follow or just skip to the questions.

What's the goal of the Exodus? Moses' call to Pharaoh—"Let my people go!"—seems to say it all: freedom! Indeed, this iconic command recurs throughout the story a notable seven times.[34] But for all its familiarity, the rest of the Bible's demand may come as a surprise. In six of the seven cases, Moses says, "Let my people go *that they may serve Me in the wilderness*."[35]

What is the nature of this service? The Hebrew in these verses, *ya'avduni*, implies a sacrificial service. The Bible makes this explicit in a question that the

Haggadah puts in the "wicked" child's mouth. "What does this service mean to you?" The verse continues, "You shall say, 'It is the Passover sacrifice to Adonai . . .'" (Exodus 12:26–27).

The Israelites did not acquire untrammeled liberty through the Exodus. They gained a more limited freedom—to worship God with the appropriate sacrificial service. Even though celebrants enjoyed a portion of the Passover offering themselves, the requirement to make the sacrifice should probably be viewed as a burden of sorts. If you didn't have a lamb or a goat, you'd have to purchase one. If your flock was small, it would be smaller yet. Even if you believed that sacrifice guaranteed divine blessing or protection, the act required a price.

The Bible itself connects sacrifice with the idea of surrendering to God something of particular value. Cain merely offered "fruit of the soil," which God rejected. Abel sacrificed "the *choicest* of the firstlings of his flock," which God accepted.[36] The language of the ultimate test to which God put Abraham makes this painfully clear. "Take your son, you favored one, Isaac, whom you love, and go to the land of Moriah, and offer him there as a burnt offering . . ." (Genesis 22:2).

We've given up these notions of sacrifice—thankfully. But important questions remain about the role of sacrifice in our lives.

For discussion

- How do you understand the concept of personal sacrifice and what role do you think it should play in our lives today?

- For most of human history animal sacrifice was central to religious practice. What do you think should take its place today?

- How do you think about the relationship between freedom and sacrifice?

- To secure our freedom should we sacrifice more?

- To draw closer to God—or to an ultimate sense of purpose—what, if anything, might we need to give up?

- Do the sacrifices we make serve a truly worthy purpose? Why or why not?

23

Elijah's Transformation: From Zealot to Folk Hero

שְׁפֹךְ חֲמָתְךָ אֶל־הַגּוֹיִם אֲשֶׁר לֹא יְדָעוּךָ
וְעַל־מַמְלָכוֹת אֲשֶׁר בְּשִׁמְךָ לֹא קָרָאוּ...

Fill Elijah's goblet and the fourth cup. The leader fills Elijah's goblet or passes it round the table so that every participant can add some wine from his or her own cup . . . We open the door for Elijah (usually a child is given this privilege) as we rise and recite:[1]
Pour out Your wrath upon the nations that do not know You, upon the governments which do not call upon Your name. For they have devoured Jacob and desolated his home. Pour out Your wrath on them; may Your blazing anger overtake them, destroy them from under the heavens of Adonai (Psalms 79:6–7, 69:25, and Lamentations 3:66).
—THE PASSOVER HAGGADAH

Upon completing Grace after the Passover meal, we reach one of the Seder's most memorable rituals—pouring the Cup of Elijah and opening the door for the prophet, hoping that he will have arrived to usher in the Messiah. In welcoming Elijah, we evoke one of Jewish folklore's most beloved figures.

In the context of the Seder, Elijah also evokes the figure of Moses, whose role in the Exodus has been strikingly minimized by the compilers of the Haggadah. But Elijah's spirit is with us more often than just at the Seder.

319

A traditional circumcision evokes the prophet through the Chair of Elijah, an empty chair placed to the right of the child, a custom that reaches back some twelve hundred years, if not more.[2] Elijah's relationship with the newborn continues: he serves as the guardian of infants for the first thirty days of life. According to the Talmud, "When a man weds a wife who is right for him, Elijah kisses him. . . ."[3] At the conclusion of every Sabbath we sing *"Eliyahu Hanavi,"* a song that urges Elijah to bring the Messiah with him speedily and in our time. Some modern Haggadot have added this song to the Seder. In the Grace after every meal (*Birkat Ha-Mazon*) we ask the Compassionate One to "send Elijah the Prophet, may he be remembered for good, to us so he may bring us good tidings of salvations and consolations."

In addition to these prescribed occasions, countless tales recount Elijah's legendary appearances over the ages. The variations of these often-miraculous tales are legion, but many revolve around the theme of an old man wrapped in his mantle who mysteriously appears to teach an ethical lesson, impart hope to those in despair, or aid the destitute.

> Ask your Seder participants to discuss what "opening the door for Elijah"
> means to them. Ask some of your senior participants to share
> their childhood recollections about Elijah and the Seder.

ELIJAH COMES TO THE SEDER

Read the section below aloud or on your own.

Elijah's connection with the Seder offers a wonderful example of the evolution of Jewish tradition: The Babylonian Talmud holds that Elijah will not come during the Sabbath or on the day before festivals. His appearance would naturally lead to special preparations that might then interfere with proper observance of the Sabbath or a festival![4] But a tenth-century midrash envisions his return on the night of the Seder after the holy day has begun.[5] The Jewish People's yearning for salvation was so powerful that it fashioned a role for Elijah at the Passover Seder, the redemptive moment par excellence.

We don't know precisely when the rituals associated with Elijah were added to the Ashkenazic Seder, but the consensus seems to be during the Middle Ages, some time after the Crusades. At around the same time, it also became customary to recite the malediction "Pour out Your wrath . . ." upon opening the door.

Scholars believe that the practice of opening the door for Elijah may have developed from an earlier custom of leaving the door ajar throughout the entire Seder to fulfill the biblical injunction that the night of Passover was "for Adonai a night of vigil to bring them out of the land of Egypt" and it should be "one of vigil for all the children of Israel throughout the ages" (Ex. 12:42).

Moses Isserles (c. 1530–1572), the great Polish commentator, held that when Jews opened their doors in foreign lands and recited the passage above, it expressed their faith that God would protect them and that Passover had indeed remained a night of vigil on God's part: "And for the merit of this faith the Messiah will come and 'pour out his wrath' upon the deniers of God."[6] But Isserles made no mention of Elijah. By contrast, the Maharal of Prague (c. 1525–1609) taught that opening the door and preparing Elijah's Cup gave concrete expression to an undying faith in the ultimate redemption.[7]

In many quarters, opening the door on Passover eve doubtless demanded faith. Throughout Europe, Passover had become an especially dangerous season for Jews. Accusations of blood libel—that Jews secretly crucified Christian children and used their blood to make matzah—were rampant. In the face of this peril, Jewish folklore taught that it was none other than Elijah who came to defend communities beset by charges of blood libel.[8] The Bible (II Kings 2:12) calls Elijah "the chariot of Israel, and its horsemen." God's prophet would stand ready to protect his people wherever danger lurked.[9]

ELIJAH'S CUP

Read the section below aloud or on your own.

The customary Cup of Elijah is also a relatively late addition to the Seder, first written about in the fifteenth century.[10] Elijah's presence at the Seder may have reflected a response to a growing sense of vulnerability, and some believe that it also attested to a quickening faith that messianic times were imminent. In explaining the late addition of Elijah's Cup to the Seder, Rabbi Menachem M. Schneerson (1902–1994), the late Lubavitcher Rebbe, said: "This custom is an expression of the Jewish People's belief in the coming of Mashiach and in the coming of Eliyahu, who will herald the imminent Redemption. The nearer we approach the time of the Redemption, the more keenly is this faithful anticipation felt in the heart of every Jew. This is why the above custom came to light and became widespread in recent generations, even though we do not find tangible evidence of it in earlier days."[11]

That mounting vulnerability and heightened messianism should occur at the same time makes perfect sense: The venerable concept of the birth pangs of the Messiah welded them together forever. According to ancient tradition, suffering signified the pain that would precede the Messiah.[12]

Why do we evoke Elijah's spirit before beginning the last four psalms of the Hallel (Psalms 115–118)? One reason is that we have just invoked his name in the *Birkat Ha-Mazon,* the Grace after Meals. But this question raises a related one. During the Seder we read the Hallel's six psalms. The Haggadah has us recite two before and four after the meal. Why? The Hallel's first two psalms, Psalms 113 and 114 (particularly Psalm 114), address themes of the Exodus from Egypt. The Hallel's last four psalms are understood as referring to the future messianic redemption. In this light, introducing those psalms with the invocation of Elijah, herald of the Messiah, makes perfect sense.[13]

THE BIBLICAL ELIJAH

Read the following story about Elijah the Prophet and
lead a discussion on the questions that follow.

According to tradition, Elijah lived during the ninth century B.C.E. The Bible tells his story in the First and Second Book of Kings. His zealous opposition to idol worship led Elijah into bitter conflict with King Ahab and Queen Jezebel. Jezebel, a Phoenician princess, came from a country that worshiped Baal. Ahab built a temple for her god in Israel so that people could worship both Baal and the God of Israel. The struggle between Elijah and the royal house reached a peak when Elijah challenged the prophets of Baal to a showdown at Mount Carmel.

Elijah said, "'How long will you keep hopping between two opinions? If Adonai is God, follow him; and if Baal, follow him!' But the people answered him not a word" (I Kings 18:21).

Elijah designed the ultimate test to reveal the true God. He and 450 prophets of Baal each brought animals to sacrifice. The true god would cause fire from heaven to consume the sacrifices.

The prophets of Baal prayed and called to their god, but nothing happened. "Elijah mocked them, saying, 'Shout louder! After all, he is a god. But he may be in conversation, he may be detained, or he may be on a journey, or perhaps he is asleep and will wake up.' So they shouted louder, and gashed themselves with knives and spears, according to their practice, until blood streamed over them" (I Kings 18:27–28). Still nothing.

Then Elijah prepared his sacrifice. "Then the fire from Adonai descended and consumed the burnt offering . . . When they saw this, all the people flung themselves on their faces and cried out: 'Adonai, alone is God; Adonai, alone is God.' Then Elijah said to them, 'Seize the prophets of Baal; let not a single one of them get away.' They seized them, and Elijah brought them down to the [brook] of Kishon and slaughtered them there" (I Kings 18:38–40).

When Jezebel found out that Elijah ordered the people to kill the prophets of Baal she tried to hunt him down and kill him. Despite the miracle at Mount Carmel, many of the people sided with Jezebel. Feeling abandoned and full of despair, Elijah wanted to die. God told him to journey through the desert for forty days and forty nights to Mount Horeb (another name for Mount Sinai). When he arrived, Elijah went into a cave and spent the night.

The word of Adonai came to him. He said to him, "Why are you here, Elijah?" He replied, "I am moved by zeal for Adonai, the God of Hosts, for the Israelites have forsaken Your covenant, torn down Your altars, and put Your prophets to the sword. I alone am left, and they are out to take my life." "Come out," He called, "and stand on the mountain before Adonai." And lo, Adonai passed by. There was a great and mighty wind, splitting mountains and shattering rocks by the power of Adonai; but Adonai was not in the wind. After the wind—an earthquake; but Adonai was not in the earthquake. After the earthquake—fire; but Adonai was not in the fire. And after the fire—a still, small voice.

—I KINGS 19:9–12

Realizing that great fiery miracles don't necessarily produce lasting spiritual change, Elijah understood that closeness to God comes more easily through an intimate, quiet, personal encounter. Elijah's spirit revived. God told Elijah to anoint a new king over Israel and to train Elisha to become the Prophet's eventual successor.

Together they continued the fight against idol worship. By the time Elijah had grown old, Elisha had become a wise and powerful prophet. At the Jordan River, "Elijah took his mantle and, rolling it up, he struck the water; it divided to the right and left, so that the two of them crossed over on dry land . . . As they kept on walking and talking, a fiery chariot with fiery horses suddenly appeared and separated one from the other; and Elijah went up to heaven in a whirlwind. Elisha saw it and cried out, 'My father, my father, the chariot of Israel, and its horsemen!'" (II Kings 2:12).

Over the centuries, Elijah became a great hero of Jewish lore and legend. In rabbinic tales, Elijah frequently offered his opinions on the intricacies of Jewish law. When legal questions were too difficult for the sages to resolve, they said, "Let the matter stand" (*teiku*). This was said to mean "the Tishbite (Elijah) will resolve difficulties and problems," or *Tishbi yetaretz kushyot u-va'ayot* (the first letter of each word spells *teiku*).

Elijah also returned to help the sages at difficult points in their lives. Some of these tales involve Rabbi Akiva and his teacher Rabbi Eliezer, two of the most important sages mentioned in the Haggadah.

Rabbi Akiva could afford only a bed of straw for Rachel, his new bride, to sleep upon. Elijah appeared before their hut dressed as a beggar, crying out for a bit of straw for *his* wife's bed.[14] Seeing that, Akiva and Rachel felt better about sleeping on straw. And it was Elijah who appeared to Eliezer and convinced him to leave the family farm and pursue his dream of studying Torah in Jerusalem. When Rabbi Eliezer died, Rabbi Akiva, his student, began his eulogy with these words, *"My father, my father, the chariot of Israel, and its horsemen."*[15] And when Akiva died at the hands of Hadrian's torturers, Elijah bore his body to a burial cave and thence to "the heavenly academy."[16]

Jewish tradition gradually transformed Elijah from a zealot to a peacemaker. No longer the slayer of heathen prophets, Elijah comes to give us hope and direction when we stand at the crossroads and, most important, brings peace and healing to a broken world.

Rabbi Joshua said, "Elijah will not come to judge between those who are ritually clean or unclean, but to remove those who have come to power through force and to bring near those who have been cast away by force. . . ." The sages say neither to remove nor to bring near, but to make peace in the world. For it is said, "Lo, I will send to you Elijah the Prophet before the coming of the awesome, fearful day of Adonai. And he shall turn the heart of the parents to the children and the hearts of the children to their parents . . ." (Mishnah, Eduyot 8:7, quoting Malachi 3:23–24).

Tonight we pray that Elijah will help us resolve our disputes with one another; enable us to open our hearts to one another; and bring peace to Israel, to her neighbors, and to all places filled with fear and hatred.

- Why do you think Jewish tradition transformed Elijah from a zealot to a peacemaker?

- What is the meaning of the idea that messianic times are associated with Elijah's turning "the heart of the parents to the children and the hearts of the children to their parents"?

- Ancient midrashim and contemporary scholars alike have discovered many similarities between Elijah and Moses.[17] How many parallels can you find between their careers? How might you explain these similarities? How are Moses and Elijah different?

THE ELIJAH PUZZLE

You may want to read this yourself, or you can use it as the basis for a discussion.
Read the two paragraphs below and then ask your guests this question:
Why do you think that Elijah, of all the figures in the Bible, became the
most popular figure in Jewish folklore? You may want to bring some
of the answers to the question below into the discussion.

Why Elijah became the most popular figure in Jewish folklore has puzzled more than a few scholars. Of all the biblical figures who could have laid claim to this role, Elijah seems one of the least likely. A man whose family the Bible never mentions, Elijah even reacts coldly when Elisha, his newly chosen disciple, wants to kiss his father and mother good-bye before starting his apprenticeship with the prophet (I Kings 19: 20).[18] Elijah was overly zealous, a champion of God rather than of his people. And for this, the third-century midrash, the *Mekhilta of Rabbi Ishmael,* chides him:

> Thus you find that there were three types of prophets. One [Jeremiah] insisted upon the honor due the Father [God] as well as the honor due the son [Israel]; one [Elijah] insisted upon the honor due the Father without insisting upon the honor due the son; one [Jonah] insisted upon the honor due the son without insisting upon the honor due the Father . . . Elijah insisted upon the honor due the Father, but did not insist on the honor due the son, as it is said: "And he [explained to God why he had fled to Mount Horeb, saying] I am moved by the zeal for Adonai, the God of Hosts, for the Israelites have forsaken Your covenant. . . ."[19]

So how did Elijah become the superhero of Jewish folklore?
Elijah's qualifications for this role are rooted in the Bible. Along with Enoch (Gen. 5:21–24), Elijah is one of the two figures the Bible describes as having risen directly to heaven without dying. "A fiery chariot with fiery horses suddenly appeared . . . and Elijah went up to heaven in a whirlwind" (II Kings 2:11). And this certainly must have caught the eye of the author of Malachi (sixth century B.C.E.), who envisioned God sending down the errant Elijah "before the coming

of the great and awesome day of Adonai" (Malachi 3:22).

Yet scholars believe that this alone does not account for Elijah's folkloric status. Here are several other explanations.

- Enoch had been so strongly identified with non-Jewish apocalypticism that Jewish tradition sought to downplay his significance by elevating that of Elijah.[20]

- Elijah's unusual role is a function of his unique name, in Hebrew *Eliyahu* (אֵלִיָּהוּ) It is the only name in the Bible that includes the two divine names: El, as in Elohim (God), and YHWH (Adonai), doubling the *hey*.[21] Befitting his name, Elijah, in the contest with the prophets of Baal, calls on God to demonstrate that "YHWH is Elohim" (I Kings 18:37) Jewish thought has long accorded the creation and continued existence of the world to a balance between the divine attributes of judgment associated with Elohim and the mercy associated with YHWH. The Elijah of legend uniquely combines these.[22] Tales of Elijah often depict him bestowing mercy upon the down and out and judgment upon the high and mighty.

- Elijah's special role at ceremonies such as circumcision and the Passover Seder serves as a kind of punishment for his excessive zeal. Elijah complained to God that the people of Israel had abandoned the covenant (*brit*) and, except for *himself*, they had all turned to idol worship. Joseph Telushkin teaches that "he who sees himself as the last Jew is fated to bear constant witness to the eternity of Israel, to be present when every male Jewish child enters the covenant, and when every Jewish family celebrates the Seder . . . Elijah stands in a long line of despairing Jews who erroneously have prophesied the end of the Jewish People."[23]

- "Elijah confronts the age-old choice between faithfulness to, and betrayal of, the ancient covenant, and he is alone during that confrontation. This is the crisis-situation of every prophet in Israel. It is, moreover, the situation of every Jew in extremis, when, looking around for allies in his desperate struggle for survival in faithfulness, he finds, like Elijah, none but the God of the covenant Himself."[24] It is the universalism of Elijah's choice and the uniqueness of his response—his willingness to subject God to a win or lose test—that makes Elijah Judaism's hero par excellence.

MODELING THE POTENTIAL TO CHANGE

Read the following passage aloud.

Let's consider one more way to understand Elijah's unrivaled folkloric status. Elijah's ascent to heaven without dying endows him, of course, with certain qualities of eternality. Yet it's ironic that Elijah of all people achieves eternal life—ironic because, after fleeing the troops Jezebel has sent to kill him, Elijah implores God to *take* his life. God eventually refuses the request and tells Elijah to "go, return [*shuv*] toward Damascus. . . ." (I Kings 19:15) and to find a disciple. The midrash explains God's displeasure with Elijah: "Elijah ought to have gone to the place in which his forefathers stood [Horeb, another name for Sinai] and prayed for mercy for Israel; he did not do so. God said to him, 'You have prayed for yourself; go return [*shuv*] toward Damascus. . . .'"[25] God is telling Elijah that his career as a prophet is drawing to a close, so he must change course. God instructs Elijah, the religious zealot, to do *teshuvah,* to abandon his self-righteousness and turn back to the world of ordinary human beings.

In terms of his own spiritual journey, Elijah has not reached the end of the road. In fact, he never will. But he knows where he's headed—back to humanity, over and over again. Eternal life assures Elijah plenty of time to ponder and mend his ways. By messianic times, Elijah, who seems to have had such little understanding of relations between parents and children, will become the one who brings about parent-child reconciliation: "And he shall turn [*heyshiv,* from the same root as *shuv*] the heart of the parents to the heart of the children, and the heart of the children to their parents . . ." (Malachi 3:24).

Elijah's story epitomizes the potential for eternal growth and change. Elijah makes the long journey from misanthrope to philanthrope. The prophet who once rejected humanity continuously reappears to enlighten those who have lost their way, to aid the weak and vulnerable. It's not punishment. It's a privilege. Elijah remembers what it was like to be lost, to feel all alone, to feel stuck in a narrow place [*maytzar, Mitzrayim,* Egypt]. He knows the heart of the stranger, because he was one. Elijah embodies the transformation of painful memories into godly behavior: "God . . . upholds the cause of the fatherless and the widow, and befriends the stranger, providing him with food and clothing. You too shall befriend the stranger, for you were strangers in the land of Egypt" (Deut. 10:17–20). Having overcome the bitterness of his own isolation, Elijah makes helping the downtrodden his mission. "Elijah becomes the Jewish alter-ego, the symbol for the whole people; exiled and tortured, but alive and hopeful."[26]

Redemption may involve salvation from external sources of oppression, but it also involves our own spiritual journey toward ultimate truth. Elijah's transformation reminds everyone around the Seder table that we, too, are free to continue our journeys.

Menachem Mendel (1787–1859), the Hasidic Rebbe of Kotsk, said, "We err if we believe that Elijah the Prophet comes through the door. Rather he must enter through our hearts and souls."[27]

THE MIRROR: A TALE OF ELIJAH AND THE SEDER

The Israel Folktale Archives at Haifa University has collected close to six hundred stories about Elijah the Prophet, more than any other figure. Read the following tale aloud at your Seder and discuss the questions below.

A pious and wealthy Jew asked his rabbi, "For about forty years I have opened the door for Elijah every Seder night waiting for him to come, but he never does. What is the reason?" The rabbi answered, "In your neighborhood there lives a very poor family with many children. Call on the man and propose to him that you and your family celebrate the next Passover in his house, and for this purpose provide him and his whole family with everything necessary for the eight days of Passover. Then on the Seder night Elijah will certainly come." The man did as the rabbi told him, but after Passover he came to the rabbi and claimed that again he had waited in vain for Elijah. The rabbi answered: "I know very well that Elijah came on the Seder night to the house of your poor neighbor. But of course you could not see him." And the rabbi held a mirror before the face of the man and said, "Look, this was Elijah's face that night."[28]

• What is this tale's message about how to bring the Messiah?

• What is the significance of the fact that the man has been waiting for forty years for Elijah to come?

• How should this revelation of Elijah influence the wealthy man?

• If acting according to the attributes of Elijah reveals the prophet, does acting according to the attributes of God reveal God?

"POUR OUT YOUR WRATH" VERSUS "GIVE UP ANGER"

Here we contrast two alternatives for the passage to be read while opening the door for Elijah. Read the paragraphs that follow and lead a discussion on the questions below.

According to traditional Haggadot, upon completing the Grace after Meals and before reciting Psalm 115, it is customary to recite a passage that begins, "Pour out Your wrath. . . ." This was added to the Haggadah in the Middle Ages, possibly during the period of the Crusades, a time of great suffering for European Jewry. According to Ashkenazic tradition, it is customary to recite these words upon opening the door for Elijah the Prophet, herald of the Messiah. This passage has generated sufficient discomfort in modern times so that many Haggadot have either deleted it or have offered alternative readings. Indeed, as early as the sixteenth century, Rabbi Eliezer ben Elijah Ashkenazi (Europe and Egypt, 1513–1585) wrote a commentary on the Haggadah that narrowly limited the target of this malediction, arguing that it applied only to those who worship idols, not to Christians and Muslims. "We are not," he wrote, "allowed to curse nations that acknowledge the Exodus from Egypt and know God even if they have not received the Torah."[29]

In addition to the traditional passage, *The Open Door,* a Haggadah published by the Reform Movement, includes the alternative below. Note that in traditional

Haggadot, the first passage functions as an introduction to the remainder of the Hallel (Psalms 115–118), which in part addresses themes of God's punishing Israel's idol-worshiping enemies and subsequently redeeming Israel.

From the traditional Haggadah:

Pour out Your wrath upon the nations that do not know You, upon the governments which do not call upon Your name. For they have devoured Jacob and desolated his home. Pour out Your wrath on them; may Your blazing anger overtake them, destroy them from under the heavens of Adonai.

—PSALMS 79:6–7, 69:25, AND LAMENTATIONS 3:66

From *The Open Door:*

Give up anger, abandon fury, put aside your wrath; it can only harm. The call to violence shall no longer be heard in your land, nor the cry of desolation within your borders. If your enemy is hungry, give him bread to eat. If she is thirsty, give her water to drink. For when compassion and truth meet, justice and peace kiss.

—PSALMS 37:8, ISAIAH 60:18, PROVERBS 25:21, AND PSALMS 85:11[30]

- Which of these passages do you prefer as a reading for opening the door for Elijah? Why?

- Are there times when it might be appropriate to vent, at least verbally, one's vengeful feelings? Similarly, are there situations in which it is unrealistic and unhealthy to "give up anger" and to feed your enemy?

- How do these passages relate to the Talmudic dictum (Sanhedrin 72a), "If one comes to kill you, rise up early to kill him?"

- Given our world today, are we better served by calling on God to support us as we strike down our enemies or as we give them bread to eat? Is there a time when both might be appropriate?

MORE THAN VENGEANCE ALONE

Consider reading the paragraphs below after your discussion.

Although it would be hard to deny the vengeful tone of "Pour out Your wrath," the midrashic source that brought these verses together points to a somewhat more nuanced reading. The *Mekhilta*, a third-century midrash from which the Haggadah often borrowed, collected three of these four verses to help answer an agonizing question.[31] After the Exodus, did God still possess the power to redeem the Jewish People? In the wake of Rome's savage crushing of the Jewish rebellions of 66–70 and 132–135 C.E., the midrash affirmed God's capacity to act and restored a measure of hope to a vanquished, exiled people.

The midrash expounds on the song the Israelites sang after they crossed the Red Sea and witnessed the destruction of Pharaoh's army. It suggests that although the song manifestly refers to events that have already transpired, a number of verbs it uses can also be understood in the future tense. The midrash wants to tell us that the Song at the Sea refers to actions that God will take in the future, not just to past history. The midrash goes on to cite other cases in which it prefers to read a verb in the future tense. "You [God] will pour out Your wrath . . ."

Each of the four verses in "Pour out Your wrath" refers to the destruction of the First Temple by the Babylonian Empire in 587 B.C.E. Forty-eight years later, that empire itself fell, and soon thereafter Jews were free to return to Israel from their exile in Babylonia. If God could redeem Israel and punish Babylonia—centuries after the Exodus—God could do so again following the defeats by Rome in the first centuries of the Common Era. The *Mekhilta's* message helped sustain hope during those dark times. It did so once again following the Crusades, when "Pour out Your wrath" entered the Haggadah. The primary issue may not have been whether or not God would punish our enemies, but whether or not God in fact retained the power to act at all.

24

Two Seder Songs: *Echad Mi Yodea* and *Chad Gadya*

אֶחָד מִי יוֹדֵעַ?

Who Knows One?

חַד גַּדְיָא . . .

One Kid …
—THE PASSOVER HAGGADAH

At our Seders, by the time we get to *Echad Mi Yodea* and *Chad Gadya*, it's pretty late and people are tired. But we summon all our energy, and with an assortment of tambourines and other percussion instruments, we bring the Seder to a rousing conclusion.[1] If these songs were nothing more than a great way to keep the kids awake—which is why many believe they were added to the Haggadah—we could happily say, *Dayyenu*! But a closer look at each of them suggests that they have something important to tell us. In this chapter we'll look at the origins and meaning of *Echad Mi Yodea* and *Chad Gadya* and at some commentary each has spawned. Questions for discussion are included throughout. Since *Echad Mi Yodea* is all about counting, we also include some number puzzles related to the Haggadah.

FOR SEDER LEADERS

A suggestion: rather than trying to discuss these songs at the end of the Seder, consider doing so before coming to the table.

ECHAD MI YODEA: MYSTERIOUS ORIGINS

Read on your own or share with your guests.

Echad Mi Yodea first appeared in a Haggadah printed in Prague in 1590, but some believe that it may actually date from the twelfth or thirteenth century. In a commentary on the Haggadah from 1791, a German rabbi wrote that he saw the following reference to the song in a prayer book dated 1406: "This song as well as *Chad Gadya*, they found hidden in walls of the study hall in Worms [in Germany] . . . and they determined that it should be sung on Passover throughout the generations."[2]

The song also appears among the records of the Inquisition from Majorca in 1678. This Marrano community was cut off from the rest of Spanish Jewry in 1391. By then, it seems, they must have known *Echad Mi Yodea*. The inquisitors believed the song was as a Jewish catechism. Fragments of the song from a repository of ancient documents, the Cairo Genizah, sometimes include the *She'ma* as a refrain, which adds weight to the claim that it may have been a catechism of sorts. Suffice it to say, *Echad Mi Yodea* has no direct connection to Passover—or any other holiday. A report from the eighteenth century notes that it had been sung during Sukkot in the south of France and it served as a wedding song for Jews in Senegal and in Cochin, India.[3]

Echad Mi Yodea may simply represent the Jewish version of a widespread folk genre—children's cumulative number songs. But according to one researcher, it may be the earliest example of this kind of song and may have "set the pattern for a number-song which has spread over two continents and been transmitted through many languages and among many nations."[4]

A NIGHT OF NUMBERS

At the beginning of the Seder, use this paragraph as a guide for a discussion.

Near the end of the Seder we'll be singing *Echad Mi Yodea*, "Who Knows One," which obviously involves a lot of numbers. The content of the song is not directly connected to Passover, but it turns out that numbers actually play a rather prominent role in the Seder. So to help get us ready for *Echad Mi Yodea*, let's think about numbers and counting in the Seder. Who can think of something in the Seder that relates to numbers or counting? Now, as we go through the Seder, please let us know if you notice anything else in the Haggadah that relates to numbers or counting.

- Why do you think there are so many elements of the Haggadah that relate to numbers or counting?

Since numbers figure so prominently in the Haggadah, here are ten number puzzles that you might wish to send out to your guests before the Seder or use during the Seder. Remember, not all Haggadot include the same text. If you want to do these puzzles (and come up with the same answers that I have), you'll need a traditional Ashkenazic Haggadah, which you can find online at www.livelyseders. com. Or you can use the ubiquitous Maxwell House Haggadah. Those puzzles marked with an asterisk require information discussed in this book, and relevant page numbers are supplied. Some of these puzzles are for youngsters, others are for adults! For answers see note 5 on page 400.

Note: These puzzles are based on the text of the Haggadah up to, but not including, Grace after Meals.

1. The number of times we wash our hands during the Seder, plus the number of times we dip according to the Four Questions, equals _____?

2. The number of "famous fours" in the Seder _____?

3. ★The number of actual questions in the Four Questions (see page 37), plus the number of questions asked by the Four Children, equals_____?

4. The number of Jacob's family members when they went down to Egypt _____?

5. The largest number mentioned in the Haggadah _____?

6. The number of different rabbinic sages mentioned in the Haggadah, minus the number of plagues in Egypt, equals _____?

7. ★The number of women mentioned in the Haggadah (see page 180), plus the number of times the Haggadah mentions Isaac, Jacob, and Esau, equals _____?

8. ★The number of times Moses' name occurs in the Haggadah (see page 214), plus the number of times the Haggadah mentions the hardening of Pharaoh's heart (see page 81), equals _____?

9. The number of steps in the Seder, plus the number of divine favors bestowed upon the Israelites in *Dayyenu*, equals _____?

10. ★The original number of the Haggadah's Four Questions (see page 39), plus the number of matzahs on the Seder plate according to the Vilna Gaon (see page 7), equals _____?

COUNTING WHAT MATTERS

Read the paragraphs below on your own or aloud and discuss the questions that follow.

The Haggadah quotes part of a biblical verse from a story about God punishing the people of Israel when King David inappropriately conducted a census.[6] This appears when the Haggadah amplifies on the meaning of God's "outstretched arm."

"Outstretched arm" is the sword, as it is written, "His sword drawn in his hand, outstretched over Jerusalem" (I Chronicles 21:16).

—THE PASSOVER HAGGDADAH

The complete verse from Chronicles reads as follows: "David looked up and saw the angel of Adonai standing between heaven and earth, with a sword drawn in his hand outstretched over Jerusalem" (I Chronicles 21:16).

• What do you make of the fact that Haggadah quotes a biblical verse that alludes to a story about the dangers of "numbering Israel?"

• How might the issue of "numbering Israel" relate to *Echad Mi Yodea?*

After discussing these questions, consider reading the following aloud.

A sixth- or seventh-century midrash about David's census may well contain some of the inspiration for *Echad Mi Yodea*. "God was displeased about the . . . [census] and He struck Israel" (I Chron. 21:7).[7] To punish Israel, God sent a destroying angel, *ha'mashchit*, the same term for the figure who slew the Egyptian firstborn (Ex. 12:23). When David saw the angel, he prayed hard! In response, the midrash describes how God reduced the duration of punishment—a devastating pestilence, *dever*, the same as the fifth plague—from seventy-two to thirty-six hours. Then, according to the midrash, a series of anthropomorphic "pleaders" appeared before God to request further mercy on Israel's behalf. In the end, God reduced the length of punishment by thirty-five hours, the number of hours associated with each of the following "pleaders."

The *seven days of the week,*
The *eight days prior to circumcision*;
The *five books of the Torah*;
The *three patriarchs*;
The *Ten Commandments*;
The *Two Tablets of the Covenant*—a total of thirty-five
  [7+8+5+3+10+2=35].

[According to the midrash,] "others suggested that in lieu of the Ten Commandments and the Two Tablets, the heads of the *twelve tribes* appeared. In any event there remained only one hour of pestilence. But, behold . . . [70,000] died in that brief time."[8]

All of the midrash's pleaders appear in *Echad Mi Yodea*. The midrash plays with the idea of counting, contrasting David's sinful numbering of Israel with the perfectly acceptable enumeration of the symbols of Jewish history and faith. These friendly pleaders symbolize the faithfulness of Jews to their tradition and the capacity of that faith to sway God. In the midrash, God eventually reduced Israel's allotted suffering from seventy-two hours to a single hour, a decrease of more than 98 percent. Jews over the millennia would surely have envied that outcome.

Though not composed for the Haggadah, *Echad Mi Yodea* fits well in it. The song's midrashic roots link it to the theme of divine punishment that befalls a people for the sins of its king, David—and Pharaoh—by means of one of the very plagues—pestilence—that God brought upon the Egyptians. And remember the initial basis for Pharaoh's animus toward the Israelites. Pharaoh determined that the Israelites "are too numerous for us" (Exodus 1:9). *Echad Mi Yodea* offers a poignant reminder to a tiny people to whom God repeatedly promised great numbers. Count what matters most, neither the size of your armies nor your population, but the objects of your faith.

THE BA'AL SHEM TOV

Read the commentary by the Ba'al Shem Tov (c. 1700–1760), founder of Hasidism, and discuss the questions that follow. Remember, in the song we begin with "Who knows one?" and end with "Who knows thirteen?"

> It was taught by the Ba'al Shem Tov that *Echad Mi Yodea* begins with knowing oneness and continues to knowing thirteen. But thirteen returns us to oneness because the Hebrew letters for one, *echad* (*alef*=1, *chet*=8, *dalet*=4), add up to thirteen. Beneath the façade of multiplicity lies the ultimate truth of the unity of all things in God.
> —YA'AKOV YOSEF OF POLNOYE (D. CIRCA 1782, POLAND) AUTHOR OF THE FIRST HASIDIC BOOK, A DISCIPLE OF THE BA'AL SHEM TOV[9]

• What do you make of the fact the song begins with "Our God is one in heaven and earth" and ends with God's thirteen attributes?

• According to the Ba'al Shem Tov, the appearance of multiplicity conceals an underlying truth of unity. How do you think about this issue?

CHAD GADYA

The Seder concludes with *Chad Gadya*. Here we'll touch on the song's history and meaning. Then we'll consider what two of Israel's most important literary figures, S.Y. Agnon and Yehuda Amichai, have written about it. We conclude with an exploration of the Haggadah's last words and their implications for a world of eternal life.

Chad Gadya first appears—written in both Yiddish and Aramaic—in a Haggadah from the late fifteenth or early sixteenth century. As with *Echad Mi Yodea*, the song may have been sung at Seders in parts of Germany several centuries earlier. Linguists believe it was composed first in Yiddish then translated, rather poorly, into the Aramaic that we still sing today.[10]

Folklorists classify *Chad Gadya* as a cumulative song similar to "There Was an Old Lady Who Swallowed a Fly" or "The House That Jack Built." It may have been based on a secular French song from the twelfth or thirteenth century or perhaps developed independently.[11] Except for the last verse, *Chad Gadya* is essentially secular. Nonetheless, Chayim Joseph David Azoulai (1724–1806), the famed Sephardic rabbi, excommunicated an individual for mocking the song. Azoulai wrote that over the generations the greatest scholars all recited *Chad Gadya*, and that the "meanings behind songs like these have been passed down from one rabbi to another" for generations.[12]

Consider holding a conversation about *Chad Gadya* before you come to the Seder table. Ask each of your guests to read a stanza aloud. Then discuss the following questions.

• Some say that *Chad Gadya* found its way into the Haggadah merely to entertain sleepy children—and maybe adults. Others argue that the song has deep meaning. What do you think?

• How would you describe the world that *Chad Gadya* depicts? In what ways does the song resonate with themes of the Seder?

• In *Chad Gadya* a cycle of violence begins when a predatory cat kills a kid that "my father bought for two *zuzim*," or a half-shekel. When the Talmud refers to a kid worth one *zuz*, it means a good fat kid.[13] A kid worth two *zuzim* must be special indeed. What do you make of the fact that the purchaser of this valuable kid did not protect it from predators? Is there a message in this? If so, what? In this context, what might it mean if the father represents God and the kid corresponds to Israel?[14]

• What do you think of the fact that the song comes at the very end of the Seder?

• *Chad Gadya* concludes with God slaughtering the Angel of Death, apparently ushering in a world of eternal life. How do you think about this concept? Do you think science may one day be able to create something approaching eternal life for human beings?

• The Seder ends with God slaughtering the Angel of Death. Below are a few words from the Haftarah for the eighth and last day of Passover. How would you compare *Chad Gadya* and this passage from Isaiah? As endings for the Seder and the festival as a whole, do you like them? Why or why not?

The wolf shall dwell with the lamb, the leopard lie down with the kid, the calf and the beast of prey, and the fatling together, with a little boy to lead them. The cow and the bear shall graze together, and the lion and the ox shall eat straw. . . . In all of My sacred mount nothing evil or vile shall be done; for the land shall be filled with devotion to Adonai as the water covers the sea.

—ISAIAH 11:6–9

INSPIRATION?

Below you will find four examples of Jewish sources containing a message or imagery related to that of *Chad Gadya*. Choose one or more to read aloud and discuss the questions that follow.

Assuredly, all who wanted to devour you shall be devoured, and every one of your foes shall go into captivity; those who despoiled you shall be despoiled, and all who pillaged you I will give up to pillage. But I will bring healing to you and cure you of your wounds—declares Adonai.

—JEREMIAH 30:16–17

He has dug a pit and deepened it, and will fall into the trap he made. His mischief will recoil upon his own head; his lawlessness will come down upon his skull.

—PSALMS 7:16–17

[Hillel] saw a skull floating on the face of the water. He said to it: "Because you drowned others they drowned you and the end of those who drowned you will be that they will be drowned."

—MISHNAH, AVOT 2:6

Ten strong things have been created in the world. The rock is hard, but the iron cleaves it. The iron is hard, but the fire softens it. The fire is hard, but the water quenches it. The water is strong, but the clouds bear it. The clouds are strong, but the wind scatters them. The wind is strong, but the body bears it. The body is strong, but fright crushes it. Fright is strong, but wine banishes it. Wine is strong, but sleep works it off. Death is stronger than all, and charity saves from death, as it is written, "Righteousness [*tzedakah*] saves from death" (Proverbs 10:2).

—BABYLONIAN TALMUD, BABA BATRA 10A.

• What parallels do you find between these sources and *Chad Gadya*?

• How do you feel about texts like these and *Chad Gadya* that suggest cycles of violence can be brought to an ultimate end by violent means? Will punishing violence with violence lead to a less violent world? Why or why not?

• To what extent do you think these texts are intended to offer victims of violence a measure of comfort? Do they comfort you? Why or why not?

CAME THE COMMENTATORS

You might ask one of your guests to do some online research about interpretations of *Chad Gadya* and share with your group what he or she has learned. Or choose one of the commentaries below. Depending on your group, consider reading aloud the brief commentary on each stanza before singing it.

STORMY LIVES

Eighteenth-century Europe produced a number of outstanding Jewish scholars who turned their attention to *Chad Gadya*, including Jonathan Eybeschuetz (c.1690–1764) and Jacob Emden (1697–1776). Both were revered as great sages and lived near one another in Germany. They also spent many years locked in bitter conflict with each other. Perhaps this helps explain their fascination with *Chad Gadya*. After all, the song chronicles a series of attacks and reprisals in a world where roles inevitably switch from predator to prey.

What was the conflict about? Eybeschuetz belonged to a conclave of influential rabbis that sought to root out heretics. In 1725 they excommunicated a group of Sabbateans. These were devotees of Shabbetai Zevi (1626–1676), the charismatic figure whose messianic claims generated such a stir throughout in the Jewish world half a century earlier. Emden, too, spent much energy ferreting out Sabbateans and in 1750 accused Eybeschuetz of belonging to the sect! Despite the community's support for Eybeschuetz, for over two decades Emden published a succession of attacks that rocked the Jewish community from Holland to Poland. Scholars still debate where the truth lies.

Before we turn to the commentaries, it's worth noting that these are brief summaries of much longer works. Eybeshuetz's commentary, full of Kabbalistic interpretations, runs almost thirty pages! His commentary focuses on Israel's trials among the nations. For Emden, the song traces the trials of an individual's soul.

JONATHAN EYBESHUETZ (C.1690–1764)[15]

One Kid—in Hebrew גדי The additional letter א (in the Aramaic), which in gematria equals one, symbolizes the oneness of God, of Israel, and the eternal covenant between God and Israel. Turn the א upside down, and it remains the same, as Israel remains faithful regardless of the reversals it has suffered throughout history.

Two *Zuzim*—usually understood as two coins, *zuz* can also be related to shifting or moving. Here it refers to two momentous acts (movements) in the life of Abraham and the Jewish People. 1) The

Covenant Between the Pieces—when God assures Abraham that his offspring will be as numerous as the stars, enslaved in Egypt, but will eventually inherit that Land of Israel; 2) The birth of Isaac.

The Cat—the enslavement of Israel by Pharaoh, likened to a cat because he does not recognize God, like a cat, says the Talmud, doesn't recognize its owner.[16]

The Dog—Amalek, who attacks the Israelites in the desert, recognizes God, but sins nonetheless.

The Stick—the staff of Moses. When Moses raised the staff, it brought the defeat of Amalek (Exodus 17:9).

The Fire—the burning of the First Temple by Nebuchadnezzar.

The Water—Torah, compared to water (Deut. 32:2). Commitment to Torah led to the rebuilding of the Temple some seventy years after its destruction.

The Ox—likened to the Greeks during the Second Temple period who discouraged Jewish practice and, according to midrashic sources, ordered Jews to "write on the horn of an ox that 'I have no portion in the God of Israel.'"[17]

The Slaughterer—the Hasmoneans who defeated the Greeks, rededicated the Temple after the Greeks defiled it, and resumed proper sacrifice.

The Angel of Death—the Roman emperor Titus, who destroyed the Second Temple and murdered many thousands of Jews, likened to Satan, whom the Talmud equates with the Angel of Death.[18]

The Holy One of Blessing—"In that day Adonai will punish, with His great, cruel, mighty sword . . . the elusive serpent. . . ." (Isaiah 27:1) and so the cycle of Jewish suffering will come to an end. "In the days to come, the Mount of Adonai's House shall stand firm above the mountains . . . And all the nations shall gaze on it with joy . . ." (Isaiah 2:2).

JACOB EMDEN (1697–1776)[19]

The Kid—the soul given to us by God our Father. A kabbalistic commentary on Gen. 38:17 ("I will send a kid from my flock . . .") explained that the kid represents the soul.[20]

Two *Zuzim*—according to Kabbalah, the two movements made by the soul as it descends from the heavenly to the terrestrial world.

Chad Gadya, Chad Gadya—O Soul, O Soul. The chorus is repeated like the repetitive lament of one in mourning.

The Cat—a creature that puts anything into its mouth, like a human infant that needs training or its base instincts will gain the upper hand and consume the kid/soul.

The Dog—another creature governed by its urges, which, if uncontrolled, lead to spoiled behavior, like an untrained child whose soul is corrupted if parents indulge insatiable desires.

The Stick—a symbol of the maturing youth's sexual urges, which, if unchecked, further damage the soul.

The Fire—burning passions further consume the soul.

The Water— Unable to extricate itself, raging torrents of foul desire sweep the soul away.

The Ox—like the goring ox, a wild individual cannot refrain from destructive behavior.

The Slaughterer—comes to torment the soul over its sinfulness.

The Angel of Death—removes the corroded soul and painfully separates it from the body, like one who separates wool from thorns.

The Holy One of Blessing—because it is only possible to atone for sins before death, God will further punish the unrepentant sinner so that death will seem painless compared to what follows.

MODERN VOICES

Choose one of the following poems to read aloud and discuss at your Seder.

From *Chad Gadya*

This poem tells us that the Cat devoured the Kid that Father bought for two zuzim.

It seems that the Cat committed an evil deed deserving punishment.

If so—the Dog did right to bite the Cat.

If so—the Stick did wrong to hit the Dog.

And the Fire did right to burn the Stick.

If so—the Water did wrong to extinguish the Fire.

And the Ox did right to drink the Water.

If so—the Slaughterer did wrong to slaughter the Ox.

And it seems the Angel of Death was right to slaughter the Slaughterer.

But in the end God comes and slaughters the Angel of Death.

It seems that the Angel of Death was right and God was not. But this is impossible to say because as the Psalm says, "God is righteous in all His ways and gracious in all His deeds" [145:17].

The solution is this:

Surely the Cat committed an evil deed when it ate the Kid.

But when a Kid and a Cat quarrel, maybe they make peace

If so—what business is it of yours, Dog, to involve yourself and render judgment here?

It seems that the Dog deserved the Stick, and the Stick did right to hit the Dog.

If so—the Fire did wrong to burn the Stick.

If so—the Water did right to extinguish the Fire.

And the Ox did wrong to drink the Water.

And the Slaughterer did right to slaughter the Ox.

And this means that the Angel of Death sinned by slaughtering the Slaughter.

Therefore, in the world to come God brings the evil inclination which is the Angel of Death who is Satan and slaughters him.[21] Thus, it seems "God is righteous in all His ways and gracious in all His deeds" [Psalm 145:17].

—SHMUEL YOSEF AGNON, 1943 (1888–1970, GALICIA AND ISRAEL),
WINNER, 1966 NOBEL PRIZE FOR LITERATURE[22]

AN ARAB SHEPHERD IS SEARCHING FOR HIS GOAT ON MOUNT ZION

An Arab shepherd is searching for his goat on Mount Zion
and on the opposite mountain I am searching
for my little boy.

An Arab shepherd and a Jewish father
both in their temporary failure.
Our voices meet
above the Sultan's Pool in the valley between us.
Neither of us wants
the child or the goat to get caught in the wheels
of the terrible *Had Gadya* machine.

Afterward we found them among the bushes
and our voices came back inside us, laughing and crying.

Searching for a goat or a son
has always been the beginning
of a new religion in these mountains.

—YEHUDA AMICHAI, 1987 (1924–2000, GERMANY AND ISRAEL),

WINNER, 1982 ISRAEL PRIZE FOR POETRY[23]

THE HAGGADAH'S LAST WORD: A WORLD OF ETERNAL LIFE

Read on your own, or consider reading
aloud after your discussion of *Chad Gadya.*

The Haggadah ends with a stunningly messianic hope. God slaughters the Angel of Death and ushers in a world of eternal life.[24] But for Judaism, it's hardly a new idea. Two prophets from the eighth century B.C.E. sounded the same note. Isaiah (25:8) said that God "will destroy death forever," and in Hosea (13:14) God promised, "I [God] will save them, redeem them from very Death."

Indeed, the traditional Jewish prayer book, often said to be Judaism's most fundamental theological textbook, echoes the same beliefs. In Grace after Meals we ask God "to make us worthy of the days of the Messiah and life in the world to come." In the traditional *Amidah*, or Eighteen Benedictions, thrice daily we thank God for "giving life to the dead." Although many associate these notions exclusively with Orthodox Judaism, they are important to the more liberal movements as well. The Reform Movement's new prayer book, for instance, has reinstated once-expurgated references to God's restoring life to the dead.[25]

Even this brief sample of sources reveals that several potentially independent ideas—the messiah, the world to come, eternal life, and resurrection of the dead—have been lumped together. How, for example, might we think about just one of these concepts, eternal life—the promise that *Chad Gadya* extends?

Chad Gadya envisions God eradicating death. How? Rather than acting independently of human beings, let's assume that God acts through us. Fashioned in God's image, we are the bearers of enormous creative potential—which we can use for good or evil. Witness the dramatically increasing pace of biomedical discovery. Over the coming centuries we will surely have the ability to vastly extend life expectancy. If, of course, we don't destroy the planet or wipe ourselves out by some other means. We can perpetuate the *Chad Gadya* cycle of death and violence or build a wholly different world. Well over two thousand years ago the composer of one of the psalms wrote a verse that we read at the Seder in the Hallel: "I shall not die, but live" (Psalms 118:17). Then a statement of profound faith, in future centuries humanity may well read these words as a prediction fulfilled.

But isn't there a fly in the ointment? If God had intended to create a world without death, how do we explain our *Chad Gadya* world where death and killing reign virtually untrammeled? Joseph B. Soloveitchik (1903–1993), the great Modern Orthodox theologian and scholar, answered this question boldly.

> When God created the world, He provided an opportunity for the work of His hands—man—to participate in His creation. The Creator, as it were, impaired reality in order that mortal man could repair its flaws and perfect it. . . . [We] are commanded to become a partner with the Creator in the renewal of the cosmos; complete and ultimate creation—this is the deepest desire of the Jewish People.[26]

We have been created in God's image, and God left us a daunting share of *tikkun olam*, mending the world. A lot of work to do. Too much, we often feel. But in taking up that task, we fulfill our human potential in the deepest sense. We also work shoulder to shoulder with one another and, as it were, with God.

So yes, *Chad Gadya* certainly entertains the children and evokes sweet family memories. But it does more. *Chad Gadya* retraces the trajectory of the Seder.

The song begins in a vicious "cat-bite-kid" world—call it Egypt—a place of domination and death. And it ends with the ultimate redemption, liberation, not just from the Pharaohs of the world, but from death itself.

The rituals of the Seder before the meal hearken back to the redemption from Egypt. After the meal, the Seder anticipates the future, the final messianic redemption. In that light, God's slaying of the Angel of Death truly deserves its place as the Haggadah's last word.[27] Getting out of Egypt was not the end of the road, it was just the beginning.

25

The Exodus from Egypt: The Question of Archeology

...וַיִּבֶן עָרֵי מִסְכְּנוֹת לְפַרְעֹה אֶת־פִּתֹם וְאֶת־רַעַמְסֵס,

. . . And they built garrison cities for Pharaoh: Pithom and Ramses (Exodus 1:11).
—THE PASSOVER HAGGADAH

In 2001, David Wolpe, a Conservative rabbi from Los Angeles, delivered a Passover sermon that many found shocking. He interpreted the holiday in light of the fact that most archeologists believe that if there were an Exodus at all, it bore little resemblance to the biblical version of the story.

After more than a century of research, archeologists have found no record of an identifiable Israelite population that resided in ancient Egypt during the period when the Exodus was to have occurred. Nor have they uncovered in the desert any of the expected remains of a migration involving a large number of people over a forty-year period. Moreover, questions have emerged about whether the people of Israel developed outside the land of Canaan, invaded that territory, and then made it their home. Recent discoveries have led many archeologists to conclude that Israel may have emerged predominantly, though not exclusively, from *within* the land of Canaan.

In this chapter, we'll take a brief look at the Exodus as a story and as history, then examine five approaches to understanding the meaning of the saga in light of questions concerning its historical accuracy.

- What difference, if any, does it make if we relate to the Exodus as a story rather than as history?

- Can the underlying truths of the biblical Exodus remain valid even if we question the historical nature of certain elements of the story?

- What are the story's most significant truths or lessons?

- Why might we feel more comfortable questioning the literal claim that God created the heavens and the earth in six days than questioning the historical truth of the biblical Exodus?

HISTORY AND STORY

Depending on the nature of your group, you may want to take turns reading aloud what follows. Ask your guests to keep the above questions in mind and, if you have not already done so, discuss them when you finish the reading.

My father was a wandering Aramean. He went down to Egypt few in numbers and sojourned there; but there he became a great and very populous nation. The Egyptians dealt harshly with us and oppressed us; they imposed heavy labor upon us (Deut. 26:5–6). So they set taskmasters over them to oppress them with forced labor; and they built garrison cities for Pharaoh: Pithom and Ramses . . . (Ex. 1:11). Pharaoh decreed, "You shall no longer provide the people with straw for making bricks . . ." (Ex. 5:7).

Like many great epics, the story of the Exodus may well contain core facts, however distantly remembered or artfully refracted. Although archeologists have questioned certain elements of the tale, they have also discovered evidence of some events that probably did occur.[1]

350

There is evidence that in ancient times people from Canaan journeyed to Egypt, where they sold members of their families into slavery in exchange for grain during all-too-frequent famines. Some of those slaves actually rose to power and established the Hyksos Dynasty that ruled Egypt from 1800 to 1550 B.C.E. Its capital was near Goshen, where Jacob and his family of shepherds reportedly settled. The Hyksos were remembered in Egyptian lore as "shepherd kings." The Hyksos were driven from power and exiled by a Pharaoh named Ahmose; one inscription accused the Hyksos of "ruling without Ra," the Egyptian sun god. Moses' name, which means "begotten" or "brought forth," is clearly Egyptian and resembles the names of many pharaohs—Ahmose, begotten by the moon, Ramses, begotten by the sun god, and so on.

A few centuries later, ancient sources report the devastation Egypt suffered when one of its Pharaohs attempted to force monotheism upon the Egyptians: "The temples of the gods and goddesses were desolated . . . their holy places were about to disintegrate having become rubbish heaps . . . The land was in grave disease. The gods have forsaken this land."[2] The epidemic that swept Egypt was called the "Canaanite" illness.

About a hundred years after this religious revolution was reversed, Ramses II embarked upon a massive construction campaign, conscripting large numbers of Semitic slaves to carry it out. He rebuilt the ancient Hyksos capital, renamed it Ramses, and erected a store city at Pithom. One tomb painting from an earlier period depicts Canaanite slaves making bricks and complaining about the absence of straw, as described in Exodus.[3]

A papyrus from this era speaks of the nighttime escape into the desert of a small number of slaves from Pharaoh's palace. It also includes orders to the border guards to retrieve them. There may well have been similar escapes by other small groups of slaves.

" . . . And Adonai drove back the sea with a strong east wind that blew all night and turned the sea into dry ground" (Exodus 14:21). Recent computer modeling at the Department of Atmospheric and Oceanic Sciences at the University of Colorado has explored the effects of wind on shallow bodies of water. (Remember, *Yam Suf*, often translated as "Red Sea," really means "Reed Sea," likely a shallow body of water.) Scientists found that the dynamics of wind setdown—"the drop in water level caused by wind stress for an extended period of time"—can create conditions remarkably similar to those described in the biblical narrative, including those that drowned the Israelites' Egyptian pursuers. When winds subside, displaced water suddenly returns as a rapidly advancing tidal bore that appears as a "wall of churning water." Indeed, surveyors working in the eastern Nile delta in 1882 reported that a strong overnight gale from the east had caused the complete disappearance of a shallow lake: "natives were walking about on the mud where the day before the fishing-boats, now aground, had been floating."[4] Even if the ancient Israelites had been experts in the dynamics of wind setdown, the perfect timing of such an event would doubtless have merited celebration!

The Bible's account of the Israelites' wandering in the desert describes their yearning for "the cucumbers, the melons, the leeks, the onions, and the garlic" they ate for free in Egypt (Num. 11:5). Writing in about 440 B.C.E., Herodotus, the Greek historian, recorded a now-lost inscription he observed on the base a pyramid built more than a thousand years before the traditional dating of the Exodus: "There is a notice in Egyptian script on the pyramid about how much was spent on radishes, onions, and garlic for the laborers. . . ."[5]

Thus, the story of the Exodus may be "true" in the sense that its general contour and many of its details correlate to real events that happened to real people. But those people may not have been Israelites, and the scale of those events may have been far smaller than that recounted in the Bible.

So how did the Exodus from Egypt become an Israelite story? Imagine that over the centuries countless numbers of Canaanites went down into Egypt as slaves and gradually identified their hopes with legends of the Hyksos slaves who rose to rule Egypt. Those old Hyksos tales were slowly interwoven with the stories of more recent migrants who became slaves to Pharaoh. Later, small groups of these slaves repeatedly escaped into the desert, where they encountered followers of YHWH.

This "Exodus group" brought their memories and stories north, where they found favor in the eyes of Israelites. They told of their slavery in Egypt, of plagues brought by God upon the Egyptians, of their miraculous escape to the desert. They told of the encounter with their new God, YHWH, who had brought them forth and whom they had come to revere. The Israelites who heard these memories were a people composed mostly of migrants to hilltop towns from Canaanite cities that had fallen on hard times. They had already known Egypt's domineering hand and were no strangers to the cycle of famine and servitude. As the eminent scholar Baruch Halpern concludes, "Small wonder [the Israelites] were also the most receptive to a cult myth [brought by the Exodus group] conditioned on the assumption of escaping bondage to the Egyptians."[6]

FIVE SAGE PERSPECTIVES ON THE EXODUS AND HISTORY

Given that the biblical narrative of the Exodus cannot be read as a history book, how are we to relate to our founding story? It's a question that deserves an answer. Below you'll find five responses. Choose one or two to read aloud for discussion.

When I read the Haggadah on the eve of Passover . . . the spirit of Moses . . . hovers before me and lifts me out of this nether world . . . I care not whether this man Moses really existed; whether his life and its activity really corresponded to our traditional account of him; whether he was really the savior of Israel and gave his people the Torah in the form in which it is preserved among us and so forth . . . We have another Moses of our own, whose image has been enshrined in the hearts of the Jewish People for generations, and whose influence on our national life has never ceased from ancient times to the present day . . . For even if you succeeded in demonstrating conclusively that the man Moses never existed, or that he was not such a man as we supposed, you would not thereby detract one jot from the historical reality of the ideal Moses—the Moses who has been our leader not only for forty years in the wilderness of Sinai, but for thousands of years in all the wildernesses in which we have wandered since the Exodus.

—AHAD HA-'AM ("ONE OF THE PEOPLE"), PEN NAME OF ASHER HIRSCH GINSBERG (1856–1927), HEBREW ESSAYIST AND ZIONIST LEADER[7]

There can be no certainty of arriving . . . at "what really happened." However, even if it is impossible to reconstitute the course of the events themselves, it is nevertheless possible to recover much of the manner in which the people participating experienced those events. We become acquainted with the meeting between this people and a vast historical happening that overwhelmed it. We become conscious of the saga-creating ardor with which the people received the tremendous event and

353

transmitted it to a molding memory . . . The meeting of a people with events so enormous that it cannot ascribe them to its own plans and their realization, but must perceive in them deeds performed by heavenly powers, is of the genuine substance of history. Insofar as the saga begins near the event, it is the outcome and record of this meeting.

—MARTIN BUBER (1878–1965), PHILOSOPHER, THEOLOGIAN, AND ZIONIST LEADER[8]

The biblical appeal to remember . . . has little to do with curiosity about the past. Israel is told only that it must be a kingdom of priests and a holy people (Ex. 19:6); nowhere is it suggested that it become a nation of historians . . . It is above all God's acts of intervention in history, and man's responses to them, be they positive or negative, that must be recalled . . . For the real danger is not so much that what happened in the past will be forgotten, as the more crucial aspect of *how* it happened. "And it shall be, when Adonai your God shall bring you into the land which He swore unto your fathers, to Abraham, to Isaac, and to Jacob, to give you great and goodly cities, which you did not build, and houses full of all good things, which you did not fill, and cisterns hewn out, which you did not hew, vineyards and olive-trees, which you did not plant, and you shall eat and be satisfied—then beware lest you forget Adonai who brought you out of the land of Egypt, out of the house of bondage [*beit avadim*]" (Deut. 6:10–12).

—YOSEF HAYIM YERUSHALMI (1932–2009), SCHOLAR OF MEDIEVAL AND MODERN JEWISH HISTORY[9]

For generations, Pesach has been passed down as history: Moses, the ten plagues, the parting of the Sea of Reeds, the miraculous deliverance. Our ancestors recited the story of the Exodus to affirm their belief that it was true and to derive faith in the God who made it happen.

In our time, most of us tell the Seder tale as sacred story rather than as historical record; we are skeptical of miracles; we are troubled by the moral implications of plague and punishment; and we seek a God commensurate with our enlarged vision of the liberation of all peoples.

Is this story true? No, not if we mean an accurate account of events that happened more or less the way they are told. But our ancestors, those who wrote the Bible and those who wrote the Haggadah, did not write history; they wrote of their experience of a Power greater than themselves that stood for freedom and against oppression.

They used myth and poetic language, couched in the context of their world of experience.

We do not live in that world, but we are the extension of the family that the Exodus created—the Jewish People. We do not tell the story of the Exodus because it is historically accurate; we tell the story because it is *our* story and we need to recover and uncover the eternal ideas that this story conveys. We take this story seriously but not literally. Pesach is the way the Jewish People celebrate, affirm, wrestle with, and work for freedom as our human destiny.

—RABBI RICHARD HIRSH (1953–), DIRECTOR
OF THE RECONSTRUCTIONIST
RABBINICAL ASSOCIATION[10]

Why should a rabbi come before a congregation on the first day of Passover and say the story you told last night at the Seder might be just a story? There is only one good reason and nothing else will justify it. It is that our rabbis insist that the seal of God is truth and that you do not serve God if you do not seek truth. It is no honor to the God who created our minds not to use them . . . If you want to pray to God you want to pray out of your faith, which means a combination of your reason and your emotion, out of the depths of your soul, and you cannot do that by closing your eyes. . . .

The story that you told at your Seder has inspired people who were searching for freedom and liberation for thousands of years. And the paradox of it is that they searched for freedom and for liberation so that they could proclaim truth, not hide it—so that their spirit could soar, so that they could be free, so they could build their religion on a foundation of what is real, on the soil of what you find, not solely on the ground of their imaginations. Ralph Waldo Emerson . . . wrote that

"God gives every human being a choice between truth and repose. Take one," he said, "you cannot have them both." And the Jewish People has never had repose. And we have never had it because we have always sought truth. *"Avadim hayinu l'pharaoh b'mitzrayim."* We were slaves to Pharaoh in Egypt. We know what it is to be slaves. We know what it is not to have freedom. That is true.

Does it matter if that sense comes to us from something that happened 3,000 years ago or 2,000 years ago? Not at all . . . I have never been in Egypt, but I know what it is to leave. If you sat at the Seder table and you felt like a slave, and you ate the matzah and you sang the songs and you were free by the time your Seder was over, then it is true. Then you don't need to be afraid of the findings of the scientists or the archeologists because in your soul it is true. Pesach has been proved true in virtually every generation of the Jewish People. Are there not people sitting in this congregation this morning who were, in a manner of speaking, slaves, and sitting here this morning are free? Don't tell me that Pesach is not true.

—RABBI DAVID WOLPE (1958–), CONSERVATIVE RABBI
AND SPIRITUAL LEADER OF SINAI TEMPLE IN WEST LOS ANGELES,
FROM HIS SERMON ON THE FIRST DAY OF PASSOVER, 2001[11]

Abraham Joshua Heschel wrote, "As a report about revelation the Bible itself is *a midrash,*" not a text "in systematic theology."[12] The same can be said about the Bible as a report about history. Its intent is to teach the deepest truths of the human spirit, not to serve as a textbook of ancient history. What does the biblical Exodus want us to learn? That we must never lose faith that evil can be overcome, no matter how deeply entrenched; that the struggle for freedom is intrinsically worthy; that though we may feel terribly weak in the face of adversity, on the most fundamental level we are not alone; and that it is our responsibility to use memories of our suffering not to inflict our wounds on others, but to build a more just world.

Proving the historical truth of the Exodus depends on digging up tangible artifacts from the ground. Discovering the spiritual truths of the Exodus depends on opening your heart to the story.

APPENDIX I

—

CHAPTER TEN OF MISHNAH PESACHIM, THE NIGHT OF PASSOVER[1]

The Mishnah was compiled in about 200 C.E. by Judah the Prince. It contains the oldest description of how Passover was celebrated following the destruction of the Second Temple in 70 C.E.

> Depending on your group, you might consider reading this aloud before your Seder.
> Make a copy for each of your guests. Read each mishnah and ask for
> one or two reactions or comments. Note that the Mishnah does not make clear
> distinctions between the Passover offering that occurred prior to the Temple's destruction
> and the Passover Seder that replaced the sacrificial offering.

- What does it feel like to read these ancient instructions of the Passover Haggadah?
- What seem to be the major differences between the Mishnah and the Haggadah?

Mishnah 10:1 On the eve of Passover, close to [the time of] *minchah* [the daily afternoon offering], a person should not eat until it gets dark. Even a poor person in Israel should not eat until [he] reclines. [Those who serve] should not give him fewer than four cups of wine even if [the funds] come from the charity plate.

Mishnah 10:2 [They] poured for him the first cup [of wine]. The House of Shammai say, "[He] says the blessing over the day [the festival] and afterward [he] says the blessing over the wine." And the House of Hillel say, "[He] says the blessing over the wine and afterward [he] says the blessing over the day."

Mishnah 10:3 [They] served—[he] dips the lettuce [*chazeret*, the vegetable used for the bitter herbs] before he reaches the bread condiment. [They] served him unleavened bread and lettuce and *charoset,* even though the *charoset* is not a [biblical] commandment. And in the Temple [they] serve him the carcass of the Passover offering.

Mishnah 10:4 [They] poured for him the second cup—and here the child asks, and if the child lacks understanding, his father instructs him.... How is this night different from all [other] nights? For on all the [other] nights we dip once, this night twice. For on all the [other] nights we eat leavened and unleavened bread, this night we eat only unleavened. For on all the [other] nights we eat meat roasted, steamed, or cooked [in a liquid, boiled], this night only roasted. According to the child's understanding, his father instructs him. [He] starts with disgrace and ends with praise; and [he] expounds from, "My father was a wandering Aramean," until he finishes the entire portion [Deuteronomy 26:5-8].

Mishnah 10:5 Rabban Gamaliel said, "Whoever did not say these three things on Passover did not fulfill his obligation: *Pesach* [the Passover offering], *matzah* [unleavened bread], and *merorim* [bitter herbs]." *Pesach*—because the Omnipresent skipped over the house of our ancestors in Egypt. *Merorim*—because the Egyptians embittered the lives of our ancestors in Egypt. *Matzah*—because they were redeemed. Therefore we are obligated to give thanks, to praise, to glorify, to crown, to exalt, to elevate the One who did for us all these miracles and took us from slavery to freedom, and let us say before him: Hallelujah [Psalm 113].

Mishnah 10:6 Up to what point does he recite [the Hallel]? The House of Shammai say, "Until 'as a happy mother of children'" [the end of Psalm 113]. And the House of Hillel say, "Until 'the flinty rock into a fountain'" [the end of Psalm 114]. And [he] seals with redemption. [He ends with a blessing formula with the motif of redemption.] Rabbi Tarfon says, "Who has redeemed us and redeemed our ancestors from Egypt and brought us to this night"— and [he] does not seal [with a concluding formula]. Rabbi Akiva says, "[One adds to the blessing:] 'Adonai our God and God of our ancestors, bring us in peace to other holy days and festivals that are approaching that we might be happy as we rebuild your city and joyful as we serve You. There we will eat from the sacrifices and Passover offerings, the blood from which will reach the wall of Your altar and please You.

And let us thank You for our redemption. Praised are You, Adonai, Who redeemed [or "redeems"] Israel.'"

Mishnah 10:7 [They] poured for him the third cup [of wine]—[he] says the blessing over his food. [At] the fourth [cup]—[he] finishes the Hallel [through Psalm 118] and says over it the blessing over the song. Between the four cups, if [he] wants to drink [further] he may drink. Between the third and the fourth, [he] should not drink.

Mishnah 10:8 After [eating from] the Passover offering, [they] do not end with *afikomen* [revelry]. [If they] fell asleep: [if it was] some of them—[they] may eat [again because the remaining individuals of the group, who stayed awake, maintained the group] and [if it was] all of them—[they] may not eat [again]. Rabbi Yossi says, "If [they] dozed— [they] may eat [again]. And if [they] slumbered—[they] may not eat [again]."

Mishnah 10:9 After midnight the Passover sacrifice imparts uncleanness to the hands; *pigul* [i.e. a sacrifice prepared with the intention of eating after the proper time] and *notar* [i.e. meat of a sacrifice that has remained uneaten beyond the allotted time]. "[If one] said the blessing over the Passover sacrifice, [one] is exempt from that over the festive sacrifice. [If one said the blessing] over the festive sacrifice, [one] is not exempt from that over the Passover sacrifice"—the words of Rabbi Ishmael. Rabbi Akiva says, "This one does not exempt that one, and that one does not exempt this one."

APPENDIX II

—

WHAT IS MIDRASH?

From ancient to modern times, midrash has embodied one of Judaism's most vibrant modes of wisdom, wondering, and creativity. The term derives from the biblical Hebrew *lidrosh*—"to search," "to seek," "to examine," or "to investigate." Later, midrash (plural: midrashim) came to signify elaboration with the intent of discovering deeper meanings or new questions behind the plain meaning of the text. The Haggadah abounds with midrash. Its phrase-by-phrase elaboration on Deuteronomy 26:5–8 ("My father was a wandering Aramean . . .") is a classic example. The debate among Rabbis Yossi the Galilean, Eliezer, and Akiva about the "true" number of plagues visited upon the Egyptians is another. Often midrash uses one biblical text to interpret another, in the process shedding new light on both. As you might expect, the miraculous events surrounding the Exodus from Egypt became the focus of enormous midrashic speculation. But remember: Midrash is meant to make a point, to stretch your thinking, not necessarily to be taken literally.

When it comes to the dates ascribed to midrashim, in this book you'll often find a reference to a particular century or two. This refers to the time when that collection of midrashim was likely compiled, but these works often contain considerably older material.

APPENDIX III

—

DIRECTIONS FOR ART MIDRASH PROJECTS

Midrash involves the process of uncovering new meaning in familiar texts or concepts. Here you can use a simple art project to explore what particular ideas or passages from the Haggadah mean to your Seder participants. Try this before your Seder begins. Distribute sheets of colored paper and glue sticks to each of your guests. Some scissors would be helpful but are not necessary.

Read aloud the particular passage that will serve as the basis for your art midrash project. Ask everyone to spend about twenty minutes making a collage that expresses something important to him or her about an idea the passage raises.

Explain that the collages can be representational or completely abstract, using shape and color to express feelings of or about one of the transitions. When you have finished, ask a few of your guests to hold up their collages, one at a time. Ask others to make a brief comment on what they think the collage may be saying. Then ask the creator of the collage to explain what he or she had in mind. Remember, the goal of this art midrash project is to explore our ideas, not to see who is the "best" artist.

Those interested in learning more about this approach may want to look at Jo Milgrom's *Handmade Midrash* (Philadelphia: Jewish Publication Society, 1992).

APPENDIX IV

—

BLESSING FOR THE NEW MOON

To be recited when the moon can be seen clearly, preferably outdoors. This blessing may be recited until the point in the month when the moon begins to wane. (See chapter 8, note 19 for more details.) The first paragraph below is from the Talmud (Sanhedrin 42a) and dates from between the third and sixth centuries. The complete service for blessing the moon begins with Psalm 148:1–6. It concludes with Psalms 121, 150, a selection from the Talmud about the blessing and then Psalm 67.

Blessed are You, Adonai our God, Sovereign of the universe, whose utterance created the heavens, the breath of His mouth all their hosts. Order and regularity He gave them so they will not deviate from their tasks. Joyfully and gladly they do the will of their Master, who does truth, whose deed is true. He told the moon to renew its crown of glory over those [He] sustained from the womb, so that like the moon, in the future, they too, will be renewed to glorify His dominion. Blessed are you God, who renews the moons.

(*Recite the following verses three times.*)

Blessed is your Molder, blessed is your Maker, blessed is your Master, blessed is your Creator.

(*Stand on toes as if dancing when reciting this verse.*)

Just as I dance toward You but cannot touch you, so may all my enemies be unable to touch me with evil.

Terror and dread descend upon them; through the might of Your arm they are as still as stone (Ex. 15:16, from the song the Israelites sang after crossing the Red Sea).

David, King of Israel, lives and endures.*

(*Participants exchange greetings:*)

David melech Yisrael chai v'kayam.

362

Shalom aleikhem, peace be with you!

Aleikhem shalom, peace be with you!

(*Recite three times.*)

May we and all Israel have a favorable omen and good fortune. Amen.

Siman tov u'mazal tov y'hei lanu u'l'chol Yisrael. Amen.

Hark! My beloved! There he comes, leaping over the mountains, bounding over hills. My beloved is like a gazelle or like a young stag. There he stands behind our wall, gazing through the window, peering through the lattice (Song of Songs 2:8–9).**

---

* The Talmud (Rosh Hashanah 25a) attributes these words to Judah the Prince, compiler of the Mishnah. He used them as a watchword to verify that his order to sanctify the new moon had been carried out. In Psalms 89:36–38 God promises that rule of the House of David shall be as enduring as the sun and the moon.

** The Song of Songs—traditionally read following the Seder and subsequently in synagogue during the festival—is often interpreted as an allegory of God's love for the Jewish People that was revealed in the redemption from Egypt. Here, the passage expresses hope for the ultimate messianic redemption.

ABBREVIATIONS AND ABBREVIATED TITLES
USED IN THIS BOOK
—

ABBREVIATIONS FOR BOOKS OF THE BIBLE

Genesis: Gen.
Exodus: Ex.
Leviticus: Lev.
Numbers: Num.
Deuteronomy: Deut.
Ecclesiastes: Eccl.

Joshua: Jos.
Jeremiah: Jer.

OTHER ABBREVIATIONS AND ABBREVIATED TITLES

BT: Babylonian Talmud.

EJ: Encyclopedia Judaica. Jerusalem: Keter Publishing House, 1972.

Etz Hayim: Etz Hayim Torah and Commentary. New York: The Rabbinical Assembly/The United Synagogue of Conservative Judaism, 2001.

Fox: The Schocken Bible: The Five Books of Moses. Translated by Everett Fox. New York: Schocken Books, 1995.

Hagadah Shelemah: Kasher, Menachem. Hagadah Shelemah. Jerusalem: Torah Shelemah Institute, 1967 (Hebrew).

Haggadah of the Sages: Safrai, Shmuel, and Safrai Ze'v. The Haggadah of the Sages. Jerusalem: Carta, 1998 (Hebrew).

Haggadah: Sources and History: Goldschmidt, E. Daniel. The Passover Haggadah: Sources and History. Jerusalem: The Bialik Institute, 1960 (Hebrew).

Legends: Ginzberg, Louis. Legends of the Jews. Philadelphia: Jewish Publication Society, 1968.

Mekhilta of Rabbi Ishmael: Mekhilta of Rabbi Ishmael. Translated by Jacob Z. Lauterbach. Philadelphia: Jewish Publication Society, 1949.

New Studies in Shemot: Leibowitz, Nehama. New Studies in Shemot. Jerusalem: The Joint Authority for Jewish Zionist Education, 1993.

Passover and Easter: Passover and Easter: Origin and History to Modern Times. Edited by Paul F. Bradshaw and Lawrence Hoffman. Notre Dame, Ind.: University of Notre Dame Press, 1999.

Pirke de Rabbi Eliezer: Friedlander, Gerald. Pirke de Rabbi Eliezer. New York: Sepher-Hermon Press, 1916; 1981.

Ramban: Ramban (Nachmanides): Commentary on the Torah. Translated by Charles B. Chavel. New York: Shilo Publishing House, 1973.

Scholar's Haggadah: Guggenheimer, Heinrich. The Scholar's Haggadah. Northvale, N.J.: Jason Aronson, 1998.

NOTES

—

Chapter 1—A Dish for the Ages: The Seder Plate

1. Arthur Schaffer, "The History of Horseradish as the Bitter Herb of Passover," in *Gesher*, 8, 1981, p. 223. You can also find this fascinating article at www.livelyseders.com. See articles of interest.

2. Maimonides, *Laws of Chametz and Matzah* 8:2.

3. The meaning of the fourth matzah has now been reinterpreted to focus on the reality of slavery as it exists in the world today by organizations such as the American Anti-Slavery Group.

4. *The Women's Seder Sourcebook: Rituals and Readings for Use at the Passover Seder*, ed. Sharon Cohen Anisfeld, et al. (Woodstock, Vt.: Jewish Lights, 2003), pp. 208-212. The practice had originally been to put a crust of bread on the Seder plate! See Rebecca Alpert, *Like Bread on the Seder Plate: Jewish Lesbians and the Transformation of Tradition* (New York: Columbia University Press, 1997), pp.1–3.

5. BT, Pesachim 115b.

6. *Seder Pesach*, section 318. The custom builds on that of Rabbi Akiva, in BT, Pesachim 108b.

7. Rabbi David Feinstein, *Laws of the Seder: The Comprehensive Kol Dodi Exposition of the Laws and Rituals of the Seder Night* (New York: Mesorah Publications, 2000), p. 42.

8. *Tosafot* to BT, Pesachim 114a, *s.v. m'tabel b'chazeret*.

9. Maimonides, *Laws of Chametz and Matzah* 8:2.

10. Mishnah, Pesachim 2:6.

11. Schaffer, "The History of Horseradish as the Bitter Herb of Passover." Opposition to the root versus the leaves of horseradish comes from Mishnah, Pesachim 2:6, which states that "one fulfills one's obligation with the stalk." This was taken to mean that which grows above rather than below the ground.

12. Bertram W. Korn, *American Jewry and the Civil War* (Jewish Publication Society, 1951), pp. 90–92.

13. Marcus Jastrow defines *karpas* as an umbelliferous plant, i.e. without a woody stem and with seed pods resembling an umbrella. Marcus Jastrow, *A Dictionary of the Targumim, the Talmud Babli and Yerushalmi, and the Midrashic Literature* (New York: Judaica Press, 1996). The word *karpas* appears in Esther (1:6), but there it means a "white cotton" fabric.

14. *Siddur R. Saadja Gaon*, ed. I. Davidson, et al. (Jerusalem: Rubin Mass. Ltd., 2000), p. 136.

15. Yosef Tabory, *The Passover Ritual Throughout the Generations* (Israel: Hakibbutz Hameuchad Publishing House, 1996), p. 263.

16. *Haggadah Shelemah*, p. 64.

17. *The Book of Maharil: Customs by Rabbi Yaacov Mulin*, ed. Shlomoh J. Spitzer (Jerusalem: Mifal Torath Chachmey Ashkenaz, 1989), p. 94 (Hebrew). See *Shulchan Arukh*, Orach Chayim, 473.4.

18. *Seder Olam Rabbah*, chapter 5, a third- or fourth-century midrash.

19. BT, Berakhot 39b.

20. Maimonides, *Laws of Chametz and Matzah* 8:6; Vilna Gaon's commentary on the *Shulchan Arukh*, Biur HaGra, Orach Chayim 473:4.

21. Orach Chayim 473:4

22. Midrash HaGadol on Ex. 1:14.

23. BT, Pesachim 114b–115a.

24. See David Feinstein, *Laws of the Seder* (Brooklyn: Mesorah Publications, 2000), p. 65.

25. See Tosefta, Pesachim 2:22 (third century) and BT, Pesachim 115a.

26. Tosafot, Pesachim 116a, *s.v. tzarikh*. Tosafot also includes almonds, *shkadim* in Hebrew, because God was diligent, *shaked*, about bringing the bondage to an end. Song of Songs includes additional references to some of these fruits. Various midrashic sources, e.g. Song of Songs Rabbah, compare the community of Israel to these fruits.

27. BT, Sotah 11b and Pesachim 116a.

28. Jerusalem Talmud 10:37d.

29. Tosafot, Pesachim 116a, *s.v. tzarikh*.

30. See David Feinstein, *Laws of the Seder*, p. 32.

31. BT, Pesachim 116b.

32. Mishnah, Pesachim 10:3.

33. BT, Pesachim 114a. There's a good deal of confusion about this, because there were two kinds of *chagigah* offerings, one slaughtered on the first day of the holiday, the fifteenth of Nisan, and the optional one slaughtered on the fourteenth of Nisan, the same day of the Passover offering. See Rashbam Pesachim 114b, *s.v. v'eched zekher*.

34. See Yael Levine Katz, "Placing a Cooked Food on the Seder Table in Commemoration of Miriam," in *All the Women Followed Her: A Collection of Writings on Miriam the Prophet and the Women of Exodus*, ed. Rebecca Schwartz (Mountain View, Calif.: Rikudei Miriam Press, 2001).

35. The most commonly cited source for this is Yoma 33b, which deals with the order in which one puts on and removes phylacteries, *tfillin*.

36. *Shulchan Arukh*, Orach Chayim, 473:3.

37. For an interesting anthropological discussion of Luria's arrangement, see Ruth Gruber Fredman, *The Passover Seder* (New York: New American Library, 1981).

38. The force of this concern seems to have diminished. The Mishnah Berurah (473:26) comments that "it may be that with respect to the maror and the *charoset* . . . the prohibition that one must not pass over mitzvot is not relevant."

39. Hayim Vital, *Sidrat Kitve Rabenu ha-Ari*, vol. 17 "Pri Etz Hayim," part 2 (Jerusalem: Yeshivat Kol Yehuda, 1987), p. 504. Ba'er Hetev, Orach Chayim 473:8.

Chapter 2—Long Road from Slavery to Freedom

1. *Haggadah: Sources and History*, pp. 7–9.

2. Isaac Mendelsohn, *Slavery in the Ancient Near East: A Comparative Study of Slavery in Babylonia, Assyria, Syria, and Palestine from the Middle of the Third Millennium to the End of the First Millennium* (New York: Oxford University Press, 1949), p. 1.

3. Antonia Loprieno, "Slaves," in *The Egyptians,* ed. Sergio Donadoni, trans. Robert Bianchi (Chicago: University of Chicago Press, 1997), p. 202.

4. Ibid. pp. 204–205.

5. Donald B. Redford, *Egypt, Canaan and Israel in Ancient Times* (Princeton: Princeton University Press, 1992), p. 209.

6. Loprieno, p. 208.

7. Moshe Weinfeld, *Social Justice in Ancient Israel and in the Ancient Near East* (Jerusalem: The Magnes Press/The Hebrew University, 1995), p. 142.

8. Chilperic Edwards, *The Hammurabi Code: And the Sinaitic Legislation,* 3rd ed. (London: Watts, 1921), paragraph 16.

9. BT, Gittin 45a, watered this down in the sense that the fugitive slave was to be brought to court and ordered to sign a promissory note to his former owner for the amount of that slave's value.

10. John Winthrop, "City on a Hill." On the web at www.mtholyoke.edu/acad/intrel/winthrop.htm. For clarity, the spelling of Winthrop's original speech has been rendered into modern English.

11. Charles Chauncey, "A Discourse on the Good News from a Far Country," in *The Pulpit of the American Revolution: Or the Political Sermons of the Period of 1776,* ed. John Wingate Thornton (Boston: Gould and Lincoln, 1860), p. 129.

12. Letter from John Adams to Abigail Adams, August 14, 1776, in *The Adams Family Papers,* on the web at www.masshist.org/digitaladams/aea/letter/.

13. Articles I, section 2, and IV, section 2. Of note, the framers avoided using any form of the word "slave" in the Constitution.

14. Samuel Elliot Morrison, *The Oxford History of the American People,* vol. 1, (New York: Penguin Books, 1972), p. 384.

15. Abraham Lincoln, *His Speeches and Writings,* ed. Roy P. Basler (New York: Da Capo Press, 1946), p. 489.

16. Martin Luther King Jr., "The Quest for Justice," on the web at www.nobel_prizes/peace/ laureates/1964/king-lecture.html.

17. See note 12.

18. *Harper's New Monthly Magazine,* 13:74, July 1856, pp. 178–186. On the web at www.digital.library.cornell.edu/m/moa. For more than you may want to know about the symbolism of the seal see David Ovason, *The Secret Symbols of the Dollar Bill: A Closer Look at the Hidden Magic and Meaning of the Money You Use Every Day* (New York: HarperCollins, 2004).

19. Mary Prince, *History of Mary Prince, A West Indian Slave* (London: Westly and Davis, 1831), in *The Classic Slave Narratives,* ed. Henry Louis Gates Jr. (New York: Penguin Books, 1987), pp. 191, 214.

20. *The Union Kommando in Auschwitz,* ed. Lore Shelley (Lanham, Md.: University Press of America, 1996), pp. 83–84.

21. Available on the web at frwebgate.access.gpo.gov/cgi-bin/getdoc.cgi?dbname= 106_senate_hearings&docid=f:69751.wais.

22. Aristotle, *Politics,* trans. Benjamin Jowett, book 3, part 4 on the web at www.eserver.org/philosophy/aristotle/politics.txt.

23. *The Historical Review of Pennsylvania,* attributed to Benjamin Franklin (Philadelphia: E. Olmsted and W. Power, 1812).

24. Abraham Lincoln, *His Speeches and Writings,* ed. Roy P. Basler (New York: Da Capo Press, 1946), p. 473.

25. Elizabeth Cady Stanton and Susan B. Anthony, *The Elizabeth Cady Stanton—Susan B. Anthony Reader: Correspondence, Writings, Speeches,* ed. Ellen Carol DuBois (Boston: Northeastern University Press, 1981), p. 154.

26. David Ben-Gurion, *Netzach Yisrael* (Tel Aviv: Ayanot, 1964), p. 25. Quoted on p. 2 of "Israel's Grand Strategy: Ben-Gurion and Israel's Next Great Debate" by Shai Feldman, delivered at the Colloquium of the Woodrow Wilson International Center for Scholars, Washington, D.C., June 15, 1988.

27. Martin Luther King Jr., "The Birth of a New Nation," Montgomery, Alabama, on the web at www.mlkonline.com/mlkhome.html.

28. Nelson Mandela, *Long Walk to Freedom: The Autobiography of Nelson Mandela* (Boston: Little, Brown and Company, 1994), p. 554. Thanks to Nadera Shalhoub Keverkian for bringing this to my attention.

29. See EJ, vol. 6, pp. 51–55, under *"dina de-malkhuta dina."*

30. Bertram W. Korn, "Jews and Negro Slavery in the Old South, 1789–1865," in *Publications of the American Jewish Historical Society,* vol. 50, 1960–1961, pp. 198–199.

31. This question became controversial in the early 1990s, when publications of the Nation of Islam grossly exaggerated the Jewish role in slavery. See Eli Faber, *Jews, Slaves and the Slave Trade: Setting the Record Straight* (New York: New York University Press, 1998), and Saul S. Friedman, *Jews and the American Slave Trade* (New Brunswick, N.J.: Transaction Publishers, 1998).

32. Kevin Bales, *Disposable People: New Slavery in the Global Economy* (Berkeley: University of California Press, 2004). The American Anti-Slavery Group's "Modern Slavery 101" is on the web at www.iabolish.org.

Chapter 3—The Four "Questions"

1. Sephardic and Yemenite Haggadot include the same questions in the following order: dipping, matzah, bitter herbs, reclining. For an excellent treatment of some of the scholarly issues surrounding the Four Questions, see Richard C. Steiner, "On the Original Structure and Meaning of *Mah Nishtannah* and the History of Its Reinterpretation," in *JSIJ,* 7, 2008, pp. 1–41. On the web at www.biu.ac.il/JS/JSIJ/7-2008/Steiner.pdf. Thanks to Louis Levine for bringing this to my attention.

2. Nehama Leibowitz, *Studies on the Haggadah,* eds. Yitshak Reiner and Shmuel Peerless (New York: Lambda Publications, 2002), p. 29.

3. *Haggadah: Sources and History,* pp. 10–13. *Haggadah of the Sages,* pp. 112–115.

4. *Haggadah of the Sages,* p. 113.

5. *Abarbanel Haggadah,* ed. Shlomo Fox, trans. Yisrael Isser Zvi Herczeg (New York: Mesorah Publications, 1990), p. 31.

6. Plato, "The Symposium," in *The Works of Plato,* trans. Benjamin Jowett (New York: Modern Library, 1928), p. 338.

7. Quoted in Sigmund Stein, "The Influence of Symposia Literature on the Literary Form of the Pesach Haggadah," in *Journal of Jewish Studies,* vol. 8, nos 1 and 2, 1957, p. 19. See also Baruch M. Bokser, "A Jewish Symposium?" in *The Origins of the Passover Seder* (Berkeley: University of California Press, 1984), chapter 5.

8. See Joseph Tabory, "Towards a History of the Paschal Meal," in *Passover and Easter,* pp. 67–68.

9. Bokser, "A Jewish Symposium?" p. 68.

10. Ibid., Appendix A: "Roasted Meat or Sacrifices after 70 C.E.?"

11. Tabory, "Towards a History," p. 71.

12. *Haggadah: Sources and History,* pp. 77–78. This manuscript is available online at www.sceti.library.upenn.edu/pages/index.cfm?so_id=2242&pageposition=7&level=4. (See folio 4v for this question.)

Chapter 4—Passover after the Temple

1. B1, Pesachim 116a. Rav and Shmuel's discussions on the Mishnah formed a central component of the Gemarah, which was compiled through about the year 500. Together, the Mishnah and the Gemarah comprise the Talmud. Actually, there are two Talmuds, one compiled in Babylonia and the other in the Land of Israel. The version of Rav's statement that appears in the Haggadah uses a different term for idol worship (*avodah zarah*) than the standard Vilna edition of the Babylonian Talmud (*gilulim*). Manuscripts of the Talmud include many variations of the exchange between Rav and Shmuel, some attributing their positions to different sages. See *Hagadah Shelemah,* pp. 20 and 22. See Joshua Kulp, "'We Were Slaves': Rava's Babylonian Haggadah," in *Conservative Judaism,* 60:3, Spring 2008, pp. 59–75. Kulp makes a good argument that Rav's disputant was Rava, a fourth century Babylonian sage, rather than Shmuel. He suggests that Rava's argument was not so much about slavery versus idol worship, but rather reflects Rava's discomfort with Rav's possible implication that living outside of the Land of Israel embodies shame or disgrace. I've stayed with Shmuel because that is the sage whose name appears in the standard printed version of the Talmud, and, as Kulp notes, in an important manuscript of the Talmud as well. A long interpretive tradition also identifies Rav's disputant as Shmuel.

2. Mishnah, Pesachim 7:2.

3. Mishnah, Beitzah 2:7.

4. Mishnah, Pesachim 10:4.

5. For details see David Arnow, "Elaborating on the Exodus," in *Conservative Judaism,* 58:4, Summer 2006, pp. 61–79. The original language in the Haggadah read: "We are

commanded to tell about the Exodus from Egypt. And all who tell of the Exodus deserve praise." The wording in our Haggadah that refers to elaborating on the story derives from David ben Joseph Abudarham, a Spanish commentator who lived in the fourteenth century.

6. The translation of the passage from Joshua follows that of the Davka Soncino Classics, CD-ROM version.

7. Genesis Rabbah 42:8, a midrash from the fifth century C.E.

Chapter 5—Five Super Sages in B'nei B'rak

1. Mishnah, Avot 2:12.

2. Mishnah, Avot 2:15; BT, Shabbat 153a.

3. Ecclesiastes Rabbah 5:4.

4. *The Fathers According to Rabbi Nathan,* trans. Judah Goldin (New Haven: Yale University Press, 1955), p. 74.

5. Ibid. p. 34.

6. Mishnah, Berakhot 1:5.

7. Mishnah, Avot 2:21.

8. Mishnah, Makkot 1:10.

9. Jerusalem Talmud, Nedarim 41:3, 9:4; Genesis Rabbah 34:14.

10. Song of Songs Rabbah 2:38.

11. BT, Berakhot 61b.

12. BT, Sanhedrin 101a and 68a.

13. EJ, vol. 8, p. 351.

14. Jonathan Sacks, *The Chief Rabbi's Haggadah* (New York: HarperCollins, 2003), p. 87. Thanks to Nigel Savage for bringing this to my attention.

15. See Sagit Mor, "Hilchot Korban Pesach O Sipur Yitziat Mitzrayim," *Zion,* 68, 2003, pp. 1–15 (Hebrew).

16. BT, Chagigah 5b.

Chapter 6—The Four Children

1. Mishnah, Pesachim 10:4.

2. The four verses usually associated with the injunction to tell your children about the story of the Exodus are Ex. 12:26, 13:8, 13:14; and Deut. 6:20. However, Ex. 10:1–2 also contains a similar injunction that refers to God's hardening of Pharaoh's heart. The Haggadah's discomfort with this theme may account for the omission of this verse from its treatment of the Four Children. (See chapter 7.)

3. *Mekhilta of Rabbi Ishmael Piskha,* 18:118–131, vol. 1, pp. 166–167.

4. *Haggadah: Sources and History,* pp. 22–29; Jerusalem Talmud, Pesachim 10:4.

5. See *Haggadah: Sources and History,* pp. 22–29; *Scholar's Haggadah,* pp. 268–278. In a personal communication, Rabbi Burton L. Visotzky argues that *otanu* likely reflected an alternative, pre-Masoretic biblical text.

6. According to this view, the Seder was at one point a "messianic meal," the chief ritual of which was eating the *afikomen,* which some claim should be translated as "the coming one." This may have inspired the Eucharist. See David Daube, "He That Cometh," St. Paul's Lecture, October 1966 (an obscure publication, but an influential article).

7. Joseph Tabory, "Towards a History," in *Passover and Easter,* p. 73.

8. Abraham Joshua Heschel, *God in Search of Man* (New York: Farrar, Straus and Giroux, 1955), pp. 337, 341. Thanks to Rabbi Michael Paley for teaching me about Heschel's insight in relation to the Four Children.

9. *Numbers Rabbah* 8.4.

10. *The Breslov Haggadah,* ed. Yehoshuah Starret (Jerusalem: Breslov Research Institute, 1989), p. 47.

11. Samson Raphael Hirsch, *The Collected Writings,* vol. 1 (New York: Phillip Feldheim, 1984), pp. 61–62.

12. Menachem M. Schneerson, *Likkutei Sichot: An Anthology of Talks,* vol. 3 (Brooklyn: Kehot Publication Society, 1987), pp. 110–119.

13. *The Journey Continues: The 1997 Ma'yan Passover Haggadah,* eds. Tamara Cohen, Sue Levi Elwell, Debbie Friedman, and Ronnie M. Horn (New York: Ma'yan: The Jewish Women's Project—The JCC of the Upper West Side, 1997), pp. 18–19.

Chapter 7—Hardening Pharaoh's Heart

1. The first section of this chapter uses the translation of the Pentateuch by Fox.

2. The Fox translation of the Pentateuch is faithful to the Hebrew, which actually uses variants of three distinct verbs to describe Pharaoh's emotional state. Some translations don't capture this nuance. Where Fox uses YHWH, I have substituted "Adonai," because it is easier to read aloud.

3. The identity of the fourth plague is unclear. The term *arov* literally means "mixture" and is generally interpreted as swarms of insects or wild beasts.

4. For modern Bible scholarship on this subject, see Brevard S. Childs, *The Book of Exodus: A Critical, Theological Commentary* (Philadelphia: Westminster Press, 1974), p. 174; David M. Gunn, "The 'Hardening of Pharaoh's Heart': Plot, Character and Theology in Exodus 1–14," in *Art and Meaning: Rhetoric in Biblical Literature,* eds.

David J. A. Clines, David M. Gunn, and Alan J. Hauser (Yorkshire, U.K.: Sheffield, 1982), pp. 72–96. For a clear schematic analysis of this motif, see Walter C. Kaiser, *Toward Old Testament Ethics* (Grand Rapids, Mich.: Zondervan, 1983), pp. 252–256.

5. Maimonides, "The Eighth Chapter," in *Ethical Writings of Maimonides,* ed. Raymond L. Weiss (New York: Dover Publications, 1975), pp. 89–90.

6. Neil Gillman, *Sacred Fragments: Recovering Theology for the Modern Jew* (Philadelphia: Jewish Publication Society, 1990), p. 191.

7. *New Studies in Shemot (Exodus),* vol. 1, p. 156.

8. Aviva Gottlieb Zornberg, *The Particulars of Rapture: Reflections on Exodus* (New York: Doubleday, 2001), pp. 104–105.

9. Jonah 4:11.

10. Jack Miles, *God: A Biography* (New York: Vintage Books, 1996).

11. *Pirke de Rabbi Eliezer,* pp. 341–342.

Chapter 8—The Festival of Spring

1. *Mekhilta of Rabbi Ishmael, Piskha* 17:100, vol. 1, p. 149. Passover often occurs on the first full moon after the vernal equinox, but due to the periodic insertion of an extra month into the Jewish calendar, it sometimes falls on the second full moon after the equinox.

2. Oded Borowski, *Agriculture in Iron Age Israel* (Winona Lake, Ind.: Eisenbrauns, 1987), p. 88.

3. Irving Greenberg, *The Jewish Way: Living the Holidays* (New York: Summit Books, 1988), p. 60.

4. Mirce Eliade, *The Myth of the Eternal Return* (New York: Pantheon Books, 1954), pp. 89, 95.

5. Stephen J. Gould, *Time's Arrow: Time's Cycle* (Cambridge: Harvard University Press, 1987), pp. 10–19.

6. Eliade, *The Myth of the Eternal Return,* p. 156

7. The blessing comes from BT, Sanhedrin 42a.

8. Mirce Eliade, *Patterns in Comparative Religion* (Cleveland: Meridian Books, 1963), pp. 155, 176.

9. Eliade, *The Myth of the Eternal Return,* p. 95.

10. Hayyim Schauss, *The Jewish Festivals: From Their Beginnings to Our Own Day* (New York: Union of American Hebrew Congregations, 1938), p. 39.

11. Scholarly inquiry into the origins of Passover is in part derived from subtle variations in the description of the festival in the Bible. For a good overview of these differences see *Etz Hayim,* pp. 1456–1459.

12. See Schauss, *The Jewish Festivals,* pp. 38–43.

13. Borowski, *Agriculture in Iron Age Israel,* pp. 158–161. The Bible provides an example of just such an event. When the people sinned, Samuel called on God to punish them by destroying their crops. "It is the season of the wheat harvest. I will pray to Adonai and He will send thunder and rain; then you will take thought and realize what a wicked thing you did. . . . Adonai sent thunder and rain that day . . ." (I Samuel 12:17-18).

14. J. B. Segal's *The Hebrew Passover: From the Earliest Times to A.D. 70* (London: Oxford University Press, 1963) provides the basis for this section on the relationship between Passover and ancient New Year's festivals.

15. Johannes Pedersen, *Israel: Its Life and Culture,* vols. 3 and 4 (London: Oxford University Press, 1940), p. 384.

16. See Glen J. Taylor, "Yahweh and the Sun: Biblical and Archeological Evidence for Sun Worship in Ancient Israel," in *Journal for the Study of the Old Testament:* Supplement Series 111 (1993): p. 91.

17. Commentary on BT, Pesachim 116a.

18. Eileen Abrams, "Grow Your Own — Barley, That Is!" in *Ecology and the Jewish Spirit: Where Nature and the Sacred Meet,* ed. Ellen Bernstein (Woodstock, Vt.: Jewish Lights, 1998), pp. 157–159.

19. According to Jewish law, it is permissible to recite the blessing over the new moon at any point in the month—when the full moon is clearly visible—until the full moon begins to wane. Due to the complexities of the Jewish calendar, the full moon sometimes occurs before the fifteenth of a Hebrew month. In that case, it would not be appropriate to recite the blessing for the new moon on Passover because the moon would already have begun to wane. The easiest way to make sure you can bless the new moon on the first Seder is to check Ezras Torah on the web at www.ezrastorah.org. Click on "Calendar" and then "Nisan."

20. *Kol Haneshamah: Shabbat Vehagim* (Wyncote, Pa.: The Reconstructionist Press, 1996), p. 332. This is actually only about half of the prayer.

21. BT, Shabbat 118b.

22. Philo, *The Special Laws,* vol. 7, ed. F. H. Colson (Cambridge: Harvard University Press, 1937), pp. 399–405.

23. Bachya ben Joseph Ibn Paquda, *Duties of the Heart,* trans. Moses Hyamson (Jerusalem: Boys Town Publishers, 1962), p. 171.

24. Rebbe Nachman of Breslav, "*Likkutei MoHaRan:* Rabbi Nachman's Wisdom," in *A Garden of Choice Fruit: 200 Classic Jewish Quotes on Human Beings and the Environment,* ed. David E. Stein (Wyncote, Pa.: Shomrei Adamah, 1991), p. 56.

25. Heschel, *God in Search of Man,* pp. 34, 36.

26. In Dov Peretz Elkins, *A Shabbat Reader: Universe of Cosmic Joy* (New York: URJ Press, 1999), p. 169.

27. *The Nation,* March 24, 2008.

Chapter 9—The Exodus as a Personal Spiritual Journey

1. See pages 48–49. This illustrates Rav's vision of where the journey leads—the end of days: a time of uninterrupted mystical cleaving to God.

2. See "Pathways of the Prophets—Life in the Fast Lane," an audiotape by Rabbi Yisrael Reisman (available through Yeshiva Tiferes Yisroel, 1271 East 35th Street, Brooklyn, NY 11210).

3. Isaiah Horowitz, *Shnei Luchot Ha-Brit, Matzah Shmurah,* 1. *Judaic Classics II.* Davka CD-ROM version (Hebrew).

4. Joel Ziff, *Mirrors in Time: A Psycho-Spiritual Journey through the Jewish Year* (Northvale, N.J.: Jason Aronson, 1996), p. 73.

5. *The Breslov Haggadah,* ed. Yehoshua Starret (Jerusalem: Breslov Research Institute, 1989), p. 54.

6. Martin Buber, *Tales of the Hasidim,* vol. 1 (New York: Schocken Books, 1947), p. 313.

7. Quoted in *Kol Haneshamah: Shabbat Vehagim: The Reconstructionist Prayer Book* (Wyncote, Pa.: The Reconstructionist Press, 1996), p. 284.

8. Warren Kenton, *Kabbalah and Exodus* (Bath, England: Gateway, 1988).

9. See Isaiah Horowitz, *Shnei Luchot Ha-Brit, Masechet Pesachim, Matzah Shmurah,* 2. *Judaic Classics Library II.* Davka CD-ROM version (Hebrew). These ideas led to the inclusion in many Ashkenazic Haggadot of a passage from Ezekiel (16:6) mentioning circumcision. See *Scholar's Haggadah,* p. 42.

10. Yehudah Leib Alter, *The Torah Commentary of the Sefat Emet,* trans. and inter. Arthur Green (Philadelphia: Jewish Publication Society, 1998), p. 390.

11. *Mekhilta of Rabbi Ishmael, Beshalach* 6:32, vol. 1, p. 234.

12. BT, Sotah 37a.

13. Martin Buber, *Moses: The Revelation and the Covenant* (Atlantic Highlands, N.J.: Humanities Press International, 1988), p. 75.

14. The Song at the Sea, the Bible's first song, begins with *aleph* (*ashir,* "I will sing . . ."), the first letter of the Hebrew alphabet. As Lawrence Kushner notes, "*Aleph* has no

sound. Only the sound you make when you begin to make every sound . . . The most basic words there are begin with the most primal sound there is." Lawrence Kushner, *The Book of Letters: A Mystical Aleph-bait* (Woodstock, Vt.: Jewish Lights, 1990), pp. 21–23.

15. There is some question as to whether the term *shira* in the context of this song refers to a musical song or a spoken form of poetry. See *The Anchor Bible: Exodus 1–18,* ed. William C. Propp (New York: Doubleday, 1998), p. 508.

16. Heschel, *God in Search of Man,* pp. 46–47, 281.

17. BT, Pesachim 118a suggests that Benediction of Song may also refer to *Yihallelukha,* a prayer that comes in the Haggadah just before Psalm 136. It refers to singing praise to God.

18. *The Breslov Haggadah,* p. 58. See also Joseph B. Soloveitchik, "Redemption, Prayer and Talmud Torah," in *Tradition,* 17:2, Spring 1978, p. 56.

19. Tamar Elad-Appelbaum, "Dancing the Unbounded Soul," Seventh Day of Passover Sermon, Temple Israel Center, White Plains, N.Y., 2010.

20. Abraham Joshua Heschel, *Man Is Not Alone* (Philadelphia: Jewish Publication, 1951), p. 153.

Chapter 10—Enslaved in Egypt

1. *Seder Olam Rabbah,* with translation and commentary by Heinrich W. Guggenheimer (Northvale, N.J.: Jason Aronson, 1998), pp. 37–41. See also Numbers 26:59.

2. *Mekhilta of Rabbi Ishmael, Pischa* 14:60, vol. 1, p. 112.

3. Moshe Weinfeld, "The Covenant of Grant in the Old Testament and in the Ancient Near East," in *Journal of the American Oriental Society,* vol. 90, 1970, pp. 184–203.

4. See Rabbi David Silber, "The Passover Haggadah—The Wandering Aramean," audiotape from the Drisha Institute, 131 West 86th Street, New York, NY 10024 (www.drisha.org/programs/tape.htm).

5. BT, Sotah 11a.

6. Thanks to Rabbi Gilbert Rosenthal for raising these issues.

7. *New Studies in Shemot,* pp. 1–11; Mordechai Winiarz, "The Reasons for the Bondage," in *The Yeshiva University Haggadah,* eds. Steven F. Cohen and Kenneth Brander (New York: Yeshiva University, 1985), pp. 48–52.

8. Genesis Rabbah 45:1.

9. Ramban, Genesis 16:6, pp. 173–174, 213.

10. Yair Zakovitch, *And You Shall Tell Your Son: The Concept of the Exodus in the Bible* (Jerusalem: Magnes Press/Hebrew University, 1991), pp. 15–45.

11. Ovadia Sforno, *Commentary on the Torah,* trans. Raphael Pelcovitz (Brooklyn: Mesorah Publications, 1997), p. 281.

12. Yitzchak Arama, *Akeydat Yitzchak,* vol. 2, trans. Eliyahu Munk (Jerusalem: Lambda Publishers, 2001), p. 304.

13. *New Studies in Shemot,* pp. 7–8.

14. E.g., Ecclesiastes Rabbah 9:18.

15. Numbers Rabbah 13:3 makes a similar point about Joseph. The BT, Chullin 60b, seems palpably dismayed that the tale of Joseph's treatment of the Egyptians was even included in the Torah.

16. *Or HaChayim* on Genesis 47:15; *Judaic Classic Library II,* Davka, CD-ROM version (Hebrew). Thanks to Elie Kaunfer for pointing out the common verb used to describe the shrewdness of both Joseph and Pharaoh.

17. For some reason, in this context, *avadim* is generally translated as "bondmen," "servants," or "serfs," instead of "slaves." *Avadim* can certainly carry all those meanings, but in this particular context "slave" seems most appropriate.

18. The Midrash, which specializes in finding relationships between similar wordings in different texts, remains amazingly silent on the connection between *v'hayinu avadim l'pharaoh* (Gen. 47:25) and *avadim hayinu l'pharaoh* (Deut. 6:21). For one of the rare contemporary comments on this, see Zakovitch, p. 39 (see note 7). On the general paucity of comment on Joseph's "reign," see W. Gunther Plaut, "The Trace of Joseph: A Commentary on Genesis 47:13–27," in *CCAR Journal,* 9:6, October 1961, pp. 29–32, 40.

19. *Etz Hayim,* p. 288.

20. BT, Shabbat 10b.

21. *The Talmud: Steinsaltz Edition,* vol. 21, Sanhedrin part 7 (New York: Random House, 1999), p. 36.

22. Zohar, Shemoth, Section 2, p. 12b. Elsewhere the Zohar (Bereshit, section 1, 142a) also sets the stolen blessing on Passover, but evinces little sympathy for Esau's tears. Genesis Rabbah (67:4) also highlights the grave consequences of Jacob's theft of his brother's blessing. Sometimes the Bible itself speaks pejoratively of how Jacob treated Esau. For example, in cataloging the evils that lead to the destruction of Jerusalem, Jeremiah (9:3) uses a wordplay involving the name of Jacob/Ya'akov: "[T]rust not even a brother! For every brother takes advantage" or is a deceitful supplanter, *ach 'akov ya'kov.* See Michael Fishbane, *Biblical Interpretation in Ancient Israel* (New York: Clarendon Press, 1985), pp. 376–379.

23. *Pirke de Rabbi Eliezer,* pp. 236–237. The midrash expands on the fact that the blessing Isaac gave to Jacob and Esau both referred to "the dew of heaven" (Gen. 27:28, 40), and that the recitation of the Prayer for Dew occurs on the first day of Passover.

Chapter 11—"Strangers in a Land Not Theirs"

1. *New Studies in Shemot,* p. 380.

2. BT, Shabbat 31a.

3. Rabbi Lester Bronstein points out that the same verbs for "crying out" and "heeding" in this verse also appear in Deut. 26:7, part of the Haggadah's principal text for telling the story of the Exodus. God will heed the cry of the stranger just as God heard our cry in Egypt.

4. Thanks to Ariella Sidelsky for her help with the composition of this blessing.

5. H. G. Enelow, *The Mishnah of Rabbi Eliezer or the Midrash of Thirty Two Hermeneutic Rules* (New York: Bloch Publishing, 1933), chapter 16, p. 301.

6. Ruth was also a Moabite, one of the groups permanently barred entry into "the congregation of Adonai" (Deuteronomy 23:4). Since the prohibition was written in the masculine, it was understood only to apply to Moabite males, not females, such as Ruth. See Mishnah Yevamot 8:3 and Sifre on Deuteronomy, 249.

7. *Pesikta Chadatta* in A. Jellinek, *Bet HaMidrasch* (Jerusalem: Sifre Wahrmann, 1967), vol. 6, p. 38.

8. Chaim Weizmann, *Trial and Error* (New York: Harper and Brothers, 1949), pp. 461–462.

9. Quoted in Shlomo Avineri, *The Making of Modern Zionism* (New York: Basic Books, 1981), p. 164.

10. *The 2008 Sikkuy Report: The Equality Index of Jewish and Arab Citizens in Israel* (www.sikkuy.org), pp. 24, 55, and 61.

11. The recitation derives from the tradition of Isaac Luria, the great sixteenth-century Kabbalist. See for example the prayer book used by Chabad, *Siddur Tehillas Hashem: According to the Nusach of the ARI Z"l* (Brooklyn: Kehot Publication Society, 1993), p. 12. The custom also appears in the prayer book of the Conservative Movement. See *Siddur Sim Shalom for Weekdays* (New York: The Rabbinical Assembly/United Synagogue of Conservative Judaism, 2002), p. 4. In Exodus 11:2, *re'a* refers to the Egyptians from whom the Israelites are told to "borrow" silver and gold.

Chapter 12—"In Every Generation . . ."?

1. This passage begins with the Hebrew word *v'hi,* literally, "and she." Most commentators hold that the pronoun refers to the promise in the previous paragraph. Zvi Yehudah Kalisher (1795–1874) suggested that *v'hi,* "and she," refers to the Shekhinah, the feminine aspects of God's immanence, often said to accompany Israel in exile. See Mayer Irwin Gruber, "The Jewish Goddess in an Orthodox Haggadah," in *Conservative Judaism,* 38:3, 1986, pp. 62–65.

2. See Rabbi Silber, "The Passover Haggadah."

3. *Haggadah of the Sages,* p. 271.

4. Steven M. Cohen, *Content or Continuity: The 1989 National Survey of American Jews* (New York: American Jewish Committee, 1991), p. 67. According to Cohen (personal communication), there is not a more recent survey that asks this question.

5. Ana-Maria Rizzuto, *The Birth of the Living God: A Psychoanalytic Study* (Chicago: University of Chicago Press, 1979).

6. Anthony Flew, "Divine Omnipotence and Human Freedom," in *New Essays in Philosophical Theology,* eds. Anthony Flew and Alasdair MacIntyre (London: SCM Press, 1955), p. 144.

7. Joseph Albo, *Sefer Ha-Ikarim,* vol. 2 (The Book of Principles), trans. Isaac Husik (Philadelphia: Jewish Publication Society, 1929), p. 206.

8. Elliot N. Dorff, *Knowing God: Jewish Journeys to the Unknowable* (Northvale, N.J.: Jason Aronson, 1992), p. 130, 148.

9. Ibid., p. 130.

10. Anson Laytner, *Arguing with God: A Jewish Tradition* (Northvale, N.J.: Jason Aronson, 1998), pp. 16–23.

11. Joseph Heinemann, *Prayer in the Talmud* (Berlin: Walter de Gruyter, 1977), p. 205.

12. Mishnah, Ta'anit 3:8.

13. For an excellent discussion that refers to many of these texts, see Marvin Fox, "Theodicy and Anti-Theodicy in Biblical and Rabbinic Literature," in *Theodicy,* ed. Dan Cohn-Sherbok (Lewiston, Maine: The Edwin Mellon Press, 1997), pp. 33–49.

14. Mishnah, Berakhot 9:2.

15. Martin Buber, *Tales of the Hasidim,* vol. 1 (New York: Schocken Books, 1947), pp. 212–213.

16. *The Jewish Moral Virtues,* eds. Eugene B. Borowitz and Frances Weinman Schwartz (Philadelphia: Jewish Publication Society, 1999), p. 300.

17. Emmanuel Levinas, "To Love the Torah More Than God," in *Loving the Torah More Than God?* ed. Franz Jozef Van Beek (Chicago: Loyola University Press, 1989), pp. 37–38.

18. Heschel, *Man Is Not Alone*, p. 151.

19. Richard Rubinstein, *After Auschwitz* (New York: Bobbs-Merrill Company, 1966), pp. 152–153.

20. David Weiss Halivni, *The Book and the Sword: A Life of Learning in the Shadow of the Holocaust* (New York: Westview Press, 1996), p. 3, unnumbered.

21. Joseph B. Soloveitchik, "*Kol Dodi Dofek:* It Is the Voice of My Beloved That Knocketh," in *Theological and Halakhic Reflections on the Holocaust,* ed. Bernard H. Rosenberg (Hoboken, N.J.: KTAV Publishing, 1992), p. 54.

22. Harold S. Kushner, *When Bad Things Happen to Good People* (New York: Schocken Books, 1981), pp. 53, 55.

23. Eliezer Berkovitz, *Faith after the Holocaust* (New York: KTAV Publishing House, 1973), p. 158.

24. Milton Steinberg, *Basic Judaism* (New York: Harcourt, Brace and World, 1947), p. 48.

25. Lawrence Kushner, *God Was in This Place and I, i Did Not Know* (Woodstock, Vt.: Jewish Lights, 1991), p. 122.

26. David Biale, *Power and Powerless in Jewish History* (New York: Schocken Books, 1986), p. 210.

Chapter 13—"Go Out and Learn . . ."

1. *Haggadah: Sources and History,* p. 30.

2. Mishnah, Sotah 7:1 and Bikkurim 3:7.

3. Moshe Weinfeld, *Deuteronomy and the Deuteronomic School* (Oxford, U.K.: Clarendon Press, 1972), pp. 32–34.

4. See Rabbi Silber, "The Passover Haggadah."

5. David Daube, "He That Cometh," St. Paul's Lecture, London, October 1966, p. 12.

6. Nehama Leibowitz, *New Studies in Devarim/Deuteronomy* (Jerusalem: The Joint Authority for Jewish Zionist Education, 1993), p. 374.

7. Baruch M. Bokser, *The Origins of the Seder: The Passover Rite and Early Rabbinic Judaism* (Berkeley: University of California Press, 1984). Bokser analyzes the evolution of the Seder as a response to the Temple's destruction. He notes (p. 72) that, for the Rabbis, "Study became the highest form of piety and a ritual in its own right. The Mishnah's requirement to expound the formulaic account of Jewish history, set out in Deuteronomy 26:5ff, reflects this new dimension of study and distinct type of encounter with the biblical text."

8. BT, Menachot 110a.

9. Joseph B. Soloveitchik, "The Nine Aspects of the Haggadah," in *The Haggadah of Yeshiva University,* eds. Steven F. Cohen and Kenneth Brander (Jerusalem: Koren Publishers, 1985), p. 8.

10. The grammatical details need not concern us here. See Leibowitz, *Studies in Deuteronomy,* pp. 269–273.

11. *Haggadah: Sources and History,* p. 34.

12. See Rashi's Torah commentary on Deuteronomy 26:5.

13. *Hagadah Shelemah,* p. 125.

14. *Or HaChayim on Deuteronomy* 26:5, Davka, CD-ROM version (Hebrew).

15. Menachem Kasher, *Torah Shelemah,* vol. 8 (Jerusalem: Torah Shelemah Institute, 1944), pp. 243–44 (Hebrew).

16. For the best discussion of all of these issues see Karin Hedner Zetterholm, *Portrait of a Villain: Laban the Aramean in Rabbinic Literature* (Leuven: Peeters, 2002).

17. Marcus Jastrow, *A Dictionary of the Targumim, the Talmud Babli and Yerushalmi, and the Midrashic Literature* (New York: Judaica Press, 1996), p. 122.

18. E.g. Tanchumah (Buber) Ekev 5, Midrash Ha' Gadol, on Gen. 31:22–33.

19. These terms appear in Genesis 31:41, 42, and 32:5. See Rabbi David Silber, "The Passover Haggadah."

20. Weinfeld, *Deuteronomy and the Deuteronomic School,* pp. 206–207.

21. Gerhard von Rad, *Old Testament Theology: The Theology of Israel's Historical Tradition,* vol. 1 (New York: Harper & Row, 1962), p. 122. See also Lawrence A. Hoffman, *Beyond the Text: A Holistic Approach to Liturgy* (Bloomington: Indiana University Press, 1987), chapter 5.

Chapter 14—Women of the Exodus

1. Exodus Rabbah 1:12 and BT, Sotah 11b (sometimes attributed to Rabbi Avira).

2. BT, Pesachim 116a. Akiva's midrash quotes the Song of Songs (8:5): "Under the apple tree I roused you; it was there your mother conceived you, there she bore you."

3. This is based on David Arnow, "Yocheved's Lesson: Decisive Action Is in Order When the World Seems Upside Down," in *Forward,* March 29, 2002.

4. The song is: "And You Shall Say: 'It Is the Sacrifice of Passover.'"

5. Tal Ilan, *Integrating Women into Second Temple History* (Tubingen: Mohr Siebeck, 1999), chapter 1.

6. Theodore Friedman, "The Shifting Role of Women, from the Bible to Talmud," in *Judaism,* 36:4, Fall 1987, p. 479; "Yocheved's Lesson," 487; Eileen Schuller, "Women of

the Exodus in Biblical Retellings of the Second Temple Period," in *Gender Difference in Ancient Israel,* ed. Peggy L. Daly (Minneapolis: Fortress Press, 1989), pp. 178–194.

7. Blake Layerle, "Meal Customs in the Greco-Roman World," in *Passover and Easter,* especially pp. 43–45. If there was indeed a trend toward excluding women from symposia, this was an element of Hellenism the Rabbis were not prepared to accept when it came to the Seder. Women's participation in the Seder is indicated from a number of sources. A pre-Talmudic legal code known as the Tosefta (Pesachim 10:4) states that "a man is commanded to make his children and his wife happy on the holiday. With what does he make them happy? With wine . . ." The BT (Pesachim 116a) indicates that if a man's son cannot ask the four questions, his wife should.

8. Judith Plaskow, *Standing Again at Sinai: Judaism from a Feminist Perspective* (San Francisco: Harper, 1991), p. 1.

9. This "synthetic midrash" combines material from the following sources: Exodus Rabbah 1:15, 1:26, 18:3; Leviticus Rabbah 1:3; BT, Sotah 12a–13a; *Mekhilta of Rabbi Ishmael, Shirata* 10:64, p 81; *Midrash HaGadol* 2:14, as quoted in *Legends,* vol. 2, p. 270; *Derech Eretz Zuta,* as quoted in *Legends,* vol. 5, pp. 95–96. Notwithstanding the references to first born sons in Ex. 4:23 and 13:12, the Bible is ambiguous as to whether the tenth plague, slaying of the Egyptian firstborn, killed just males as is commonly understood. The legend that Pharaoh's daughter, Bitya, was spared the last plague because she rescued Moses from the Nile reflects a midrashic tradition that this plague struck both males and females. See for example *Pesikta Rabbati* 17:5 (W.G. Braude, p. 368) and the *Shulchan Arukh* (470:1). Thanks to Alvan and Elie Kaunfer for bringing these two sources to my attention.

10. Suzanne Scholz, "The Complexities of 'His' Liberation Talk: A Literary Feminist Reading of the Book of Exodus," in *Exodus to Deuteronomy: A Feminist Companion to the Bible* (Second Series), eds. Athalya Brenner and Carole R. Fontaine (Sheffield, U.K.: Sheffield Academic Press, 2000), pp. 26–27.

11. Ramban (Gen. 2:9), pp. 70–71. Also see Maimonides, *Guide of the Perplexed,* ed. Sholomo Pines (Chicago: University of Chicago Press, 1963), pp. 23–26, part 1 chapter 2.

12. Martin Buber, "The Tree of Knowledge," in *On the Bible,* ed. Nahum Glatzer (Syracuse: Syracuse University Press, 2000), p. 21.

13. Exodus Rabbah 18:6.

14. Fox. All four of these passages have been ascribed to the J source, an author thought to have lived in Judea between 848 and 722 B.C.E. See Richard Elliott Friedman,

Who Wrote the Bible? (New York: Harper & Row, 1987), pp. 246–251. Common authorship suggests that the use of these terms expresses a subtle, but intentional, linkage of Eden and Exodus.

15. BT, Sotah 11b, compares the posture of a birthing woman to that of a potter. In quoting Jeremiah 18:3 in which the prophet describes God as a potter, the Talmud points to the godliness of women's role in procreation.

16. This "synthetic midrash" combines material from the following sources: BT, Sotah 13a; Genesis Rabbah 94:9; Exodus Rabbah 5:13; Deuteronomy Rabbah 11:7; and Ecclesiastes Rabbah 9:28. For Serakh's words to Jacob, see *Midrash HaGadol,* ed. Mordecai Margulies (Jerusalem: Mosad HaRav Kook, 1947), p. 766, on Genesis 45:26. For the confrontation between Serakh and ben Zakkai, see Jacob Neusner, *Pesikta de-Rav Kahana: An Analytical Translation,* vol. 1 (11:13) (Atlanta: Scholars Press, 1987). For two excellent and comprehensive treatments of Serakh, see "Serah bat Asher: The Transformative Power of Aggadic Invention," in Leila Leah Broner, *From Eve to Esther: Rabbinic Reconstructions of Biblical Women* (Louisville: Westminster John Knox Press, 1994), pp. 42–60; and Rachel Adelman, "Serakh bat Asher: Songstress, Poet, and Woman of Wisdom," in *Torah of Our Mothers,* eds. Ora Wiskind Elper and Susan Handelman (New York: Urim Publications, 2000), pp. 218–243. See also Aviva Gottlieb Zornberg, *The Beginning of Desire: Reflections on Genesis* (New York: Doubleday, 1995), pp. 280–283.

17. The midrash elaborates on the actions of a bold and "clever woman" described in II Samuel 21.

18. Phyllis Trible, "Bringing Miriam Out of the Shadows," in *Bible Review* 5:1, February 1989, p. 23.

19. Moses Isserles, gloss on the *Shulchan Arukh* (299:10), the great sixteenth-century legal code.

20. The lyrics pertaining to Miriam were composed by Leila Gal Berner.

21. *ArtScroll Tanakh* (New York: Mesorah Publications, 1996).

22. Thanks to Riva Silverman for many of these insights.

Chapter 15—The Ten Plagues

1. The identity of the fourth plague is unclear. The term *arov* literally means "mixture" and is generally interpreted as swarms of insects or wild beasts.

2. Although the above list of the plagues may sound familiar, identifying the ten plagues in the Book of Exodus is not so simple. Indeed, Psalms 78 and 105 enumerate seven plagues, each with a slightly different list. Rabbi Yehuda's acronym asserts the primacy

of this particular enumeration of the plagues. For an excellent treatment of the plagues, including their literary structure, see Nachum M. Sarna, *Exploring Exodus* (New York: Schocken Books, 1986), chapter 4.

3. *Torat Chaim* vol. on Exodus (7:24) (Jerusalem: Mossad Harav Kook, 1993), p. 83 (Hebrew). *Etz Hayim* (p. 362) supports this position. Regarding the fourth plague, it comments: "For the first time, a clear distinction is made between the Egyptians and the Israelites."

4. Ramban, Exodus 8:18.

5. Elazar ben Judah of Worms (c. 1176–1238), *Drasha L'Pesach*, ed. Simcha Emanuel (Jerusalem: Mekize Nirdamim, 2006), p. 101.

6. *The Book of Maharil: Customs by Rabbi Yaacov Mulin*, ed. Shlomoh J. Spitzer (Jerusalem: Mifal Torath Chachmey Ashkenaz, 1989), p. 106.

7. *The Yeshiva University Haggadah*, p. 19. The attribution to Abarbanel's Haggadah commentary, *Zevach Pesach*, is widespread but appears erroneous. Goldschmidt (*Passover Haggadah*, Tel Aviv: Schocken, 1947, p. 22) attributes this interpretation to Samson Raphael Hirsch and Edouard Baneth. Baneth writes: "[The wine] is removed because each plague that our persecutors suffered to bring about our freedom diminished the joy of our liberation . . . The custom breathes the spirit of the essence of Judaism." Baneth, *Der Sederabend* (Berlin: M. Poppelauer, 1904), p. 28. Thanks to Peter Reimold for translating the German.

8. *Legends*, vol. 3, pp. 22–25. Midrash *Va-Yosha*, pp. 39–40.

9. *Yalkut Shimoni* on *Emor*, 654, quoted in *The Book of Legends*, no. 111 (*Sefer Ha-Aggadah*), eds. Hayim Nahman Bialik and Yehoshua Hana Ravnitzky, trans. William G. Braude (New York: Schocken Books, 1992), p. 499.

10. Franz Rozenzweig, *The Star of Redemption* (Notre Dame: Notre Dame Press, 1985, 1921), p. 317.

11. See also Samuel E. Lowenstamm, *The Evolution of the Exodus Tradition* (Jerusalem: Magnes Press/Hebrew University, 1992), pp. 111–128.

12. *New Studies in Shemot*, pp. 170–177. Leibowitz (p. 171) mentions that these ten references to knowing Adonai correspond to the Ten Commandments given to the Israelites. For a midrashic treatment, see *Pesikta Rabbati* (Piskha 21:20), trans. William G. Braude (New Haven: Yale University Press, 1968), pp. 446–447.

13. This is the first time in the Bible that God speaks through a human intermediary and the first time God seeks to overcome human skepticism. See Jack Miles, *God: A Biography*, pp. 102–103.

14. Exodus 8:6; 8:18; 9:14; 9:29.

15. For a fascinating discussion of whether Pharaoh eventually comes to know God, see Zornberg, *The Particulars of Rapture,* p. 152.

16. H. H. Schmid, "Creation, Righteousness, and Salvation," in *Creation in the Old Testament,* ed. Bernhard W. Anderson (Philadelphia: Fortress Press, 1984), p. 105.

17. It has been argued that the plagues involved a chain of natural events. Occasional super-floods washed down red microorganisms from the Ethiopian highlands, upsetting the ecology of the Nile. Frogs sought higher ground, etc. See Greta Hort, "The Plagues of Egypt," in *Zeitschrift Für Die Alttestamentliche Wissenchaft* vol. 69, 1957, pp. 84–103, and vol. 70, 1958, pp. 48–59 (English). Many scholars have rejected this approach, because the relevant biblical passages are thought to derive from different sources and because the plagues as recounted in Psalms 78 and 105 differ in number and sequence from those in Exodus (and from each other). This suggests distinct oral traditions about the plagues that would not fit with the naturalistic explanation of the plagues as they occur in Exodus. See Propp, ed. *The Anchor Bible: Exodus 1–18,* p. 347.

18. S.G.F. Brandon, *Creation Legends of the Ancient Near East* (London: Hodder and Stoughton, 1963), pp. 16–17.

19. Exodus Rabbah 22:1. A related version of this midrash appears in BT, Sotah 11a.

20. Mishnah, Avot 5:1. Ziony Zevit, "Three Ways to Look at the Ten Plagues," in *Bible Review* 6:3, June 1990, p. 23. These pronouncements refer to the ten occurrences of *vay-omer* ("and He said") in the context of God's creation of the cosmos in Genesis. In the Bible, precise identification of some of the things most taken for granted, such as the ten plagues and the Ten Commandments, proves challenging. So, too, with the ten utterances of creation. Zevit lists the following: Genesis 1:3, 6, 9, 11, 14, 20, 24, 26, 28, 29.

21. This material comes primarily from three sources: Ziony Zevit, "The Priestly Redaction and Interpretation of the Plague Narrative in Exodus," in *The Jewish Quarterly Review* 66:4, April 1976, pp. 193–211; Ziony Zevit, "Three Ways to Look at the Ten Plagues" (see note 19); and Terrence E. Fretheim, part III "The Plagues," in *Exodus* (Louisville: John Knox Press, 1991).

22. This appears in several psalms, such as 74 and 80, in Job 26:1–13, and in sections of Isaiah, including 51:9–10.

Chapter 16—Moses in the Haggadah

1. For a more extensive treatment of this subject see, David Arnow, "The Passover Haggadah: Moses and the Human Role in Redemption," in *Judaism,* 55, 2006. (See www.livelyseders.com, "Moses and the Haggadah.") This article ascribes the origins of this myth to a misunderstanding of a commentary by the Vilna Gaon. This commen-

tary may well reflect his animus toward Hasidism and what he believed was a dangerous tendency to deify the movement's holy men. For a contrasting treatment of Moses in the Haggadah, see David Henshke, "'The Lord Brought Us Forth from Egypt': On the Absence of Moses in the Passover Haggadah," *AJS Review*, 31, 2007, pp. 61–73.

2. Shmuel and Ze'ev Safrai, *Haggadah of the Sages*, English edition (Jerusalem: Carta, 2009), p. 124.

3. Mamonides, *Laws of Chametz and Matzah* 7:2.

4. *Mekhilta of Rabbi Ishmael*, vol. 1, p. 251, *Beshalach* 7:110.

5. Mishnah Avot 5:6. The other objects were: the mouth of the earth that swallowed Korah (Numbers 16:30); Miriam's well (Numbers 21:16–18); Balaam's talking ass (Numbers 22:28); the rainbow (Genesis 9:13); manna; the Shamir, a worm that cut stone; the text of the Ten Commandments; the writing with which the commandments were incised; and the actual tablets of the commandments.

6. BT, Sanhedrin 38b identifies "the messenger" as Metatron and suggests that Metatron was the guardian angel of sorts whom God sent to protect Israel (Exodus 23:20–23). Medieval commentators likewise identify Metatron as "the messenger." See Nachmanides on Exodus 12:12 and the Haggadah commentaries of Yom Tov ben Abraham Ishbili and Shimon ben Tzemach Duran in *Haggadat Torat Chayim*, ed. Mordecai Leib Katznelbogen (Jerusalem: Mosad Harav Kook, 1998), pp. 107–108.

7. *Mekhilta of Rabbi Ishmael*, vol.1, p. 53, *Pischa* 7:28; vol. 2, pp. 231–232, *Bachodesh* 5:20.

8. See Daniel Boyarin, *Border Lines: The Partition of Judaeo-Christianity* (Philadelphia: University of Pennsylvania Press, 2004).

9. Jubilees is one of many ancient texts known as Pseudepigrapha and Apocrypha that were excluded from Jewish and many Christian canonical traditions. The word *mastema* appears in Hosea 9:7, 8.

10. Sifre on Deuteronomy, piska 42.

11. The Samaritan Bible reads: "*He* will grant the rain . . ."

12. Deuteronomy Rabbah 11:4.

13. Midrash Lekach Tov, V'zot Ha'brachah 61b. See Samuel E. Loewenstamm, "The Death of Moses," in *Studies on the Testament of Abraham*, ed. George W. E. Nickelsburg (Missoula, Mont.: Scholars Press, 1976), pp. 185–186.

14. For a midrash on this subject, see pp. 293–294.

15. BT, Sotah 11b (sometimes attributed to Rabbi Avira).

16. The Yemenite tradition places these phrases in a different order, and the Sephardic tradition eliminates the last phrase.

17. From the point of view of Jewish law, it's worth noting that a festival cancels many of the rites of mourning.

18. On the fifteenth of Nisan, the first night of Passover, Esther arranged a "wine feast" for the king and approached him for a fateful audience. She requested his permission for a second wine feast the next night, at which she intended to engineer Haman's downfall. Esther's plan succeeded, and the king executed Haman on the sixteenth of Nisan, the second day of Passover.

19. Scholars disagree about whether the Song of Songs refers to God. Some render *shalhevet'ya* (8:6) as "flame of God"; others as "blazing flame."

20. Michael Strassfeld, *The Jewish Holidays: A Guide and Commentary* (New York: Harper & Row, 1985), p. 197. There are many other Passover/Purim parallels. The Talmud (Shabbat 88a) asserts that at Sinai the Israelites accepted the Torah under divine coercion. They only accepted it freely with the events of Purim. Thanks to David Goshen for bringing this text to my attention.

21. *Mekhilta of Rabbi Ishmael*, vol. 1, p. 249. *Beshalach* 7:89.

22. *Mekhilta of Rabbi Ishmael*, vol. 1, p. 141, *Pischa* 16:171.

23. William G. Braude, *Pesikta de-Rab Kahana*, (Philadelphia: Jewish Publication Society, 2002), p. 412.

24. William G. Braude, *Pesikta Rabbati* (New Haven: Yale University Press, 1968), vol. 2, p. 608.

25. William G. Braude, *The Midrash on Psalms* (New Haven: Yale University Press, 1959), vol. 2, p. 228.

Chapter 17—*Dayyenu*

1. The Haggadah first refers to a "new song" before we sing the first two psalms of the Hallel. As we thank God for bringing us from slavery to freedom . . . from darkness to great light . . . we say, "So let us sing *a new song* to God." The phrase recurs near the end of the blessing over the second cup of wine, just after these two Psalms: "And we will thankfully acknowledge You with *a new song* for our redemption and for the ransoming of our lives." The first is in the feminine form (*shira chadashah*) and the second is masculine (*shir chadash*), both of which occur in the Bible. A fifth- or sixth-century midrash, Song of Songs Rabbah 1:36, explains this by comparing the cycle of Israel's travails—burdened, freed, burdened, freed—to the burden of bearing children. "Because Israel's pains are like those of a female in childbirth, they utter a song before God [*shirah* in the feminine form], but in the world to come, because they will no longer suffer such pains, they will utter a song [*shir*] in the masculine form."

Precisely when these phrases entered the Haggadah is hard to say. The first appears in the Machzor Vitry from the eleventh or twelfth century and the second in Haggadot of the ninth-century Babylonian Geonim.

2. Augustine of Hippo, *Sermons* 336, 1 PL 38, 1472.

3. Denominations differ on the question of using musical instruments on holidays. Orthodoxy forbids this, Reform permits it. In 1970 the Conservative Movement's Committee on Jewish Law and Standards approved the use of acoustic instruments. In Reconstructionist and Conservative synagogues, practice varies.

4. The sources are: Exodus Rabbah 23:4 and *Mekhilta of Rabbi Ishmael, Piskha Shirta,* 2:16, Lauterbach, vol. 2, p. 2. The former counts the Song at the Sea as the first song. The second cites Isaiah 30:29: "For you, there shall be singing as on a night when a festival is hallowed." This source claims that the Israelites sang Hallel on the night of Passover in Egypt. See also Genesis Rabbah 6:2, BT, Pesachim 95b, and Rashi on Isaiah 30:29.

5. The description of Solomon's construction of the Temple shares this view. It began "in the four hundred and eightieth year after the Israelites left the land of Egypt" (I Kings: 6:1). Excluding a few instances in the Five Books of Moses, this is the only event in the rest of the entire Bible that is dated in relation to the Exodus! The Torah itself dates a few events in relation to the Exodus, such as the death of Aaron (Numbers 33:38) and Moses' address to the Israelites at the beginning of Deuteronomy (1:3). Nahum M. Sarna, *Exploring Exodus: The Origins of Biblical Israel* (New York: Schocken Books, 1986), pp. 100–102.

6. Jacob ben Asher (Spain, fourteenth century) seems to have been the first to refer to a midrashic tradition that found fifteen divine praises in the Song at the Sea. He notes that in the daily liturgy the Song at the Sea precedes *Yishtabach,* which also includes fifteen praises of God (Tur, Orach Chayim, 51). Ben Asher and other medieval commentators seem to have been familiar with a midrashic source on this subject that has since been lost. The midrash may have been related to Midrash Hagadol on Ex. 15:19, which discusses the Song at the Sea as the basis for why the daily *Amidah* includes eighteen blessings.

7. Louis Finkelstein, "Pre-Maccabean Documents in the Passover Haggadah," in *Harvard Theological Review,* vol. 36, Jan. 1943, pp. 1–38, especially pp. 1–8.

8. Psalms 78 and 105 and Nehemiah 9 also include Exodus reviews. See Theodore A. Bergren, "The Tradition History of the Exodus-Review in 5 Ezra 1," in *Of Scribes and Sages: Early Jewish Interpretation and Transmission of Scripture,* vol. 2. ed. Craig Evans (London: T & T Clark International, 2004), pp. 34–50. Some scholars maintain that

Dayyenu was the model for a series of Christian Exodus reviews that cast Jews in a distinctly negative light. Others argue that *Dayyenu* was a response to these Christian polemics. See Israel J. Yuval, "Easter and Passover as Early Jewish-Christian Dialogue," in *Passover and Easter,* pp. 98–124. A case for either of these positions can certainly be made. The fact Hebrew Scripture itself includes some Exodus reviews that depict Israel as grateful and others that focus on Israel's ingratitude suggests that these biblical sources themselves may have informed both *Dayyenu* and negative Christian Exodus reviews.

9. Piskaot 337 and 339. Deut. Rabbah 4:7 is worth comparing. "Israel said to God: 'Master of the Universe, *Let me exult and rejoice in Your faithfulness* (Psalms 31:8) . . . for if You had exacted punishment from the Egyptians and not given us their riches we would still have cause to exult and rejoice; our joy [is all the greater] now that You have given us their riches." The midrash uses a similar form with regard to events in the life of Joseph in Egypt.

10. *Mekhilta of Rabbi Ishamel, Beshalach* 2:108, vol. 1, p. 195.

11. *Mekhilta of Rabbi Ishamel, Shirata* 7:20, vol. 2, p. 55. This is one of the earliest appearances in rabbinic literature of the word *dayyenu*. Ironically, it comes from the lips of Pharaoh! As far as I know, commentators on the Haggadah have overlooked the relationship between *Dayyenu* and these sources from the *Mekhilta*.

12. Lev. Rabbah 35:12. For the translation of Malachi, see JPS and *The Jerusalem Bible*, Jerusalem: Koren, 1986.

13. Rabbi Yom Tov ben Abraham Ashbili, Ritba (Spain, c. 1250–1330) comments on Isaiah 26:4 that *b'yah*, usually read "in God," can be read "in fifteen" if one uses the numerical values of the letters in the word *yah—yod* (10) *hey* (5). Abarbanel (1437–1508) mentions the favors described in Ezekiel 16:9–13. See Menachem Kasher, Haggadah *Shelemah*, p. 55, note to source 587.

14. Middot 2:5.

15. E.g. Song of Songs Rabbah, 1:55. For the commentary attributed to Rashbam, see *Haggadah Shel Pesach, Torat Chayim* (Jerusalem: Mossad Harav Kook, 1998), pp. 133-140.

16. BT, Shabbat 145b–146a. See Byron L. Sherwin, "Original Sin: Is It Sufficient for Us?" in *Mo'ed*, vol. 13, 2003.

17. Deuteronomy Rabbah 4:4, Exodus Rabbah 25:12. See Menachem Kasher, *The Israel Haggadah* (New York: American Biblical Encyclopedia Association, 1957), p. 137.

18. See Daniel Landes in *My People's Passover Haggadah*, eds. Lawrence Hoffman and David Arnow (Woodstock, Vt.: Jewish Lights, 2008), vol. 2, p. 68.

Chapter 18—Reliving the Exodus

1. Thanks to Nigel Savage of Hazon for teaching me about the relationship between this prayer and the Exodus.

2. *Legends,* vol. 2, p. 375 and vol. 5, p. 439. This combines three sources: The *Mekhilta of Rabbi Ishmael* (*Masechet Pischa* 13 on Exodus 12:34); *Mekhilta of Rabbi Shimon bar Yochai* (24); and the *Targum Yerushalmi* on Exodus 12:34.

Chapter 19—Israel and the Haggadah

1. There are different traditions about when these complaints occurred. *Seder Olam Rabbah* (chapter 9), an ancient rabbinic chronology, and medieval commentators including Shmuel ben Meir and Ibn Ezra place the events in the fortieth year in the desert. Others place them much earlier.

2. Thanks to Rabbi Gordon Tucker for bringing this issue to my attention.

3. Scholars differ as to Rashi's stance on the fifth cup, referred to in some manuscripts of the Talmud. Goldschmidt (*Haggadah: Sources and History,* p. 66) believes that Rashi based his position on the fact that the Mishnah only mentions four cups of wine and therefore Rashi "emended" versions of the Talmud referring to a fifth cup as simply erroneous. Guggenheimer (*Scholar's Haggadah,* p. 367) asserts that Rashi merely preferred the version of the Talmud associated with the ancient Babylonian academy of Pumbedita, which held to four cups, over that of Sura, which allowed an optional fifth cup.

4. The concept first finds expression in the Babylonian Talmud (Ta'anit 5a). "The Holy One, blessed be He, said, 'I will not enter the heavenly Jerusalem until I can enter the earthly Jerusalem.' Is there then a heavenly Jerusalem? Yes; for it is written, 'Jerusalem [is] built up like a city knit together'" (Psalms 122:3). Here, the heavenly Jerusalem is not a substitute for the earthly city, but will in fact be built only *after* God restores the mundane city.

5. Song of Songs Rabbah 2:20.

6. Benjamin Segal, *Returning: The Land of Israel as a Focus in Jewish History* (Jerusalem: Department of Education and Culture of the World Zionist Organization, 1987), p. 124.

7. Ibid. p. 131.

8. For the omission in Saadiah's Haggadah, see *Haggadah of the Sages,* p. 280. Thanks to Rabbi Gilbert Rosenthal for suggesting this line of inquiry.

9. Joseph B. Soloveitchik, "The Nine Aspects of the Haggadah," in *The Yeshiva University Haggadah,* p. 11.

10. For the former view, see Irving Greenberg, *The Jewish Way* (New York: Summit Books, 1988), pp. 56, 424. For the latter, see Shlomo Riskin, "Lesson of the

Haggadah in Our Present War Against Terror." *Shabbat Hadagol Drasha,* 2002. CD-ROM by Ohr Torah Stone Institutions, (212) 935-8672. As Rabbi Riskin pointed out in a personal communication, the notion of drinking a cup without the traditional blessing over wine is common in Sephardic practice, which includes that blessing only for the first and third cups.

11. Joseph Tabory, *The Passover Ritual throughout the Generations* (Israel: Hakibbutz Hameuchad Publishing, 1996), p. 330 (Hebrew).

12. Menachem Kasher, *The Israel Passover Haggadah* (New York: The Sentry Press, 1962), p. 334. The *Shulchan Arukh* (481:1), an authoritative legal code from the sixteenth century, renders a fifth cup optional.

13. See Tabory, *The Passover Ritual throughout the Generations,* pp. 323–341.

14. Theodore Herzl, *Altneuland,* trans. Paula Arnold (Haifa: Haifa Publishing Company, 1960), p. 156. Thanks to Madeleine Arnow for bringing this to my attention.

15. For a discussion of Kasher and the fifth cup see, *Studies on the Haggadah from the Teachings of Nechama Leibowitz,* eds. Yitshak Reiner and Shmuel Peerless (New York: Urim Publications, 2002), p. 11.

16. Riskin, "Lessons of the Haggadah."

17. Leonard S. Cahan, ed., *Siddur Sim Shalom* (New York: Rabbinical Assembly/United Synagogue of Conservative Judaism, 1998), p. 149.

18. Kasher, *Israel Passover Haggadah,* p. 335.

19. Amos Elon, *Herzl* (New York: Schocken Books, 1986), p. 16.

20. *The Jewish Case Before the Anglo-American Committee of Inquiry on Palestine: Statement and Memoranda* (Jerusalem: The Jewish Agency for Israel, 1947), p. 65.

21. Mishnah, Pesachim 10:6.

22. *New York Times,* August 29, 2003, p. 8

23. Nir Hasson, "If the Vilna Gaon Was Right, the 3rd Temple Is on Its Way," www.haaretz.com, November 30, 2009.

Chapter 20—The Restoration of Wonder

1. The JPS Tanakh translates *moftim* as "portents." In this chapter, I've followed the Artscroll rendering: "wonders."

2. Thanks to Rabbi Lester Bronstein for pointing this out.

3. Yair Zakovitch, *The Concept of the Miracle in the Bible* (Tel Aviv: MOD Books, 1991), pp. 9–20. See also *Divine Intervention and Miracles in Jewish Theology,* ed. Dan Cohn-Sherbok (Lewiston, Maine: The Edwin Mellon Press, 1996).

4. Moshe Weinfeld, *Social Justice in Ancient Israel and in the Ancient Near East* (Jerusalem: The Magnes Press/The Hebrew University, 1995), pp. 14–15.

5. Thanks to Rabbi Alfredo Borodowski for pointing out this disagreement between Gersonides and Abarbanel.

6. David Hume, *Enquiries Concerning the Human Understanding and Concerning the Principles of Morals,* ed. L. A. Selby-Bigge (London: Oxford University Press, 1966, 1902), pp. 114–115, note 1. Although Hume did not rule out the possibility of miracles, he believed their probability to be extremely low: The test is whether false testimony of the miraculous would be more miraculous than the event itself (p. 116).

7. *The Random House Dictionary of the English Language* (New York: Random House, 1987).

8. BT, Shabbat 32a.

9. Jerusalem Talmud, Berakhot 5:2, as quoted in Ephraim Urbach, *The Sages: Their Concepts and Beliefs* (Cambridge: Harvard University Press, 1975), p. 112.

10. Mishnah, Berakhot 9:1. The Gemarah (Berakhot 54a) illustrates this with reference to the place where the Israelites crossed the Red Sea.

11. BT, Niddah 31a.

12. BT, Chullin 90b.

13. As quoted in Urbach, *The Sages,* pp. 111–112.

14. Buber, *Tales of the Hasidim,* vol. 2, p. 315.

15. Heschel, *God in Search of Man,* p. 46.

16. BT, Pesachim 109a.

17. Maimonides, *The Guide of the Perplexed,* trans. Shlomo Pines (Chicago: The University of Chicago Press, 1963), Book 2, chapter 6, pp. 263–264.

18. Ramban (vol. on Exodus 13:6) pp. 172, 174.

19. Benedict de Spinoza, *A Theologico-Political Treatise,* trans. R.H.M. Elwes (New York: Dover Publications, 1951), p. 91.

20. Umberto Cassuto, *A Commentary on the Book of Exodus* (Jerusalem: The Magnes Press/Hebrew University, 1967), pp. 167–168.

21. Heschel, *God in Search of Man: A Philosophy of Judaism,* p. 49. Chapter 4, "Wonder," is an absolute gem.

22. Robert N. Goldman, *Einstein's God* (Northvale, N.J.: Jason Aronson, 1997), p. 24.

23. Michael Graetz, "Metaphors for God," in *Conservative Judaism,* 51:2, Winter 1999, p. 69.

24. Abraham Joshua Heschel, *The Prophets* (Philadelphia: Jewish Publication Society, 1955), p. 186.

25. Lawrence Kushner, "Opening Your Eyes," in *The Book of Miracles: A Young Person's Guide to Jewish Spirituality* (Woodstock, Vt.: Jewish Lights, 1997), pp. 15–18.

26. Vol. 2, p. 21.

Chapter 21—"Blessed Are You . . . Who Redeemed Us"

1. Maimonides, "Epistle to Yemen," in *A Maimonides Reader,* ed. Isadore Twersky (Philadelphia: Behrman House, 1972), pp. 459–460.

2. Gershom Scholem, *Sabbatai Sevi: The Mystical Messiah* (Princeton: Princeton University Press, 1973), p. 652.

3. Ibid., pp. 459, 460. Shabbetai Zevi's breaking Jewish law upset some; others found justification for it in rabbinic statements, such as this one in BT, Shabbat 151b: "Rabbi ben Eliezer [active in the late second century] said: 'In the messianic era, there is neither merit nor guilt.'"

4. Buber, *Tales of the Hasidim,* vol. 1, pp. 78–79.

5. David G. Roskies, *The Literature of Destruction* (Philadelphia: Jewish Publication Society, 1989), pp. 403–404.

6. EJ, vol. 14, p. 1. The two principal Hebrew words associated with redemption derive from two roots, *pey-dalet-hey* and *gimel-alef-lamed.* Both can be associated with either human or divine agency. The first is more general and does not imply any special relationship between redeemer and redeemed. The second refers to the next of kin "who acts to maintain the validity of his extended family group by preventing any breaches form occurring within it" (p. 1).

7. Weinfeld, *Social Justice in Ancient Israel,* p. 141.

8. Ibid., p. 80.

9. Ibid., pp. 15, 88, 81.

10. David Daube, *The Exodus Pattern in the Bible* (London: Faber and Faber, 1963), chapter 5.

11. In Egypt, the first known appearance of the term "slave" occurs in a religious context, "servant of god." The reference dates from the Old Kingdom, between 2630 and 2213 B.C.E. See Antonio Loprieno, "Slaves," in *The Egyptians,* ed. Sergio Donadoni (Chicago: University of Chicago Press, 1997), p. 195.

12. *Pischa,* 5:14, vol. 1, p. 34.

13. *Pikudei,* 9 (Warsaw version). This midrash obviously builds on Rabbi Akiva's tale described in BT, Sotah 11b. See pages 11–12.

14. The most common explanation for raising the cup of wine—one directly linked to the idea of redemption—sees it as fulfilling a verse from Psalms that we recite at the Seder during Hallel: "I will raise the cups of deliverance and invoke the name of

Adonai" (Psalms 116:13). Aside from lifting our cups prior to reciting the blessings over each cup of wine, many Haggadot direct us to do so prior to the passages that begin "And this is the promise that sustained us . . ." and (just before Hallel) "We must therefore thank, praise, honor . . ." Scholars often attribute the custom to Isaac Luria and the Kabbalists of the sixteenth century. See, for example, Scholar's Haggadah, p. 286 and Haggadah: Sources and History, p. 120. But according to Elazar ben Judah of Worms (c. 1176–1238), Jews in Germany already practiced the custom. See Elazar ben Judah of Worms, *Drasha L'Pesach*, ed. Simcha Emanuel (Jerusalem: Mekize Nirdamim, 2006), p. 99.

15. Jacob Neusner, *The Talmud of the Land of Israel: A Preliminary Translation and Explanation*, vol. 13 (Chicago: University of Chicago Press, 1991), pp. 476–477. This and the following excerpts from the Jerusalem Talmud come from the same source. For Neusner's interpretation, see p. 589, note 20.

16. Mordecai M. Kaplan, *The Meaning of God in Modern Jewish Religion* (New York: Berhman's Jewish Book House, 1937), pp. 45, 52–54.

17. Martin Buber, *On the Bible* (Syracuse: Syracuse University Press, 2000), p. 12.

18. Heschel, *God in Search of Man,* pp. 312–313, 380.

19. Abraham Isaac Kook, *"Orot,"* in *The Zionist Idea*, ed. Arthur Hertzberg (New York: Atheneum Books, 1959), pp. 420, 425. Thanks to Rabbi Michael Paley for bringing this selection to my attention.

20. David Arnow, "In Every Generation, Finding Redemption in the Seder," in *Forward,* April 18, 2003. It is reprinted here with permission.

21. Maimonides, *"Mishne Torah:* The Laws of Kings and Wars 12:5," in *A Maimonides Reader,* ed. Isadore Twersky (New York: Behrman House, 1972), pp. 225–226.

22. Yaffa Eliach, *Hasidic Tales of the Holocaust* (New York: Vintage Books, 1982), p. 19.

Chapter 22—Passover without a Seder?

1. Mishnah, Pesachim 10:6.

2. Deuteronomy 27:12.

3. Qur'an Sura 2: 124; 37:102–105. Although the Qur'an does not specify which son was to be sacrificed, Islamic tradition identifies him as Ishmael.

4. *Mekhilta of Rabbi Ishmael*, vol. 1 p. 57, *Piskha* 7:78. For fascinating discussions of the relationship between the binding of Isaac and Passover, see Geza Vermes, *Scripture and Tradition in Judaism* (Leiden: Brill, 1961), pp. 193–227 and Jon D. Levenson, *The Death and Resurrection of the Beloved Son* (New Haven: Yale University Press, 1993), pp.

173–199. See also Elie Kaunfer, "Torah Reading as a Weapon: Rosh Hashanah and the Akedah" at www.livelyseders.com, articles of interest.

5. *Mekhilta de-Rabbi Shimon Bar Yohai*, ed. W. David Nelson (Philadelphia: Jewish Publication Society, 2006), p. 6, Sanya 2:2.

6. E.g. Jubilees 17:15–16 and Exodus Rabbah 15:11.

7. Thanks to Rabbi Michael Goldman of Temple Israel Center, White Plains, N.Y., for this idea.

8. Josephus and the Talmud offer exaggerated reports of Passover celebrations involving millions of people. See Josephus, *The Jewish War* (6:9:3), trans. G. A. Williamson (London: Penguin Books, 1981), pp. 371–372. Also see BT, Pesachim 64a–b. One study suggests that, in fact, only a small fraction of the population made the pilgrimage to Jerusalem. See Shmuel Safrai, *Ha'aliya l'regel b'yemai ha'bayit ha'sheni* (Tel Aviv: Am Ha'sefer, 1965), chapter 1. According to the Mishnah, the Temple Court where the sacrifice took place was approximately 200 by 280 feet—just over one-and-a-quarter acres—and filling it three times accommodated everyone wishing to offer a sacrifice (Mishnah, Midot 5:1 and Pesachim 5:5). For an overview of modern scholarship on the Temple, see *Temple and Worship in Biblical Israel*, ed. John Day (London: T&T Clark: 2005).

9. *The Jewish War* (5:5:6), p. 304.

10. Ibid. (6:9:3), pp. 371–372.

11. Ibid. (2:1:1), p. 120.

12. Ibid. (6:9:3), pp. 371–372.

13. Mishnah, Pesachim 5:5 explains this by a verse from the ancient description of the festival that we considered earlier: "[A]ll the assembled congregation of the Israelites shall slaughter it . . ." (Exodus 12:6). The Mishnah interpreted the "*assembled congregation* of the *Israelites*" as referring to three separate groups.

14. II Chronicles 30:17 and 35:6 indicate that there was a time when the Levites rather than the Israelites themselves carried out the sacrifice. Rabbinic sources do not reflect this practice, e.g. Mishnah, Pesachim 5:6. Although the Mishnah (Zevachim 3:1) indicates that non-priests could slaughter sacrifices, it may be that this primarily occurred on Passover when the number of pilgrims offering sacrifices was particularly high. This Mishnah indicates that women could also slaughter animals for sacrifice. Thanks to Rabbi Gordon Tucker for clarifying these issues.

15. Philo, *On the Life of Moses*, ed. and trans. F. H. Colson and G. H. Whitaker (Cambridge: Harvard University Press), 2:224.

16. Mishnah, Chullin 1:2.

17. Mishnah, Pesachim 5:5.

18. Leviticus 3:3–4.

19. Mishnah, Pesachim 5:9.

20. BT, Pesachim 65b.

21. Mishnah, Pesachim 7:1.

22. Mishnah, Pesachim 8:3.

23. Jubilees 49:6. This is the first mention of wine in connection with the Passover celebration.

24. BT, Pesachim 116a. He reports that merchants of Jerusalem would cry out, "Come and take spices for the mitzvah [of *charoset*]."

25. BT, Pesachim 85b.

26. Henri Hubert and Marcel Mauss, *Sacrifice: Its Nature and Function* (Chicago: University of Chicago Press, 1964), p. 100. Originally published in 1898.

27. Ibid., pp. 98–99.

28. See Gordon Tucker, "Sacrifices," in *Etz Hayim*, p. 1447.

29. *The Jewish Study Bible*, Adele Berlin and Marc Zvi Brettler eds., (New York: Oxford University Press, 2004).

30. *The ArtScroll Siddur* (Brooklyn, N.Y.: Mesorah Publications, 1984), p. 471 (Ashkenazic). The Conservative Movement's prayer book is similar but without the reference to "fire-offerings." Prayer books published by the Reform and Reconstructionist Movements include a version of the prayer that omits the reference to the Temple. The Mishnah (Tamid 5:1) and Talmud (Berakhot 11b) both indicate that priests recited a version of this prayer during the Second Temple period.

31. Maimonides, *The Guide of the Perplexed*, trans. Shlomo Pines (Chicago: University of Chicago Press, 1963), III:32, p. 526.

32. Everett Fox, *The Five Books of Moses* (New York: Schocken Books, 1995), p. 508.

33. Arnold Eisen, *Taking Hold of Torah: Jewish Commitment and Community in America* (Bloomington: University of Indiana Press, 2000), pp. 78–79. Thanks to Rabbi Noah Arnow for bringing this source to my attention.

34. Exodus 5:1; 7:16, 26; 8:16, 9:1, 13; 10:3. The translation of the verse follows the 1917 JPS rendering in place of the 1985 JPS translation, which uses "worship" rather than "serve."

35. The only variation is this: "Let my people go that they may celebrate a festival for Me in the wilderness" (Exodus 5:1). The phrase "let my people go" also appears in Exodus 8:17 and 10:4, but not as a command.

36. Genesis 4:3–5.

Chapter 23—Elijah's Transformation

1. *Passover Haggadah: The Feast of Freedom* (New York: The Rabbinical Assembly, 1982), p. 101. There is enormous variation in how contemporary Haggadot refer to Elijah's cup. For a discussion of how modern Haggadot approach this passage, see Debra Reed Blank, "*Sh'fokh Hamatkha* and *Eliyahu* in the Haggadah: Ideology in Liturgy" in *Conservative Judaism,* 40:2, Winter 1987/1988, pp. 73–86.

2. The earliest reference to Elijah's presence at circumcisions is found in the eighth-century midrash *Pirke de Rabbi Eliezer,* chapter 29, pp. 213–214.

3. Derekh Eretz Rabbah 1 (one of the "minor" tractates of the BT), quoted in *The Book of Legends,* eds. H. N. Bialik and Y. H. Ravnitzky, trans. William G. Braude (New York: Schocken Books, 1992), p. 617, no. 32.

4. BT, Pesachim 13a.

5. Exodus Rabbah 18:12: "Why does He call it 'a night of watching'? (Ex. 12:47). Because, on that night, He performed great things for the righteous, just as He had wrought for Israel in Egypt. On that night, He saved Hezekiah, Hananiah and his companions, Daniel from the lions' den, and on that night Messiah and Elijah will be made great" [or revealed, as some readings suggest].

6. *Hagadah Shelemah,* p. 180. (*Shulchan Arukh*, Orach Chayim, 480, the Order of the Fourth Cup.) Isserles brings this interpretation in the name of Rabbanu Israel Bruna (mid-fifteenth century, known as the Mahariv). The *Shulchan Arukh* makes no specific mention of any of the rituals associated with Elijah. See also *Scholar's Haggadah,* p. 366.

7. Judah Loew Ben Bezalel, the Maharal of Prague, *Divrai Nigidim* (Noble Words), p. 155, Judaic Classics, Davka CD-ROM version (Hebrew).

8. Yisroel Yaakov Klapholtz, part II, chap. 9, "Elijah Saves from a Blood Libel," in *Stories of Elijah the Prophet* (B'nei B'rak, Israel: Pe'er Hasefer Publishers, 1973).

9. See A. M. Beek, "The Chariots and the Horsemen of Israel," in *Oudtestamentische Studien,* vol. 17, 1972, pp. 1–10. Beek observes that Elisha's curious designation of Elijah as "Israel's chariots and its horsemen" evokes imagery of the Exodus from Egypt in which references to Pharaoh's pursuit of Israel with his chariots and horsemen occur six times in the fourteenth chapter of Exodus alone.

10. *Scholars Haggadah,* pp. 365–366.

11. Menachem Mendel Schneerson, *From Exile to Redemption: Chassidic Teachings of the Lubavitcher Rebbe and the Preceding Rebbeim of Chabad,* vol. 1 (Brooklyn: Kehot Publication Society, 1992), p. 99.

12. BT, Sanhedrin 98b.

13. BT, Pesachim 118a.

14. BT, Nedarim 50a.

15. BT, Sanhedrin 68a.

16. Midrash Eileh Ezkerah, a martyrology from early medieval times, some of which is read on the afternoon of Yom Kippur. See David G. Roskies, *The Literature of Destruction: Jewish Responses to Catastrophe* (Philadelphia: Jewish Publication Society, 1988), p. 64.

17. For an excellent discussion of this, see Rabbi David Silber, "Moses and Elijah: A Study in Leadership," audiotape from the Drisha Institute. *Pesikta Rabbati* (Piskha 4), a collection of midrashim from the sixth to seventh centuries C.E., includes the definitive rabbinic comparison between Moses and Elijah. It lists dozens of similarities. *Pesikta Rabbati,* vol. 1, ed. and trans. William G. Braude (New Haven: Yale University Press, 1968), pp. 1, 82–88.

18. To Elisha's request, Elijah replies, "Go return. What have I done to you?" (I Kings 19:20). Rashi interprets this as follows: "**Go return** from following me, for **what have I done to you** that you should follow me?"

19. *Mekhilta of Rabbi Ishmael, Piskha* 1:88–97, vol. 1, pp. 8–9.

20. Dov Noy, "Forward," in *Tales of Elijah,* ed. Peninah Schram (Northvale, N.J.: Jason Aronson, 1997), p. xiv.

21. Ibid., p. xv.

22. See Genesis Rabbah (12:15) for the balance between justice and mercy. The *Zohar* (Shemoth, section 2, p. 216b), the mystical text from the thirteenth century, provides an intriguing interpretation of the *Sh'ma,* Judaism's credal statement on the unity of God: "The words, 'Adonai our God' [YHWH—*Elohainu*] are to reunite God's attributes . . . This is the method of avowing the unity of God practiced by Rab Hamnuna the Venerable, who learnt it from his father, who had it from his master, and so on, till it came from the mouth of Elijah."

23. Joseph Telushkin, *Biblical Literacy* (New York: William Morrow and Company, 1997), pp. 257–258.

24. Emile Fackenheim, *Encounters between Judaism and Modern Philosophy* (New York: Basic Books, 1973), p. 9. Thanks to Rabbi Gordon Tucker for bringing this to my attention.

25. Midrash Zuta Song of Songs 8:4, quoted in Aharon Wiener, *The Prophet Elijah in the Development of Judaism* (London: Routledge & Kegan Paul, 1978), pp. 48–49.

26. Gerson D. Cohen, *Studies in the Variety of Rabbinic Cultures* (Philadelphia: Jewish Publication Society, 1991), p. 35.

27. Yitzchak Sender, *The Commentator's Pesach* (New York: Feldheim Publishers, 1996), p. 220.

28. Wiener, *The Prophet Elijah,* p. 139. The tale is attributed to a Hasidic circle in Israel.

29. See Eliezer ben Elijah Ashkenazi, *Maase Hashem* (Warsaw: n.p., 1871), part 2, p. 37. Ashkenazi's view is all the more important because it was repeated in a commentary on the *Shulchan Arukh* (sixteenth century), perhaps Judaism's most influential law code. That commentary, *Be'er Hagolah*, was written by Moshe Rivkes (d. c 1671/72) and appears in all printed versions of the *Shulchan Arukh* (*Choshen Mishpat*, 425:5). See Neta Ecker Rosinger, "Universalism in the Thought of Eliezer Ashkenazi" (Doctoral Dissertation, August, 2010, Haifa University), p. 259.

30. *The Open Door: A Passover Haggadah,* ed. Sue Levi Elwell (New York: Central Conference of American Rabbis, 2002), pp. 85–87.

31. *Mekhilta of Rabbi Ishmael, Shirata* 6:69, vol. 2, p. 48. For more see "Pour Out Your Wrath" by David Arnow on www.livelyseders.com, articles of interest.

Chapter 24—Two Seder Songs

1. For the issue of playing instruments on holidays, see page 389, note 3.

2. This was the study hall of Elazar ben Judah of Worms (c. 1165–1230).

3. See Goldschmidt, p. 98; Safrai and Safrai (English version), pp. 165–167; and Menachem Zvi Fox, "The History of the Songs 'Echad Mi Yodea' and 'Chad Gadya' in Israel and the World," in *Asufot*, vol. 2, 1988, pp. 201-225 (Hebrew).

4. Leah Rachel Clara Yoffie, "Songs of the 'Twelve Numbers' and the Hebrew Chant of 'Echod Mi Yodea,'" in *The Journal of American Folklore*, vol. 62, 1949 , p. 411.

5. 1. 2+2+4; 2. Four Questions, Four Children, Four Cups of Wine =3 3. 1+3=4; 4. 70; 5. 400—years of enslavement (Gen. 15:13); 6. 10-10=0; 7. 0+3+6+2=11; 8. 1+0=1; 9. 15+15=30 (Some Haggadot combine *motzi* and *matzah* into one step, making 14 rather than 15 steps.); 10. 3+2=5.

6. Traditional Jews remain reluctant to number Israel. The Talmud warns, "It is forbidden to count Israel even for [the purpose of fulfilling] a commandment" (Yoma 22b). To avoid counting Jews for a minyan, traditional Jews designate those present with a word from a biblical verse that contains ten words, often Psalm 28:9.

7. II Samuel 24 contains a parallel version of the story. The problematic nature of the census has perplexed scholars in part because in Chronicles, Satan incites David to carry it out, and in Samuel, God does so.

8. Pesikta Rabbati 11:3. See also the Midrash Samuel 31:3 and Midrash on Psalms 17:4. These midrashim elaborate on the story as it appears in II Samuel 24:12-17.

9. *Sefer Ya'akov Yosef* (Jerusalem: Agudat Beit V'yeliphali, 1973), vol. 1, on parashat Vayakel, p. 253.

10. Chone Szmeruk, "The Earliest Aramaic and Yiddish Version of the 'Song of the Kid' (*Khad Gadye*)," in *The Field of Yiddish*, ed. Uriel Weinreich (New York: Linguistic Circle of New York, 1954), pp. 214-218.

11. William Wells Newell, "The Passover Song of the Kid and an Equivalent from New England," *Journal of American Folklore*, vol. 18, 1905, pp. 33–48, see p. 43.

12. *Chayim Sha'al* 1:28 (Bar Ilan Responsa Project 17.) It is interesting that Azoulai attributes this statement about passing down the meaning of songs from one generation of rabbis to the next to Elazar ben Judah of Worms. It was behind the walls of his study hall that the parchment referring to *Echad Mi Yodea* and *Chad Gadya* was reputedly found. See note 2, above.

13. See Rashi on BT, Berakhot 44b, v. *bar zuz*.

14. Thanks to Madeleine Arnow for raising this last question.

15. Haggadah *Shel Pesach Ma'amar Yehonatan* (Jerusalem: Ma'arekhet Noam Ha'torah, 1985).

16. BT, Horayot 13a.

17. Genesis Rabbah 2:4.

18. BT, Baba Batra 16a.

19. J. D. Eisentsein, *Otzar Perushim V'tziurim Haggadah Shel Pesach* (Israel: n.p., 2005).

20. Moses Alshekh (1508–1600), *Sefer Torat Moshe* (Warsaw: 1879), Vayeshev.

21. Agnon alludes here to the Babylonian Talmud, Baba Batra 16a.

22. Shmuel Yosef Agnon, *Takhrikh shel Sipurim* (Jerusalem: Schocken, 1984), p. 147. First published in *Ha'Aretz*, 1943, prior to Passover. English translation by David Arnow.

23. Yehuda Amichai, *Poems of Jerusalem* (Jerusalem: Schocken, 1987), p. 143.

24. For an outstanding treatment of this subject, see Neil Gillman, *The Death of Death: Resurrection and Immortality in Jewish Thought* (Woodstock, Vt.: Jewish Lights, 1997).

25. *Mishkan T'filah: A Reform Siddur* (New York: Central Conference of American Rabbis, 2007), p. 246.

26. Joseph B. Soloveitchik, *Halakhic Man* (Philadelphia: Jewish Publication Society, 1983), pp. 105 and 107.

27. For a good discussion of *Chad Gadya*, including a comparison of interpretations, see Kenneth Brander, "An Analysis of *Had Gadya*," in *The Journal of Jewish Music and Liturgy*, vol. 17, 1994.

Chapter 25—The Exodus from Egypt

1. In addition to cited works, this essay synthesizes material from the following sources: *Exodus: The Egyptian Evidence,* eds. Ernest S. Frerichs and H. Lesko, eds. (Winona

Lake, Ind.: Eisenbrauns, 1997); Ronald Hendel, "The Exodus in Biblical Memory," in *Journal of Biblical Literature,* 120:4, 2001, pp. 601–622; Donald B. Redford, "An Egyptological Perspective on the Exodus Narrative," in *Egypt, Israel, Sinai: Archaeological and Historical Relationships in the Biblical Period,* ed. Anson F. Rainey (Tel Aviv: Tel Aviv University Press, 1987); Nahum M. Sarna, "Israel in Egypt: The Egyptian Sojourn and the Exodus," in *Ancient Israel,* rev. ed. Hershel Shanks (Washington, D.C.: Biblical Archaeological Society, 1999); Hershel Shanks, "Did the Exodus Really Happen?" in *Moment,* vol. 102, October 2001, pp. 62–65.

2. Jan Assmann, *Moses the Egyptian: The Memory of Egypt in Western Monotheism* (Cambridge: Harvard University Press, 1997), p. 27.

3. *The Rise of Ancient Israel,* ed. Hershel Shanks (Washington, DC: Biblical Archeology Society, 1992), color plate II, facing p. 22.

4. Carl Drews and Weiqing Han, "Dynamics of Wind Setdown at Suez and the Eastern Nile Delta," in *PloS One,* August 2010, vol. 5, no. 8. Quotations are found on pp. 1, 2, and 10. www.plosone.org/article/info%3Adoi%2F10.1371%2Fjournal.pone.0012481.

5. Herodotus, *The Histories,* trans. Robin Waterfield (New York: Oxford University Press, 1998), p. 145.

6. Baruch Halpern, "The Exodus from Egypt: Myth or Reality," in *The Rise of Ancient Israel,* p. 106.

7. Ahad Ha-'Am, "Moses" (1904), in *Selected Essays of Ahad Ha-'Am,* trans. Leon Simon (New York: Atheneum, 1970), pp. 308–309.

8. Buber, *Moses,* p. 16.

9. Yosef Hayim Yerushalmi, *Zakhor: Jewish History and Jewish Memory* (Seattle: University of Washington Press, 1982), pp. 10–11.

10. Richard Hirsh, "Is This Story True?" in *A Night of Questions: A Passover Haggadah,* eds. Joy Levitt and Michael Strassfeld (Elkins Park, Pa.: Reconstructionist Press, 2000), p. 21.

11. Transcribed from an audiotape supplied by Sinai Temple.

12. Heschel, *God in Search of Man,* p. 185.

Appendix I—Chapter Ten of Mishnah Pesachim, The Night of Passover

1. With a few exceptions, this translation follows that of Baruch M. Bosker, *The Origins of the Seder,* pp. 29–32. Bokser's translation is based on the Kaufmann manuscript of the Mishnah, which dates from the thirteenth century. This manuscript is considered the best such manuscript and lacks additions from the Gemarah or the Haggadah that have found their way into the "standard" Mishnah.

SELECT BIBLIOGRAPHY

—

Alter, Judah Aryeh Leib. *The Language of Truth: The Torah Commentary of the Sefat Emet.* Translated and interpreted by Arthur Green. Philadelphia: Jewish Publication Society, 1998.

Anisfeld, Sharon Cohen, Tara Mohr, and Catherine Spector, eds. *The Women's Seder Sourcebook: Rituals and Readings for Use at the Passover Seder.* Woodstock, Vt.: Jewish Lights, 2003.

———. *The Women's Passover Companion: Women's Reflections on the Festival of Freedom.* Woodstock, Vt.: Jewish Lights, 2003.

Babylonian Talmud, Midrash Rabbah, and the *Zohar.* Davka CD-ROM version. Soncino Translation.

Bokser, Baruch M. *The Origins of the Seder: The Passover Rite and Early Rabbinic Judaism.* Berkeley: University of California Press, 1984.

———. "Changing Views of Passover and the Meaning of Redemption According to the Palestinian Talmud." *Journal of the Association for Jewish Studies,* 10:1 (Spring 1985). 1–18.

Borowski, Oded. *Agriculture in Iron Age Israel.* Winona Lake, Ind.: Eisenbrauns, 1987.

Bradshaw, Paul F., and Lawrence H. Hoffman, eds. *Passover and Easter: Origin and History to Modern Times.* Notre Dame, Ind.: University of Notre Dame Press, 2000.

Brumberg-Kraus, Jonathan. "Meals as Midrash: A Survey of Ancient Meals in Jewish Studies Scholarship." On the web at acunix.wheatonma.edu/jkraus/articles/MealsasMidrash.htm.

Buber, Martin. *Moses: The Revelation and the Covenant.* Translated by Michael Fishbane. Atlantic Highlands, N.J.: Humanities Press International, 1988.

Cassuto, Umberto. *A Commentary on the Book of Exodus.* Translated by I. Abrahams. Jerusalem: Magnes Press, 1967.

Cohen, Jeffrey M. *Let My People Go: Insights to Passover and the Haggadah.* Northvale, N.J.: Jason Aronson, 2002.

Cohen, Nachman. *The Historical Haggadah.* Yonkers, N.Y.: Torah Lishmah Institute, 2002.

Daube, David. *The Exodus Pattern in the Bible.* London: Faber and Faber, 1963.

Feinstein, David. *The Laws of Passover.* Brooklyn: Mesorah Publications, 2000.

Fredman, Ruth Gruber. *The Passover Seder.* New York: New American Library, 1983.

Gaster, Theodor H. *Festivals of the Jewish Year: A Modern Interpretation and Guide.* New York: Morrow Quill Paperbacks, 1978.

Ginzberg, Louis. *Legends of the Jews.* Philadelphia: Jewish Publication Society, 1963.

Goldschmidt, E. Daniel. *The Passover Haggadah: Its Sources and History.* Jerusalem: The Bialik Institute, 1960 (Hebrew).

Goodman, Amy and Philip, eds. *Passover Anthology.* Philadelphia: Jewish Publication Society, 2003.

Greenberg, Irving. *The Jewish Way: Living the Holidays.* New York: Summit Books, 1988.

Guggenheimer, Heinrich. *The Scholar's Haggadah: Ashkenazic, Sephardic, and Oriental Versions.* Northvale, N.J.: Jason Aronson, 1998.

Haggadat Torah Chaim. Jerusalem: Mossad Harav Kook, 1998 (Hebrew).

Hauptman, Judith. "How Old Is the Haggadah?" *Judaism,* 51:1 (Winter 2002): 3–18.

Hoffman, Lawrence A. *Beyond the Text: A Holistic Approach to Liturgy.* Bloomington: Indiana University Press, 1987.

Hoffman, Lawrence A., and David Arnow, eds. *My People's Passover Haggadah: Traditional Texts, Modern Commentaries, Volume 1.* Woodstock, Vt.: Jewish Lights, 2008.

Hoffman, Lawrence A., and David Arnow, eds. *My People's Passover Haggadah: Traditional Texts, Modern Commentaries, Volume 2.* Woodstock, Vt.: Jewish Lights, 2008.

Homolka, Walter. "God Is Thy Rescue As the Central Message of the Seder Ritual." *European Judaism,* 30:2 (Autumn 1997): 72–85.

Isaac, Benjamin, and Aharon Oppenheimer. "The Revolt of Bar Kochba: Ideology and Modern Scholarship." *Journal of Jewish Studies,* 36:1 (Spring 1985): 33–60.

Kasher, Menachem. *Hagadah Shelemah.* Jerusalem: Torah Shelemah Inst., 1967 (Hebrew).

Klein, Mordell. *Passover.* Jerusalem: Keter Books, 1973.

Laufer, Nathan. *Leading the Passover Journey: The Seder's Meaning Revealed, the Haggadah's Story Retold.* Woodstock, Vt.: Jewish Lights, 2005.

Leibowitz, Nehama. *New Studies in Shemot.* Jerusalem: World Zionist Organization, 1986.

Lieber, David L., and Jules Harlow, eds. *Etz Hayim: Torah and Commentary.* Philadelphia: Jewish Publication Society, 2001.

Maimonides. *Mishneh Torah: The Laws of Chametz and Matzah.* Translated by Eliyahu Touger. New York: Moznaim Publishing Corporation, 1988.

Mekhilta of Rabbi Ishmael. Translated by Jacob Z. Lauterbach. Philadelphia: Jewish Publication Society, 1949.

Mihaly, Eugene. "The Passover Haggadah as PaRaDiSe." *CCAR Journal,* 13:5 (April 1966): 3–27.

Nachmanides. *Ramban (Nachmanides): Commentary on the Torah.* Translated by Charles B. Chavel. New York: Shilo Publishing, 1974.

Nadich, Judah. *The Legends of the Rabbis: Volume 2: The First Generation After the Destruction of the Temple and Jerusalem.* Northvale, N.J.: Jason Aronson, 1994.

_____. *Rabbi Akiva and His Contemporaries.* Northvale, N.J.: Jason Aronson, 1998.

Olitzky, Kerry M. *Preparing Your Heart for Passover: A Guide for Spiritual Readiness.* Philadelphia: Jewish Publication Society, 2003.

Pirke de Rabbi Eliezer. Translated by Gerald Friedlander. New York: Sepher-Hermon Press, 1981.

Propp, William C. *Exodus 1–18: A New Translation with Introduction and Commentary.* (Anchor Bible, Volume 2) New York: Anchor, 1999.

Raphael, Chaim. *A Feast of History: The Drama of Passover Through the Ages.* New York: Gallery Books, 1972.

Safrai, Shmuel, and Ze'v Safrai. *The Haggadah of the Sages.* Jerusalem: Carta, 1998 (Hebrew).

Sarna, Nahum M. *Exploring Exodus: The Origins of Biblical Israel.* New York: Schocken Books, 1996.

Schauss, Hayyim. *The Jewish Festivals: A Guide to Their History and Observance.* New York: Schocken Books, 1996.

Segal, J. B. *Hebrew Passover from the Earliest Times to A.D. 70.* London: Oxford University Press, 1963.

Silber, David. "The Passover Haggadah/The Wandering Aramean." New York: Drisha Institute Tape Project (audiotape), 1994. Available at www.drisha.org.

Soloveitchik, Joseph D. "Redemption, Prayer, Talmud, Torah." *Tradition,* 17:2 (1978): 55–72.

Stein, Siegfried. "The Influence of the Symposia Literature on the Literary Form of the Haggadah." *Journal of Jewish Studies,* 7:1 and 2 (1957): 13–44.

Strassfeld, Michael. *The Jewish Holidays: A Guide and Commentary.* New York: Harper & Row, 1985.

Tabory, Joseph. *The Passover Ritual throughout the Generations.* Tel Aviv, Israel: Hakibbutz Hameuchad Publishing House, 1996 (Hebrew).

Urbach, Ephraim E. *The Sages: Their Concepts and Beliefs.* Cambridge: Harvard University Press, 1987.

Walzer, Michael. *Exodus and Revolution.* New York: Basic Books, 1985.

Waskow, Arthur O., and Phyllis O. Berman. *Freedom Journeys: The Tale of Exodus and Wilderness across Millenia.* Woodstock, Vt.: Jewish Lights, 2011.

Wolfson, Ron. *Passover: The Family Guide to Spiritual Celebration,* 2nd. Ed. Woodstock, Vt.: Jewish Lights, 2003.

Ziff, Joel. *Mirrors in Time: A Psycho-Spiritual Journey through the Jewish Year.* Northvale, N.J.: Jason Aronson, 1997.

Zornberg, Avivah Gottlieb. *The Particulars of Rapture: Reflections on Exodus.* New York: Image Books, 2002.

HAGGADOT OF INTEREST

Birnbaum, Philip. *The Passover Haggadah.* New York: Hebrew Publishing Company, 1976.

Cohen, Tamara R. *The Journey Continues: The Ma'yan Passover Haggadah.* New York: May'an: The Jewish Women's Project, 2000.

Dishon, David, and Noam Zion. *A Different Night: The Family Participation Haggadah.* Jerusalem: Shalom Hartman Institute, 1997. (See also Dischon and Zion, *Leader's Guide to the Family Participation Haggadah.*)

Elias, Joseph. *Haggadah.* New York: Mesorah Publications, 2000.

Elwell, Sue Levi, ed. *The Open Door: A Passover Haggadah.* New York: Central Conference of American Rabbis, 2002.

Geffen, David, ed. *American Heritage Haggadah.* Jerusalem: Gefen Books, 1997.

Herczeg, Yisrael I., ed. *Abarbanel Haggadah: The Passover Haggadah with the Commentary of Don Issac Abarbanel (Artscroll Mesorah Series).* Translated by Shlomo Fox. New York: Mesorah Publications, 1990.

———. *Haggadah: Vilna Gaon, Artscroll Mesorah Series.* New York: Mesorah Publications, 1999.

Hoffman, Lawrence A., and David Arnow, eds. *My People's Passover Haggadah: Traditional Texts, Modern Commentaries, Volume 1.* Woodstock, Vt.: Jewish Lights, 2008.

Hoffman, Lawrence A., and David Arnow, eds. *My People's Passover Haggadah: Traditional Texts, Modern Commentaries, Volume 2.* Woodstock, Vt.: Jewish Lights, 2008.

Kasher, Menachem M. *Israel Passover Haggadah.* New York: Sentry Press, 1950.

Leibowitz, Nechama, and Yitshak Reiner, eds. *Studies on the Haggadah: From the Teachings of Nechama Leibowitz.* New York: Urim Publications, 2002.

Levitt, Joy, and Michael Strassfeld, eds. *A Night of Questions: A Passover Haggadah.* Elkins Park, Pa.: Jewish Reconstructionist Federation, 2000.

Mykoff, Moshe, ed. *The Breslov Haggadah.* Translated by Yehoshua Starret. Jerusalem and New York: Breslov Research Institute, 1989.

Rabbinowicz, Rachel Anne. *Passover Haggadah: The Feast of Freedom.* New York: United Synagogue Book Service, 1982.

Riskin, Shlomo. *The Passover Haggadah: With a Traditional and Contemporary Commentary.* New York: KTAV Publishing House, 1984.

Sacks, Jonathan. *The Chief Rabbi's Haggadah.* London: HarperCollins, 2003.

Silber, David, with Rachel Furst. *A Passover Haggadah: Go Forth and Learn.* Philadelphia: Jewish Publication Society, 2011.

INDEX

PERMISSIONS

—

"Is This Story True?" by Richard Hirsh, from *A Night of Questions: A Passover Haggadah*, © 2000 by the Reconstructionist Press, Elkins Park, PA. Used with permission of the Reconstructionist Press.

Translation of the "Prayer for Dew," *Kol Haneshamah: Shabbat Vehagim*, © 1994 by the Reconstructionist Press, Elkins Park, PA. Used with permission of the Reconstructionist Press.

"Metaphors for God," by Michael Graetz, *Conservative Judaism*, volume 51, number 2, Winter 1999, pp. 69–70, © by The Rabbinical Assembly, reprinted with permission.

"A Prayer for Peace," *Siddur Sim Shalom*, used with permission of the Rabbinical Assembly.

"The Four Daughters," by Tamara Ruth Cohen, Rabbi Sue Levi Elwell, and Ronnie Horn. Reprinted with permission from *The Journey Continues: The Ma'yan Passover Haggadah*, 1997.

Mir'yam Han'viah, © 1989 by Leila Gal Berner, from *The Ma'yan Passover Haggadah*, 1997. Used with permission of the composer.

Kos Miryam Ritual, Composed by Matia Rania Angelou and Janet Berkenfield. © Matia Rania Angelou Used with permission of Matia Rania Angelou. Matia Rania Angelou credits Stephanie Loo with inspiring the creation of this ritual.

"Opening Your Eyes," from *The Book of Miracles* by Lawrence Kushner, © 1987 by the UAHC Press. Reprinted with permission of the UAHC Press.

"Sermon for the First Day of Passover 2001," by Rabbi David Wolpe. Used with permission of Rabbi Wolpe.

Page from the Sarajevo Haggadah, © Zemaljski Musej Bosne I Hercegovine Sarajevo (The National Museum of Bosnia and Herzegovina in Sarajevo). Reproduced with permission of the copyright holder.

Chapter 10 of Mishnah Pesachim (the Kaufmann Manuscript), translated by Baruch Bokser. *The Origins of the Seder: The Passover Rite and Early Rabbinic Judaism*, by Baruch Bokser, © 1984 by the Regents of the University of California. Reprinted with permission of the University of California Press.

"Give up anger . . . ," alternative to *Sh'fokh chamatkha*. *The Open Door: A Passover Haggadah*, © 2002 by the Central Conference of American Rabbis. Selections are used with permission of the Central Conference of American Rabbis.

The Book and the Sword: A Life of Learning in the Shadow of Destruction by David Weiss Halivni. © 1996 by Perseus Books Group. Reproduced with permission of Perseus Books Group, via Copyright Clearance Center.

"An Arab Shepherd Is Searching for His Goat on Mount Zion," by Yehuda Amichai, in *The Selected Poetry of Yehuda Amichai, Newly Revised Expanded Edition* (Berkeley: University of California Press, 1996). Reprinted with permission of University of California Press via Copyright Clearance Center.

"*Chad Gadya*," by Shmuel Yosef Agnon, in *Takhrikh shel Sipurim* (Jerusalem: Schocken, 1984), p. 147. Reprinted with permission. © Schocken Publishing House, Tel Aviv, Israel.

Notes

Notes

Notes

Congregation Resources

Empowered Judaism: What Independent Minyanim Can Teach Us about Building Vibrant Jewish Communities
By Rabbi Elie Kaunfer; Foreword by Prof. Jonathan D. Sarna
Examines the independent minyan movement and the lessons these grassroots communities can provide. 6 x 9, 224 pp, Quality PB, 978-1-58023-412-2 **$18.99**

Spiritual Boredom: Rediscovering the Wonder of Judaism *By Dr. Erica Brown*
Breaks through the surface of spiritual boredom to find the reservoir of meaning within. 6 x 9, 208 pp, HC, 978-1-58023-405-4 **$21.99**

Building a Successful Volunteer Culture
Finding Meaning in Service in the Jewish Community
By Rabbi Charles Simon; Foreword by Shelley Lindauer; Preface by Dr. Ron Wolfson
Shows you how to develop and maintain the volunteers who are essential to the vitality of your organization and community. 6 x 9, 192 pp, Quality PB, 978-1-58023-408-5 **$16.99**

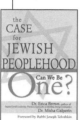

The Case for Jewish Peoplehood: Can We Be One?
By Dr. Erica Brown and Dr. Misha Galperin; Foreword by Rabbi Joseph Telushkin
6 x 9, 224 pp, HC, 978-1-58023-401-6 **$21.99**

Inspired Jewish Leadership: Practical Approaches to Building Strong Communities
By Dr. Erica Brown 6 x 9, 256 pp, HC, 978-1-58023-361-3 **$24.99**

Jewish Pastoral Care, 2nd Edition: A Practical Handbook from Traditional & Contemporary Sources *Edited by Rabbi Dayle A. Friedman, MSW, MAJCS, BCC*
6 x 9, 528 pp, Quality PB, 978-1-58023-427-6 **$30.00**

Rethinking Synagogues: A New Vocabulary for Congregational Life
By Rabbi Lawrence A. Hoffman, PhD 6 x 9, 240 pp, Quality PB, 978-1-58023-248-7 **$19.99**

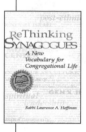

The Spirituality of Welcoming: How to Transform Your Congregation into a Sacred Community *By Dr. Ron Wolfson* 6 x 9, 224 pp, Quality PB, 978-1-58023-244-9 **$19.99**

Children's Books

What You Will See Inside a Synagogue
By Rabbi Lawrence A. Hoffman, PhD, and Dr. Ron Wolfson; Full-color photos by Bill Aron
A colorful, fun-to-read introduction that explains the ways and whys of Jewish worship and religious life. 8½ x 10¼, 32 pp, Full-color photos, Quality PB, 978-1-59473-256-0 **$8.99**
For ages 6 & up (A book from SkyLight Paths, Jewish Lights' sister imprint)

Because Nothing Looks Like God
By Lawrence Kushner and Karen Kushner Introduces children to the possibilities of spiritual life. 11 x 8½, 32 pp, Full-color illus., HC, 978-1-58023-092-6 **$17.99** *For ages 4 & up*

Board Book Companions to *Because Nothing Looks Like God*
5 x 5, 24 pp, Full-color illus., SkyLight Paths Board Books *For ages 0–4*

How Does God Make Things Happen? 978-1-893361-24-9 **$7.95**

What Does God Look Like? 978-1-893361-23-2 **$7.99**

Where Is God? 978-1-893361-17-1 **$7.99**

The Book of Miracles: A Young Person's Guide to Jewish Spiritual Awareness
Written and illus. by Lawrence Kushner
6 x 9, 96 pp, 2-color illus., HC, 978-1-879045-78-1 **$16.95** *For ages 9–13*

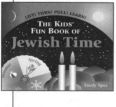

In God's Hands *By Lawrence Kushner and Gary Schmidt* 9 x 12, 32 pp, Full-color illus., HC, 978-1-58023-224-1 **$16.99**

In Our Image: God's First Creatures *By Nancy Sohn Swartz*
9 x 12, 32 pp, Full-color illus., HC, 978-1-879045-99-6 **$16.95** *For ages 4 & up*

Also Available as a Board Book: **How Did the Animals Help God?**
5 x 5, 24 pp, Full-color illus., Board Book, 978-1-59473-044-3 **$7.99** *For ages 0–4*
(A book from SkyLight Paths, Jewish Lights' sister imprint)

The Kids' Fun Book of Jewish Time
By Emily Sper 9 x 7½, 24 pp, Full-color illus., HC, 978-1-58023-311-8 **$16.99**

What Makes Someone a Jew? *By Lauren Seidman*
Reflects the changing face of American Judaism.
10 x 8½, 32 pp, Full-color photos, Quality PB, 978-1-58023-321-7 **$8.99** *For ages 3–6*

Children's Books by Sandy Eisenberg Sasso

Adam & Eve's First Sunset: God's New Day
Explores fear and hope, faith and gratitude in ways that will delight kids and adults—inspiring us to bless each of God's days and nights.
9 x 12, 32 pp, Full-color illus., HC, 978-1-58023-177-0 **$17.95** *For ages 4 & up*

Also Available as a Board Book: **Adam and Eve's New Day**
5 x 5, 24 pp, Full-color illus., Board Book, 978-1-59473-205-8 **$7.99** *For ages 0–4*
(A book from SkyLight Paths, Jewish Lights' sister imprint)

But God Remembered: Stories of Women from Creation to the Promised Land
Four different stories of women—Lilith, Serach, Bityah and the Daughters of Z—teach us important values through their faith and actions.
9 x 12, 32 pp, Full-color illus., Quality PB, 978-1-58023-372-9 **$8.99** *For ages 8 & up*

Cain & Abel: Finding the Fruits of Peace
Shows children that we have the power to deal with anger in positive ways. Provides questions for kids and adults to explore together.
9 x 12, 32 pp, Full-color illus., HC, 978-1-58023-123-7 **$16.95** *For ages 5 & up*

For Heaven's Sake
Heaven is often found where you least expect it.
9 x 12, 32 pp, Full-color illus., HC, 978-1-58023-054-4 **$16.95** *For ages 4 & up*

God in Between
If you wanted to find God, where would you look? This magical, mythical tale teaches that God can be found where we are: within all of us and the relationships between us. 9 x 12, 32 pp, Full-color illus., HC, 978-1-879045-86-6 **$16.95** *For ages 4 & up*

God Said Amen
An inspiring story about hearing the answers to our prayers.
9 x 12, 32 pp, Full-color illus., HC, 978-1-58023-080-3 **$16.95** *For ages 4 & up*

God's Paintbrush: Special 10th Anniversary Edition
Wonderfully interactive, invites children of all faiths and backgrounds to encounter God through moments in their own lives. Provides questions adult and child can explore together. 11 x 8½, 32 pp, Full-color illus., HC, 978-1-58023-195-4 **$17.95** *For ages 4 & up*

Also Available as a Board Book: **I Am God's Paintbrush**
5 x 5, 24 pp, Full-color illus., Board Book, 978-1-59473-265-2 **$7.99** *For ages 0–4*
(A book from SkyLight Paths, Jewish Lights' sister imprint)

Also Available: **God's Paintbrush Teacher's Guide**
8½ x 11, 32 pp, PB, 978-1-879045-57-6 **$8.95**

God's Paintbrush Celebration Kit
A Spiritual Activity Kit for Teachers and Students of All Faiths, All Backgrounds
9½ x 12, 40 Full-color Activity Sheets & Teacher Folder w/ complete instructions
HC, 978-1-58023-050-6 **$21.95**
8-Student Activity Sheet Pack (40 sheets/5 sessions), 978-1-58023-058-2 **$19.95**

In God's Name
Like an ancient myth in its poetic text and vibrant illustrations, this award-winning modern fable about the search for God's name celebrates the diversity and, at the same time, the unity of all people.
9 x 12, 32 pp, Full-color illus., HC, 978-1-879045-26-2 **$16.99** *For ages 4 & up*

Also Available as a Board Book: **What Is God's Name?**
5 x 5, 24 pp, Full-color illus., Board Book, 978-1-893361-10-2 **$7.99** *For ages 0–4*
(A book from SkyLight Paths, Jewish Lights' sister imprint)

Also Available in Spanish: **El nombre de Dios**
9 x 12, 32 pp, Full-color illus., HC, 978-1-893361-63-8 **$16.95**

Noah's Wife: The Story of Naamah
When God tells Noah to bring the animals of the world onto the ark, God also calls on Naamah, Noah's wife, to save each plant on Earth. Based on an ancient text.
9 x 12, 32 pp, Full-color illus., HC, 978-1-58023-134-3 **$16.95** *For ages 4 & up*

Also Available as a Board Book: **Naamah, Noah's Wife**
5 x 5, 24 pp, Full-color illus., Board Book, 978-1-893361-56-0 **$7.95** *For ages 0–4*
(A book from SkyLight Paths, Jewish Lights' sister imprint)

Spirituality/Women's Interest

The Divine Feminine in Biblical Wisdom Literature: Selections Annotated & Explained *Translation & Annotation by Rabbi Rami Shapiro* 5½ x 8½, 240 pp, Quality PB, 978-1-59473-109-9 **$16.99** *(A book from SkyLight Paths, Jewish Lights' sister imprint)*

The Quotable Jewish Woman: Wisdom, Inspiration & Humor from the Mind & Heart *Edited by Elaine Bernstein Partnow* 6 x 9, 496 pp, Quality PB, 978-1-58023-236-4 **$19.99**

The Women's Haftarah Commentary: New Insights from Women Rabbis on the 54 Weekly Haftarah Portions, the 5 Megillot & Special Shabbatot *Edited by Rabbi Elyse Goldstein* 6 x 9, 560 pp, Quality PB, 978-1-58023-371-2 **$19.99**

The Women's Torah Commentary: New Insights from Women Rabbis on the 54 Weekly Torah Portions *Edited by Rabbi Elyse Goldstein* 6 x 9, 496 pp, Quality PB, 978-1-58023-370-5 **$19.99**; HC, 978-1-58023-076-6 **$34.95**

New Jewish Feminism: Probing the Past, Forging the Future *Edited by Rabbi Elyse Goldstein; Foreword by Anita Diamant* 6 x 9, 480 pp, HC, 978-1-58023-359-0 **$24.99**

Spirituality/Crafts
(from SkyLight Paths, Jewish Lights' sister imprint)

Beading—The Creative Spirit: Finding Your Sacred Center through the Art of Beadwork *By Wendy Ellsworth*
Invites you on a spiritual pilgrimage into the kaleidoscope world of glass and color. 7 x 9, 240 pp, 8-page full-color insert, b/w photos and diagrams, Quality PB, 978-1-59473-267-6 **$18.99**

Contemplative Crochet: A Hands-On Guide for Interlocking Faith and Craft *By Cindy Crandall-Frazier; Foreword by Linda Skolnik*
Will take you on a path deeper into your crocheting and your spiritual awareness. 7 x 9, 208 pp, b/w photos, Quality PB, 978-1-59473-238-6 **$16.99**

The Knitting Way: A Guide to Spiritual Self-Discovery *By Linda Skolnik and Janice MacDaniels* Shows how to use knitting to strengthen your spiritual self. 7 x 9, 240 pp, b/w photos, Quality PB, 978-1-59473-079-5 **$16.99**

The Painting Path: Embodying Spiritual Discovery through Yoga, Brush and Color *By Linda Novick; Foreword by Richard Segalman*
Explores the divine connection you can experience through art. 7 x 9, 208 pp, 8-page full-color insert, b/w photos, Quality PB, 978-1-59473-226-3 **$18.99**

The Quilting Path: A Guide to Spiritual Self-Discovery through Fabric, Thread and Kabbalah *By Louise Silk* Explores how to cultivate personal growth through quilt making. 7 x 9, 192 pp, b/w photos, Quality PB, 978-1-59473-206-5 **$16.99**

The Scrapbooking Journey: A Hands-On Guide to Spiritual Discovery *By Cory Richardson-Lauve; Foreword by Stacy Julian*
Reveals how this craft can become a practice used to deepen and shape your life. 7 x 9, 176 pp, 8-page full-color insert, b/w photos, Quality PB, 978-1-59473-216-4 **$18.99**

Travel

Israel—A Spiritual Travel Guide, 2nd Edition: A Companion for the Modern Jewish Pilgrim *By Rabbi Lawrence A. Hoffman, PhD* 4¾ x 10, 256 pp, Illus., Quality PB, 978-1-58023-261-6 **$18.99**
Also Available: **The Israel Mission Leader's Guide** 5½ x 8½, 16 pp, PB, 978-1-58023-085-8 **$4.95**

Twelve Steps

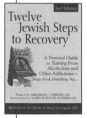

100 Blessings Every Day: Daily Twelve Step Recovery Affirmations, Exercises for Personal Growth & Renewal Reflecting Seasons of the Jewish Year *By Rabbi Kerry M. Olitzky; Foreword by Rabbi Neil Gillman, PhD* 4½ x 6½, 432 pp, Quality PB, 978-1-879045-30-9 **$16.99**

Recovery from Codependence: A Jewish Twelve Steps Guide to Healing Your Soul *By Rabbi Kerry M. Olitzky* 6 x 9, 160 pp, Quality PB, 978-1-879045-32-3 **$13.95**

Twelve Jewish Steps to Recovery, 2nd Edition: A Personal Guide to Turning from Alcoholism & Other Addictions—Drugs, Food, Gambling, Sex ... *By Rabbi Kerry M. Olitzky and Stuart A. Copans, MD; Preface by Abraham J. Twerski, MD* 6 x 9, 160 pp, Quality PB, 978-1-58023-409-2 **$16.99**

Ecology/Environment

A Wild Faith: Jewish Ways into Wilderness, Wilderness Ways into Judaism
By Rabbi Mike Comins; Foreword by Nigel Savage 6 x 9, 240 pp, Quality PB, 978-1-58023-316-3 **$16.99**

Ecology & the Jewish Spirit: Where Nature & the Sacred Meet
Edited by Ellen Bernstein 6 x 9, 288 pp, Quality PB, 978-1-58023-082-7 **$18.99**

Torah of the Earth: Exploring 4,000 Years of Ecology in Jewish Thought
Vol. 1: Biblical Israel & Rabbinic Judaism; Vol. 2: Zionism & Eco-Judaism
Edited by Rabbi Arthur Waskow Vol. 1: 6 x 9, 272 pp, Quality PB, 978-1-58023-086-5 **$19.95**
Vol. 2: 6 x 9, 336 pp, Quality PB, 978-1-58023-087-2 **$19.95**

The Way Into Judaism and the Environment *By Jeremy Benstein, PhD*
6 x 9, 288 pp, Quality PB, 978-1-58023-368-2 **$18.99**; HC, 978-1-58023-268-5 **$24.99**

Graphic Novels/History

The Adventures of Rabbi Harvey: A Graphic Novel of Jewish Wisdom and Wit in the
Wild West *By Steve Sheinkin* 6 x 9, 144 pp, Full-color illus., Quality PB, 978-1-58023-310-1 **$16.99**

Rabbi Harvey Rides Again: A Graphic Novel of Jewish Folktales Let Loose in the
Wild West *By Steve Sheinkin* 6 x 9, 144 pp, Full-color illus., Quality PB, 978-1-58023-347-7 **$16.99**

Rabbi Harvey vs. the Wisdom Kid: A Graphic Novel of Dueling
Jewish Folktales in the Wild West *By Steve Sheinkin*
Rabbi Harvey's first book-length adventure and toughest challenge.
6 x 9, 144 pp, Full-color illus., Quality PB, 978-1-58023-422-1 **$16.99**

The Story of the Jews: A 1,000-Year Adventure A Graphic History Book
By Stan Mack 6 x 9, 288 pp, Illus., Quality PB, 978-1-58023-155-8 **$16.99**

Grief/Healing

Facing Illness, Finding God: How Judaism Can Help You and Caregivers
Cope When Body or Spirit Fails *By Rabbi Joseph B. Meszler*
Will help you find spiritual strength for healing amid the fear, pain and chaos of
illness. 6 x 9, 208 pp, Quality PB, 978-1-58023-423-8 **$16.99**

Midrash & Medicine: Healing Body and Soul in the Jewish Interpretive
Tradition *Edited by Rabbi William Cutter, PhD; Foreword by Michele F. Prince, LCSW, MAJCS*
Explores how midrash can help you see beyond the physical aspects of healing to
tune in to your spiritual source. 6 x 9, 352 pp, HC, 978-1-58023-428-3 **$29.99**

Healing from Despair: Choosing Wholeness in a Broken World
By Rabbi Elie Kaplan Spitz with Erica Shapiro Taylor; Foreword by Abraham J. Twerski, MD
5½ x 8½, 208 pp, Quality PB, 978-1-58023-436-8 **$16.99**; HC, 978-1-58023-360-6 **$21.99**

Healing and the Jewish Imagination: Spiritual and Practical Perspectives on
Judaism and Health *Edited by Rabbi William Cutter, PhD*
6 x 9, 240 pp, Quality PB, 978-1-58023-373-6 **$19.99**; HC, 978-1-58023-314-9 **$24.99**

Grief in Our Seasons: A Mourner's Kaddish Companion *By Rabbi Kerry M. Olitzky*
4½ x 6¼, 448 pp, Quality PB, 978-1-879045-55-2 **$15.95**

Healing of Soul, Healing of Body: Spiritual Leaders Unfold the Strength & Solace
in Psalms *Edited by Rabbi Simkha Y. Weintraub, LCSW*
6 x 9, 128 pp, 2-color illus. text, Quality PB, 978-1-879045-31-6 **$16.99**

Mourning & Mitzvah, 2nd Edition: A Guided Journal for Walking the Mourner's
Path through Grief to Healing *By Rabbi Anne Brener, LCSW*
7½ x 9, 304 pp, Quality PB, 978-1-58023-113-8 **$19.99**

Tears of Sorrow, Seeds of Hope, 2nd Edition: A Jewish Spiritual Companion for
Infertility and Pregnancy Loss *By Rabbi Nina Beth Cardin*
6 x 9, 208 pp, Quality PB, 978-1-58023-233-3 **$18.99**

A Time to Mourn, a Time to Comfort, 2nd Edition: A Guide to Jewish
Bereavement *By Dr. Ron Wolfson; Foreword by Rabbi David J. Wolpe*
7 x 9, 384 pp, Quality PB, 978-1-58023-253-1 **$19.99**

When a Grandparent Dies: A Kid's Own Remembering Workbook for Dealing
with Shiva and the Year Beyond *By Nechama Liss-Levinson, PhD*
8 x 10, 48 pp, 2-color text, HC, 978-1-879045-44-6 **$15.95** *For ages 7–13*

Inspiration

The Seven Questions You're Asked in Heaven: Reviewing and Renewing Your Life on Earth *By Dr. Ron Wolfson*
An intriguing and entertaining resource for living a life that matters.
6 x 9, 176 pp, Quality PB, 978-1-58023-407-8 **$16.99**

Happiness and the Human Spirit: The Spirituality of Becoming the Best You Can Be *By Rabbi Abraham J. Twerski, MD*
Shows you that true happiness is attainable once you stop looking outside yourself for the source. 6 x 9, 176 pp, Quality PB, 978-1-58023-404-7 **$16.99**; HC, 978-1-58023-343-9 **$19.99**

A Formula for Proper Living: Practical Lessons from Life and Torah
By Rabbi Abraham J. Twerski, MD
Gives you practical lessons for life that you can put to day-to-day use in dealing with yourself and others. 6 x 9, 144 pp, HC, 978-1-58023-402-3 **$19.99**

The Bridge to Forgiveness: Stories and Prayers for Finding God and Restoring Wholeness *By Rabbi Karyn D. Kedar* 6 x 9, 176 pp, HC, 978-1-58023-324-8 **$19.99**

The Empty Chair: Finding Hope and Joy—Timeless Wisdom from a Hasidic Master, Rebbe Nachman of Breslov *Adapted by Moshe Mykoff and the Breslov Research Institute*
4 x 6, 128 pp, Deluxe PB w/ flaps, 978-1-879045-67-5 **$9.99**

The Gentle Weapon: Prayers for Everyday and Not-So-Everyday Moments—Timeless Wisdom from the Teachings of the Hasidic Master, Rebbe Nachman of Breslov *Adapted by Moshe Mykoff and S. C. Mizrahi, together with the Breslov Research Institute*
4 x 6, 144 pp, Deluxe PB w/ flaps, 978-1-58023-022-3 **$9.99**

God Whispers: Stories of the Soul, Lessons of the Heart *By Rabbi Karyn D. Kedar*
6 x 9, 176 pp, Quality PB, 978-1-58023-088-9 **$15.95**

God's To-Do List: 103 Ways to Be an Angel and Do God's Work on Earth
By Dr. Ron Wolfson 6 x 9, 144 pp, Quality PB, 978-1-58023-301-9 **$16.99**

Jewish Stories from Heaven and Earth: Inspiring Tales to Nourish the Heart and Soul *Edited by Rabbi Dov Peretz Elkins* 6 x 9, 304 pp, Quality PB, 978-1-58023-363-7 **$16.99**

Life's Daily Blessings: Inspiring Reflections on Gratitude and Joy for Every Day, Based on Jewish Wisdom *By Rabbi Kerry M. Olitzky* 4½ x 6½, 368 pp, Quality PB, 978-1-58023-396-5 **$16.99**

Restful Reflections: Nighttime Inspiration to Calm the Soul, Based on Jewish Wisdom *By Rabbi Kerry M. Olitzky and Rabbi Lori Forman* 4½ x 6½, 448 pp, Quality PB, 978-1-58023-091-9 **$15.95**

Sacred Intentions: Daily Inspiration to Strengthen the Spirit, Based on Jewish Wisdom *By Rabbi Kerry M. Olitzky and Rabbi Lori Forman* 4½ x 6½, 448 pp, Quality PB, 978-1-58023-061-2 **$15.95**

Kabbalah/Mysticism

Ehyeh: A Kabbalah for Tomorrow
By Rabbi Arthur Green, PhD 6 x 9, 224 pp, Quality PB, 978-1-58023-213-5 **$18.99**

The Flame of the Heart: Prayers of a Chasidic Mystic
By Reb Noson of Breslov; Translated and adapted by David Sears, with the Breslov Research Institute
5 x 7¼, 160 pp, Quality PB, 978-1-58023-246-3 **$15.99**

The Gift of Kabbalah: Discovering the Secrets of Heaven, Renewing Your Life on Earth
By Tamar Frankiel, PhD 6 x 9, 256 pp, Quality PB, 978-1-58023-141-1 **$16.95**

Kabbalah: A Brief Introduction for Christians
By Tamar Frankiel, PhD 5½ x 8½, 208 pp, Quality PB, 978-1-58023-303-3 **$16.99**

The Lost Princess & Other Kabbalistic Tales of Rebbe Nachman of Breslov
The Seven Beggars & Other Kabbalistic Tales of Rebbe Nachman of Breslov
Translated by Rabbi Aryeh Kaplan; Preface by Rabbi Chaim Kramer
Lost Princess: 6 x 9, 400 pp, Quality PB, 978-1-58023-217-3 **$18.99**
Seven Beggars: 6 x 9, 192 pp, Quality PB, 978-1-58023-250-0 **$16.99**

Seek My Face: A Jewish Mystical Theology *By Rabbi Arthur Green, PhD*
6 x 9, 304 pp, Quality PB, 978-1-58023-130-5 **$19.95**

Zohar: Annotated & Explained *Translation & Annotation by Dr. Daniel C. Matt; Foreword by Andrew Harvey* 5½ x 8½, 176 pp, Quality PB, 978-1-893361-51-5 **$15.99**
(A book from SkyLight Paths, Jewish Lights' sister imprint)

See also *The Way Into Jewish Mystical Tradition* in The Way Into… Series.

Meditation

Jewish Meditation Practices for Everyday Life
Awakening Your Heart, Connecting with God
By Rabbi Jeff Roth
Offers a fresh take on meditation that draws on life experience and living life with greater clarity as opposed to the traditional method of rigorous study.
6 x 9, 224 pp, Quality PB, 978-1-58023-397-2 **$18.99**

The Handbook of Jewish Meditation Practices
A Guide for Enriching the Sabbath and Other Days of Your Life
By Rabbi David A. Cooper Easy-to-learn meditation techniques.
6 x 9, 208 pp, Quality PB, 978-1-58023-102-2 **$16.95**

Discovering Jewish Meditation: Instruction & Guidance for Learning an Ancient
Spiritual Practice *By Nan Fink Gefen, PhD* 6 x 9, 208 pp, Quality PB, 978-1-58023-067-4 **$16.95**

Meditation from the Heart of Judaism: Today's Teachers Share Their Practices,
Techniques, and Faith *Edited by Avram Davis*
6 x 9, 256 pp, Quality PB, 978-1-58023-049-0 **$16.95**

Ritual/Sacred Practices

The Jewish Dream Book: The Key to Opening the Inner Meaning of
Your Dreams *By Vanessa L. Ochs, PhD, with Elizabeth Ochs; Illus. by Kristina Swarner*
Instructions for how modern people can perform ancient Jewish dream practices and dream interpretations drawn from the Jewish wisdom tradition.
8 x 8, 128 pp, Full-color illus., Deluxe PB w/ flaps, 978-1-58023-132-9 **$16.95**

God in Your Body: Kabbalah, Mindfulness and Embodied Spiritual Practice
By Jay Michaelson
The first comprehensive treatment of the body in Jewish spiritual practice and an essential guide to the sacred.
6 x 9, 272 pp, Quality PB, 978-1-58023-304-0 **$18.99**

The Book of Jewish Sacred Practices: CLAL's Guide to Everyday &
Holiday Rituals & Blessings *Edited by Rabbi Irwin Kula and Vanessa L. Ochs, PhD*
6 x 9, 368 pp, Quality PB, 978-1-58023-152-7 **$18.95**

Jewish Ritual: A Brief Introduction for Christians
By Rabbi Kerry M. Olitzky and Rabbi Daniel Judson
5½ x 8½, 144 pp, Quality PB, 978-1-58023-210-4 **$14.99**

The Rituals & Practices of a Jewish Life: A Handbook for Personal Spiritual
Renewal *Edited by Rabbi Kerry M. Olitzky and Rabbi Daniel Judson*
6 x 9, 272 pp, Illus., Quality PB, 978-1-58023-169-5 **$18.95**

The Sacred Art of Lovingkindness: Preparing to Practice
By Rabbi Rami Shapiro 5½ x 8½, 176 pp, Quality PB, 978-1-59473-151-8 **$16.99**
(A book from SkyLight Paths, Jewish Lights' sister imprint)

Science Fiction/Mystery & Detective Fiction

Criminal Kabbalah: An Intriguing Anthology of Jewish Mystery &
Detective Fiction *Edited by Lawrence W. Raphael; Foreword by Laurie R. King*
All-new stories from twelve of today's masters of mystery and detective fiction—sure to delight mystery buffs of all faith traditions.
6 x 9, 256 pp, Quality PB, 978-1-58023-109-1 **$16.95**

Mystery Midrash: An Anthology of Jewish Mystery & Detective Fiction
Edited by Lawrence W. Raphael; Preface by Joel Siegel
6 x 9, 304 pp, Quality PB, 978-1-58023-055-1 **$16.95**

Wandering Stars: An Anthology of Jewish Fantasy & Science Fiction
Edited by Jack Dann; Introduction by Isaac Asimov
6 x 9, 272 pp, Quality PB, 978-1-58023-005-6 **$18.99**

More Wandering Stars: An Anthology of Outstanding Stories of Jewish Fantasy and
Science Fiction *Edited by Jack Dann; Introduction by Isaac Asimov*
6 x 9, 192 pp, Quality PB, 978-1-58023-063-6 **$16.95**

Spirituality

Repentance: The Meaning and Practice of *Teshuvah*
By Dr. Louis E. Newman; Foreword by Rabbi Harold M. Schulweis; Preface by Rabbi Karyn D. Kedar
Examines both the practical and philosophical dimensions of *teshuvah*, Judaism's core religious-moral teaching on repentance, and its value for us—Jews and non-Jews alike—today. 6 x 9, 256 pp, HC, 978-1-58023-426-9 **$24.99**

Tanya, the Masterpiece of Hasidic Wisdom
Selections Annotated & Explained
Translation & Annotation by Rabbi Rami Shapiro; Foreword by Rabbi Zalman M. Schachter-Shalomi
Brings the genius of *Tanya*, one of the most powerful books of Jewish wisdom, to anyone seeking to deepen their understanding of the soul.
5½ x 8½, 240 pp, Quality PB, 978-1-59473-275-1 **$16.99**
(A book from SkyLight Paths, Jewish Lights' sister imprint)

Aleph-Bet Yoga: Embodying the Hebrew Letters for Physical and Spiritual Well-Being
By Steven A. Rapp; Foreword by Tamar Frankiel, PhD, and Judy Greenfeld; Preface by Hart Lazer
7 x 10, 128 pp, b/w photos, Quality PB, Lay-flat binding, 978-1-58023-162-6 **$16.95**

A Book of Life: Embracing Judaism as a Spiritual Practice
By Rabbi Michael Strassfeld 6 x 9, 544 pp, Quality PB, 978-1-58023-247-0 **$19.99**

Bringing the Psalms to Life: How to Understand and Use the Book of Psalms
By Rabbi Daniel F. Polish, PhD 6 x 9, 208 pp, Quality PB, 978-1-58023-157-2 **$16.95**

Does the Soul Survive? A Jewish Journey to Belief in Afterlife, Past Lives & Living with Purpose *By Rabbi Elie Kaplan Spitz; Foreword by Brian L. Weiss, MD*
6 x 9, 288 pp, Quality PB, 978-1-58023-165-7 **$16.99**

First Steps to a New Jewish Spirit: Reb Zalman's Guide to Recapturing the Intimacy & Ecstasy in Your Relationship with God *By Rabbi Zalman M. Schachter-Shalomi with Donald Gropman* 6 x 9, 144 pp, Quality PB, 978-1-58023-182-4 **$16.95**

Foundations of Sephardic Spirituality: The Inner Life of Jews of the Ottoman Empire
By Rabbi Marc D. Angel, PhD 6 x 9, 224 pp, Quality PB, 978-1-58023-341-5 **$18.99**

God & the Big Bang: Discovering Harmony between Science & Spirituality
By Dr. Daniel C. Matt 6 x 9, 216 pp, Quality PB, 978-1-879045-89-7 **$16.99**

God in Our Relationships: Spirituality between People from the Teachings of Martin Buber *By Rabbi Dennis S. Ross* 5½ x 8½, 160 pp, Quality PB, 978-1-58023-147-3 **$16.95**

The Jewish Lights Spirituality Handbook: A Guide to Understanding, Exploring & Living a Spiritual Life *Edited by Stuart M. Matlins*
What exactly is "Jewish" about spirituality? How do I make it a part of my life? Fifty of today's foremost spiritual leaders share their ideas and experience with us.
6 x 9, 456 pp, Quality PB, 978-1-58023-093-3 **$19.99**

Judaism, Physics and God: Searching for Sacred Metaphors in a Post-Einstein World
By Rabbi David W. Nelson 6 x 9, 352 pp, Quality PB, inc. reader's discussion guide, 978-1-58023-306-4 **$18.99**; HC, 352 pp, 978-1-58023-252-4 **$24.99**

Meaning & Mitzvah: Daily Practices for Reclaiming Judaism through Prayer, God, Torah, Hebrew, Mitzvot and Peoplehood *By Rabbi Goldie Milgram*
7 x 9, 336 pp, Quality PB, 978-1-58023-256-2 **$19.99**

Minding the Temple of the Soul: Balancing Body, Mind, and Spirit through Traditional Jewish Prayer, Movement, and Meditation *By Tamar Frankiel, PhD, and Judy Greenfeld*
7 x 10, 184 pp, Illus., Quality PB, 978-1-879045-64-4 **$18.99**

One God Clapping: The Spiritual Path of a Zen Rabbi *By Rabbi Alan Lew with Sherril Jaffe*
5½ x 8½, 336 pp, Quality PB, 978-1-58023-115-2 **$16.95**

The Soul of the Story: Meetings with Remarkable People
By Rabbi David Zeller 6 x 9, 288 pp, HC, 978-1-58023-272-2 **$21.99**

There Is No Messiah ... and You're It: The Stunning Transformation of Judaism's Most Provocative Idea *By Rabbi Robert N. Levine, DD*
6 x 9, 192 pp, Quality PB, 978-1-58023-255-5 **$16.99**

These Are the Words: A Vocabulary of Jewish Spiritual Life
By Rabbi Arthur Green, PhD 6 x 9, 304 pp, Quality PB, 978-1-58023-107-7 **$18.95**

Spirituality/Prayer

Making Prayer Real: Leading Jewish Spiritual Voices on Why Prayer Is Difficult and What to Do about It *By Rabbi Mike Comins*
A new and different response to the challenges of Jewish prayer, with "best prayer practices" from Jewish spiritual leaders of all denominations.
6 x 9, 320 pp, Quality PB, 978-1-58023-417-7 **$18.99**

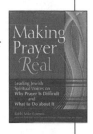

Witnesses to the One: The Spiritual History of the *Sh'ma*
By Rabbi Joseph B. Meszler; Foreword by Rabbi Elyse Goldstein
6 x 9, 176 pp, Quality PB, 978-1-58023-400-9 **$16.99**; HC, 978-1-58023-309-5 **$19.99**

My People's Prayer Book Series: Traditional Prayers, Modern Commentaries *Edited by Rabbi Lawrence A. Hoffman, PhD*
Provides diverse and exciting commentary to the traditional liturgy. Will help you find new wisdom in Jewish prayer, and bring liturgy into your life. Each book includes Hebrew text, modern translations and commentaries from all perspectives of the Jewish world.

Vol. 1—The *Sh'ma* and Its Blessings
    7 x 10, 168 pp, HC, 978-1-879045-79-8 **$24.99**
Vol. 2—The *Amidah* 7 x 10, 240 pp, HC, 978-1-879045-80-4 **$24.95**
Vol. 3—*P'sukei D'zimrah* (Morning Psalms)
    7 x 10, 240 pp, HC, 978-1-879045-81-1 **$29.99**
Vol. 4—*Seder K'riat Hatorah* (The Torah Service)
    7 x 10, 264 pp, HC, 978-1-879045-82-8 **$23.95**
Vol. 5 *Birkhot Hashachar* (Morning Blessings)
    7 x 10, 240 pp, HC, 978-1-879045-83-5 **$24.95**
Vol. 6—*Tachanun* and Concluding Prayers
    7 x 10, 240 pp, HC, 978-1-879045-84-2 **$24.95**
Vol. 7—Shabbat at Home 7 x 10, 240 pp, HC, 978-1-879045-85-9 **$24.95**
Vol. 8—*Kabbalat Shabbat* (Welcoming Shabbat in the Synagogue)
    7 x 10, 240 pp, HC, 978-1-58023-121-3 **$24.99**
Vol. 9—Welcoming the Night: *Minchah* and *Ma'ariv* (Afternoon and
    Evening Prayer) 7 x 10, 272 pp, HC, 978-1-58023-262-3 **$24.99**
Vol. 10—Shabbat Morning: *Shacharit* and *Musaf* (Morning and
    Additional Services) 7 x 10, 240 pp, HC, 978-1-58023-240-1 **$24.99**

Spirituality/Lawrence Kushner

I'm God; You're Not: Observations on Organized Religion & Other Disguises of the Ego
    6 x 9, 256 pp, HC, 978-1-58023-441-2 **$21.99**

The Book of Letters: A Mystical Hebrew Alphabet
    Popular HC Edition, 6 x 9, 80 pp, 2-color text, 978-1-879045-00-2 **$24.95**
    Collector's Limited Edition, 9 x 12, 80 pp, gold-foil-embossed pages, w/ limited-edition silkscreened
    print, 978-1-879045-04-0 **$349.00**

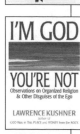

The Book of Miracles: A Young Person's Guide to Jewish Spiritual Awareness
    6 x 9, 96 pp, 2-color illus., HC, 978-1-879045-78-1 **$16.95** *For ages 9–13*

The Book of Words: Talking Spiritual Life, Living Spiritual Talk
    6 x 9, 160 pp, Quality PB, 978-1-58023-020-9 **$18.99**

Eyes Remade for Wonder: A Lawrence Kushner Reader *Introduction by Thomas Moore*
    6 x 9, 240 pp, Quality PB, 978-1-58023-042-1 **$18.95**

God Was in This Place & I, i Did Not Know: Finding Self, Spirituality and
    Ultimate Meaning 6 x 9, 192 pp, Quality PB, 978-1-879045-33-0 **$16.95**

Honey from the Rock: An Introduction to Jewish Mysticism
    6 x 9, 176 pp, Quality PB, 978-1-58023-073-5 **$16.95**

Invisible Lines of Connection: Sacred Stories of the Ordinary
    5½ x 8½, 160 pp, Quality PB, 978-1-879045-98-9 **$15.95**

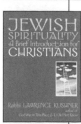

Jewish Spirituality: A Brief Introduction for Christians
    5½ x 8½, 112 pp, Quality PB, 978-1-58023-150-3 **$12.95**

The River of Light: Jewish Mystical Awareness
    6 x 9, 192 pp, Quality PB, 978-1-58023-096-4 **$16.95**

The Way Into Jewish Mystical Tradition
    6 x 9, 224 pp, Quality PB, 978-1-58023-200-5 **$18.99**; HC, 978-1-58023-029-2 **$21.95**

Theology/Philosophy/The Way Into... Series

The Way Into... series offers an accessible and highly usable "guided tour" of the Jewish faith, people, history and beliefs—in total, an introduction to Judaism that will enable you to understand and interact with the sacred texts of the Jewish tradition. Each volume is written by a leading contemporary scholar and teacher, and explores one key aspect of Judaism. The Way Into... series enables all readers to achieve a real sense of Jewish cultural literacy through guided study.

The Way Into Encountering God in Judaism
By Rabbi Neil Gillman, PhD

For everyone who wants to understand how Jews have encountered God throughout history and today.

6 x 9, 240 pp, Quality PB, 978-1-58023-199-2 **$18.99**; HC, 978-1-58023-025-4 **$21.95**

Also Available: **The Jewish Approach to God:** A Brief Introduction for Christians
By Rabbi Neil Gillman, PhD

5½ x 8½, 192 pp, Quality PB, 978-1-58023-190-9 **$16.95**

The Way Into Jewish Mystical Tradition
By Rabbi Lawrence Kushner

Allows readers to interact directly with the sacred mystical texts of the Jewish tradition. An accessible introduction to the concepts of Jewish mysticism, their religious and spiritual significance, and how they relate to life today.

6 x 9, 224 pp, Quality PB, 978-1-58023-200-5 **$18.99**; HC, 978-1-58023-029-2 **$21.95**

The Way Into Jewish Prayer
By Rabbi Lawrence A. Hoffman, PhD

Opens the door to 3,000 years of Jewish prayer, making anyone feel at home in the Jewish way of communicating with God.

6 x 9, 208 pp, Quality PB, 978-1-58023-201-2 **$18.99**

Also Available: **The Way Into Jewish Prayer Teacher's Guide**
By Rabbi Jennifer Ossakow Goldsmith

8½ x 11, 42 pp, PB, 978-1-58023-345-3 **$8.99**

Download a free copy at www.jewishlights.com.

The Way Into Judaism and the Environment
By Jeremy Benstein, PhD

Explores the ways in which Judaism contributes to contemporary social-environmental issues, the extent to which Judaism is part of the problem and how it can be part of the solution.

6 x 9, 288 pp, Quality PB, 978-1-58023-368-2 **$18.99**; HC, 978-1-58023-268-5 **$24.99**

The Way Into *Tikkun Olam* (Repairing the World)
By Rabbi Elliot N. Dorff, PhD

An accessible introduction to the Jewish concept of the individual's responsibility to care for others and repair the world.

6 x 9, 304 pp, Quality PB, 978-1-58023-328-6 **$18.99**; 320 pp, HC, 978-1-58023-269-2 **$24.99**

The Way Into Torah
By Rabbi Norman J. Cohen, PhD

Helps guide you in the exploration of the origins and development of Torah, explains why it should be studied and how to do it.

6 x 9, 176 pp, Quality PB, 978-1-58023-198-5 **$16.99**

The Way Into the Varieties of Jewishness
By Sylvia Barack Fishman, PhD

Explores the religious and historical understanding of what it has meant to be Jewish from ancient times to the present controversy over "Who is a Jew?"

6 x 9, 288 pp, Quality PB, 978-1-58023-367-5 **$18.99**; HC, 978-1-58023-030-8 **$24.99**

Theology/Philosophy

Jewish Theology in Our Time: A New Generation Explores the Foundations and Future of Jewish Belief *Edited by Rabbi Elliot J. Cosgrove, PhD; Foreword by Rabbi David J. Wolpe; Preface by Rabbi Carole B. Balin, PhD*
A powerful and challenging examination of what Jews can believe—by a new generation's most dynamic and innovative thinkers.
6 x 9, 240 pp, HC, 978-1-58023-413-9 **$24.99**

Maimonides, Spinoza and Us: Toward an Intellectually Vibrant Judaism
By Rabbi Marc D. Angel, PhD A challenging look at two great Jewish philosophers and what their thinking means to our understanding of God, truth, revelation and reason. 6 x 9, 224 pp, HC, 978-1-58023-411-5 **$24.99**

The Death of Death: Resurrection and Immortality in Jewish Thought
By Rabbi Neil Gillman, PhD 6 x 9, 336 pp, Quality PB, 978-1-58023-081-0 **$18.95**

Doing Jewish Theology: God, Torah & Israel in Modern Judaism *By Rabbi Neil Gillman, PhD*
6 x 9, 304 pp, Quality PB, 978-1-58023-439-9 **$18.99**; HC, 978-1-58023-322-4 **$24.99**

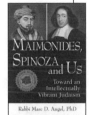

Ethics of the Sages: Pirke Avot—Annotated & Explained
Translation & Annotation by Rabbi Rami Shapiro 5½ x 8½, 192 pp, Quality PB, 978-1-59473-207-2 **$16.99***

Hasidic Tales: Annotated & Explained *Translation & Annotation by Rabbi Rami Shapiro*
5½ x 8½, 240 pp, Quality PB, 978-1-893361-86-7 **$16.95***

A Heart of Many Rooms: Celebrating the Many Voices within Judaism
By Dr. David Hartman 6 x 9, 352 pp, Quality PB, 978-1-58023-156-5 **$19.95**

The Hebrew Prophets: Selections Annotated & Explained
Translation & Annotation by Rabbi Rami Shapiro; Foreword by Rabbi Zalman M. Schachter-Shalomi
5½ x 8½, 224 pp, Quality PB, 978-1-59473-037-5 **$16.99***

A Jewish Understanding of the New Testament *By Rabbi Samuel Sandmel; Preface by Rabbi David Sandmel* 5½ x 8½, 368 pp, Quality PB, 978-1-59473-048-1 **$19.99***

Jews and Judaism in the 21st Century: Human Responsibility, the Presence of God and the Future of the Covenant *Edited by Rabbi Edward Feinstein; Foreword by Paula E. Hyman*
6 x 9, 192 pp, Quality PB, 978-1-58023-374-3 **$19.99**; HC, 978-1-58023-315-6 **$24.99**

A Living Covenant: The Innovative Spirit in Traditional Judaism
By Dr. David Hartman 6 x 9, 368 pp, Quality PB, 978-1-58023-011-7 **$25.00**

Love and Terror in the God Encounter: The Theological Legacy of Rabbi Joseph B. Soloveitchik *By Dr. David Hartman* 6 x 9, 240 pp, Quality PB, 978-1-58023-176-3 **$19.95**

The Personhood of God: Biblical Theology, Human Faith and the Divine Image
By Dr. Yochanan Muffs; Foreword by Dr. David Hartman
6 x 9, 240 pp, Quality PB, 978-1-58023-338-5 **$18.99**; HC, 978-1-58023-265-4 **$24.99**

A Touch of the Sacred: A Theologian's Informal Guide to Jewish Belief
By Dr. Eugene B. Borowitz and Frances W. Schwartz
6 x 9, 256 pp, Quality PB, 978-1-58023-416-0 **$16.99**; HC, 978-1-58023-337-8 **$21.99**

Traces of God: Seeing God in Torah, History and Everyday Life *By Rabbi Neil Gillman, PhD*
6 x 9, 240 pp, Quality PB, 978-1-58023-369-9 **$16.99**

We Jews and Jesus: Exploring Theological Differences for Mutual Understanding *By Rabbi Samuel Sandmel; Preface by Rabbi David Sandmel* 6 x 9, 192 pp, Quality PB, 978-1-59473-208-9 **$16.99***

Your Word Is Fire: The Hasidic Masters on Contemplative Prayer
Edited and translated by Rabbi Arthur Green, PhD, and Barry W. Holtz
6 x 9, 160 pp, Quality PB, 978-1-879045-25-5 **$15.95**

I Am Jewish
Personal Reflections Inspired by the Last Words of Daniel Pearl
Almost 150 Jews—both famous and not—from all walks of life, from all around the world, write about many aspects of their Judaism.
Edited by Judea and Ruth Pearl 6 x 9, 304 pp, Deluxe PB w/ flaps, 978-1-58023-259-3 **$18.99**
Download a free copy of the *I Am Jewish Teacher's Guide* at www.jewishlights.com.

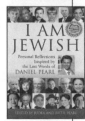

Hannah Senesh: Her Life and Diary, The First Complete Edition
By Hannah Senesh; Foreword by Marge Piercy; Preface by Eitan Senesh; Afterword by Roberta Grossman
6 x 9, 368 pp, b/w photos, Quality PB, 978-1-58023-342-2 **$19.99**

*A book from SkyLight Paths, Jewish Lights' sister imprint

Judaism / Christianity / Interfaith

Christians & Jews—Faith to Faith: Tragic History, Promising Present, Fragile Future *By Rabbi James Rudin*
A probing examination of Christian-Jewish relations that looks at the major issues facing both faith communities.   6 x 9, 288 pp, HC, 978-1-58023-432-0 **$24.99**

How to Do Good & Avoid Evil: A Global Ethic from the Sources of Judaism *By Hans Küng and Rabbi Walter Homolka* Explores how the principles of Judaism provide the ethical norms for all religions to work together toward a more peaceful humankind.   6 x 9, 224 pp, HC, 978-1-59473-255-3 **$19.99***

Getting to the Heart of Interfaith: The Eye-Opening, Hope-Filled Friendship of a Pastor, a Rabbi and a Sheikh
By Rabbi Ted Falcon, Pastor Don Mackenzie and Sheikh Jamal Rahman
Presents ways we can work together to transcend the differences that have divided us historically.   6 x 9, 192 pp, Quality PB, 978-1-59473-263-8 **$16.99***

Claiming Earth as Common Ground: The Ecological Crisis through the Lens of Faith *By Rabbi Andrea Cohen-Kiener*   6 x 9, 192 pp, Quality PB, 978-1-59473-261-4 **$16.99***

Modern Jews Engage the New Testament: Enhancing Jewish Well-Being in a Christian Environment *By Rabbi Michael J. Cook, PhD*   6 x 9, 416 pp, HC, 978-1-58023-313-2 **$29.99**

The Changing Christian World: A Brief Introduction for Jews
By Rabbi Leonard A. Schoolman 5½ x 8½, 176 pp, Quality PB, 978-1-58023-344-6 **$16.99**

Christians & Jews in Dialogue: Learning in the Presence of the Other
By Mary C. Boys and Sara S. Lee
6 x 9, 240 pp, Quality PB, 978-1-59473-254-6 **$18.99**; HC, 978-1-59473-144-0 **21.99***

Disaster Spiritual Care: Practical Clergy Responses to Community, Regional and National Tragedy *Edited by Rabbi Stephen B. Roberts, BCJC, and Rev. Willard W. C. Ashley Sr., DMin, DH*
6 x 9, 384 pp, HC, 978-1-59473-240-9 **$40.00***

Healing the Jewish-Christian Rift: Growing Beyond Our Wounded History
By Ron Miller and Laura Bernstein 6 x 9, 288 pp, Quality PB, 978-1-59473-139-6 **$18.99***

How to Be a Perfect Stranger, 5th Edition: The Essential Religious Etiquette Handbook *Edited by Stuart M. Matlins and Arthur J. Magida*
6 x 9, 432 pp, Quality PB, 978-1-59473-294-2 **$19.99***

InterActive Faith: The Essential Interreligious Community-Building Handbook
Edited by Rev. Bud Heckman with Rori Picker Neiss
6 x 9, 304 pp, Quality PB, 978-1-59473-273-7 **$16.99**; HC, 978-1-59473-237-9 **$29.99***

Introducing My Faith and My Community
The Jewish Outreach Institute Guide for the Christian in a Jewish Interfaith Relationship
By Rabbi Kerry M. Olitzky 6 x 9, 176 pp, Quality PB, 978-1-58023-192-3 **$16.99**

The Jewish Approach to Repairing the World (*Tikkun Olam*)
A Brief Introduction for Christians *By Rabbi Elliot N. Dorff, PhD, with Rev. Cory Willson*
5½ x 8½, 256 pp, Quality PB, 978-1-58023-349-1 **$16.99**

The Jewish Connection to Israel, the Promised Land: A Brief Introduction for Christians *By Rabbi Eugene Korn, PhD* 5½ x 8½, 192 pp, Quality PB, 978-1-58023-318-7 **$14.99**

Jewish Holidays: A Brief Introduction for Christians *By Rabbi Kerry M. Olitzky and Rabbi Daniel Judson* 5½ x 8½, 176 pp, Quality PB, 978-1-58023-302-6 **$16.99**

Jewish Ritual: A Brief Introduction for Christians *By Rabbi Kerry M. Olitzky and Rabbi Daniel Judson* 5½ x 8½, 144 pp, Quality PB, 978-1-58023-210-4 **$14.99**

A Jewish Understanding of the New Testament *By Rabbi Samuel Sandmel;*
Preface by Rabbi David Sandmel 5½ x 8½, 368 pp, Quality PB, 978-1-59473-048-1 **$19.99***

Righteous Gentiles in the Hebrew Bible: Ancient Role Models for Sacred Relationships *By Rabbi Jeffrey K. Salkin; Foreword by Rabbi Harold M. Schulweis; Preface by Phyllis Tickle*
6 x 9, 192 pp, Quality PB, 978-1-58023-364-4 **$18.99**

Talking about God: Exploring the Meaning of Religious Life with Kierkegaard, Buber, Tillich and Heschel *By Rabbi Daniel F. Polish, PhD* 6 x 9, 160 pp, Quality PB, 978-1-59473-272-0 **$16.99***

We Jews and Jesus: Exploring Theological Differences for Mutual Understanding
By Rabbi Samuel Sandmel; Preface by Rabbi David Sandmel
6 x 9, 192 pp, Quality PB, 978-1-59473-208-9 **$16.99**

*A book from SkyLight Paths, Jewish Lights' sister imprint

Social Justice

There Shall Be No Needy
Pursuing Social Justice through Jewish Law and Tradition
By Rabbi Jill Jacobs; Foreword by Rabbi Elliot N. Dorff, PhD; Preface by Simon Greer
Confronts the most pressing issues of twenty-first-century America from a deeply Jewish perspective.
6 x 9, 288 pp, Quality PB, 978-1-58023-425-2 **$16.99**; HC, 978-1-58023-394-1 **$21.99**
Also Available: **There Shall Be No Needy Teacher's Guide**
8½ x 11, 56 pp, PB, 978-1-58023-429-0 **$8.99**

Conscience: The Duty to Obey and the Duty to Disobey
By Rabbi Harold M. Schulweis
This clarion call to rethink our moral and political behavior examines the idea of conscience and the role conscience plays in our relationships to government, law, ethics, religion, human nature, God—and to each other.
6 x 9, 160 pp, Quality PB, 978-1-58023-419-1 **$16.99**; HC, 978-1-58023-375-0 **$19.99**

Judaism and Justice: The Jewish Passion to Repair the World
By Rabbi Sidney Schwarz; Foreword by Ruth Messinger
Explores the relationship between Judaism, social justice and the Jewish identity of American Jews.
6 x 9, 352 pp, Quality PB, 978-1-58023-353-8 **$19.99**; HC, 978-1-58023-312-5 **$24.99**

Spiritual Activism: A Jewish Guide to Leadership and Repairing the World
By Rabbi Avraham Weiss; Foreword by Alan M. Dershowitz
6 x 9, 224 pp, Quality PB, 978-1-58023-418-4 **$16.99**; HC, 978-1-58023-355-2 **$24.99**

Righteous Indignation: A Jewish Call for Justice *Edited by Rabbi Or N. Rose, Jo Ellen Green Kaiser and Margie Klein; Foreword by Rabbi David Ellenson, PhD*
Leading progressive Jewish activists explore meaningful intellectual and spiritual foundations for their social justice work.
6 x 9, 384 pp, Quality PB, 978-1-58023-414-6 **$19.99**; HC, 978-1-58023-336-1 **$24.99**

Spirituality/Women's Interest

New Jewish Feminism: Probing the Past, Forging the Future
Edited by Rabbi Elyse Goldstein; Foreword by Anita Diamant
Looks at the growth and accomplishments of Jewish feminism and what they mean for Jewish women today and tomorrow.
6 x 9, 480 pp, HC, 978-1-58023-359-0 **$24.99**

The Divine Feminine in Biblical Wisdom Literature
Selections Annotated & Explained
Translation & Annotation by Rabbi Rami Shapiro
5½ x 8½, 240 pp, Quality PB, 978-1-59473-109-9 **$16.99**
(A book from SkyLight Paths, Jewish Lights' sister imprint)

The Quotable Jewish Woman: Wisdom, Inspiration & Humor from the Mind & Heart
Edited by Elaine Bernstein Partnow 6 x 9, 496 pp, Quality PB, 978-1-58023-236-4 **$19.99**

The Women's Haftarah Commentary: New Insights from Women Rabbis on the 54 Weekly Haftarah Portions, the 5 Megillot & Special Shabbatot
Edited by Rabbi Elyse Goldstein Illuminates the historical significance of female portrayals in the Haftarah and the Five Megillot.
6 x 9, 560 pp, Quality PB, 978-1-58023-371-2 **$19.99**

The Women's Torah Commentary: New Insights from Women Rabbis on the 54 Weekly Torah Portions
Edited by Rabbi Elyse Goldstein
Over fifty women rabbis offer inspiring insights on the Torah, in a week-by-week format.
6 x 9, 496 pp, Quality PB, 978-1-58023-370-5 **$19.99**; HC, 978-1-58023-076-6 **$34.95**

See Passover for *The Women's Passover Companion: Women's Reflections on the Festival of Freedom* and *The Women's Seder Sourcebook: Rituals & Readings for Use at the Passover Seder.*

Life Cycle
Marriage/Parenting/Family/Aging

The New Jewish Baby Album: Creating and Celebrating the Beginning of a Spiritual Life—A Jewish Lights Companion
By the Editors at Jewish Lights; Foreword by Anita Diamant; Preface by Rabbi Sandy Eisenberg Sasso
A spiritual keepsake that will be treasured for generations. More than just a memory book, *shows you how—and why it's important*—to create a Jewish home and a Jewish life. 8 x 10, 64 pp, Deluxe Padded HC, Full-color illus., 978-1-58023-138-1 **$19.95**

The Jewish Pregnancy Book: A Resource for the Soul, Body & Mind during Pregnancy, Birth & the First Three Months *By Sandy Falk, MD, and Rabbi Daniel Judson, with Steven A. Rapp* Medical information, prayers and rituals for each stage of pregnancy. 7 x 10, 208 pp, b/w photos, Quality PB, 978-1-58023-178-7 **$16.95**

Celebrating Your New Jewish Daughter: Creating Jewish Ways to Welcome Baby Girls into the Covenant—New and Traditional Ceremonies *By Debra Nussbaum Cohen; Foreword by Rabbi Sandy Eisenberg Sasso* 6 x 9, 272 pp, Quality PB, 978-1-58023-090-2 **$18.95**

The New Jewish Baby Book, 2nd Edition: Names, Ceremonies & Customs—A Guide for Today's Families *By Anita Diamant* 6 x 9, 320 pp, Quality PB, 978-1-58023-251-7 **$19.99**

Parenting as a Spiritual Journey: Deepening Ordinary and Extraordinary Events into Sacred Occasions *By Rabbi Nancy Fuchs-Kreimer, PhD* 6 x 9, 224 pp, Quality PB, 978-1-58023-016-2 **$17.99**

Parenting Jewish Teens: A Guide for the Perplexed
By Joanne Doades Explores the questions and issues that shape the world in which today's Jewish teenagers live and offers constructive advice to parents.
6 x 9, 176 pp, Quality PB, 978-1-58023-305-7 **$16.99**

Judaism for Two: A Spiritual Guide for Strengthening and Celebrating Your Loving Relationship *By Rabbi Nancy Fuchs-Kreimer, PhD, and Rabbi Nancy H. Wiener, DMin; Foreword by Rabbi Elliot N. Dorff, PhD*
Addresses the ways Jewish teachings can enhance and strengthen committed relationships. 6 x 9, 224 pp, Quality PB, 978-1-58023-254-8 **$16.99**

The Creative Jewish Wedding Book, 2nd Edition: A Hands-On Guide to New & Old Traditions, Ceremonies & Celebrations *By Gabrielle Kaplan-Mayer* 9 x 9, 288 pp, b/w photos, Quality PB, 978-1-58023-398-9 **$19.99**

Divorce Is a Mitzvah: A Practical Guide to Finding Wholeness and Holiness When Your Marriage Dies *By Rabbi Perry Netter; Afterword by Rabbi Laura Geller* 6 x 9, 224 pp, Quality PB, 978-1-58023-172-5 **$16.95**

Embracing the Covenant: Converts to Judaism Talk About Why & How *By Rabbi Allan Berkowitz and Patti Moskovitz* 6 x 9, 192 pp, Quality PB, 978-1-879045-50-7 **$16.95**

The Guide to Jewish Interfaith Family Life: An InterfaithFamily.com Handbook *Edited by Ronnie Friedland and Edmund Case* 6 x 9, 384 pp, Quality PB, 978-1-58023-153-4 **$18.95**

A Heart of Wisdom: Making the Jewish Journey from Midlife through the Elder Years *Edited by Susan Berrin; Foreword by Rabbi Harold Kushner* 6 x 9, 384 pp, Quality PB, 978-1-58023-051-3 **$18.95**

Introducing My Faith and My Community: The Jewish Outreach Institute Guide for the Christian in a Jewish Interfaith Relationship *By Rabbi Kerry M. Olitzky* 6 x 9, 176 pp, Quality PB, 978-1-58023-192-3 **$16.99**

Making a Successful Jewish Interfaith Marriage: The Jewish Outreach Institute Guide to Opportunities, Challenges and Resources *By Rabbi Kerry M. Olitzky with Joan Peterson Littman* 6 x 9, 176 pp, Quality PB, 978-1-58023-170-1 **$16.95**

A Man's Responsibility: A Jewish Guide to Being a Son, a Partner in Marriage, a Father and a Community Leader *By Rabbi Joseph B. Meszler* 6 x 9, 192 pp, Quality PB, 978-1-58023-435-1 **$16.99**; HC, 978-1-58023-362-0 **$21.99**

So That Your Values Live On: Ethical Wills and How to Prepare Them *Edited by Rabbi Jack Riemer and Rabbi Nathaniel Stampfer* 6 x 9, 272 pp, Quality PB, 978-1-879045-34-7 **$18.99**

Holidays/Holy Days

Who by Fire, Who by Water—Un'tanch Tokef
Edited by Rabbi Lawrence A. Hoffman, PhD
Examines the prayer's theology, authorship and poetry through a set of lively essays, all written in accessible language.
6 x 9, 272 pp, HC, 978-1-58023-424-5 **$24.99**

Rosh Hashanah Readings: Inspiration, Information and Contemplation
Yom Kippur Readings: Inspiration, Information and Contemplation
Edited by Rabbi Dov Peretz Elkins; Section Introductions from Arthur Green's These Are the Words
An extraordinary collection of readings, prayers and insights that will enable you to enter into the spirit of the High Holy Days in a personal and powerful way, permitting the meaning of the Jewish New Year to enter the heart.
Rosh Hashanah: 6 x 9, 400 pp, Quality PB, 978-1-58023-437-5 **$19.99**; HC, 978-1-58023-239-5 **$24.99**
Yom Kippur: 6 x 9, 368 pp, Quality PB, 978-1-58023-438-2 **$19.99**; HC, 978-1-58023-271-5 **$24.99**

Jewish Holidays: A Brief Introduction for Christians
By Rabbi Kerry M. Olitzky and Rabbi Daniel Judson
5½ x 8½, 176 pp, Quality PB, 978-1-58023-302-6 **$16.99**

Reclaiming Judaism as a Spiritual Practice: Holy Days and Shabbat
By Rabbi Goldie Milgram 7 x 9, 272 pp, Quality PB, 978-1-58023-205-0 **$19.99**

7th Heaven: Celebrating Shabbat with Rebbe Nachman of Breslov
By Moshe Mykoff with the Breslov Research Institute
5⅛ x 8¼, 224 pp, Deluxe PB w/ flaps, 978-1-58023-175-6 **$18.95**

Shabbat, 2nd Edition: The Family Guide to Preparing for and Celebrating the Sabbath *By Dr. Ron Wolfson*
7 x 9, 320 pp, Illus., Quality PB, 978-1-58023-164-0 **$19.99**

Hanukkah, 2nd Edition: The Family Guide to Spiritual Celebration
By Dr. Ron Wolfson 7 x 9, 240 pp, Illus., Quality PB, 978-1-58023-122-0 **$18.95**

The Jewish Family Fun Book, 2nd Edition: Holiday Projects, Everyday Activities, and Travel Ideas with Jewish Themes *By Danielle Dardashti and Roni Sarig; Illus. by Avi Katz*
6 x 9, 304 pp, 70+ b/w illus. & diagrams, Quality PB, 978-1-58023-333-0 **$18.99**

The Jewish Lights Book of Fun Classroom Activities: Simple and Seasonal Projects for Teachers and Students *By Danielle Dardashti and Roni Sarig*
6 x 9, 240 pp, Quality PB, 978-1-58023-206-7 **$19.99**

Passover

My People's Passover Haggadah
Traditional Texts, Modern Commentaries
Edited by Rabbi Lawrence A. Hoffman, PhD, and David Arnow, PhD
A diverse and exciting collection of commentaries on the traditional Passover Haggadah—in two volumes!
Vol. 1: 7 x 10, 304 pp, HC, 978-1-58023-354-5 **$24.99**
Vol. 2: 7 x 10, 320 pp, HC, 978-1-58023-346-0 **$24.99**

Leading the Passover Journey: The Seder's Meaning Revealed, the Haggadah's Story Retold *By Rabbi Nathan Laufer*
Uncovers the hidden meaning of the Seder's rituals and customs.
6 x 9, 224 pp, Quality PB, 978-1-58023-399-6 **$18.99**; HC, 978-1-58023-211-1 **$24.99**

The Women's Passover Companion: Women's Reflections on the Festival of Freedom
Edited by Rabbi Sharon Cohen Anisfeld, Tara Mohr and Catherine Spector; Foreword by Paula E. Hyman
6 x 9, 352 pp, Quality PB, 978-1-58023-231-9 **$19.99**; HC, 978-1-58023-128-2 **$24.95**

The Women's Seder Sourcebook: Rituals & Readings for Use at the Passover Seder
Edited by Rabbi Sharon Cohen Anisfeld, Tara Mohr and Catherine Spector
6 x 9, 384 pp, Quality PB, 978-1-58023-232-6 **$19.99**

Freedom Journeys: The Tale of Exodus and Wilderness across Millennia
By Rabbi Arthur O. Waskow and Rabbi Phyllis O. Berman 6 x 9, 288 pp, HC, 978-1-58023-445-0 **$24.99**

Passover, 2nd Edition: The Family Guide to Spiritual Celebration
By Dr. Ron Wolfson with Joel Lurie Grishaver 7 x 9, 416 pp, Quality PB, 978-1-58023-174-9 **$19.95**

About Jewish Lights

People of all faiths and backgrounds yearn for books that attract, engage, educate, and spiritually inspire.

Our principal goal is to stimulate thought and help all people learn about who the Jewish People are, where they come from, and what the future can be made to hold. While people of our diverse Jewish heritage are the primary audience, our books speak to people in the Christian world as well and will broaden their understanding of Judaism and the roots of their own faith.

We bring to you authors who are at the forefront of spiritual thought and experience. While each has something different to say, they all say it in a voice that you can hear.

Our books are designed to welcome you and then to engage, stimulate, and inspire. We judge our success not only by whether or not our books are beautiful and commercially successful, but by whether or not they make a difference in your life.

For your information and convenience, at the back of this book we have provided a list of other Jewish Lights books you might find interesting and useful. They cover all the categories of your life:

Bar/Bat Mitzvah
Bible Study / Midrash
Children's Books
Congregation Resources
Current Events / History
Ecology / Environment
Fiction: Mystery, Science Fiction
Grief / Healing
Holidays / Holy Days
Inspiration
Kabbalah / Mysticism / Enneagram

Life Cycle
Meditation
Men's Interest
Parenting
Prayer / Ritual / Sacred Practice
Social Justice
Spirituality
Theology / Philosophy
Travel
Twelve Steps
Women's Interest

Stuart M. Matlins

Stuart M. Matlins, Publisher

Or phone, fax, mail or e-mail to: **JEWISH LIGHTS Publishing**
Sunset Farm Offices, Route 4 • P.O. Box 237 • Woodstock, Vermont 05091
Tel: (802) 457-4000 • Fax: (802) 457-4004 • www.jewishlights.com
Credit card orders: (800) 962-4544 (8:30AM–5:30PM ET Monday–Friday)
Generous discounts on quantity orders. SATISFACTION GUARANTEED. Prices subject to change.